HACKING EXPOSED™
COMPUTER FORENSICS
SECOND EDITION
REVIEWS

"This book provides the right mix of practical how-to knowledge in a straightforward, informative fashion that ties all the complex pieces together with real-world case studies. With so many books on the topic of computer forensics, *Hacking Exposed Computer Forensics, Second Edition*, delivers the most valuable insight on the market. The authors cut to the chase of what people must understand to effectively perform computer forensic investigations."
—**Brian H. Karney, COO, AccessData Corporation**

"*Hacking Exposed Computer Forensics* is a 'must-read' for information security professionals who want to develop their knowledge of computer forensics."
—**Jason Fruge, Director of Consulting Services, Fishnet Security**

HACKING EXPOSED™ COMPUTER FORENSICS SECOND EDITION

AARON **PHILIPP**
DAVID **COWEN**
CHRIS **DAVIS**

New York   Chicago   San Francisco
Lisbon   London   Madrid   Mexico City
Milan   New Delhi   San Juan
Seoul   Singapore   Sydney   Toronto

The McGraw·Hill Companies

Cataloging-in-Publication Data is on file with the Library of Congress.

McGraw-Hill books are available at special quantity discounts to use as premiums and sales promotions, or for use in corporate training programs. To contact a representative, please e-mail us at bulksales@mcgraw-hill.com.

Hacking Exposed™ Computer Forensics, Second Edition

1234567890 DOC DOC 019

ISBN   978-0-07-262677-4
MHID   0-07-162677-8

Sponsoring Editor	**Proofreader**
Jane K. Brownlow	Susie Elkind
Editorial Supervisor	**Indexer**
Janet Walden	Karin Arrigoni
Project Editor	**Production Supervisor**
LeeAnn Pickrell	George Anderson
Acquisitions Coordinator	**Composition**
Joya Anthony	EuroDesign - Peter F. Hancik
Technical Editor	**Illustration**
Louis S. Scharringhausen, Jr.	Lyssa Wald
Copy Editor	**Art Director, Cover**
Lisa Theobald	Jeff Weeks

To my mom and dad, thanks for teaching me to follow my dreams. To my sister, Renee, for always being there for me. To all of my friends and teachers at The University of Texas at Austin, for making me what I am and showing me what I can be. Hook 'em Horns!

—*Aaron*

To my daughter, I can't wait to meet you. To my wife, thank you for supporting me through the second edition. To my mom and dad, thank you for your enthusiasm for a book you will never read. To my friends at G-C, thank you for all the hard work.

—*Dave*

About the Authors

Aaron Philipp

Aaron Philipp is a managing consultant in the Disputes and Investigations practice at Navigant Consulting, which assists domestic and global corporations and their counsel who face complex and risky legal challenges. In this capacity, he provides consulting services in the fields of computer forensics and high-tech investigations. Mr. Philipp specializes in complex computer forensic techniques such as identification and tracing of IP theft, timeline creation, and correlation relating to multiparty fraud and reconstruction of evidence after deliberate data destruction has occurred that would nullify traditional computer forensic methodology. Mr. Philipp was previously Managing Partner of Affect Computer Forensics, a boutique forensics firm based in Austin, Texas, with offices in Dallas, Texas, and Hong Kong. Affect's clients include the nation's top law firms, FORTUNE 500 legal departments, and government investigatory agencies. In addition, Mr. Philipp is a regular speaker at technology and legal conferences around the world. He has been internationally recognized for his work, with citations of merit from the governments of Taiwan and South Africa. Mr. Philipp has a B.S. in computer science from The University of Texas at Austin.

David Cowen, CISSP

David Cowen is the co-author of the best-selling *Hacking Exposed Computer Forensics* and the *Anti-Hacker Toolkit, Third Edition*. Mr. Cowen is a Partner at G-C Partners, LLC, where he provides expert witness services and consulting to Fortune 500 companies nationwide. Mr. Cowen has testified in cases ranging from multimillion-dollar intellectual property theft to billion-dollar antitrust claims. Mr. Cowen has over 13 years of industry experience in topics ranging from information security to computer forensics.

Chris Davis

Chris Davis has trained and presented in information security and certification curriculum for government, corporate, and university requirements. He is the author of *Hacking Exposed Computer Forensics, IT Auditing: Using Controls to Protect Information Assets,* and *Anti-Hacker Toolkit,* and he contributed to the *Computer Security Handbook, Fifth Edition.* Mr. Davis holds a bachelor's degree in nuclear engineering technologies from Thomas Edison and a master's in business from The University of Texas at Austin. Mr. Davis served eight years in the U.S. Naval Submarine Fleet, onboard the special projects Submarine NR-1 and the USS Nebraska.

About the Contributing Authors

Todd K. Lester is a director in the Disputes and Investigations practice of Navigant Consulting (PI), LLC, which assists domestic and global corporations and their counsel who face complex and risky legal challenges. He is an Accredited Senior Appraiser (ASA) in business valuation and a Certified Fraud Examiner (CFE) with over 20 years of experience in forensic accounting, litigation consulting, damages analysis, business valuation, and business investigations. Mr. Lester has conducted financial investigations of accounting irregularities, fraud, and other misconduct in a wide variety of domestic and international forums. He also has extensive experience advising clients in complex litigation and disputes on the financial, accounting, and data analysis aspects of multifaceted damages calculations, especially where complex databases and business systems are involved. Prior to joining Navigant Consulting, Mr. Lester was a director in the Financial Advisory Services practice of PricewaterhouseCoopers. He holds a bachelor's of business administration in finance/international business, a B.A. in biology, and an MBA from The University of Texas.

Jean Domalis has over eight years of investigative experience, focusing on digital forensic techniques in the areas of IP theft, corporate espionage, embezzlement, and securities fraud. Ms. Domalis was previously a senior consultant with Navigant Consulting, where she participated as a key member of teams undertaking multinational forensic investigations in the United States, Canada, and Asia. Ms. Domalis came to Navigant with the acquisition of Computer Forensics, Inc., one of the nation's premier computer forensics boutique firms. Ms. Domalis attended the University of Washington.

John Loveland specializes in providing strategic counsel and expert witness services on matters related to computer forensic investigations and large end-to-end discovery matters. He has over 18 years of experience in consulting multinational corporations and law firms and has led or contributed to over 100 investigations of electronic data theft and computer fraud and abuse and to the collection of electronic evidence from hard drives, backup tapes, network servers, cell phones and BlackBerries, and other storage media. Mr. Loveland was the founder and president of S3 Partners, a computer forensics firm based in Dallas, which was acquired by Fios, Inc., in 2003. He is currently managing director in the Computer Forensics and Electronic Discovery Services practice for Navigant Consulting in Washington, D.C. and oversees the practice's operations in the Mid-Atlantic region.

David Dym has been a private computer forensics consultant for several years, providing services at G-C Partners, LLC. Forensic services have included evidence collection, recovery, and analysis for clients of top firms in the United States as well as companies in the banking and mining industry. Mr. Dym has over nine years of experience with programming, quality assurance, enterprise IT infrastructure, and has experience with multiple network, database, and software security initiatives. Mr. Dym has built and managed multiple teams of programmers, quality assurance testers, and IT infrastructure administrators. He has participated in dozens of projects to develop and deploy custom-developed business software, medical billing, inventory management, and accounting solutions.

Rudi Peck has been a private computer forensic consultant for the last several years providing services at G-C Partners, LLC. Forensic services have included evidence collection, recovery, and analysis for clients of several top firms in the United States as well as companies in the banking industry. Mr. Peck has over a decades worth of experience in programming, software production, and test engineering with an extensive background in Window's security. Mr. Peck has designed several security audit tools for companies and provided contract development work for the Center of Internet Security.

Rafael Gorgal is a partner with the firm of G-C Partners, LLC, a computer forensics and information security consultancy. He is the three-term past president of the Southwest

Chapter, High Technology Crime Investigations Association, and has extensive experience in analyzing digital evidence. He has conducted numerous forensic investigations, developed methodologies for use by incident response teams, and managed teams of forensic consultants. He has also developed computer forensic curriculum currently being taught to both private sector and law enforcement investigators. Mr. Gorgal has taught information security at Southern Methodist University, the University of California at Los Angeles, and the National Technological University.

Peter Marketos is a partner at Haynes and Boones, LLP, who practices commercial litigation in the firm's Dallas office. He represents clients as both plaintiffs and defendants in business disputes from trial through appeal. Mr. Marketos has tried many cases to juries and to the bench, obtaining favorable verdicts in disputes involving corporate fraud, breach of contract, breach of fiduciary duty, and theft of trade secrets. He has developed substantial expertise in the discovery and analysis of electronic evidence through the use of technology and computer forensics.

Andrew Rosen is president of ASR Data Acquisition & Analysis, LLC. He offers unique litigation support services to the legal, law enforcement, and investigative communities. With over a decade of experience in the recovery of computer data and forensic examination, Mr. Rosen regularly provides expert testimony in federal and state courts. Along with training attorneys and law enforcement officials in computer investigation techniques, Mr. Rosen frequently speaks and writes on emerging matters in the field. He has a worldwide reputation for developing cutting-edge computer-crime investigative tools and is frequently consulted by other professionals in the industry.

About the Technical Editor

Louis S. Scharringhausen, Jr., is the director of Digital Investigations for Yarbrough Strategic Advisors in Dallas, Texas, where he is responsible for directing, managing, and conducting digital investigations and electronic discovery projects. Mr. Scharringhausen was a special agent for the U.S. Environmental Protection Agency's Criminal Investigation Division (USEPA-CID) for ten years, conducting complex, large-scale environmental investigations. For five of those years, he was a team leader for USEPA-CID's prestigious National Computer Forensics Laboratory-Electronic Crimes Team, conducting forensic acquisitions and analysis in support of active investigations. After leaving the public sector in January 2007, Mr. Scharringhausen worked with Navigant Consulting, Inc., where he was an integral part of a digital forensics team that focused on fraud and intellectual property investigations before coming to Yarbrough Strategic Advisors. He has participated in numerous training sessions for Guidance Software, Access Data, the National White Collar Crimes Center, and the Federal Law Enforcement Training Center, among others. He holds the EnCase Certified Examiner endorsement (EnCE) and a B.S. in environmental science from Metropolitan State College of Denver.

AT A GLANCE

CONTENTS

Part II   Collecting the Evidence

Part III Forensic Investigation Techniques

Part IV   Presenting Your Findings

Part V　Putting It All Together

ACKNOWLEDGMENTS

"A good writer possesses not only his own spirit but also the spirit of his friends."
—Friedrich Nietzsche

We simply could not have done this without the help of many, many people. It was an amazing challenge to coordinate the necessary depth of corporate, legal, criminal, and technical expertise across so many subjects. Many old and new friends donated knowledge, time, techniques, tools, and much more to make this project a success. We are truly grateful to each of you.

The wonderful and overworked team at McGraw-Hill is outstanding. We sincerely appreciate your dedication, coaching, and long hours during the course of this project. Jane Brownlow, this book is a result of your tireless dedication to the completion of this project. You are truly one of the best in the business. We would also like to extend a big round of thanks to Joya Anthony, our acquisition coordinator and honorary coxswain. Thanks to LeeAnn Pickrell for seeing us through to the finish line.

A special thank you goes to Jean Domalis, Todd Lester, John Loveland, and Louis Scharringhausen for their contributing work and thorough reviews. Jean, as always, your work is fantastic. You truly play to a standard in everything you do and it shows. Todd, you went above and beyond and the book is a world better for it. John, thank you for the vision and strategic input on the structure of the new sections. Louis, your attention to detail and desire to know the right answer is a huge asset. You were a fantastic technical editor.

Lastly, a special note of remembrance for Bill Siebert. He wrote the foreword for the first edition of the book, donating his time when none of us knew how the book would be received. Unfortunately Bill passed in December 2008. Bill, you and your family are in our thoughts.

—*The Authors*

I would like to thank my fellow authors for their tireless work and many long nights getting this book done.

Thanks to everyone at Navigant Consulting. A special thanks to the entire Austin office, especially Travis Casner, Cade Satterfield, Adam Scheive, and Zarin Behramsha for their assistance with the research on the new sections. Also, a special note of thanks to Kris Swanson and Todd Marlin for ideas and guidance throughout both this book and our other case work.

John, Jean, and Louis, I am proud to say that we were on the same team. You guys are great. John, you have always had my back, and I have learned a ton from you. Here is to success and building it the right way.

To Susan and Lauren, I cannot express my gratitude enough for your patience with me as Todd and I worked on the book weekend after weekend. Todd, thanks for everything, not just the book. You do the Longhorn nation proud and I *will* beat you one of these years at the Shiner GASP. Na zdorov'e.

Thanks to Fr. Patrick Johnson for all the sage advice and for reminding me of the importance of balance in life. St. Austin Catholic Parish in Austin, Texas, has truly become an anchor in my life.

Thanks to Chris Sweeny, Jonathan McCoy, and all of my teammates and brothers on the University of Texas Rugby Team. You taught me mental toughness, brotherhood, the value of perseverance, and how to never give up.

Thanks to Larry Leibrock and David Burns for introducing me to forensics and treating me so well while I was at the McCombs School of Business. And to every one of my computer science professors for showing me how much I still have to learn.

A huge thank you to Robert Groshon and Bradley O. Brauser for believing in me all those years ago.

Thanks to Peggy Cheung for being such a great friend. Your selling me the 2006 Rose Bowl tickets at face value goes as one of the greatest demonstrations of friendships I have ever witnessed. I am very sorry I stopped texting you game updates in the third quarter, and I still have no idea how much that phone call to Hong Kong cost me.

Finally, I would like to give another thank you to my family, my mother and father who gave me my first computer when I was seven, and my sister Renee.

—*Aaron Philipp*

INTRODUCTION

"This is not an incident response handbook." This was the first line of the introduction for the first edition. Little did we know at the time how much computer forensics would change since the book was first published in 2004. Computer forensics is changing the way investigations are done, even investigations previously thought to be outside the four corners of technology investigations.

If you look at what happened with the economy in 2008 and 2009, the subprime mortgage meltdown, the credit crisis, and all of the associated fraud that has been uncovered, you can see the vital role that computer forensics plays in the process. Before the prevalence of technology in corporations, all investigators had to go on were paper documents and financial transactions. With the addition of computer forensics as a tool, we can better identify not only what happened at a certain point in time, but also, in some cases, the intent of the individuals involved. Multibillion-dollar fraud schemes are being blown open by the discovery of a single e-mail or thumb drive. Computer forensics is front and center in changing the way these investigations are conducted.

HOW THIS BOOK IS ORGANIZED

We have broken this book into five parts, reflective of the different stages of the investigation.

Part I: Preparing for an Incident

This section discusses how to develop a forensics process and set up the lab environment needed to conduct your investigation in an accurate and skillful manner. In addition, it lays the technical groundwork for the rest of the book.

Part II: Collecting the Evidence

These chapters teach you how to effectively find, capture, and prepare evidence for investigation. Additionally, we highlight how the law applies to evidence collection.

Part III: Forensic Investigation Techniques

This section illustrates how to apply recovery techniques to investigations from the evidence you have collected across many platforms and scenarios found in corporate settings. We introduce field-tested methods and techniques for recovering suspect activities.

Part IV: Presenting Your Findings

The legal environment of technical forensics is the focus of this section. We discuss how you will interact with council, testify in court, and report on your findings. In many ways, this is the most important part of the forensics process.

Part V: Putting It All Together

This section is all about the application of what we've discussed in the earlier parts of the book. We look at different types of investigations through the lens of computer forensics and how it can help create the bigger picture.

The Basic Building Blocks: Attacks and Countermeasures

This format should be very familiar to anyone who has read a *Hacking Exposed* book before. How we define attacks and countermeasures for forensics, however, is a bit different than in past books.

This is an attack icon.

In previous *Hacking Exposed* books, this icon was used to denote a type of attack that could be launched against your network or target. In this book, the attack icon relates to procedures, techniques, and concerns that threaten to compromise your investigation.

For instance, failing to properly image a hard drive is labeled an attack with a very high risk rating. This is because you are going to see it often; it is not difficult to create an image, and if you accidentally write to the disk when you are imaging, your whole investigation may be compromised, no matter what else you do correctly.

Popularity:	*The frequency with which you will run across this attack or technique in an investigation—1 being most rare and 10 being widely seen.*
Simplicity:	*The effort or degree of skill involved in creating an attack or technique—1 being quite high and 10 being little or involving no effort or skill.*
Impact:	*The potential damage to an investigation if you miss this detail—1 being trivial or no measurable damage and 10 being certain loss of evidence or equivalent damage.*
Risk Rating:	**The preceding three values are averaged to give the overall risk rating, representing the risk to the investigation's success.**

This is a countermeasure icon.

In this book, the countermeasure icon represents the ways that you can ensure correct completion of the investigation for the attack. In our hard drive example, this would mean correctly hashing the drive and verifying the hash after you have taken the image.

Other Visual Aides

We have also made use of several other visual icons that help point out fine details or gotchas that are frequently overlooked.

NOTE ————————————————————————————————————

TIP ————————————————————————————————————

CAUTION ————————————————————————————————————

ONLINE RESOURCES

Forensics is a constantly changing field. In addition, there are things we weren't able to include because they were outside the scope of the book. For these reasons, we have created a Web site that contains additional information, corrections for the book, and electronic versions of the things discussed in these pages. The URL is www.hackingexposedforensics.com.

In addition, if you have any questions or comments for the authors, feel free to e-mail us at authors@hackingexposedforensics.com.

We hope that you visit the Web site to keep up-to-date with the content in the book and the other things we think are useful. E-mail us if you have any questions or comments; we'd love to hear from you.

A FINAL WORD TO OUR READERS

As we said in the first edition, this book is about what happens after the incident response has taken place and during the nights of prolonged investigation to find the truth. When we wrote the first edition of the book, we had a fundamental tenet: Write a clear handbook for performing investigations of computer-related fraud. Five years and a world of technology later, that principle still guides us and is more important than ever. When applied properly, computer forensics applies a new level of transparency and accountability to traditional investigations that we haven't seen in the past. It is our sincere hope that this book can assist, even if in a very small way, this transparency and accountability take root.

That being said, we hope you enjoy reading this book as much as we did writing it. Thank you for taking the time to read what we have to say and good luck in all your investigations!

—*The Authors*

PART I

PREPARING FOR AN INCIDENT

CASE STUDY: LAB PREPARATIONS

Since its founding seven years ago, AcmeTech had seen its share of ups and downs. Started near the end of the tech bubble, the company's early days were a long way from the glitzy, go-go days of the dot.com heydays with fancy offices with $1000 Herman Miller chairs and product launch parties featuring the Dave Matthews Band. No, AcmeTech's early days could be described best as "scrappy." But the company succeeded where others failed primarily because it had what many didn't: a "killer app." It also had an aggressive salesperson who did his best to ensure that every Fortune 500 CIO had seen the application and wanted it.

Seven years later, that one application had grown into a suite of applications and the company's sales force had grown to 100 sales representatives in 10 countries. Leading the sales team was Herb Gouges, the same salesperson who, by sheer force of personality, got the company its first customer. Herb was now a seasoned veteran and was in high demand as a technology salesperson. While sales were booming, Herb was more than a little frustrated with AcmeTech management. He was one of the initial employees (and arguably one of its most important), yet he had received only a small amount of company stock. Worse, as the company grew, management reduced Herb's commissions—fairly typical of a growing company but still frustrating to Herb. He was approached by a headhunter recruiting for a new technology company with a product competing with AcmeTech's. Herb liked the product and the company but was concerned with having to start his sales efforts from scratch. While a non-compete agreement prevented him from soliciting directly from AcmeTech's customers, Herb knew he could work "behind the scenes" at his new firm and direct his AcmeTech customers to the new product. All he needed was information: customer lists and data, pricing models, service agreement templates, and so on.

Cashing Out

The plan worked. Mr. Gouges and a small cadre of helpers compromised more than 60 computers across dozens of locations, and unsuspecting users suffered hundreds of thousands in monetary damages—these people lost some serious cash.

It wasn't long before the U.S. Secret Service got involved and traced the source of the damages to Mr. Gouges. After capturing the suspect, they further discovered that Herb was taking advantage of ACME Services' computers, but they did not yet know how. The Secret Service notified ACME Services quietly to control any potential negative publicity for the publicly traded company. Acting as a silent partner, the Secret Service coordinated with ACME Services to bring in outside help.

In the meantime, the judge released Mr. Gouges on bail. The story wasn't over yet.

Preparing for a Forensics Operation

Before starting an investigation of any case, we have a thorough understanding of the forensics process, technical training, and proper lab preparation. These are critical to the success of an investigation. All the technicians assigned to our unit are required to have the necessary training and background to understand and conduct investigations. The training ensures that technicians avoid frequently made mistakes, such as turning on the computer to "check it out and see if anything important is in there."

Our team runs a secure lab and a formal case-management system. Before we started on the ACME case, we validated all the tools in the lab and neatly tucked the portable hardware units into the flyaway kits. We were ready to go when the call came to us. Our case-management system lets us handle the case and organize the evidence as it is returned to the lab. We control a large number of systems, tracking where the systems go and assigning the systems unique numbers with the proper documentation attached. This enables us to compare notes quickly and understand similarities found in multiple computers.

Rapid Response

Our flyaway kit includes a fully portable system with write blockers and extra drive bays ready to copy data. We also carry a standard set of tools and hardware used for our investigations. The standard set helped immensely when we needed to re-create our working system onto five new computers to handle all the systems we had to image. Having the tools and paperwork ready beforehand was critical to the rapid response demanded by the customer, especially considering the number of computers we had to investigate.

Solid process controls, training, preparations, and case management allowed us to respond quickly and efficiently. Our success in this case depended on our investment in a deeper understanding of how case operations work and how we could get the system to tell us the information we needed to know.

CHAPTER 1

THE FORENSICS PROCESS

fo·ren·sics (fə-rŏn´sĭks, -zĭks) *n. (used with a sing. verb)* The use of science and technology to investigate and establish facts in criminal or civil courts of law.

Corporate espionage. Illicit images. Violations of corporate policy. Hacking attempts. Work in information technology for even a short amount of time and you will find yourself dealing with one of these situations. When an incident occurs, the inevitable first words from management will be "What happened?" Apply computer forensics correctly and you answer that question in a way that is technically, legally, and analytically sound. To meet this goal, a forensics investigator must combine time-tested forensic techniques, legal framework, investigative skill, and cutting-edge technology to determine the facts.

Forensics is, first and foremost, a legal process. Depending on the investigation, you must understand and apply a vast array of legal concepts and precedents, such as chain of custody, spoilage of evidence, and dealing with production of evidence in court. If this sounds daunting, that's because it is. If the crime is heinous enough, a lawyer will call on you to take the stand and testify about your investigation, your findings, and your qualifications as an investigator. If you do not perform the investigation with dedication to the process, technical details, and legal issues required, the facts that you uncover are useless. In the extreme, criminals get away, corporate secrets are leaked, and the investigator is held with a fiduciary responsibility for the mistakes made during the investigation. To put it in more concise terms, *Be prepared*. Have a process, understand what you know and what you don't know, and create a list of who to call when the investigation exceeds your knowledge of either the technical or legal issues.

TYPES OF INVESTIGATIONS

Determining the type of investigation you are conducting is vital in discerning the correct process to follow. Each type of investigation has its own set of pitfalls, and knowing the parameters for the investigation you are conducting will help you avoid them. For the purposes of this book, investigations are divided into four main categories: theft of trade secrets, corporate or employee malfeasance, external breach, and civil litigation.

● Theft of Trade Secrets

Popularity:	10
Simplicity:	10
Impact:	8
Risk Rating:	**9**

By far the most common type of forensic investigation is that of theft of trade secrets. *Black's Law Dictionary* defines a trade secret as "Information that is not generally known or ascertainable, provides a competitive advantage, has been developed at the [company's] expense and is the subject of [the company's] intent to keep it confidential." A trade secret may be a patent, trademark, or other intellectual property, or it may be something as simple yet important as a customer list or proposal template. The classic example of a trade secret is the formula for Coca-Cola.

Trade secrets are protected by law, and employees and other entities are prohibited from stealing them or making them available to the others. Despite this prohibition, employee theft of trade secrets is rampant. It typically occurs when an employee or a group of employees leave a company to work for a competitor. Everyone wants a leg up, and for the employee that might mean taking competitive intelligence to his new employer. Depending on the nature of the information taken, this can have serious consequences for the owner of the stolen information in terms of lost customers, contracts, revenues, and so on. Because of this, and because most trade secrets today are stored electronically, internal and external forensic investigators deal with this issue more than any other. Depending on the nature of the information stolen, these cases can be very fast-moving investigations because of the potentially negative financial impact on the company.

While these investigations may start as an internal investigation, they can quickly turn into litigation in the form of temporary restraining orders and lawsuits. As a result, an investigator must assume from the outset that the evidence collected in a theft of trade secrets matter will be ultimately presented in court and should use defensible technical methods and follow appropriate processes.

Corporate or Employee Malfeasance

Popularity:	8
Simplicity:	6
Impact:	5
Risk Rating:	6

Investigations into malfeasance on the part of a company, an individual, or a group of employees can take one of three forms: internal, external such as a governmental investigation, or quasi-internal such as a board of director's investigation of senior executives. These investigations require an element of secrecy, as the suspects are typically active employees who are in violation of the law or corporate policy. The simple knowledge that an investigation is occurring would be enough for the suspects to destroy evidence, potentially causing more harm. The clandestine nature of these investigations makes them different and challenging. Alternative means of evidence collection may be employed to preserve the secrecy of the investigation. Forensic activities may take place without the knowledge of the company's IT department, making the investigation even more complicated. And because the information gathered may ultimately end up being used in a criminal case, the methods must be rigorous and unassailable.

External Breach

Popularity:	5
Simplicity:	9
Impact:	10
Risk Rating:	6

You are most likely familiar with this type of an investigation because it's typically the one that gets all the headlines. Individuals from outside the company penetrate the company's network to exploit the data or the network itself for commercial gain, retaliation, or purely for fun. To the extent that customer data such as transaction information or financial records are involved, these types of hacking incidents can be very harmful to a company's reputation and can open it up to expensive regulatory action and litigation. Theft of credit card information from banks and Social Security numbers from universities are famous examples of external breaches. Time is of the essence in these situations. But while steps must be taken to secure the breach, an investigator must be mindful that these steps do not, if at all possible, compromise the investigation that will ensue. Too often we have seen the remediation and the investigation occur sequentially when in reality they should occur simultaneously. Documentation in these investigations is critical, as it is important to ensure that the evidence is preserved so that it can be used in future civil or criminal litigation.

Civil Discovery

Popularity:	8
Simplicity:	6
Impact:	5
Risk Rating:	6

Civil discovery is less of an investigation and more of a step in the litigation process. Our legal system allows parties to litigation the opportunity to review documents in support of or in refutation of a legal claim. This means that if one company sues another, each is entitled to review the other company's documents that are deemed to be relevant to the case. For example, in the case of a theft of trade secrets, the competitive firm is allowed to review all the evidence collected during the investigation that relates to the theft. Forensic investigators may be asked to identify and produce electronic data from their company to comply with a discovery request or review the evidence provided by the opposing company to establish proof of the company's claim.

While the pace of civil discovery may be slower than an investigation into an external breach, the importance of well-documented processes and methods remains critical. Either side may make an issue over how the evidence was collected and produced. Should the judge agree that the processes used were negligent, the company could suffer

A Special Note About Criminal Investigations

While any one of the aforementioned investigations can rise to the level of a criminal act, they are most likely to occur in instances of corporate malfeasance and external breach. These investigations are often for the highest stakes. The suspect's livelihood and/or the company's reputation and even viability are on the line, and every aspect of the investigation is scrutinized and reworked multiple times. Accuracy is paramount, with attention to the process and documentation a close second.

Know your process, know your tools, and above all know your limits. For an internal investigator, these cases can be particularly problematic as the pressure to muddle or even suppress the truth can be intense. In these situations, it's best to encourage the use of an external forensic investigator. As an external forensic investigator, be judicious in selecting in which criminal matters you get involved. These cases play out in the media, with the latest happenings of the court showing up on the 6 o'clock news. Credibility of the investigator is also at a premium, and if you don't have the proper credentials and background to testify properly on your findings, your credibility will be destroyed on the stand in a very public forum.

in the courtroom. We've seen entire cases thrown out or monetary sanctions imposed as a result of faulty methods used in the preservation or collection of relevant data.

Determining the Type of Investigation

Knowing the type of case you are dealing with defines how you conduct your investigation. This determination is never as easy as it sounds. Cases can escalate in the blink of an eye. You don't want to get in a situation where evidence has to be thrown out because you took the situation too lightly and didn't fully think through what type of case you were dealing with. Always treat a new case with the same standard procedures you know are tested and true. This simple guiding principle, although not followed as often as we'd like to believe, can save an investigator immeasurable grief down the line.

THE ROLE OF THE INVESTIGATOR

What makes a good computer forensics investigator? The ability to be creative in the discovery of evidence, rigorous in the application of a disciplined process, and understanding of the legal issues that are involved every step of the way. However, other factors play into the equation, depending on the investigation's context. Stories of investigators who ruined or destroyed a case because of incompetence or arrogance are all too familiar. You must have a complete understanding of the risks when you embark on a case.

Investigator Bias

Popularity:	7
Simplicity:	9
Impact:	8
Risk Rating:	8

The investigator must play the role of an unbiased third party. Think of it in terms of traditional forensic sciences. For example, if the scientist performing a blood test in a violent crime case is friends with the suspect, the results of the test will be considered dubious at best. The same holds for computer forensics. As those who have been on the stand in this position will attest to the fact that you must be unbiased. If the opposing counsel can create the impression that you are biased, you will be embarrassed on the stand or in deposition. This is particularly true of internal forensic investigators. If you are perceived to be operating solely in the best interest of your employer and not to the furtherance of the truth, you'll become raw meat to a good opposing counsel. Internal investigators need to take even more steps to ensure the integrity and completeness of their analysis than even external investigators do to overcome this perceived bias.

 Resolving Bias

Always practice full disclosure with your clients, internal and external. Discuss with them potential conflicts of interest. If you had dinner at the suspect's house two years ago, make sure they know about it. If the other side knows about it but your guys don't, you are in for a bad time during and after deposition. Don't be afraid to recommend a third-party firm or investigator who can conduct the investigation in an unbiased manner.

Investigator Qualifications

Popularity:	6
Simplicity:	7
Impact:	9
Risk Rating:	7

The investigator must be qualified to perform the analysis in a skillful manner. For criminal investigations, the law enforcement examiners go through rigorous training seminars to become skilled in the art. Experts who have a track record in the industry and who have enough credentials to imply competency often conduct civil investigations. Commonly, IT administrators conduct internal investigations, or in the case of large-scale corporations, a special division of the company is employed. Don't make the mistake of assuming that you're qualified to be a forensic examiner just because you're a skilled IT manager. I have been a party to many dinners and outings where experienced investigators tell war stories about going against "newbies." These stories always end badly for the newbie. Don't be the subject of one of these stories. If you are not properly qualified and credentialed to perform the investigation, the court will throw out your findings and you will be in a world of hurt with your superiors.

Investigator Use of Evidence

Popularity:	6
Simplicity:	7
Impact:	9
Risk Rating:	7

Evidence is a tricky thing. The best rule of thumb is that if you didn't empirically find the evidence through hands-on investigation, don't use it. Hearsay is not admissible in a court of law, and we all know what happens when you make assumptions. The best course of action is to treat every investigation as a blank slate with no prior knowledge. Begin an investigation with an open mind, and take the unsubstantiated words of others with a grain of salt. The tools and the processes exist for a reason; use them and trust them. The more that politics and personal agendas influence your analysis, the less credible your results become in court.

Investigator Liability

Popularity:	6
Simplicity:	7
Impact:	9
Risk Rating:	7

If you ignore the caveats and decide to conduct the investigation, you are financially and legally liable if it becomes a civil or criminal case and you are not doing a corporate investigation. In the best case, the courts throw out the analysis and a third party conducts another investigation. In civil cases, you may be liable for loss damages resulting from the destruction or inadmissibility of evidence. All those high-priced lawyers that your company is using to go after someone will soon be coming after you. In criminal cases, you can be tried for negligence and serve jail time.

Being a Good Investigator

Know your limits, and don't be afraid to call in qualified professionals if the situation requires it. This may sound basic, but practice with your tools. Constantly revalidate your processes for handling evidence and test the results of your tools. You must be able to execute flawlessly when the time comes. This is a hard lesson that most rookie investigators learn in their first deposition when the opposing counsel's experts contest them. They leave the deposition with egos deflated, wishing that they had finished reading this book.

ELEMENTS OF A GOOD PROCESS

The task of a computer forensics investigator is difficult. It is one of the most adversarial occupations in information technology. You will have every aspect of your technical competency and methods scrutinized to their very core. As such, it is imperative that you use a deterministic, repeatable process that is clear, concise, and simple. Adherence to this process is the examiner's greatest asset. Deviate from it, and your investigation will be for naught. Having a defined, proven process means you show several elements:

- Cross-validation of findings
- Proper evidence handling
- Completeness of investigation
- Management of archives
- Technical competency
- Explicit definition and justification for the process
- Legal compliance
- Flexibility

This list will become your lifeline the day you either take the stand yourself or hand off the investigation to authorities who will pursue it further. These items are the difference between an effective, expedient investigation and playing around with a neat piece of software. Software is good, and while your friends may be impressed with your comprehensive knowledge of the latest in-vogue forensic tool, the opposing counsel, and more importantly the judge, will not.

Cross-validation

Whenever possible, rely on more than one tool to back up your findings. Cross-validation is one of the key tools available to the forensic investigator. If you trust only one tool in your investigation, you live and die by that tool. If the opposing counsel can rip holes in the single tool you use, it doesn't matter how solid your investigative process is. A member of law enforcement once told me that he would assume that he could win cases based solely on the fact that the defense used a tool he knew had several holes. You can mitigate this type of situation by cross-validating findings with multiple toolsets. Better still, have another skilled investigator test your results independently and attempt to validate your findings.

Proper Evidence Handling

A good rule to follow as a forensic investigator is the same one taught to all incoming medical students: First, no do harm. Computer evidence is notoriously subject to the "observer effect": the mere act of viewing data on a system without using proper forensic techniques can cause the data in the system to change. You must be able to show that the evidence you present in court is exactly the same as the evidence that existed at the time it was collected. That means you must not modify the evidence in any way as part of your investigation.

The forensic investigator must always be aware of the chain of custody of evidence after collection. It is vital that you show who had access to the evidence, what they did with it, and that no tampering with the evidence occurred. Become familiar with the different cryptographic hashing functions, such as MD5 and SHA-1. These algorithms act like fingerprints, allowing you to show mathematically that the evidence is the same today as the day the investigator collected it. Also, always keep records of who accesses evidence, when they access the evidence, and what they do with it. This will help to refute evidence injection arguments that the opposing counsel may make during litigation.

Completeness of Investigation

When conducting an investigation, a forensics investigator has to be able to show that she conducted the search for evidence in a complete manner. Lawyers hate new evidence brought up days before court time that they didn't know about. The clients they represent hate it even more when that new evidence causes them to lose the case. Know what you know and know what you don't know. Follow your counsel's direction on what evidence to look for and don't go outside the scope of that. But use a process that ensures that you will locate every piece and reference to that evidence. If you don't use a solid, tested process for evidence collection, analysis, and reporting, you will miss evidence.

Management of Archives

In the legal world, just because a judge has ruled does not mean the case is over. An investigator may be asked to rework a case months or years after the initial investigation. This makes it imperative always to ensure that proper archiving and case management is part of the process. If counsel comes back six months after a ruling asking you to rework a case for the appeal, you must be able to fulfill that request. This means proper document retention, data storage, and backup policies. As with your initial testimony, you will be required to show proper evidence handling and authenticity of the data. The last thing you want as an investigator is to formally request the opposing counsel for an image of a hard drive because your process didn't include proper retention procedures.

Technical Competency

Have a complete technical understanding of everything you do. The surefire way to lose a case is to justify your actions by saying, "That's what the tool says to do." Challenge your tool's assumptions. If you do settle on a specific toolset, understand the tradeoffs that the developers made when designing the tool. Know your toolset's weaknesses and strengths so you can stand by it when questioned.

A prime example of this is the way that the novice investigator treats digital signatures. It is common for someone with a basic understanding of a cryptographic hash to make the statement that "each dataset will create a unique hash." While this statement is true as a matter of practice, the "birthday attack" shows that this can be subverted. If you understand hashing and are familiar with the birthday attack, it is easy to address this subversion when questioned. If you don't understand these basics, you will be torn apart by the opposing expert.

The birthday attack is based on the fact that if you continually change input datasets, the resulting hash will be the same alarmingly more often than one would expect. Its name is derived from the fact that with 23 people in a room, there is approximately a 50 percent chance that two of them share a birthday on the same day of the year.

Explicit Definition and Justification for the Process

Hardware malfunctions. Software crashes. You must conduct your investigation in a manner that allows you to retrace all your steps. You must follow a discrete and clear path while performing an investigation that is easily explainable to a judge and opposing counsel. If you end up questioned on your methodology and the line of thinking that led you to the results you are presenting, you have to justify yourself. Do this by showing the steps and walking others through the investigation. If, when questioned on your methods, you can't provide clear evidence that they were correct, the investigation was for naught.

Legal Compliance

Always ensure that your process conforms to the laws in the jurisdiction of the investigation. For an internal corporate investigation, ensure that it complies with the corporate policies set forth. The most technically creative and astute investigations are meaningless if they don't adhere to the legal rules of the case. Talk to the lawyers or the corporate higher-ups. Get feedback on how the investigation should proceed, the type of evidence desired, and where the legal or corporate policy landmines exist. Remember that at the end of the day, the role of the investigator is a supporting role in a much bigger play. Talk to the legal or corporate experts and don't perform the investigation in a vacuum.

Flexibility

Every investigation is different. Each has its own set of requirements and pitfalls. The process that you use to conduct investigations must be able to cope with change. A common issue with rookie examiners is reliance on just one tool. If an investigation requires you to find evidence on technology not supported by the tool, your process is worthless. Make sure you design your process to handle new technologies and requirements that may pop up as the investigation continues, and as you take on new investigations.

DEFINING A PROCESS

Now that you know what makes a good forensic investigator and what the elements of a sound process are, let's define a process. The remainder of the chapter will focus on the process used by the Electronic Discovery Reference Model (EDRM). The EDRM is an industry working group that was created in May 2005 to create an industry standard process for the analysis and production of electronic data. It is sound and has been tested in both legal and technical aspects. In addition, it is flexible enough to handle the diverse requirements that you may see as an investigator.

Following are the relevant stages of the EDRM:

1. Identification

2. Collection and preservation

3. Analysis

4. Production and presentation

When applied correctly, these steps can guide you to a complete and justifiable investigation. They have been tested in court time and time again, with years of refinement.

 The EDRM working group comprises industry members from all areas of electronic discovery and forensics (including the two authors of this book). For more information on the EDRM project, visit www.EDRM.net.

To understand the process as a whole, you must understand what each step in the methodology entails.

Identification

This first phase of the process details what you do when you're presented with a case and need to determine a course of action. Five core steps guide you through the initial identification phase:

1. *Determine scope and quantity of the data.* This requires that you, as the investigator, work with the individuals requesting the examination to determine what the investigation will cover and approximately how much data the investigation will entail.

2. *Identify repositories.* Before beginning an investigation but after determination of the scope, you must identify the location of data that could potentially

hold evidence. This could be anything from personal computers to enterprise servers, personal digital assistants (PDAs), or cell phones. At this point, you need to determine whether you have the tools you need to complete the examination properly.

3. *Strategize preservation.* Once you determine where the data to examine is stored, you must decide what steps will be required to protect that data at all costs. If it can be shown that the data was modified outside normal business processes after the incident occurred, you will have problems justifying your findings. This preservation action must occur as quickly as feasible. As will be discussed in later chapters, accomplishing this depends on the circumstances of the investigation; no hard-and-fast rule applies to every case.

4. *Establish chain of custody.* After protecting the evidence, it is a legal requirement that chain of custody be established. As discussed earlier, this entails creating a record of who did what to the data when. The longer you wait to establish chain of custody, the more difficult it is to trace the findings back to the original data. You must be able to show that the data is unmodified and that every attempt to access and interpret it was logged.

5. *Preview the data.* Only after the completion of steps 1 through 4 should you preview the data in a manner that guarantees it is not changed. This allows you to prepare for the acquisition phase of the process, when you will create a forensic copy of the data for the purpose of investigation and interpretation. Be very careful to use only forensically approved tools, as standard interfaces such as Windows Explorer can cause inadvertent modifications to things such as file metadata.

Collection and Preservation

This is the point at which you will actually collect the data in a forensically sound manner for conducting the investigation. Detailed discussion of this phase occurs in later chapters. However, at a broad level, four core steps are involved in this phase of the process:

1. *Identify the source media.* Data is stored on media, and you need to know what type of data is stored and how to access it. While this step sounds obvious, some pitfalls can occur. This issue can be especially problematic when you are presented, for example, with 15-year-old tape backups and no one has a clue in what format or media the tape is actually stored. Creativity and ingenuity are paramount in such situations.

2. *Select acquisition parameters.* Establish the parameters required for proper imaging. The type of case and legal requirements placed upon the investigator will determine this. To use an old construction analogy, some jobs require a hammer and some require a screwdriver. Know what you are dealing with and act appropriately.

3. *Create the image.* After you have determined the media and set your parameters, create the image. The image creation process must ensure that it hasn't modified the data and that the image is complete. You must have metadata to accompany the image so that you can validate this process.

4. *Authenticate.* The purpose of this phase is to determine whether the image that you have created is identical to the original data. The reliable way to accomplish this is through metadata cryptographic hashes. Before you create the image, create a hash of the original data in its pristine state. Immediately after you create the image, create a hash of the image data. These two hashes must match; if they don't, you did something wrong and you will lose the case. It is also important that these hashes exist outside the data. If you place the hash inside the data to be imaged, you will alter the original data and thus invalidate your image and your investigation. Also, ensure that the hashing algorithm you choose is sufficiently secure. A simple checksum is too easy to spoof for evidence verification. The two common algorithms used in this step are the MD5 and the SHA-1 algorithms. While the forensics community battles about which is better, at the end of the day as long as you can justify your usage of your flavor of choice, either will be OK to use in practice.

Analysis

After you have determined what data you need to examine and have forensically verified images of that data, you can begin analysis. This is the meat of the investigation. The entire second part of this book addresses this phase, so we discuss it only at a broad level here. The key thing to keep in mind whenever performing analysis is completeness. Always be sure that you have looked in every nook and cranny and that you haven't missed anything relevant. Lawyers hate it when opposing counsel finds new evidence that destroys your case. Be complete and creative; unconventional thinking will help greatly in this phase.

Production and Presentation

After you complete your investigation, you will probably have come up with evidence and information relevant to the case. Other people are interested in these findings, especially those paying your bill. This phase is discussed at length in the third part of the book. In general, just remember to keep it simple. To test how well you articulate your case, find the least technically competent member of your family and explain your findings to him or her. If you accomplish that goal successfully, you are ready to present the data to counsel. Lawyers are lawyers and CEOs are CEOs; if you find yourself having to describe the intricacies of the latest image format to them, you probably haven't distilled the findings sufficiently. For highly technical investigators, this can be the most difficult phase of the process, so tread with care.

AFTER THE INVESTIGATION

After you have detailed your findings and the case has concluded, you must archive the data and findings because you may have to readdress the case in the future. The manner in which you go about this varies case to case. Ask yourself the following three questions to determine how to archive the data:

- *How much?* Some cases will require that you archive the complete images and datasets used in the investigation. For some cases, such as large-scale corporate cases, complete archival is either cost-prohibitive or impossible. Work with those who are directing the case to determine how much data and which datasets need archiving for the possibility of future issues.

- *How long?* How long you need to keep the archives around depends again on the case. The lawyers or executives involved in the case will have knowledge of the process of wrapping up a case and the timeline for things such as appeals. Discuss this with them and create a plan that accommodates this timeline. Destroying evidence too soon after a case concludes can have disastrous consequences.

- *How likely?* Try to determine the likelihood that the case will be appealed or escalated. If it seems like an appeal is inevitable, archive as much as possible to prepare for the appeal. If it looks as though a case will be escalated, such as an internal investigation resulting in a wrongful termination suit, consider that as well. As with the previous two questions, look to counsel or the executive in charge of the case for guidance on this issue.

Once you have answered these questions, you are ready to design an archival solution for the case. The goal is to create a time capsule, a bundle that contains archived data, the proper documentation such as process checklists, chain of custody records, and the results and findings. Place this bundle in an environment-proof storage location. The last thing you need is to lose a case because a fire ruined your evidence. Archival details are covered in Chapter 3. With all things like this, a little prevention goes a long way.

CHAPTER 2

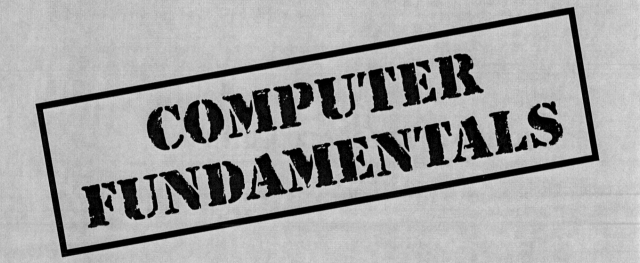

COMPUTER FUNDAMENTALS

As with any discipline, the key to employing effective computer forensics is a firm grasp and complete understanding of the fundamentals. Opposing counsel loves nothing more than to rip apart the credibility of an expert witness by playing "stump the chump" with obscure facts about storage media or operating system (OS) internals. For some, this chapter will be a crash course in the internal workings of computer technologies. For others, it will serve as a refresher course. Either way, this chapter offers a technical foundation to the rest of the book.

Before you can effectively complete investigations on any operating system, you must understand how a hard drive stores information and how the OS uses that hard drive. In addition, more exotic technologies such as flash memory and PDA RAM have their own sets of pitfalls. If you don't understand the fundamental concepts discussed in this chapter, you will not be able to complete a defensible investigation.

In addition, if you are called upon to perform a deposition or testify on the witness stand, this chapter will help serve as a crib sheet for testimony. A friend of mine was once asked, while on the stand, "What type of file system do floppy disks use in MS-DOS 6.0?" by opposing counsel to try to rattle him. The answer to this question is FAT12, and because he knew his stuff, he answered correctly. Floppy disks use a file system different from that of hard drives in the old DOS scheme. With all the point-and-click forensics tools available today, it is tempting to forgo learning details like this. However, this is a perfect example of how a complete understanding of the basics can protect you while you're under fire on the witness stand.

We wrote this chapter to serve as a reference. The night before you are scheduled to give testimony, dust off this book and reread this chapter. It will help prepare you for what is to come.

THE BOTTOM-UP VIEW OF A COMPUTER

As my "Introduction to Computing Science" professor once said, the essence of modern computing is abstracting complexity. The modern computer is much like the human body. Different modules each perform simple tasks; put them together in the right way, and amazingly complex tasks can be completed. A heart pumps blood. The lungs move air around. Eyes process light to create images. These are very basic tasks that work simultaneously to sustain life. Computers work in a similar way. A processor performs operations. A hard disk stores 1s and 0s. A video card converts those 1s and 0s to signals a monitor can understand. Put them together and you get the computer and all the possibilities that go along with it. Figure 2-1 shows a modular illustration of a computer, from the application that balances your checkbook to the processor that crunches the numbers.

It's All Just 1s and 0s

1s and 0s seem simple enough, but these numbers are the building blocks for every computing technology and application in existence. Known as the *binary number system*,

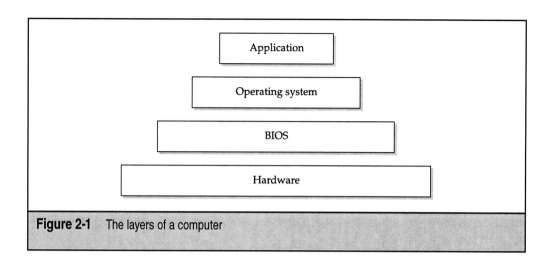

Figure 2-1   The layers of a computer

they are used in conjunction with transistors to create Boolean algebraic equations. The operations that these transistors can perform are AND, OR, NOT, and various combinations of those basic operators.

NOTE   To reduce the total number of transistors actually used, most processors today create all their operations with NAND gates as the basic building block. If you are interested in learning more, consult an elementary computer architecture book.

Once these operations are defined, you can take the 1s and 0s and create a combinatorial network that performs conventional math functions (addition, subtraction, and so on). Figure 2-2 shows how the Boolean operations combine to add two, 1-bit numbers (what is known as a *1-bit adder*).

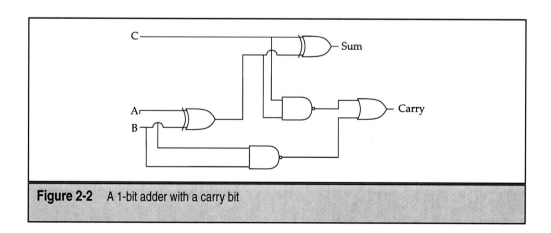

Figure 2-2   A 1-bit adder with a carry bit

After you have built an adder, you can use it and the Boolean operations to perform addition, subtraction, multiplication, and division. You can also hook the adders together to add 8-, 16-, or 32-bit numbers, as most modern processors do. In the race to have the fastest benchmark numbers on the market, computer builders have added specialized operations into computers that allow them to perform certain types of operations quickly. In fact, the staggering number of transistors on modern processors is a result of the need for specialized operations. While detailed descriptions of the complete modern processor is outside the scope of this book, the following table shows the number of transistors per chip to give you an idea of the complexity of these technologies.

Processor	Year Created	Number of Transistors
Intel 8080	1974	6000
Intel 80486	1989	1,200,000
Intel Pentium	1993	3,100,000
Intel Pentium IV	2000	42,000,000

Furthermore, in the past few years, we have seen the addition of multiple cores to processors. This means that instead of a single chip containing a single Pentium chip, for instance, a single "dual core" chip will contain the equivalent of two Pentium chips. The current "arms race" in processor development seems to be centering around this concept of multiple cores and the idea of getting as many as possible onto a single chip. We are now starting to see 4, 8, 16 and even 64 on a single chip.

Learning from the Past: Giving Computers Memory

Now that we have the ability to perform mathematical operations on numbers, we need a way to load and store the results of these operations. This is where memory comes in. Computers use two basic types of memory: volatile and nonvolatile. Volatile memory is difficult to retrieve when the computer is turned off. Examples of this type of memory are main memory (RAM, or Random Access Memory) and cache memory. Nonvolatile memory is not difficult to retrieve when the computer is turned off. This is usually the secondary memory source, such as hard disks or flash memory. Figure 2-3 shows the interaction of the various types of memory and how they move information in a computer.

Volatile Memory

You can think of volatile memory as a scratch pad that the computer uses when evaluating data. The most fundamental unit of this type of memory is the *flip-flop*, shown in Figure 2-4. As the name suggests, a flip-flop can store a 1 or a 0 while the computer is on, and the computer can flip the stored value when it needs to store a different value.

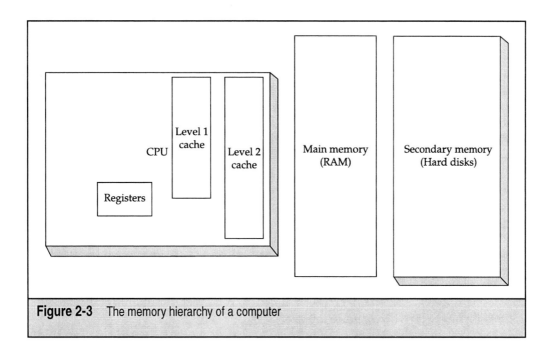

Figure 2-3   The memory hierarchy of a computer

If you hook together eight flip-flops, you can store an 8-bit number. In the common nomenclature, a series of these flip-flops is known as a *register*. By combining this with the adder described earlier, you can add two numbers and store the result for later use.

Registers hold a very small amount of data and are used only when the computer needs to store temporary values during multiple-step operations. For larger pieces of data, a second level of memory must be used, and this is where RAM comes in. RAM memory

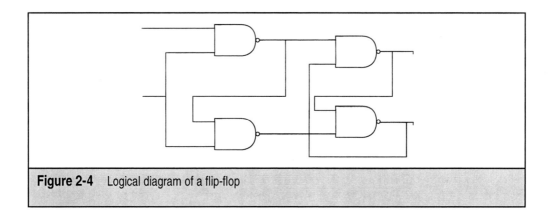

Figure 2-4   Logical diagram of a flip-flop

is outside the processor and can hold a very large amount of data while the computer is on. The downside to this type of memory, however, is the delay time the processor incurs when loading and storing data in RAM. Because of this lag time and the adverse effects on performance, most modern processors have what is known as a *cache*, which you can think of as an intermediate step between the registers and the main memory. It's slower than the registers but not nearly as slow as accessing main memory.

Nonvolatile Memory

Nonvolatile memory is used when data needs to be stored even if the computer is turned off. The most common type of media used in nonvolatile memory is magnetic media, such as a hard disk. The upside to magnetic media is that it can be purchased cheaply in comparison to volatile memory. The downside, however, is that it is incredibly slow in comparison. Magnetic media actually has moving parts: the typical hard drive has platters that spin around with a tiny magnetic head changing charges on the platter from positive to negative, which represent the binary 1s and 0s. Even though today's hard drives have been able to achieve mind-blowing speed, their inherent design prevents them from ever being as fast as volatile memory by an order of magnitude. Because of this speed difference, computers are designed to minimize the number of times that something has to be written out to this secondary memory.

However, since nonvolatile memory is so much cheaper than RAM, secondary memory is also often used as swap space for the processor. This presents a unique opportunity for the investigator, because you can go back through the hard drive, find the swap file, and take apart the memory of the computer to locate evidence that would otherwise be destroyed or obfuscated. The specific way to do this varies from operating system to operating system and is discussed in more detail in Chapters 6, 7, and 8. In fact, most of your time as an investigator will be spent going through nonvolatile memory. Due to the timing of forensic investigations (you get the computers days, weeks, and sometimes months after the fact), very rarely will you have the opportunity to access the RAM in a form that is usable during an investigation. The different types of memory that a computer can use are detailed later in this chapter in "Types of Media"; it's well worth your time to learn each type completely.

Basic Input and Output System (BIOS)

Now that we have created a processor and memory for the processor to use, we need to create a way for software to talk to the hardware and work with other peripherals. The BIOS provides simple methods for software to interact with hardware. When you first turn on the computer, the BIOS runs a series of self checks (called the *Power On Self Test*, or *POST*) and then turns control over to the operating system. This transition occurs by way of what is called the Master Boot Record (MBR) on the hard drive, a topic that will be discussed in detail in Part II. An effective BIOS manages the allocation of resources (via interrupt requests, or IRQs, and direct memory access, or DMA) to the peripherals and handles basic security measures. Some of the more modern BIOS features are power management and digital rights management (DRM). The BIOS provides only raw access to the resources; it does nothing to manage or allocate those resources for performance. Its function is strictly to act as the interface between the OS and the hardware.

The Operating System

The OS is by far the most complex piece of software on any given computer. It acts as the translation layer between the end-user applications and the BIOS or hardware. The OS manages the users, the memory, the applications, and the processor time on the computer. A well-written OS can breathe new life into an old computer, same as a poorly written one can bog down even the fastest of machines. As an investigator, I recommend that you spend time learning the mainstream OSs inside and out.

 Learning about an OS is not a trivial task. Windows XP has more than 5 million lines of code. The file system, the swap space, and the memory map are all artifacts of the OS installed on the machine. We devote Chapters 6, 7, and 8 to discussions of various operating systems.

The Applications

Applications are why you use a computer in the first place. They balance our checkbooks, allow us to browse the Internet, or entertain us with games, movies, or other activities. From a forensics perspective, it is beneficial for you to become familiar with the ins and outs of a few select applications. Understanding the way that office applications create and delete documents, how e-mail programs work, and how web browsers access the Internet will help you track down evidence that you can use in your investigation. Chapters 11 and 12 are dedicated to various applications that you will see again and again in your time as an investigator.

TYPES OF MEDIA

As discussed in the preceding section, investigations will focus primarily on the secondary memory area—hard disks, CD-ROMs, tape backups, and most other types of commonly used storage. Each of these types of media has its own nuances and pitfalls in an investigation. Let's look at the three most common types of media—magnetic, optical, and RAM—in detail.

 If you are conducting an investigation in a legal capacity (as an action in a lawsuit, in a formal third-party investigation, and so on), it is vital that you not only understand the different types of media but also the laws that govern what you can ask for and what you can't. We discuss this topic more in Chapters 14 and 15.

Magnetic Media

You will spend the majority of your time dealing with magnetic media, including hard disks, floppy disks, and tape backups. Zip disks and other such large-capacity portable disks are just variations on the structure of the hard disk or floppy disk. The theory for all of these types is the same: Some kind of metal or magnetic surface holds a series of positive or negative magnetic charges. This series represents 1s or 0s, depending on the charge of the magnet. When data is changed on the media, the magnetic charge is changed. This means several things: First, there are moving parts, and moving parts are susceptible to breaking. Always have backups. Second, the media is open to being affected by external magnets. This means that your forensic lab procedures and storage policies must consider this, and you must be able to prove that this hasn't happened when dealing in a court of law.

Hard Disk Drives

Popularity:	10
Simplicity:	6
Impact:	10
Risk Rating:	9

If you learn the complete architecture for just one media type, make it the hard drive. Ninety percent of an investigator's time will be spent imaging, searching, or wiping hard drives, and none of these are as easy as they might seem. How do you know the image of a hard drive is an exact duplicate? What is slack space? What is your wiping procedure? Until you can answer these questions and fully justify your answers, don't even attempt an investigation. Let's break down a hard drive's components and how those components interact.

Physical Parts of the Hard Drive

Before we look at how data is stored on a hard drive, we need to talk a bit about the physical components of the drive. Hard drives are marvels of modern engineering. Imagine a plane traveling Mach 1 with an altitude of about 2 feet above the runway. This is the rough equivalent to what a hard drive does every time it spins up and reads or writes data. Figure 2-5 shows the parts of a hard drive.

Platters   Platters are the circular discs that actually store the data. A single hard drive will include multiple platters often made of some aluminum alloy, but newer drives use a glass or ceramic material. These platters are covered with a magnetic substrate so that they can hold a magnetic charge. Hard drive failures rarely occur within the platters. In fact, nine times out of ten, if you send a drive off to a data recovery firm, it will take the drive apart and mount the platters in a new drive assembly to retrieve the data from them.

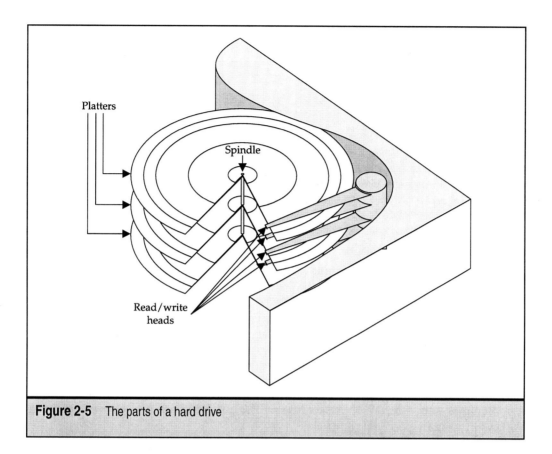

Figure 2-5   The parts of a hard drive

Read and Write Heads   Tiny magnetic read and write heads change and read the magnetic state on the platters. Think of these in the same way you think of a needle on an old LP record player or a laser on a CD-ROM player. In this case, the head is a copper coil that has charges pushed through it. This creates a magnetic field that can either read or write data. Because there are multiple platters, multiple heads are used. Typically, to optimize the usage of the platter, both the top and bottom of the platter's surface are used. For performance purposes and for better reliability, all the heads are hooked together and move in unison. This way, data can be read simultaneously from multiple platters. These are so compactly designed that they must be assembled in a clean room, because even a single stray particle can disrupt the head alignment.

Head Actuator   For many years, this was a major source of failure for hard drives. The two types of head actuators are stepper motor and voice coil. Old hard drives (less than

100MB) used stepper motor actuators, which were nothing short of terrible: if you didn't park the heads before moving the drive, you broke it; if you didn't recalibrate the disk by formatting it after you cleared it, you broke the drive; if you used the hard drive too much, you broke it. Look at the thing wrong and you broke it! Over time, these actuators would "forget" where they were on the hard disk and you'd lose all your data. On the opposite side of the equation are the voice coil actuators. These correct themselves if they get lost on the platter using grey code. In addition, they don't have to be parked before a hard drive is spun down.

NOTE   Grey codes are an alternative binary numbering system in which only 1 bit changes from one number to the next. Grey codes are particularly useful in mechanical encoders, since a slight change in position affects only 1 bit. Using a typical binary code, up to n bits could change, and slight misalignments between reading elements could cause wildly incorrect readings.

Spindle Motor   As you may have guessed, the spindle motor spins the platters. These motors are engineered to very strict standards, since they have to be able to maintain precise speeds and must not vibrate. These motors rotate at a constant rate (such as 3600, 4200, 7200, 10,000, or even as high as 15,000 RPM). A feedback loop is set up inside the motor to ensure that it rotates at exactly the correct speed. On older hard drives, the motor was on the bottom of the drive, but now they are built into the hub of the platters to conserve space and allow for more platters in the drive.

Hard Drive Interface   The hard drive interface is the protocol used by the hard drive to communicate with a host computer or network. Following are the types of interfaces commonly used by personal computers:

- **PATA/EIDE (Parallel Advanced Technology Attachment/Enhanced Integrated Drive Electronics)**   PATA, also referred to as EIDE, is the old standard for connecting hard drives and other devices to the motherboard using a ribbon cable and a 40-pin connector. These types of drives are typically hooked up externally to a computer using USB or Firewire converter. You may occasionally encounter these drives installed in older computers.

- **SATA (Serial Advanced Technology Attachment)**   SATA is the serial interface that has come to replace PATA. It uses a much narrower cable and has faster data transfer speeds. These drives can be connected internally to the motherboard or externally as eSATA, USB, or Firewire converters.

- **SCSI (small computer system interface)**   SCSI drives are often seen in servers and RAID controllers, but occasionally you'll find personal computers with them as well, although they are quickly being replaced by SATA. SCSI can be used as both an external and internal interface.

- **SAS (Serial-Attached SCSI)**   SAS drives are the progression of SCSI drives into a point-to-point serial protocol. SAS also offers faster transfer speeds over its predecessor in addition to using a narrower cable. More devices can also be supported on the SAS bus. It's worth noting that SATA devices can be hooked up to SAS controllers.

Storing Data on the Hard Drive

Now that you have a grasp on what parts are inside the metal enclosure, let's focus on the platters and how they store the data. Modern hard drives hold a massive amount of information. Over the years, a structure has developed that optimizes the speed that this data is read off the drive. Figure 2-6 shows a cross-section of the platters.

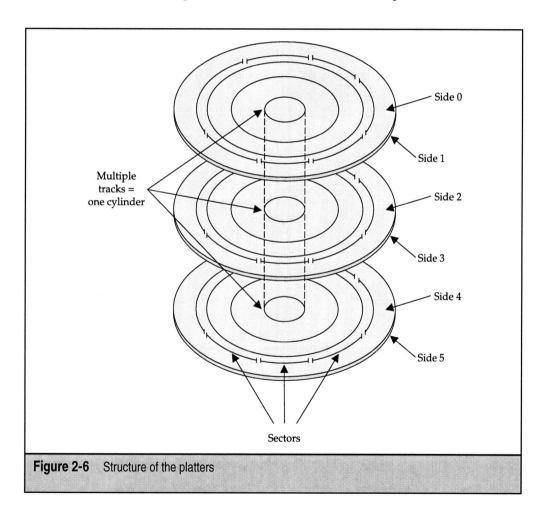

Figure 2-6   Structure of the platters

A very logical and structured layout controls how data is stored on rotational magnetic media. Three basic units denote position of data on a hard disk: head, sector, and cylinder.

Head   The head came about when multiple platters were added to the hard drive assembly. The head number corresponds to the platter that holds the data.

Sector   The name sector is derived from the mathematical term for a pie-shaped division of a circle (think of a triangle with one vertex at the center of the circle and two on the circle itself). This term was chosen because sectors were originally broken out in this shape on the physical disk. Each sector contains 512 bytes of user data and some extra bits for error-correction and metadata. A sector is the "atomic unit" of a hard disk: it's the smallest unit of data that a hard disk can effectively read. On older hard disks, the actuator couldn't handle having different numbers of sectors for each track. Because of this, the shape of the sector was maintained and the density of the bits on the platter was lessened as you went to the edge of the disk. This changed with zone-density recording, where a variable number of sectors could be included per track. Sectors are rolled up into units known as clusters when a file system is placed on the disk—that will be discussed in more detail in the OS-specific chapters (Chapters 6, 7, and 8) when we talk about the different file systems.

Track/Cylinder   Think about a phonograph needle traveling around an LP. Now think about the concentric rings inside a tree. Tracks on a hard disk are laid out in the same fashion. These are the actual streams of data that are written to the hard drive. On multi-head hard drives, the cylinder is the combination of each track on all platters that can be accessed with the head in a certain position.

Logical Block Addressing

Large Block Addressing (LBA) happens when engineers guess about maximum limits—and guess wrong. LBA is a "hack" to get around the upper limit placed on drive size by the IDE bus system. Old IDE drives incurred a 504MB limit on how much data could be accessed. To get around this, hard-drive manufacturers figured out a way to "lie" to the BIOS about the size of the disk. Instead of addressing things by cylinder, sector, and head, only one value is used for sector number. This is similar to a phone number. The traditional system has a country code, area code, and then a local phone number. The LBA equivalent of this gives everyone in the world a local phone number without an area code or country code. The reason this works is because it leaves the geometry translation to the drive itself (which isn't limited to 504MB), instead of allowing the BIOS or bus to do it.

Floppy Disks

Popularity:	3
Simplicity:	6
Impact:	6
Risk Rating:	**5**

Floppy disks are the eight-tracks of the computing world. Most people have used them and very few people have fond memories of the experience. These workhorses can be kicked, warped, melted, poked, and suffer any other number of abuses and they still keep going. While they aren't used much anymore, you will still run across them if you are working on an investigation with a timeframe that goes far enough back. For instance, several years ago I worked an investigation that required us to look at data from 1988, on large 5.25-inch floppies. These drives and associated media are similar in structure and form to the hard disk. As you can see in Figure 2-7, many of the same parts are used in both designs.

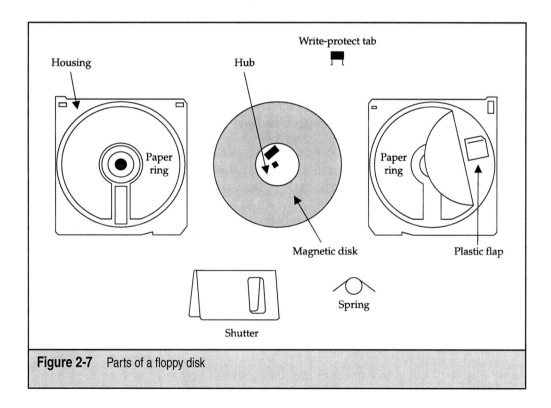

Figure 2-7   Parts of a floppy disk

Just like the parts, the actual structure of the disk is similar to a one-platter hard disk. The platter is encased in either a hard or soft plastic cover that protects the storage disk inside. In the upper corner of the disk is a notch that can be set to write-protect the disk. The main difficulty you may have in a forensics investigation involving floppy disks is the formatting. OS and file system vendors created interesting ways to store more information on the disks than they could previously hold. The typical 3.5-inch disk would hold 1.44MB of data, but by using compression or extra sectors on the disk, an extra half meg of storage could be squeezed on. Woe be the investigator who has to figure out one of these cryptic methods of storing data on the disk. They are poorly documented and more than a few different ways are used to store on the disk, with no real identifying marks.

TIP   If you do find yourself in one of these "historic" investigations and run across a type of media for which you don't have a reader, may I suggest your local thrift store. I have yet to be disappointed by the varied and complete collection of drives and media you either forgot about or never knew existed. And it can all be yours for a very reasonable price and good cause.

Working with Rotational Media

You will spend the majority of your time during investigations working with hard drives. Unfortunately, these are the trickiest of media to manage and investigate, and you'll encounter a ton of pitfalls when dealing with imaging, investigating, and documenting such media. The long and short of it is this: Always use forensically designed and validated tools when you deal with disks. Some tools on the market claim to pull complete disk images, but fail to do so. Other programs claim to wipe drives completely, but don't. If you go up against an expert who is out to make your life hard, he or she will try to derail your investigation by placing bad data in end sectors and playing games with the media in general. Know the drives and layout inside and out. Use tools that you understand completely and know exactly how they work, and they'll do what you expect them to do.

Tape Backup Drives

Popularity:	7
Simplicity:	2
Impact:	8
Risk Rating:	6

While working in the server group of a large computer manufacturer, I learned the value of good, regular backups. It is rare these days to find a server that doesn't have some form of tape backup unit attached to it for data recovery purposes. Given the fact that data such as e-mail and office documents are normally centralized on these servers, you will probably be dealing with an investigation of a tape backup at some point in the future. Start crying now. The number of different hardware drive types, software packages that perform backups, and the percentage of backups that actually succeed make pulling evidence off a tape drive a dicey proposition at best. Let's look at three of the most common drive types: DAT, DLT, and LTO.

Digital Audio Tape (DAT) Drives

DAT drives are among the most common type of tape drives. They are more often referred to by their data recovery name, Digital Data Storage (DDS). As you can see from the following table, several generations of DDS drives exist, each with its own transfer rates and capacities.

Standard	Transfer Rate	Capacity
DDS	550 KBps	2GB
DDS-1	1.1 MBps	2GB
DDS-2	1.1 MBps	4GB
DDS-3	2.2 MBps	12GB
DDS-4	4.8 MBps	20GB

These drives were originally created for use in high-end audio applications, but after a few tweaks for robustness, they now work well for backups. They employ a helical scan technique that allows data to be tightly packed on the media, requiring less actual tape than traditional tape methods. As a tradeoff, however, they experience a lot of friction when writing to the tape. This causes the tape head to gain residue over time and can actually silently hamper the writing of data onto the tape. Also, when you are dealing with these drives, keep in mind the difference between a DDS and a DAT. The DAT is held to a much lower standard of quality and manufacturing than the DDS. DATs can cause problems down the line with tape breakage and loss of data.

Digital Linear Tape (DLT) and Super DLT

As its name implies, the DLT technology relies on a linear recording method. The tape itself has either 128 or 208 total tracks. The capacities and transfer rates of the drives vary based on the generation and format of the DLT drive, as shown in the following table.

Standard	Transfer Rate	Capacity
DLT2000	1.25 MBps	15GB
DLT4000	1.5 MBps	20GB
DLT7000	5 MBps	35GB
DLT8000	6 MBps	40GB
SDLT 220	11 MBps	110GB

These tracks are written in pairs along the entire length of the tape. The heads are then realigned, and two more tracks are written in the opposite direction. This process continues until the tape is full. The design of the DLT drive is a bit different because it has only one spindle in the tape itself. The other spindle is in the drive and the tape is wound back onto the cartridge upon ejection. This design is superior to DAT because it places less tension on the tape with less friction, and thus the drive requires less maintenance and has a lower failure rate. The super DLT is essentially the same technology, but it uses a combination of optics and magnetism (laser-guided magnetic recording, or LGMR) to increase the precision of the tape.

Linear Tape-Open (LTO)

LTO drives also uses a linear recording method. It is an open standard that was developed jointly by Hewlett-Packard, IBM, and Seagate. LTO tapes were initially designed to come in two form factors: Accelis and Ultrium. The Accelis was designed for fast data access, but it did not become as popular as the more widely known Ultrium, which is known for its high capacity. This made the Ultrium more practical for use due to increasing hard disk drive capacity and decreasing hard drive prices. The Accelis never became commercially available, while the Ultrium is now a top competitor for DLT due to its higher transfer rates and data capacity. Several generations of LTO drives also exist, as shown in the following table.

Standard	Transfer Rate	Capacity
LTO-1	15 MBps	100GB
LTO-2	40 MBps	200GB
LTO-3	80 MBps	400GB
LTO-4	120 MBps	800GB
SDLT 220	11 MBps	110GB

Multi-loaders

Many times, the amount of data that needs to be backed up exceeds the capacity of a single tape. In such cases, multi-tape loader mechanisms are used. These can be anything from two-tape contraptions to advanced robotic arms that sling tapes around. From an investigator's standpoint, make sure you always find out not only what multi-loader was used, but also how the software stored data on the multiple tapes. Working with an archive created on a multi-loader is a tricky proposition and usually requires that you purchase hardware and software similar to what was used to create the archive. This gets expensive quickly, so make sure your contract has a clause stipulating that the client pays for materials.

Working with Tape Drives

Working with tape drives boils down to two simple questions: What type of tapes are being used, and what software created the archive? If you can easily answer these questions, you are home free, because you will be able to pull the archive off the tapes. Unfortunately, more often than not, you will be handed a pile of tapes created many years ago, before any of the current staff was employed. Someone will hand you a box, give you his or her best guess as to how it was created, and wish you good luck. Chapter 10 discusses in detail how to manage and investigate such situations.

Optical Media

I can still remember getting my first CD-ROM drive, eagerly awaiting what would happen when I saw my first full-motion video, roughly the size of a postage stamp with sound recorded in a tin can. I think it involved a growing plant. These days, optical media is everywhere in the forms of CD-ROM and DVD. With the widespread ability for users to burn their own discs, such media are finding their way into more and more court cases. Chances are you will deal with them either directly as evidence or as a transport mechanism for opposing counsel to give you evidence during discovery. It's important that you understand how these technologies work and how they can be manipulated.

 CD-ROM

Popularity:	6
Simplicity:	4
Impact:	8
Risk Rating:	6

The CD-ROM, shown in Figure 2-8, is the father of the optical revolution. These discs use a red laser as the read mechanism to extract data off the drive. Like hard disks, CD-ROMs use high and low polarization to set the bits of data; however, CDs have reflective pits that represent the low bit. If the pit is nonexistent, the data is a 1; if the pit exists, it's a 0.

The laser mechanism actually detects how far into the disc the beam has gone and how it is refracted to determine whether the pit exists. This explains why getting a scratch or smudge on a disc renders it erroneous. The laser becomes "confused" as to the data and "punts." As density was the limiting factor on hard drives, laser wavelength is the limiting factor for capacity on these discs. Red is the largest of the visible spectrum, meaning that a red laser-based drive will be able to store the least amount of data. CD-ROMs have their own file system that is independent of the operating system. This is

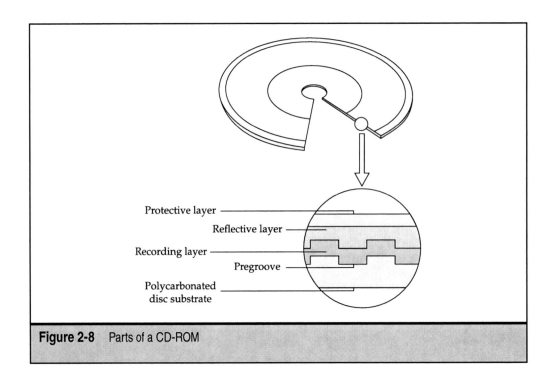

Protective layer

Reflective layer

Recording layer

Pregroove

Polycarbonated disc substrate

Figure 2-8 Parts of a CD-ROM

commonly referred to as the *Joliet file system*, and with certain parts of the disc populated, the disc can become bootable. The standard size for a CD-ROM disc is 650MB, but it can be written "outside of tolerance" to hold more data.

Digital Video Disc (DVD)

Popularity:	6
Simplicity:	4
Impact:	8
Risk Rating:	6

In function, DVDs are similar to CD-ROM technology with some tweaks. First, DVDs use a much more precise laser. Since the laser has a smaller wavelength, the data density is much greater, so the disc can hold more data. The entire DVD holds up to 4.8GB of data. The structure of a DVD is shown in Figure 2-9.

In addition, DVDs use a multilayer system that allows multiple discs to be overlaid onto one disc. The setup is much like the platters on a hard disk. The laser is focused on the layer holding the data being read, allowing it to pull data from only that layer. In

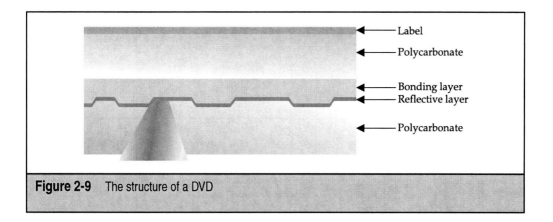

Figure 2-9   The structure of a DVD

addition to this multi-layering, you may have heard of HD-DVD or Blu-ray. These technologies use a blue laser to read the data, with a much smaller wavelength. The computer applications of these technologies allow for as much as 50GB to be stored on a single disc.

Working with Optical Media

Working with optical media from a forensics standpoint is a bit easier than working with other types of media, because the media is inherently read-only, which means you have to do much less work to show that the data on the disc hasn't been modified. Even so, you should make sure that you never work with originals, no matter how tempting it may be. Make a copy and archive the original in accordance with your evidence storage policy.

If you are exporting files to a CD or DVD, watch out for filename and file path limitations. Because of the file system type used on these media, you may encounter issues with characters, filenames, and/or file path lengths that are fine on other file systems. If you do come across this, we recommend using either a filename translation spreadsheet or some type of archiving system (zip, tar, and so on).

Memory Technologies

If you have used a digital camera, an MP3 player, or a PDA/smartphone, you have used a memory technology. These are the memory cards and cartridges that store the pictures, music, and data for these devices. As you can imagine, they often become evidence in investigations, so it's a good idea for you to understand how they work and what you are up against.

USB Flash Drives

Popularity:	10
Simplicity:	6
Impact:	8
Risk Rating:	**8**

USB flash drives are also known as *thumb drives*. They are the keychains, necklaces, and doodads that have become the gift of choice for people in the IT world. While a thorough understanding of how these drives work requires an electrical engineering degree, here is the digest version. Flash drives have no moving parts. Each bit is set by using a two-transistor cell, and the value is changed in each cell using a technique called *Fowler-Nordheim tunneling*. The memory bank then communicates with the computer using a controller and USB interface, much like a hard disk communicates over IDE or SCSI. An important thing to remember about these drives is that some of them have a physical switch that forces a read-only mode. Use this whenever you are extracting data for investigation.

SmartMedia

Popularity:	4
Simplicity:	7
Impact:	6
Risk Rating:	**5**

Also known as the solid-state floppy-disk card (SSFDC), the SmartMedia card was developed by Toshiba. They range in capacity from 2MB to Multiple GB, with physical dimensions of 45 mm long, 37 mm wide, and less than 1 mm thick. These cards have a very small NAND electrically erasable programmable read-only memory (NAND EEPROM) sandwiched between a plastic base card and a gold plate of contacts. Write protection is performed using a small metallic sticker placed in the upper corner of the card. These cards write and erase data in very small chunks, in 256- to 512-byte increments. This allows for fast and reliable data transfer, but be aware that their size and design can create problems with ruggedness and they will break.

CompactFlash Cards

Popularity:	6
Simplicity:	5
Impact:	7
Risk Rating:	6

CompactFlash cards were developed by SanDisk in 1994. They are very similar in design and function to SmartMedia cards but vary in several ways. First, they are thicker, which increases the lifetime of the card in the real world. Second, they are not just dumb memory; they have a controller built into the card itself. The storage capacity varies from 8MB to Multiple GB and the controller can take the load off slower computers. Another type of flash cards are xD-Picture cards. xD cards are used primarily by Olympus and Fujifilm and use a proprietary format.

Sony Memory Sticks

Popularity:	6
Simplicity:	5
Impact:	7
Risk Rating:	6

Memory sticks are the Beta tapes of the flash memory world. In fact, the memory stick was designed by the same company that brought us Beta. Sony broke ranks with flash memory standards and created its own standard for its devices. The memory stick has a very distinctive form factor and color—it looks like a purple stick of gum. The first generation of the memory stick maxed out at 128MB, but later revs took the capacity up to 1GB. In addition, Sony introduced its MagicGate technology, which placed DRM technology inside the stick itself. These memory sticks have a slider that denotes the read-only mode.

Working with Memory Technologies

From a forensics standpoint, the whole thing can be summed up in one word: *read-only*. Most of these technologies have a hardware-level read-only mode. Always, always take advantage of this feature to prevent modification of the data. Make sure read-only mode is a part of your methodology even before inspecting the media. Another main problem with flash memory is getting an adequate reader. For the most part, this is an easy task, but you may end up obtaining some exotic or obsolete flash memory card that requires a reader that is not easily obtained. Learn what you are working with and how to set it to read-only as quickly as possible once you find out what you are going to be given. Also, sometimes pulling an accurate image from one of these devices can be a tricky process. Chapter 13 will cover this topic in more depth.

CHAPTER 3

FORENSIC LAB ENVIRONMENT PREPARATION

In this chapter, we discuss four components that work together to make your lab's output successful: the physical lab, forensic hosts, forensic tools, and case management. Each of these work in conjunction with the others to preserve, identify, and extract evidence:

- The lab's security, host computers, tools, and case management affect your forensic capabilities. Having the appropriate protections, documentation, storage mechanisms, room requirements, and environmental conditions aid in the successful discovery and preservation of evidence.

- Computer platforms used for forensic acquisition and analysis vary in usefulness and usability. They also vary from inexpensive homegrown platforms to extremely expensive, proprietary, prebuilt specialty machines.

- Hardware and software tools used during the investigation can make or break your case. You need to understand what tools will yield the results you need for your case. Your decision to use open-source or proprietary tools also plays a role in this discussion.

- Solid case-management practices provide the foundation for conducting and archiving the investigation.

THE ULTIMATE COMPUTER FORENSIC LAB

The very nature of this assertion should grab your attention, because it is impossible for us to know the particular circumstances you might face. How can we possibly know the best mix of equipment, policies, personnel, qualifications, and myriad other criteria that will produce the ultimate lab for your organization? The best forensic lab for you is a careful combination of cost and effectiveness. This chapter provides a short education on the best resources for a well-equipped lab as well as the pitfalls often found in homegrown forensic labs and how to counteract them. Keep in mind that our focus is on the corporate lab, not labs found in law enforcement or government agencies.

What Is a Computer Forensic Laboratory?

The computer forensic laboratory houses the equipment and suspect media in a secure environment for day-to-day operations. You must consider a number of necessary components when designing your lab. The physical lab size, placement, security controls, policies, and procedures vary depending on your organizational needs. Small companies that handle the occasional civil case may not need more than an office behind a locked door and an inexpensive, fireproof safe. A corporation with tens of thousands of employees may have a substantial case load containing several dozen investigations each week. The differences here are obvious and include time, money, and resources necessary to sustain operations. You must design the right lab for your needs.

Forensic Lab Security

Ask yourself the following questions: How difficult would it be to compromise evidence in your lab? How many people have access to the lab? If a janitor came into your organization and visited late at night, would your evidence storage and processing facility be subject to compromise? Multiple attack vectors exist to destroy or alter evidence in your lab, and as a computer forensics examiner, you should account for these in your lab environment. They present a direct threat to the preservation, or integrity, of your evidence. You must protect both physical and network access to your lab and provide the appropriate environmental safeguards to protect the evidence.

Spoliation of Evidence Through Lab Network Access

Popularity:	3
Simplicity:	5
Impact:	10
Risk Rating:	6

The threat from curious and malicious crackers, hackers, and rogue employees grows because of the increased technical proficiency and curiosity of the workforce. A computer on an isolated network is protected from open access to hackers, viruses, and other malicious threats. If a trusted computer were placed on an open network without protection, the computer would no longer be trusted because it would present an opportunity for compromise. Protection from malicious network access is very important. Simply put, if the trusted platform is compromised over the network, the evidence findings may be in jeopardy. In the corporate environment, some initial level of protection is usually present. However, you must also consider isolating the corporate network from the forensic lab with an air gap (physical isolation) or at least a firewall (network isolation).

Granted, proper preservation procedures will document the authenticity of the evidence and therefore protect against the argument that the evidence was tampered with. However, lots of components must line up—the discovery of the evidence must be reproducible, the authenticity of the evidence must be verifiable, and the examiner must follow proper procedures and not take shortcuts. You do not want to find yourself in a deposition trying to explain why your lab network's security is careless and poor.

Spoliation of Evidence Through Lab Physical Access

Popularity:	9
Simplicity:	9
Impact:	10
Risk Rating:	9

Perhaps one of the easiest methods used to destroy or tamper with civil evidence is simply walking into a lab and taking it. Depending on circumstances, this may be easier than you think. Multiple books and self-proclaimed experts in the market discuss several methods for "social engineering" their way into a building to conduct malicious behavior. Unfortunately, in some cases, not even this bit of effort is required to compromise the sanctity of an organization's evidence. If a company doesn't take the time to place evidence in a secure location, how much credibility does that build for the company? What does this say about how well the company understands the value of critical evidence?

Spoliation of Evidence from Poor Environmental Safeguards

Popularity:	3
Simplicity:	10
Impact:	10
Risk Rating:	8

Fires, floods, and other disasters spell out a bad day in the lab, especially if no one has thought in advance about the risk mitigation of such disastrous events. A low rating represents the popularity, or likelihood, that this type of event will take place. However, note the rating for impact! Impact is a huge consideration in both a large corporate lab and a smaller company that desperately depends on the evidence findings.

Like insurance, nobody likes to pay for security, but should something happen—and it may—you need to be prepared. If you have not conducted a basic physical survey of your lab, you are needlessly jeopardizing your equipment, records, archives, storage, and any pending internal and external cases.

Protecting the Forensic Lab

The security stakes for the large corporation are possibly much higher than those for a small organization, and so is the expectation for lab controls and policies. However, small companies must still adhere to common sense and "best practices." A wealth of information is available about lab security, including the information in this chapter. Take the time and inventory the critical components needed for your lab. We will discuss some of these components in this chapter, but this is not meant to be an exhaustive review.

Protecting the Forensic Lab's Network Access

The traditional school of thought is to isolate the examining computer completely from the network. However, some tools on the market are causing a shift in the way networks are used. These tools preview suspect computers prior to a formal examination in an effort to triage and determine the need for further investigation. An example of such a tool is EnCase Enterprise from Guidance Software, which allows a computer forensics examiner to examine a computer for documents, images, and other data (including volatile data) over the network without having to acquire the hard drive. (The advantages of a remote investigations tool are enormous and discussed in Chapter 5.) Consider the implications of leaving your analysis host on the network, unprotected, while you're examining evidence. It's an excellent practice to remove any doubt up front and affirm the integrity of your lab through carefully documented practices and formal lab policies regarding how your forensic hosts are used.

Using the Internet during an investigation is a powerful tool, and in several cases the Net has proved to be enormously beneficial in helping to understand a suspect's behaviors and interests. However, you should always access the Internet on a separate, segmented network. Many professional labs use three separate computers:

- One for Internet access
- One for administration
- One for evidence, testing, and training

Bottom line: Protect the integrity of your forensic lab from the rest of the corporate network. If possible, use a separate, standalone computer for Internet access during an investigation.

 ## Protecting the Forensic Lab's Physical Access to Evidence

The degree of security and access control required depends on the nature, sensitivity, and importance of the investigated evidence for your organization. If you are protecting information you believe may lead to a criminal investigation, you should increase the control of the material in question. Depending on the potential severity of the cases your organization will handle, you may be interested in the following types of access control considerations to help deter, detect, or defend possible asset compromise.

Remember also that there are multiple ways to skin a buffalo. The end result is that you want to minimize your risk. The following example illustrates this point.

Structural Design

Some time ago, a young office administrator received sexually suggestive e-mails from an anonymous e-mail address. After several weeks of receiving the e-mails, the offended office administrator began to suspect a fellow coworker in her group. The forensic examiner for the investigation covertly reviewed the suspect's drive and found remnants of web-based e-mail. The web-based e-mail clearly contained sexually explicit language directed toward the office administrator. When the examiner reported the findings to HR, the suspect was immediately called into the HR office, where HR staff were waiting on the examiner to print out the e-mail remnants. This should have been an easy task.

Unfortunately, the forensic examiner was locked out of the lab. The office held the critical evidence that HR needed to view so that they could settle the allegation of sexual harassment. Frustrated, the forensic examiner asked a coworker to look up the number of the manager who had the backup key for the office.

The coworker looked at the locked office door and said, "Young Grasshopper, go around the door, not through the door." A minute later, the investigator watched as the coworker climbed over the wall and dropped through the ceiling, landing on the office floor.

Structural design can be as complicated as erecting a concrete and steel bunker capable of withstanding category F5 tornadoes, or it may be as simple as mitigating the structural risk with locked containers and strict policies that ensure evidence is locked in a protected enclosure, such as a small safe, when the investigator is no longer working on the evidence. The perimeter walls of the forensic lab should not just partition the lab from the rest of the building, extending to just above the ceiling. They must extend all the way to the next floor deck. Otherwise, someone could easily climb over the wall into the forensic lab, as the example illustrates.

Again, multiple methods can be used for achieving the end result. If the walls cannot be extended, consider ways you can secure the ceiling entrance. For high-security forensic labs such as those you would expect from a consulting services organization or a large corporate environment, the room should be alarmed, and not with just contacts on the doors. Properly placed motion sensors will detect a door opening as well as a person climbing through the roof or over the wall. In both cases, the alarm signal could go to the onsite guard and police.

Locks, Doors, and Windows

Two components are necessary for creating effective lock-out controls. The first component is the physical lock, and the second component is controlling access to the authentication components to make the lock function. In simple terms, the door to your house has a "good enough" quality deadbolt that will keep out most criminals looking for a quick crime of opportunity. You control access to the authentication piece (the key) by allowing your children and spouse to have a key, but not your neighbors.

Locks for your forensic lab should be made of high-grade materials and specialized for high-security protection. Several types of locks on the market require multiple forms of authentication prior to operating. The authentication means vary as widely as requiring a special key, PIN code, fingerprint, proximity badge, and other such methods. You must make the best decision based on the materials you control in your environment and the resources available to build out your lab. In short, your protection mechanisms need to be defensible as reasonable precautions used to protect the evidence and the lab under your control.

Additional considerations for doors and windows prevent them from getting easily bypassed. Doors should either hinge from the inside or have specialty hinges that prevent a person from removing the pin in the hinge and popping out the door. Windows and other glass should be too small for a person to fit through.

Evidence Lockers

Evidence lockers provide additional protection beyond the physical barrier provided by the perimeter of the lab. With strict policy controls, such as locking away original evidence at all times when an investigator is not in the lab, you help ensure that your evidence is protected from tampering and physical disaster. Large case processing facilities typically have a room within a room for holding and working on evidence; however, this is not practical in most resource-constrained corporate environments. An evidence locker can be as sophisticated as a keyless, multi-compartmentalized system used by some police agencies, or as simple as a locking, fireproof safe available at your local office supply store. (For some inexpensive solutions, check out SentrySafe online at www.sentrysafe. com.) An inexpensive safe costing a few hundred dollars can accommodate several dozen hard drives, while more expensive safes can easily run in the tens of thousands of dollars.

The important message here is to protect your evidence. Standard backup procedures also apply. Whether your gig is investigating civil or criminal cases, you simply cannot afford to lose evidence. Take the time to find a secure method that works for you.

Policies and Procedures

In addition to obvious physical protections, policy and procedural requirements are necessary for controlling access to the lab. Access control lists (ACLs) determine who has access to the lab and who is allowed to escort others into the lab. Ideally, every entrance and exit to the lab contains a log that is initialed or signed by the people entering and exiting the lab. At a minimum, anyone not associated with the lab, as in not specifically listed on the ACL, should log his or her entrance, escort, date, time, and reason for entering the lab.

All of this tracking is especially true for evidence. Evidence must be traceable from the moment the media was confiscated to preserve the all-important chain of custody, as discussed in Chapter 1.

 ## Protecting the Forensic Lab from Environmental Damage

Perhaps one of the worst ways to lose evidence is through an unforeseen natural disaster. Prepare up front and design protections into your lab in case of a potential problem.

Fire Protection

If your lab is located in a commercial facility, you should have automatic fire suppression. Take into account where the sprinkler or suppression agent dispensers are located, and plan accordingly. If you are using a locked enclosure with splash-proof vents, serious smoke damage will follow the fire as the smoke pours into the vents. For very little money, fireproof enclosures can protect your investments in specialized gear, licensed software, special operating system builds, and especially key evidence.

If you don't have experience with fire suppression or you don't know how to protect your assets, spend some time with your site's physical security manager or your local fire marshal. They are usually quite helpful and happy that you would bother to learn best practices in advance. Additionally, they will be able to look at your particular location and help determine any peculiarities you may have and need to solve.

Flooding

Like fire, if flooding occurs in your area, caused by leaks or something tipping off the fire-suppression system, you need to ensure that your critical evidence is properly protected. Look for an evidence safe that has a water-tight seal, and be mindful of water pipes running in the ceiling above your lab.

Temperature Control

Keep your equipment from overheating and prolong your equipment's life by using efficient ventilation and temperature controls. Given the confined spaces in many labs and the heat produced by the equipment, this is a must.

Power Protection

Surge protectors and uninterruptible power supplies (UPSs) should be a given by now. Protect your equipment from power surges caused by lightning with a good surge protector. Keep your equipment safe and running during power surges and outages with a solid UPS.

FORENSIC COMPUTERS

Once the lab is constructed—or in most cases, designated—your next step is to determine what kinds of cases the lab will handle and what resources are available to the department developing the forensic team.

Components of a Forensic Host

Host computers are the physical computer hardware and operating systems that host the forensic tools used by the examiner. The hardware will vary in scope and usage depending on the needs and budget of the examiner.

As a rule, examiners need lots of processing power. This isn't because they are power hungry, but because some forensic tools require lots of processing power. Recommended additional components include a large monitor, external drive bays, device adapters, and CD-R/DVD burners. The large monitor will help you view extensive data simultaneously. Adapters for USB, SCSI (Small Computer Standard Interface), FireWire, and flash media are recommended, and a fast burner will help you copy and archive data. Additionally, include ample storage for all the evidence and generous onboard memory to work with the data. Fast drives such as SATA (Serial Advanced Technology Attachment) and SCSI, ideally on a controller separate from the OS drive, are worth the investment. Consider external hard drives for large data acquisitions. Provide yourself the additional horsepower with a fast bus, fast RAM, and only the software necessary to carry out investigations. Use quality components when possible.

The operating system used will depend on the comfort level of the user, the tools used, and, in some cases, the examiner's budget.

Wrong or Poorly Configured Hardware

Popularity:	6
Simplicity:	5
Impact:	8
Risk Rating:	6

The consequences of investigating a civil or criminal case with the wrong equipment sometimes suffers you only the time and ingenuity to overcome the shortfall. Other times, however, it may cost you your investigation. Learning that you need a SCSI adapter at 3:00 A.M. in Bumford, Texas, is a bad situation. Other bad circumstances include not having enough storage, memory, adaptors, and other necessary equipment for your organization's needs.

Understand Your Computer's Role

Forensic hosts can play multiple roles. In purist environments, the acquisitions computer is always separate from the analysis computer. However, most corporate environments currently use the same machine for acquisitions and analysis. Whatever the environment, prepare yourself before you need the gear. Buy the appropriate cables, readers, or accessories to interface with the hardware in your environment, and make certain that your analysis machine can handle the workload.

For many investigators, a small shuttle computer may suffice for a mobile unit, whereas others feel hampered by the single PCI slot and will carry a fully equipped mid-tower computer to an onsite call. Still other investigators prefer a laptop, and they can successfully triage, grab, and work with data effectively within those constraints. Keep an eye on the market, as new computers and form factors are coming out all the time.

Acquisition Units

Acquisition host computers need lots of drive storage. If you're short on funds, an older computer that's deemed inadequate for everyday use makes an excellent acquisition and duplication host. An internal removable drive bay or an external drive bay connected via FireWire or USB 2.0 is recommended. Note that some old hardware write-blockers hook up only through a SCSI connection.

Analysis Units

Analysis host computers need lots of memory and processing power as they perform the brunt of the work with the forensic examiner on the machine. Because computer time is cheap and the examiner's time is not, it is a good idea to invest money in an excellent analysis host. This will maximize the examiner's time while minimizing frustration. If your organization has the funds, multiple hosts may break up the investigation to get specific tasks completed quicker than serially feeding the tasks through the same host.

Also consider the surrounding environment, and ensure that the examiner has access to all the same software and equipment normally used in the environment. For example, if tapes are used in the environment, it makes sense to equip the investigator with the same access to hardware. Likewise, if the hardware used by the workforce supports certain high-end tools or software packages, the forensic investigator should have access to these types of tools or software packages.

Mobile Units

The forensic examiner might need to visit remote sites in your organization. A forensic services organization providing forensic acquisition and examination services at a customer's premises needs a highly mobile workstation. In addition, companies with multiple branch offices, manufacturing facilities, and storage facilities often need mobile workstations capable of performing onsite investigations.

Often, large corporations employ only a handful of trained forensic investigators. This small group of people is forced to travel, in some cases worldwide, to perform acquisitions (and sometimes investigations) onsite. A correctly built and configured mobile workstation is a tremendous asset to the investigator.

If this is your role, you will appreciate a smaller, more compact workstation than a full-sized desktop computer. A laptop can be configured to work well if only a few hosts need to be acquired or analyzed. If more than a few hosts need to be acquired, consider using portable hardware duplicating tools such as Forensic Talon from Logicube and HardCopy by Voom Technologies. These devices are small and portable, and they typically have data capturing speeds of 3 gigabytes per second or faster.

Hardware Components for a Mobile Investigator   The following components will help a mobile investigator:

- An internal or standalone external drive bay can offer plenty of storage. If you are going to use a laptop, consider using a laptop with a built-in FireWire. This allows you to use the available PCMCIA slot.

- A hard, solid storage case built for traveling will protect your gear while you're on the move. Make certain the case locks or can accept a padlock.

- A USB expansion card makes it effortless to add other components such as a printer or multi-card reader.

- A wide array of adapters protects you from making last-minute trips.

- A multi-card reader for different kinds of flash media can come in handy, especially if you are working covertly in a corporate environment.

- Hardware write-blockers such as FastBlock by Intelligent Computer Solutions (ICS) prevent writing data accidentally to your source media during the acquisition phase.

- Paraben Forensics' Device Seizure Toolbox is a top-notch product for personal digital assistants (PDAs) and cell phones. If you even remotely think you will face a PDA during an investigation, the product is worth the money. Paraben also offers the ability to acquire cell phone data, and the company is constantly updating its products. As previously mentioned, hardware duplicating tools are often useful, depending on what you want to accomplish.

Depending on your established method and available tools, each situation might require a different acquisition technology.

The "Poor Man's Shop"

If your management has not allocated enough funds, or if it's a new group, you can save money by sharing hardware between the acquisitions workstation and the analysis workstation. You can also configure inexpensive hardware with open-source Linux and run freeware tools. Linux will run well on old hardware. The most important component in a "poor man's shop" is the technical competence of the examiner. Keep in mind that you can always start out with limited tools and hardware and grow your abilities over time.

Commercially Available Hardware Systems

A number of commercial hardware systems are available, and they are excellent if you can afford them, but they aren't necessary to do the job. At the end of the day, the forensic computer spends most of its time waiting on the examiner to press the next key. If you get bored, graph the average CPU utilization during an investigation. That said, commercial systems can provide several benefits:

- Professional support is available for examiners, should you ever run into hardware problems.
- Lots of horsepower helps handle large case loads and heavy data manipulation.
- Preconfigured computers are in many cases loaded and guaranteed to work with popular forensic software such as EnCase, SMART, or other tools.

The large drawback to commercial systems is that they are usually extremely expensive. They can cost tens of thousands of dollars with all the extras. Check out http://forensic-computers.com to see some prebuilt forensic computers.

Do-It-Yourself Hardware Systems

Do-it-yourself systems can be any size or shape and can run any operating system you choose. Though this is not for the faint of heart, they are not difficult to build. Such hardware systems can save you a tremendous amount of money and offer you the flexibility you may need to buy exactly the components you want. With a little patience and knowledge, you can design and build a formidable lab machine. If you just want the design and not the build part, then check out some of the prebuilt systems from DELL that may be loaded with everything you want. Hardware recommendations include the following:

- Extremely fast dual processor and front-side bus
- Extra memory for heavy analysis work
- Extra hard drive space for the operating system, programs, tools, and data output
- Removable drive bay for quickly changing hard drives
- Additional hard drive and controller to move acquired data, extracted information, or tools to a different hard drive from the OS
- Drives that are fast SCSI or SATA hard drives on their own controller
- A wide array of adapters
- Excellent video card for large monitors and for quickly reviewing hundreds of images
- Multiple connections for FireWire and USB
- Standalone external FireWire or USB drive enclosure that accepts SATA, IDE, and laptop drives
- SCSI connection if needed
- Extra SATA/IDE controller(s) going to a hardware write-block device(s) of your choice (such as those made by Intelligent Computer Solutions, at www.icsforensic.com)
- Heavy-duty, fast printer
- Multi-card reader for different kinds of Flash memory
- Ultra-fast CD and DVD burners
- For some, a tape backup
- Depending on your case load, a large file server on a local network to store media images while you work with them

Data Storage

Now that you have all of this data, how are you going to store it? Most forensic labs do not have the monetary resources to purchase large Storage Area Network (SAN) or Network Attached Storage (NAS) systems, government agencies excluded. Many corporations are getting space on the SAN or NAS as a shared resource, and reasonably priced mini-SANs are appearing on the market. If either of these options doesn't work for you, you will have to get creative. To address this need, you have several options depending on how much you want to spend. For all of these options, it's assumed your storage needs are greater than the current largest SATA disk.

Cheapest Storage

The least expensive option is to create a large RAID (Redundant Array of Inexpensive Disks) set from a couple of internal RAID cards; these are now sold at most computer stores. We recommend making a hardware RAID for each card and then combining them with a software RAID 0 to allow the operating system to access the RAIDs as a single disk, giving you more storage. Other methods include using a couple of IDE drives with Windows software RAID or logical volumes across a number of physical disks.

Cheap Storage

The next step up would be an external SATA RAID. SATA drives are always less expensive than SCSI drives, but SCSI busses and drives are also faster. So these external RAID units allow you to take between 2 and 15 SATA drives and create a RAID disk that will be shown through the SCSI interface as a single disk to the operating system. These units can also be daisy-chained. We use the Promise SuperTrack Series (www.promise.com) and can get up to 16 terabytes per 16-drive unit.

Not-so-cheap Storage

Once you have outgrown multiple 16-terabyte boxes and need multiple servers to access a single set of data, you have outgrown most of the inexpensive solutions. At this point, you need to move to a NAS (Network Attached Storage) or a SAN system, or to a distributed file system, such as GFS and OpenGFS for Linux and DFS for Windows. SAN systems are always more expensive than NAS systems. We would recommend the units from Equallogic (www.equallogic.com) and BlueArc (www.bluearc.com). These units are not cheap; they typically cost at least $20,000, but they will allow you to grow your lab environment. More information about NAS and SAN systems can be found in Chapter 10.

FORENSIC HARDWARE AND SOFTWARE TOOLS

This is almost a misnomer, because many so-called "forensic tools" were created for uses outside the forensics field. A forensic tool produces useful, reproducible, and verifiable results. Forensic tools can be divided into two large classes of tools: hardware and software.

Using Hardware Tools

Forensic hardware tools include every hardware element outside the traditional host, such as the specialized cables, write-blockers, drive-dupers, and other gear that allows forensic software tools to work. The forensic lab in your organization should be able to assess common digital storage devices rapidly. If your organization uses SCSI hard drives on production servers, you should be able to deal with SCSI drives. If you have other common storage mechanisms, consider whether it makes sense for you to include those capabilities in the lab.

A forensically sound write-blocker allows data to travel in one direction only, like a diode or check valve. One version, FASTBLOC, is detected automatically if you use EnCase. A note is added to the case log stating you used hardware write protection.

Another nice tool is the Image MASSter Solo 3 Forensic system, a hardware duplication device that will image a suspect's hard drive onto another hard drive with full cryptographic verification. The target drive can hold multiple images from more than one suspect drive and can also be put into 640MB Linux-DD chucks for input into other programs. This device copies data at speeds close to 3 GB/minute, depending on the source and destination hard drive spindle speed.

Using Software Tools

Software tools fall into many categories, depending on how you want to break them down. Some tools are multipurpose tools that can cover more than one scenario. EnCase, SMART, FTK, and TCT are all multipurpose tools. Something definitely to consider is the value of having and using a robust multipurpose tool. Consider a Swiss Army Knife. You want to have a tool that has all the blades you may ever need, even if you don't use them all at first.

Other tools are highly specialized, such as X-Ways WinHex. If you need a hex editor, WinHex is one of the best tools on the market. If you need to view e-mail, this is the wrong tool.

One frequently asked question we encounter is how to verify a tool for use in forensic investigations. Initiatives are underway at NIST to validate certain tools. Additionally, the Scientific Working Group on Digital Evidence (SWGDE) aims to provide guidelines for validation testing. You can find the latest SWGDE public documents, including the SWGDE Validation Guidelines, online at http://www.swgde.org/documents.html.

Some of the tool categories we will cover in this book include the following:

- Acquisition tools
- Data discovery tools
- Internet history tools
- Image viewers
- E-mail viewers
- Password-cracking tools
- Open source tools
- Mobile device tools (PDA/cell phone)
- Large storage analysis tools

More than one tool can usually do the job, but depending on your skill level, familiarity, and comfort, some tools are more effective for particular uses than others.

The important result is that you can get your work done efficiently with verifiable and well-documented results.

THE FLYAWAY KIT

Following is a list of suggestions for additional equipment to include in a basic tool kit for use in offsite searches. Given that your circumstances may vary, use your best judgment when deciding what to take with you.

Small Tool Kit   Remember that you may need a small tool kit to dismantle the computer. Make sure you include assorted screwdrivers, pliers, wire snips, and a small flashlight in your flyaway kit. It can be frustrating after a long airplane getaway to a remote location to realize you don't have the right tools in your bag.

Digital Camera with Date/Time Stamp   A digital camera with a date/time stamp ensures that you know exactly how the scene was laid out before you started your work. In covert collections, a digital camera will help you reposition the office papers, photos, and other personal items found on top of the computer you are investigating. In some cases, these images may help you remember something you forgot or bring attention to something you need to revisit.

Notepad and Forms   Always carry a notepad to jot down information about who is in the room and what they have to say about the computer's usage. Also include notes on what is happening in the room, the date and time of incremental events, where everything is located, and details on how you are performing your search and seizure. An evidence or property log is great for recording details of computer and component makes, models, and serial numbers. Prepared forms will make sure you include everything in the rush or drudgery of responding.

Permanent Markers and Labels   Permanent markers and labels will help you tag components as they are removed.

Antistatic Bags   If you are removing and carrying a hard drive back to the lab, consider taking along appropriate protective means to carry the drive back safely to the office, such as anti-static bags and a small padded box. If you are traveling with only a few drives, hand-carry them on the plane if you do not have a sufficient protective enclosure for the drives. Most hard drives were not made for the rough handling they would surely get in the belly of the airplane storage area.

Policies and Procedures   Copies of appropriate policies and procedures should be standard in your flyaway kits, including policies confirming your right to perform your job and standard procedures making sure you are thorough. Having these will help answer questions by workers who do not know you and have questions about what you are doing with the computers. A well-written checklist included with your procedures can be a blessing. Include a contact person at the local site to ensure you have access to resources.

Equipment Manuals and Guides   You might digitally store or carry appropriate manuals for your own gear or the equipment you will encounter. Search-and-seizure guides or other notes may also help you respond to the incident.

CASE MANAGEMENT

You clear off your desk following the victory of completion of an investigation, and the phone rings. It's HR out of Boston, and they need you to answer some questions about the case you just completed. They are worried about a potential wrongful termination lawsuit. Now what? Where do you go from here? Where was that summary report? What happened to that hard drive? How was that information found? Case management is the practice of organizing, working with, and archiving information produced during an investigation.

Poor Case Management

Popularity:	7
Simplicity:	7
Impact:	9
Risk:	8

Unfortunately, many companies have extremely poor case management practices. When it comes to locating a file associated with a particular case, the difficulty and lack of controls can make the task nearly impossible. Ask many companies to locate the hard drive they had a couple of months ago, and good luck! You need those locked-away case findings if a terminated employee decides to file suit against your organization.

Effective Case Management

No matter the size or the number of investigations you handle, effective case management is essential to organizing your data and supporting documentation in a manner that is safe, preserved, and retrievable. Several important points to consider include the types of investigations you commonly encounter, the volume, and the number of people in your lab.

Some standard daily practices can make your life easier. Use standardized forms for all of your tracking needs. This practice provides consistency in the lab and saves you time. Clearly label all hard drives, other media, and components you wish to store. They can be stored together however you wish as long as they are protected and organized. For example, you can place critical hard drive originals used during the investigation inside anti-static wrapping and then inside manila envelopes. The envelopes fit nicely inside plastic containers or on a shelf in a fireproof safe.

 In medium to large labs dealing with multiple ongoing investigations, it helps to have one individual and a backup responsible for case archival and retrieval to maintain consistency. This is an organizational decision based on your needs and resources. An experienced and efficient examiner can handle five to seven cases simultaneously. If you have more than four or five people on your team, you want to consider seriously reassigning or hiring examiners to handle all of your case-management administration.

Entire courses and disciplines are involved in effective case management. If you have a large caseload and you don't have formal case management procedures in place, you might want to research our Web site, www.hackingexposedforensics.com, for more information and links to other sites.

Misplacing Evidence

Popularity:	4
Simplicity:	9
Impact:	9
Risk:	8

On the surface, this risk sounds like a no-brainer. "How could I ever lose a vital hard drive?" It takes only one such mistake to realize the catastrophic results of losing a vital piece of evidence in a high stakes case. Furthermore, consider the fast-paced nature of the industry in terms of how many cases an investigator will work on at a time, as well as the long layovers between events on a case, and you can see how vital keeping track of case files and evidence using something other than memory can be.

Effective Evidence Handling

Chain of custody isn't just a good idea, it's the law. You can maintain your evidence logs in many ways—from keeping handwritten manual logs to using software databases and bar-coding systems. What method you use depends on the size of your organization and the amount of evidence you typically handle. The important thing is to maintain a chain of custody to demonstrate that you have positive control of the evidence.

Proper chain of custody should show the following:

- Identify the people who handle the evidence at every step of the investigation.

- Document what actions/procedures were performed on the evidentiary item and how it was collected (for example, removal of a hard drive from a computer).

- Document when the evidence was collected and when/if the evidence was transferred to the custody of another party.
- Show where the evidence was collected and where is it being stored.
- Indicate the reason the evidence was collected.

A lot of discussion among forensics professionals deals with how to maintain and track evidence. Any sufficiently large organization will have knock-down, drag-out fights about how to number evidence and what the numbers mean. At the end of the day, it really doesn't matter how evidence is numbered, as long as it is consistent across all the investigations and the evidence numbering system is designed to prevent collisions (the same evidence number being used for multiple cases/images). For our purposes, random or sequential numbering has worked just as well as anything else out there. Remember that this is a process issue and not a technology one, and choose wisely. Once a numbering system has been chosen, you can implement it in cases in multiple ways.

Traditional Tracking Systems

You can use numerous ways to track your evidence as you proceed with your investigation. As mentioned, you can use handwritten logs. Many sample chain of custody forms are available to the public (a sample is included in this book). Logs should be kept in a secure location near or with your evidence. This makes it convenient for you to update your logs as you handle the evidence while keeping it in a protected area. Be sure to keep backup copies of your forms in a separate, but equally secure, location in case damage occurs to the original copies.

Automated Tracking Systems

If your organization typically handles large-scale investigations, you may need an evidence tracking system that is more automated. A number of available software systems can automatically generate evidence numbers, labels, and bar codes to attach to your evidence. They can also be used to create databases in which to track your evidence. These types of systems typically use scanners and simplify the evidence-tracking process by reducing the amount of paperwork and time needed. However, these systems can be expensive and may not be ideal for organizations running on smaller budgets. Many organizations use a combination of paper logs and computer databases. What is important is that your chosen method properly documents the entire history of possession in a way that maintains the chain of custody.

Improper Evidence Destruction

Popularity:	3
Simplicity:	5
Impact:	9
Risk:	6

Often the case data that is dealt with is highly confidential and proprietary. As such, you, as an investigator, should be concerned not only with the preservation of evidence when required, but also the destruction of evidence when the case is over and you have counsel's request to destroy the data. You only need to look at the anecdotal stories of hard drives purchased on eBay and the personal information contained on them to understand why proper attention needs to be given to destruction procedures as well.

Proper Destruction of Evidence

At some point, your case is going to wrap up and the time will come for you to destroy your case files. You may have a protective order that states how you must dispose of any work data you have generated during the case. Depending on your organization, you may need to obtain a directive from your client as to how they would like you to dispose of case data. At any rate, your organization should have a retention policy that states how long you keep case files, what materials you retain, how/when files are destroyed, and who destroyed them.

File destruction can occur in many ways. If your organization is small, a paper-shredder may suffice and you can wipe your own storage media in-house. Larger organizations typically outsource their data destruction to companies that specialize in these services, as they have the capacity to shred large amounts of paper documents, in addition to destroying storage media such as CD/DVD discs, backup tapes, and hard drives. Either way, you should keep documentation as to what you destroyed, the method you used, when it was destroyed, and who performed the work.

BONUS: LINUX OR WINDOWS?

We leave it up to you to impose the final verdict about which operating system to use. In general, we suggest basing your decision on your organization's policy, types of investigations, and resources, and your current OS understanding. We also recommend downloading and installing Linux for the experience. Take the time to kick around a few commands. If your department is short on funds, Linux is an excellent platform to use despite the initial learning curve.

On the flip side, Windows is easy to use, familiar, and has an excellent repository of tools available if you have the capital to acquire them.

Linux Benefits	Windows Benefits
Hardware devices are treated as files, which make imaging and MD5 verification easy. Supports multiple file systems. Supports read-only mode of files and volumes natively. Bootable Linux CDs such as Helix or customized Knoppix versions are free and full of useful tools. Basic forensic utilities such as DD for imaging, file for file identification, and MD5 for verifying are all native to the OS. A fully usable Linux install can be done on a fast Pentium computer.	Most users are familiar with it. Native environment for data in most investigations. Some specialized tools run only on Windows.
Linux Drawbacks	**Windows Drawbacks**
User must learn new platform. Some specialized tools will run only on Windows.	Limited file system support. Requires special boot disk or write-blocker. Licensing.

PART II

COLLECTING THE EVIDENCE

CASE STUDY: THE COLLECTIONS AGENCY

We received a phone call Thursday at 3 P.M. Then, at 5 P.M., we were notified that we were being deployed to New York City to meet with client personnel the next morning. Within that two-hour period, we were to gather up our personal items, such as clothes and other effects. We also had to bring along all of our paperwork and equipment packed and ready for the plane. Our advance preparations paid off, and we made it out on the last flight that night.

Preparations

With preparations in hand from Part I, we had our portable system in its air travel–safe container. We called it "The Heavy" because the box was plastered with multiple stickers warning would-be lifters how much the box weighed. The Heavy carried the imaging and preview systems, extra hard drives, write blockers, and other assorted parts. We also carried precompleted paperwork along with templates in case we needed to print more paperwork from our laptops. Waking up in New York that morning, we rushed to an 8 A.M. meeting with the client.

Revelations

At 10 A.M. Friday, after a two-hour meeting, what was supposed to be a simple, two-day operation revealed its true nature. Instead of the original and simple two-system collection for which our company deployed us, a larger pattern quickly emerged. Shortly after examining the first two systems, the controlled samples exposed the need to visit each of the systems across the company's network and throughout the city.

Collecting Evidence

The extent of the damage was clearly larger than anyone expected, and it was necessary for us to collect and image for preservation and analysis each of these computers. We began to collect systems throughout the city and visited 63 hard drives in four days.

We worked quietly and split the load between us and our corporate office. We kept systems we knew the suspect had used onsite in New York for immediate analysis and sent systems we knew were only affected but not used by the suspect to the lab for imaging. Once again, the preplanning from Part I allowed us to scale from three systems to more than ten systems working in parallel. Imaging continued around the clock. One of our portable systems was used so much and jarred so hard during acquisitions that the fan broke off in transit and the processor overheated to the point that the chip cracked.

The goal was to analyze the impact of the situation and preserve relevant data to minimize the legal risk to the client and client's duty to preserve. Moreover, we needed to identify the potential ongoing damage from the suspect. Life was about to get interesting.

CHAPTER 4

FORENSICALLY
SOUND EVIDENCE
COLLECTION

E vidence collection is the most important part of the investigation of any incident, and it's even more important if the evidence will find its way into a court of law. No matter how good your analysis, how thorough your procedures, or how strong your chain of custody, if you cannot prove to the court that you collected your evidence in a forensically sound matter, all your hard work won't hold up and will be wasted.

In this chapter, we discuss several types of collections, also called *acquisitions* or *imaging* (short for forensic imaging), scenarios that might play out in your day-to-day investigative duties. We cover the most common scenario, collecting evidence from a single system, and discuss some common mistakes that are made while collecting evidence. Other types of imaging are covered throughout the rest of the book.

COLLECTING EVIDENCE FROM A SINGLE SYSTEM

Popularity:	10
Simplicity:	8
Impact:	10
Risk Rating:	9

A *single system* in this context can include any type of *x86*-based system, such as desktop and laptop computers and possibly lower-end servers. I say *possibly* because in most cases a higher-end server may contain a RAID set, which is discussed in detail in Chapter 10. A single system may include IDE (Integrated Device Electronics), SATA (Serial AT Attachment), or SCSI (Small Computer System Interface) drives and may have a wide assortment of peripherals attached to it; in this section, we focus on collecting evidence from IDE, SATA, or SCSI hard drives.

Typically during an investigation, you should power down any system that you are about to acquire and boot it into a safe operating system environment or remove the hard drive(s) and attach the drive(s) to some sort of hardware-based write blockers and to your own forensic system. However, at times you may want to keep the system powered on and acquire the information from the active memory, but that is outside the scope of this section and should not be attempted by anyone who does not feel confident enough in his or her procedures to defend his or her actions in court.

After reading the previous chapters, you should have a good understanding of the basic tools and issues that exist in the forensics process. You can now use that knowledge to go through the process of collecting evidence from a single system. While we attempt to cover the most popular tools in use today, more are available, and there is no reason why any particular tool or technology that is documented to conform to your forensic needs could not be used in this generic framework.

We use the terms *suspect system* and *forensic system* to distinguish between the system from which you are collecting data and the system on which you will be performing your forensic analysis, respectively.

Step 1: Power Down the Suspect System

Powering down the suspect system allows you to state on the record and in your documentation that you've established a time and date upon which no other modifications will occur in the system. It is important that you are able to prove that nothing you do in the course of your collection, analysis, and reporting modifies the original evidence. If you cannot prove this, your findings may be dismissed.

 Never rely on the power buttons on the front panel of a computer case to power off a system, as many systems today by default will go into stand-by mode when these buttons are pressed. Instead, remove the power cord from the system and wait until the power supply fan stops spinning to continue. If LEDs on the motherboard stay lit after shutdown, they should turn off in about 20 seconds.

Step 2: Remove the Drive(s) from the Suspect System

Look inside the system to determine what drive(s) exist and remove them, even if they are not currently attached to any cabling. Create a Chain of Custody form and fill in the fields described in Table 4-1. You will typically want to document one sheet per drive you have removed.

Depending on your level of comfort in reliably describing and re-creating the technology present in the suspect system, you may want to take photographs of all of the drive connections, cable connections to the case, and general work area for future use. Photos, however, are not required for admittance into court. Whether or not you choose to take pictures is up to your discretion, as well as your company's policies regarding investigations. (See the sidebar "Legal Brief: Admissibility of Images," later in this chapter.)

 You can also leave the drives in the system and acquire them with some forensically safe boot disks/ CD-ROMs/thumb drives. We do not recommend this, however, until you have experience with the tools and the time to test them.

Field	Description
Manufacturer	The manufacturer of the removed drive, as found on the drive label
Model	The model of the removed drive, as found on the drive label
SN	The unique serial number of the drive itself, as found on the drive label
Evidence Description	The full name of the suspect and the type of drive technology with which you are dealing: Parallel ATA (IDE)/SCSI/Serial ATA (IDE)

Table 4-1   Drive Information Fields for Chain of Custody Form

Step 3: Check for Other Media

At this point, the drives are removed and the system is powered off; you now need to look in the floppy drive, zip drive, and any other drive that does not require power to function and is located on the system to see whether any storage media is still located in the drive. This media should be considered evidence and handled as such. Remove all of the media found in the system (at least the media you can remove when the drives are powered down) and fill out the Chain of Custody form for each piece of media removed from the suspect system.

Also, if you have the authority and right to search the suspect's work area, you should check all drawers, folders, cabinets, and briefcases in the area for evidence.

 You should always check corporate policies before attempting to search a suspect's work area, as this could be an area of potential liability for you and your employer.

Step 4: Record BIOS Information

At this point, the drives are removed and you have identified and removed the media in the system. You can now safely boot up the system to check the BIOS information.

In the Chain of Custody form, enter information about the BIOS of the system; you can typically access this information by pressing ESC, DEL, F2, F9, F10, or F11 during the initial boot screen, but this varies radically depending on the system manufacturer, so always try to search the system manufacturer's Web site ahead of time to determine how to access this information. Once you've accessed the BIOS information, you need to record the system time and date in the Chain of Custody form. The BIOS time is important because it can radically differ from the actual time and time zone set for the geographical area in which you are located. The importance of the BIOS time will vary by the file system (NTFS stores Greenwich Mean Time) and operating system, as some will update the time using network time servers. If the BIOS time is different, you need to note this and then adjust the times of any files you recover from the image to determine the actual time and date they were created, accessed, or modified.

After the power has been restored to the system, eject all media contained in drives that cannot be operated without power (such as some CD-ROMs and DVD-ROMs) and remove them. Then fill out a separate Chain of Custody form for each of the items removed. If you forget to eject the CD-ROM before powering it down, do not worry, because most CD-ROMs can be opened by sticking the end of a paper clip in the tiny hole near the eject button.

Step 5: Forensically Image the Drive

At this point, your steps stop being generic to any system. Here, we go into specifics about tools and technologies used in the imaging process; if you want to emulate this process with tools and technologies not discussed here, do so with caution and only after reading all of the procedures described here to identify similar feature sets you'll need to enable.

Modifying Original Evidence

Popularity:	*10*
Simplicity:	*10*
Impact:	*10*
Risk Rating:	*10*

Be warned that the next steps lead you into the most risky part of your endeavor (other than carpal tunnel from filling out all of the documentation): actual access to the original evidence drive(s). Any time you access the original media, you must take precautions to avoid writing to it. How easy is it to write to the drive accidentally? Consider the following possibilities, which each add information to the drive:

- Booting up the suspect system in Windows with the drive still in it
- Using an unmodified DOS boot disk
- Mounting the drive read/write in Linux
- Booting up the forensic system in Windows with the original drive attached to it
- Plugging in the original drive with a USB/FireWire hard drive enclosure in Windows
- Choosing the wrong drive to write to when collecting evidence

If any of these scenarios play out, you could be facing disaster. You may write to the original evidence and change a large amount of system times that you need to rely on in the analysis phase. This could lead to unverifiable evidence and your suspect walking away—unless you have a good attorney or established repeatable processes and you have created a well-documented investigation. (You did do that, right?)

Legal Briefs: The Chain of Custody

What does *chain of custody* mean? The chain of custody is a document that details who has had possession and access, thus custody, of the document. The chain of custody is not unique to computer forensics; in fact, it exists in any criminal investigation for which evidence of some type is collected. The chain of custody provides proof that the evidence you have collected during an investigation has not been accessed by anyone else since you collected it, and it provides proof, via documentation, that no one else could have changed the evidence without your knowledge. This is especially important in cases for which you have only an image of a suspect's system and not the original drive to refer to.

Countermeasure: Procedures and Tools for Preventing Modification

If you use any of the following tools or procedures, you will have created a verifiable image of a suspect system—and kept yourself out of trouble.

Step 5a: Wipe Image Drives Before Using Them

Before you use a drive to store an image, you should always use some kind of wiping software to clean the drive of any previous evidence. The wiping process allows you to state to a court that any evidence found in your investigation came from the forensic image and is not a remnant of any other evidence collected and stored on the drive. This is accomplished by overwriting every sector on the drive; what data is used to overwrite the drive varies from vendor to vendor. The most basic tools allow you to overwrite a single character sequence, while the most advanced tools use US Department of Defense (DOD) guidelines for random sequences of multiple writes to the disk before finishing. (More information about DOD guidelines for disk sanitizing can be found at www.dss .mil/isec/chapter8.htm.)

In most cases, a single wipe using a single-character sequence will suffice, and that is demonstrated next.

Note that you do not have to wipe a drive in order to use any of the imaging tools we cover in this book. The reason you do not have to wipe the drive is that our tools create a file(s) that contains the image of the drive instead of duplicating sector by sector the contents of the drive. If, however, you previously stored extracted evidence, notes, or personal data on this drive, it is still good practice to wipe it as any opposing attorney may request access to it in the future.

Wipe a Drive Using EnCase   EnCase provides drive wiping as a standard feature of the software, but it can write only a static set of data out to the drive. This means that if you follow the examples in this chapter, the drive will contain *00* for every sector on the disk. Remember that if you choose to re-create this sector, the tools covered in this book cannot be used to recover the data you have wiped.

1. Attach the image drive you want to wipe to your system. In this case, you don't need to be concerned about modifying the contents of the disk, since you are about to overwrite all of it.

2. Load EnCase in Windows. When wiping using EnCase, the licensed version is not needed; in this case, you can use EnCase in unlicensed or acquisition mode.

3. In EnCase, choose Tools | Wipe Drive.

4. In the Wipe Drive dialog box shown here, make sure that Local Devices is selected under Source. Leave the defaults under Include, and then click Next.

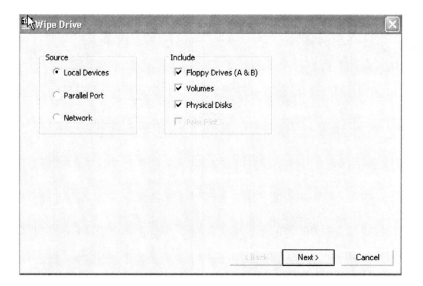

5. You are presented with a list of available drives to overwrite. Notice that the drive from which you booted is not available; this prevents you from accidentally overwriting your system drive. (Older versions of EnCase did allow you to overwrite your system drive, so be careful and know your software.) Select the drive you want to wipe and click Next.

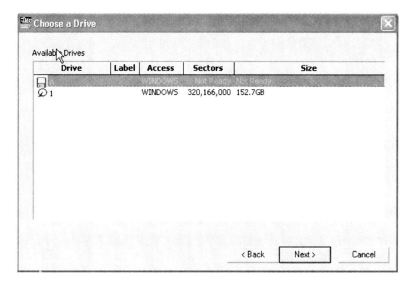

EnCase will not allow you to overwrite a drive that has EnCase evidence files on it. The best way to get around this quickly is to SHIFT-DELETE the EnCase evidence files.

6. The next window, shown in the next illustration, shows wiping options. The Wipe Char entry represents the character that will be written to all the sectors of the drive; you can leave this set at the default 00. The start and stop sectors are set automatically by EnCase and should be correct, so you can leave these at the default settings unless you want to overwrite just a partition and you know which sectors make up the partition. The Verify Wiped Sectors checkbox allows you to specify whether or not the EnCase program checks to determine that all sectors were successfully wiped at the end of the process; checking this box will result in a longer wipe time but verified results. Depending on your level of comfort with EnCase and the contentiousness of the investigation, you can decide whether or not to choose this option. For now, accept the defaults and click Finish.

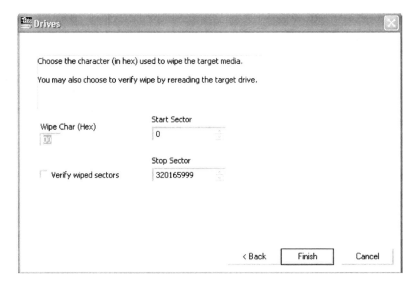

7. You are prompted to type YES in uppercase letters to verify that you want to wipe this drive. Type **YES**.

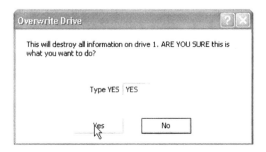

8. The drive then wipes the disk; you can click the bottom-left progress bar to discover how much time remains in the wiping process. Upon completion of the wiping process, a summary message box, shown next, pops up to let you know that drive wiping has completed successfully.

Note that while EnCase is capable of wiping the drive, it does not claim to be a full wiping utility. As such, it will not wipe the last cylinder on the drive. This is normally not an issue. If, however, this becomes an issue for your investigation, use one of the other wiping tools mentioned in this book; we recommend wiping with Linux, as described next.

Wipe a Drive with Linux   Windows and EnCase are not the only operating systems and tools you can use to wipe a drive. Using Linux, you can wipe a drive using the standard distribution tool dd using the following command:

```
dd if=/dev/random of=/dev/<image drive>
```

Where *image drive* is the device to write to, such as hda1 or sda1.

The command would read random values from the virtual device /dev/random and then write them to the drive specified, from the beginning of the drive until the end.

Step 5b: Forensically Image the Drive with an EnCase DOS Boot Disk

Here you'll create an EnCase DOS boot disk using the EnCase program. If you do not have an image for the EnCase DOS boot disk, you can download it. Guidance Software offers boot disks that you can download at www.guidancesoftware.com/support/downloads.shtm (under the Drivers section).

1. Choose Tools | Create Boot Disk in EnCase and follow the prompts.

2. Power down the system.

3. Reattach the suspect drive to the system.

NOTE When acquiring evidence in DOS, you may find that the types of connections that you can read from are very limited. Most DOS USB and FireWire drivers use too much memory for DOS acquires and tend to use only the local IDE or SCSI drive connections. You don't need to worry about writing to the suspect drive at boot time, though, because the modified DOS boot disk prevents you from writing to the drive without unlocking the drive in the EnCase software. This means that using an EnCase DOS boot disk, instead of acquiring a drive in Windows, saves you the cost of acquiring a write-blocker for these types of acquisitions.

4. Boot up the system using the EnCase DOS boot disk; depending on the version of EnCase you're using, you will either go directly into EnCase for DOS or to the command prompt. At the command prompt, enter **en** and press RETURN.

5. You should see the EnCase DOS Version interface.

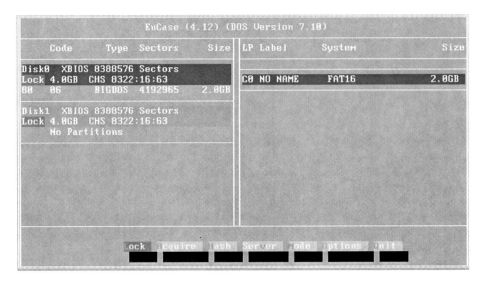

Unlock the disk to which you will be writing the image of the suspect drive by highlighting Lock, pressing ENTER, and choosing the disk drive to unlock (in this case, we're unlocking Disk1), as shown here:

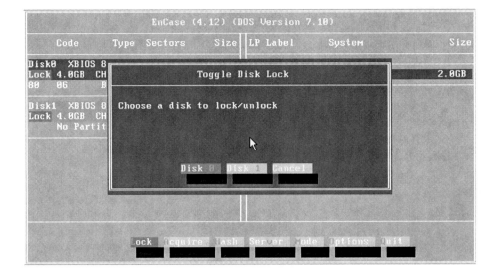

6. Your screen should now look like the following illustration, with the suspect drive (Disk1) shown as locked and the drive to which you want to write the image (Disk0) unlocked.

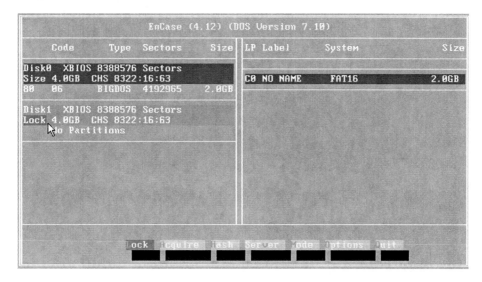

7. Select Acquire and choose the suspect drive (Drive1). You can move between options by pressing the TAB key. After you have selected the suspect drive, press ENTER.

8. Provide the path to the directory on the image drive to which you want the image of the suspect drive to be written and the name of the image file, and then press ENTER. Before you choose OK, make sure that the drive you are writing to is FAT16 or FAT32, as DOS cannot read from or write to drives of other file systems. You must also make sure that enough free space is available on the destination drive to hold the image. The image will always be about 2K larger than the suspect drive for case-specific information EnCase stores in the file, so never try to image a suspect drive to another drive of the same or a smaller size without using compression.

9. Type in a case number for your image. Use a unique number for each case you work on to help you keep track of your evidence. In this case, type **he** for hacking exposed, as shown here. Then click OK.

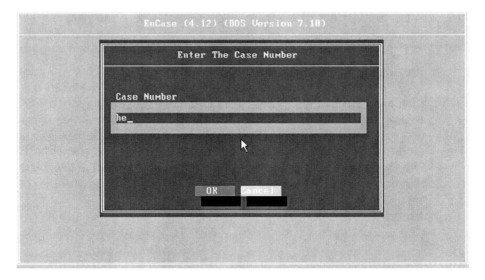

10. Type in the examiner's name. Click OK.

11. Now enter the evidence number and click OK. Like the case number, this needs to be unique, except here it needs to be unique only for the case. Since this is our first image in the *he* case, assign it evidence number 0. The next image created in this case would be evidence number 1, then evidence number 2, and so on.

NOTE If you are working with another person, make sure you divvy up your evidence numbers early on, because you cannot change them inside the image file after you have created the image. This approach works only with small cases. When you work on larger cases, you should look into implementing the case management techniques we talk about in Chapter 3.

12. Enter a description of the case. Normally, you would type in the name of the suspect or any other identifying information about the system. This information will be displayed in place of a name within EnCase when you analyze the system later. Click OK.

13. Enter the correct time according to the investigator, in case the system BIOS shows an incorrect time set; you must make sure your image creation time reflects the true time as the investigator knows it. If the BIOS time is correct, accept it and click OK, as shown next:

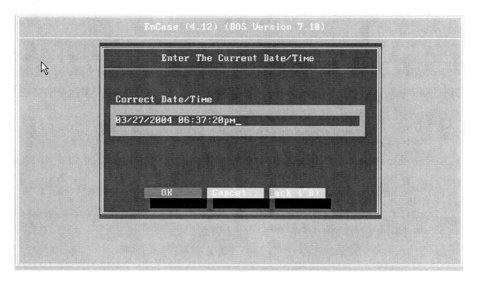

14. Enter any other notes about the system. Enter the serial number of the hard drive and any other notes that might be handy to know later.

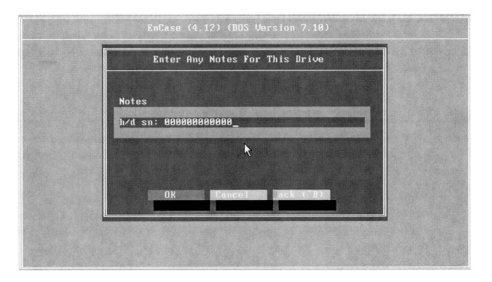

15. Now you must decide whether or not to compress the image. If speed is your primary concern, you probably should not compress the image at this point, as this can take a bit longer. However, if you have the time, you should choose Yes to compress the drive so you can fit more images on a single image drive.

16. Next, you're asked whether you want to make an MD5 hash of the drive; you should always choose Yes. Creating the MD5 hash and storing it in the image file is what lets the EnCase evidence file authenticate and thus verify itself in future accesses. It also allows you to testify to the fact that the image of the suspect drive has not changed during the course of your investigation.

17. Choose whether you want to set a password on the image. This is a good idea if for no other reason than to prevent other parties from getting bored and reviewing evidence files, or more seriously, if you are concerned about external parties or unauthorized individuals viewing the evidence. Click OK when you're done, and you'll be asked to reenter the password to confirm it.

18. When you are asked for the number of sectors to acquire, you should normally accept the default value and click OK.

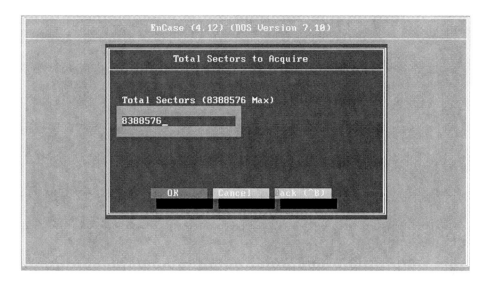

19. Now choose the maximum size that a single segment of the image file should consume. The image will be divided among multiple files that will span the contents of the suspect drive. The size of those pieces will determine how you can move them around. The default of 640MB is good, as it supports the size of the smallest recordable CD. We recommend using the 640MB size. Click OK.

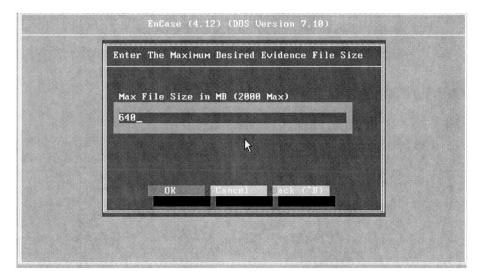

20. A status bar on the bottom of the screen appears with an estimate of the time remaining, as shown next. Review all of the information you have entered, as it is summarized here for you. If you see any incorrect information, cancel the imaging now by restarting the system; then restart this process from the beginning. Once you have created the image, you cannot change the information you entered.

21. After you have successfully completed the imaging, power off the system, remove the image drive, and place it and the suspect drives in static-proof bags.

Alternative Methods for Imaging

Image the Drive Using the FastBloc Hardware Write-Blocker and EnCase   Imaging systems outside of DOS allow you to take advantage of memory ranges beyond 640K and offer the ability to write to NTFS drives. However, imaging systems in operating systems such as Windows require that you take extra precautions. Specifically, you need a hardware-level write-blocker. Upon attaching a new piece of media to a Windows system, Windows will automatically attempt to write some system-level data to the drive. Allowing this to happen would defeat all the work you've put into your forensics effort up to that point. Using a hardware write-blocker in line between the system and the suspect drive allows you to state to the court without a doubt that you prevented any modification of the original evidence during your imaging. Hardware write-blockers work by preventing a write command from ever reaching the drive itself; instead, they return a true value to the operating system and do not pass on the command. This physically prevents your system from modifying your evidence.

You can image the drive using a FastBloc write-blocker by following these steps:

1. Attach the suspect drive to the FastBloc hardware write-blocker.
2. Attach the FastBloc hardware to your imaging system.
3. Load EnCase.
4. Click Acquire.
5. You are prompted to choose the source of the data, as shown next. In this case, leave the defaults as they are; we are going to image a local drive attached to the FastBloc device. (In Chapter 5, we cover acquiring drives over networks.) Leave the Include checkboxes set to their defaults. Click Next.

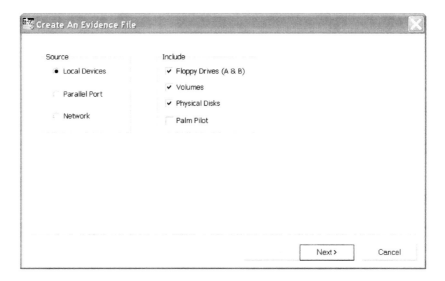

6. In the Choose A Drive screen, select the drive you will be imaging. The FastBloc device has been identified as "GSI FastBloc," as shown next. Select that drive. Note that you select the icon for the physical disk and not the volume E. The physical disk gives you a complete image of the drive, while the volume E would give you an image of only one logical partition. You should always choose to image the physical disk to reduce the risk of missing data.

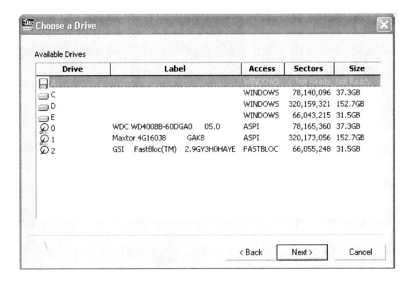

7. At the Identification screen, you'll notice that you're required to supply the same information you supplied for the EnCase DOS version, but here the fields are all on one screen. Fill out all fields as shown here and click OK.

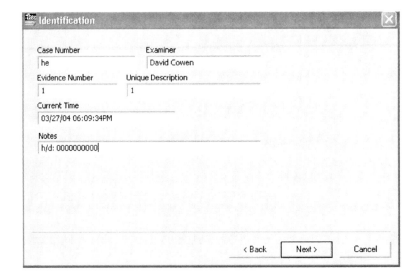

8. In the Output File screen, choose the options shown in the following illustration. Make sure you set the Evidence File Path to your image drive, and then click Finish.

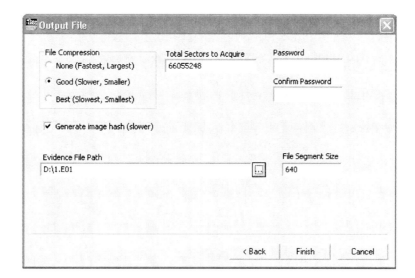

9. The image will now be acquired. You can view the status of the acquisition by double-clicking the blinking status bar on the bottom-left of the screen. You can also cancel imaging from this dialog box:

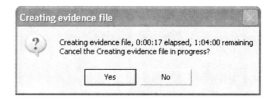

10. After a message box tells you that imaging is completed, click OK and then remove the suspect drive from the system and place it in an anti-static bag for storage.

Image the Drive Using Linux and dd   Unlike Windows, Linux will not write to any device attached to it, nor does it attempt to determine the file system and mount any device attached to it. Instead, you can image a suspect drive in Linux without the use of a hardware write-blocker using the following steps (although there is nothing wrong with using a write-blocker):

1. Power down the Linux system.

2. Attach the suspect drive to the Linux system.

3. Power up the Linux system.

4. Determine the device name of the suspect drive. You can normally do this by inspecting the messages log or viewing /proc/partitions.

5. Run the following command to image the device:

   ```
   dd if =/dev/<suspect drive> of=</some dir/imagename>
   ```

6. This creates a single file that is an image of the entire physical disk of the suspect drive. Here *suspect drive* represents the device name of the suspect drive, such as /dev/sda or /dev/hdb, and */some dir/imagename* is the full path and name of the file to which you want the image to be written.

7. Create an MD5 hash of the drive using the following commands.

   ```
   md5sum </some dir/imagename>
   ```

8. Then use

   ```
   md5sum /dev/<suspect drive>
   ```

9. Compare the results to verify that the image is complete.

10. Power down the Linux system and place the suspect drive in an anti-static bag for storage.

 NOTE   A modified version of dd, dcfldd, is also available. This version of dd has been modified for a forensic examiner. For more information, go to http://dcfldd.sourceforge.net/.

Image the Drive Using SMART   SMART is the only commercial Linux forensic suite available today. SMART, written by ASRdata and found at www.asrdata.com, is a forensic suite that is capable of performing all the common forensic tasks performed by other products such as EnCase. In addition, SMART gives you the power of the Linux operating system. When an image is accessed through SMART, it can be mounted as a local file system and browsed and searched with all of the open-source tools available to the investigator.

Here's how you image a drive in SMART:

1. Power down the Linux system.

2. Attach the suspect drive to the Linux system.

3. Power up the Linux system.

4. Load SMART.

5. Choose the device you want to acquire; then right-click it and choose Acquire.

6. In the Acquire window, select the number of copies of the device you want to make and the hashing algorithm you would like to use. As shown next, one copy will be made using the MD5 hashing algorithm.

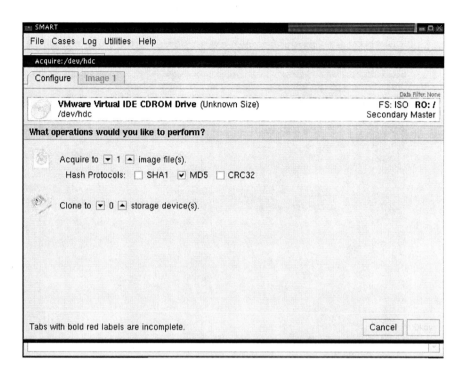

7. Click the Image 1 tab and type in the name of the image and its description.

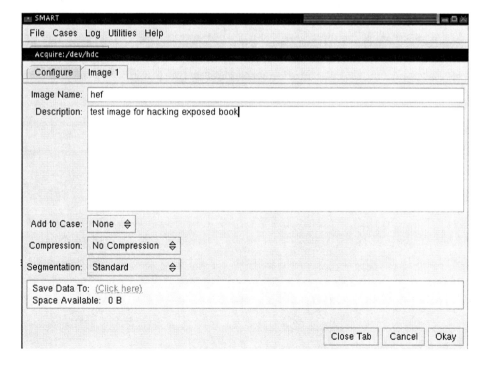

8. Click the area next to Save Data To and choose the directory where this data should be stored, as shown next. Click Okay and the imaging begins.

Image the Drive Using Helix   Helix is an open-source Linux LiveCD distribution maintained by e-fense, Inc., that comes modified not to mount drives on boot, thus creating a read-only environment. This distribution was available free but is now available for a fee from www.e-fense.com/helix. Here's one way to image a drive in Helix:

1. Power down the system.
2. Attach the suspect drive to the Linux system.
3. Place the CD-ROM in the system.
4. Power up the Linux system.
5. Click the link Boot Into The Helix Live CD.

6. Choose Applications | Forensics & IR | Adepto.

7. Type in your name and a unique evidence name for this image; then click Go.

8. Choose the drive you are going to acquire, and note the information provided in your chain of custody; then click the Acquire tab.

9. Fill in the Image Name field to match the evidence name you used in step 7.

10. Fill in the Image Notes field to include whose computer this is and any additional information about it.

11. In the Mount Point field, type the name of the directory to which you are going to write the data on your disk, or type in an external device you have already mounted.

12. Select the Use Advanced Options checkbox and make any adjustments as you see fit.

13. Click Start.

14. When the image is successfully created, "IMAGE VERIFIED" is displayed.

Image the Drive Using FTK Imager   AccessData provides a free Windows-based forensic-imaging tool named FTK Imager, available at www.accessdata.com/downloads.html. FTK Imager not only allows you to create an image in multiple evidence formats (EnCase, SMART, Raw, Sparse), but it also allows you to access images, export and recover deleted files from images, and convert images from one type to another. With FTK Imager, you can take advantage of the USB write-protect feature introduced in Windows XP SP2 to create images of USB connected drives in Windows. Here's how to do it:

1. Download the registry modification files located at www.howtogeek.com/howto/windows-vista/registry-hack-to-disable-writing-to-usb-drives/.

2. Access the Disable USB Write hack to prevent writing to the original evidence drive.

3. Attach your original evidence drive to your computer via a USB enclosure or a device of your choice.

4. Load the FTK Imager.

5. Choose File | Create Disk Image to open the Select Source dialog box.

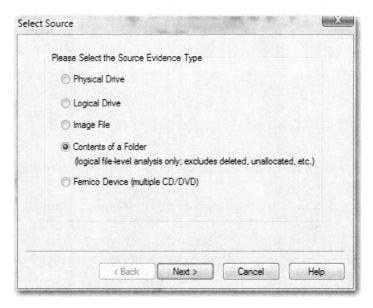

6. Select Physical Drive, and then click Next.

7. In the Select Drive dialog box, choose the physical drive to acquire and then click Finish.

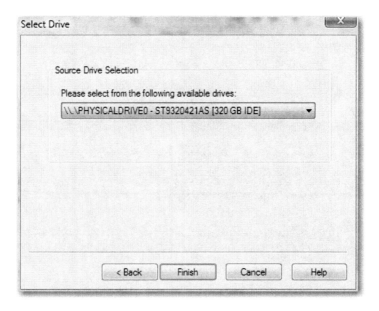

8. In the Create Image dialog box, click Add.

9. In the Select Image Type dialog, select the image type; choose Raw (dd), as all forensic tools support it. Then click Next.

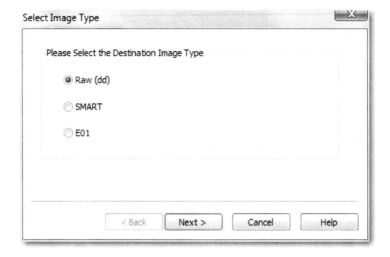

10. In the Evidence Item Information dialog, fill in the information about the original evidence drive; then click Next.

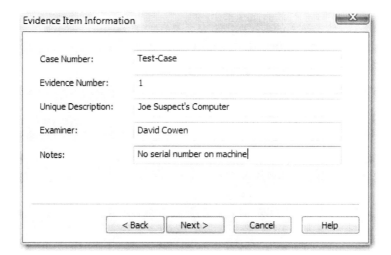

11. In the Select Image Destination dialog, type the directory where you want to store the image and type in a name for the image. Then click Finish.

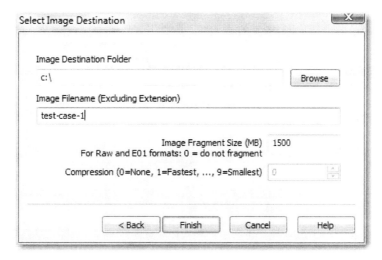

12. Click Start to start creating the image. You'll see a dialog box similar to the one shown next.

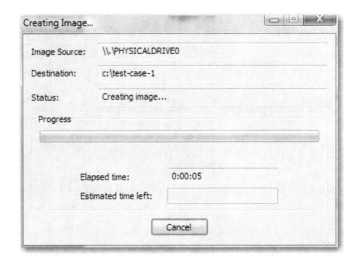

13. After the drive is imaged, FTK Imager will let you know whether the hashes matched.

14. Unplug the USB device.

15. Run the Enable USB Write registry modification. You downloaded it in step 1.

 If you want to make a copy of a running system, you can also do this using FTK Imager. Place the executable on a thumb drive and then attach it to the suspect system along with your storage drive or network share attached. Then follow all the same steps in this section except for the USB write-blocking.

Step 6: Record Cryptographic Hashes

You have successfully created images of your suspect media. You now need to record the cryptographic hashes created by your imaging programs. A *cryptographic hash* is any mathematical function that can take in a varying length of data to create a fixed-length output that mathematically represents the entire data set in such a way that it is statistically infeasible that two different data sets could ever have the same result. Typically, we use MD5, or Message Digest 5, as our cryptographic hash function, since it is an industry standard within the forensic world.

This is a very important step. The MD5 hash that is created will allow you to demonstrate that not only does the image you have created have an exact one-for-one correspondence with the original suspect drive, but that any analysis that you perform has not modified the image in any way and thus represents the same data that would have been extracted from the original suspect drive. If one bit of the contents of the drive is changed, the MD5 hash will be different.

Step 7: Bag and Tag

Now that you have completed the collection and imaging process, you need to label the drive that your forensic image has been written to and store it in a safe place. Although you can use any type of labeling, we recommend that you use some kind of peel-and-stick preprinted drive label so you can easily work with your image drives without worrying about the labels falling off. For a safe storage place, we recommend at a minimum that you place the drive in an anti-static bag. The bagged and tagged image drive should then be stored in a location with no access to unauthorized personnel. Specifically, you must be able to testify to the fact that the image drive was placed in some kind of locked room, filing cabinet, or drawer to which only you and other authorized individuals have access.

The suspect drive at this point may or may not be bagged and tagged for remote storage, depending on your scenario. A properly validated image drive will stand as original evidence in a court of law, so the suspect drive becomes a supplemental source of verification and recovery if the image drive(s) were to fail. While we recommend that you store the suspect drive with the image drive, on many occasions this may not be possible, and the actual drive will be returned back into operation in the suspect system. We would like to reiterate at this point that you should avoid using the original drive in the future and access only the forensic image.

Move Forward

Now that you have created your image(s) and documented your evidence, you can move forward with the next part of your investigation, the analysis—that is, of course, if you are lucky enough to have a case that involved only one system. Otherwise, you will have a lot more evidence to collect and systems to work with. Forensics is a *science*, and with such a strong word comes a lot of paperwork. If you are the type of person who cannot stay organized enough to keep up with this paperwork, you may want to hand the case over to someone who can. Repeatable processes are what will stand up in court and are the things that you should consider implementing as quickly as possible.

Unverifiable Images

Popularity:	10
Simplicity:	10
Impact:	10
Risk Rating:	10

Now that you have an image and a hash of an image, do you have any way of putting these two together? Hopefully, your answer is yes. If no, you just created an image of a system that will be difficult to use as evidence. According to the federal rules of evidence, an image must have some kind of automated mechanism that allows for a duplicate to be shown to be an exact copy of the original. In the computer forensics world, this usually comes down to some kind of hash, typically MD5, and a mechanism that allows for continuous self-validation of the evidence you create. By *self-validation*, we mean that within the contents of the image it can be seen and proven that the image has not been modified without referring back to the original suspect media.

 ## Countermeasure: Image Verification

You can verify an image in a number of ways, but depending on the tool you used to create the image, you may be limited to one.

Verifying an Image with EnCase

If you have added an Image to an EnCase case, it will automatically begin verifying your image. However, you can manually verify the image after acquiring it from within the acquisition or unlicensed version using the following steps:

1. Load EnCase.
2. Choose Tools | Verify Single Evidence File.
3. Choose the icon of the evidence file you want to verify and click Open.
4. The verification status will appear on the bottom-left of the EnCase window. The verification should show 0 errors. The verification is now completed.

Verifying a Raw Image

If you have a raw image created with a tool such as dd, you can still verify the image. Retrieve the previously documented hash that you created when you first created the dd image, and then run the following command in Linux:

```
md5sum "image file"
```

The md5sum should be the same as the hash you created earlier.

COMMON MISTAKES IN EVIDENCE COLLECTION

Examiners make several common mistakes in evidence collection. Some are technical and others are procedural. Reading this section will alert you to what investigators have learned are easily avoidable pitfalls. We hope that you can avoid the mistakes of others by following the advice in this section.

System Downtime

Popularity:	7
Simplicity:	10
Impact:	7
Risk Rating:	8

Most people are not familiar with computer forensic processes, and they will not understand that a system will have to be down for some time while it is imaged. On average, a DOS acquire images at about 10GB an hour, without compression. In an EnCase acquire in Windows, you can expect 20GB an hour, without compression. Compressing during acquisition is actually slower in DOS than acquiring without compression. Acquiring with compression in Windows can be fast if your processor is at least a Pentium 4 or equivalent. Linux acquires are faster than either, as they do not have the overhead of the evidence file creation that EnCase brings, but Linux imaging is still a lengthy process. Hardware imaging devices, if they are available, advertise even faster transfer rates but the downtime risk still exists.

Countermeasure: Communicate with Clients

Make sure that you communicate with your client(s), and make sure that the client, internally or externally, tells you how large the drive is and to what type of system it is attached. This way, you can respond to the client with an estimate of the downtime depending on the acquisition methodology used for the system. It could be that you decide to create the image at night or that the user can use another system while you image his or her system.

Some mission-critical systems, however, cannot be taken offline. In these cases, you have to go to the judge and opposing counsel to attempt to work out an arrangement to produce backups of the live system. The best way to prevent unnecessary conflicts is to communicate as much information about the process as you can without divulging any sensitive information.

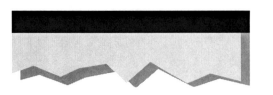

CHAPTER 5

REMOTE INVESTIGATIONS AND COLLECTIONS

In today's business climate, corporations face an array of security issues on a daily basis, including wrongful termination lawsuits, e-discovery requests, employee performance issues, whistle-blower investigations, intellectual property theft, and employee harassment issues. In addition, new government regulations hold organizations to updated standards for securing and responding to incidents in their environments. These types of challenges are forcing current forensic approaches to evolve because traditional forensic investigative techniques cannot meet the increasing demand. Not only has the forensic practitioner's workload increased, but global logistics, extremely large data sets, increased network complexity, workplace privacy, legal issues, and unrealistic time frames are impacting his or her ability to perform investigations.

This chapter discusses a number of approaches and tools designed for the changing investigative landscape. Moreover, this chapter touches on many of the technical, legal, and organizational challenges that come with utilizing some of these newer investigative methods.

PRIVACY ISSUES

Before you carry out any type of remote investigation or collection, ensure that the appropriate end user policies are in place. In performing an investigation, you must consider the issue of "reasonable expectation of privacy" and how the corporate culture may affect your remote investigation. Many organizations don't want their employees to think they are being watched continually because it lowers morale. Therefore, you must employ effective controls and methods to protect the corporation and its employees.

Pitfall: Violating Private-sector Workplace Privacy

Popularity:	5
Simplicity:	8
Impact:	9
Risk Rating:	7

If an employer does not have a clearly defined policy related to an employee's expectation of privacy or an *Acceptable Use Policy (AUP)* when an individual logs on to a company-owned computer or network, the employee may claim a reasonable expectation of privacy.

The courts generally look at two areas when evaluating workplace searches:

- The employer's justification for conducting the search
- The employee's reasonable expectation of privacy

Companies with poorly defined policies and procedures expose themselves to liability. Employees may be able to claim that their expectations of privacy were reasonable and their rights were violated.

Countermeasure: Correctly Written Acceptable Use Policies

It is critical that an AUP be written and implemented effectively. The AUP must indicate to a user that any private, non-business-related activities are at the user's own risk, and the user should have no expectations of privacy. Employers should consider obtaining a signed document from each employee that acknowledges receipt and understanding of the corporate policies and procedures. This may help to strengthen an employer's position should an employee challenge the expectation of privacy issue.

In the sections that follow, we discuss two major types of remote forensic capabilities: remote investigations and remote collections. A remote *investigation* is the practice of actually performing the investigation, such as keyword searching and file hashing on the remote machine. A remote *collection* is the practice of actually going across the network to take a forensic image of the remote machine for preservation and future examination purposes.

REMOTE INVESTIGATIONS

A remote investigation is the practice of actually performing an investigation on a remote machine. In most cases, you'll want to investigate the machine before carrying out the remote collection. That way, you can verify the presence of suspect artifacts on the remote machine before collecting data.

One of the biggest challenges facing forensic investigators is how to access and investigate the suspect media prior to performing any level of forensic collection. It is still considered acceptable practice to acquire the machine's image and then begin your analysis. However, such traditional approaches that involve collecting evidence before analyzing it make it almost impossible to conduct large-scale legal discovery and fraud cases without devoting considerable resources and disrupting business. This can be both costly and time-consuming, especially if the machines are located in a number of remote offices. Several tools are available, however, that allow investigators to analyze a network computer forensically without having to travel to the computer's location and bring it offline to acquire its hard drive.

With the remote investigative capabilities available today, the forensic examiner can, from a secure location, carry out many of the standard investigative tasks discussed in other chapters—forensic imaging, examining file signatures, performing keyword searches and file hashing, viewing deleted files and images, reviewing forensic artifacts, reviewing registries, copying files to the examiner workstation, and generating reports of suspect information.

 To conduct a remote investigation, the investigator needs to configure and deploy the appropriate software in advance. The tools discussed next have at least an examiner component that resides on the investigator's machine and an agent component that resides on the target machine that will be investigated. In the case of EnCase Enterprise, a third component is required for authentication purposes.

Remote Investigation Tools

Three remote forensic analysis tools are EnCase Enterprise Edition, Paraben Enterprise (P2EE), and ProDiscover. The breadth of analysis varies depending on the technology used to carry out the remote investigation. No matter which tool you use, ensure that the appropriate security controls are in place.

 NOTE You should test and deploy the remote investigative technology in your environment well in advance of actual use. The last thing you want to be doing is deploying agents to machines that you should be examining immediately.

Remote Analysis with EnCase

To perform remote analysis with EnCase, follow these steps:

1. Log on to EnCase Enterprise Edition from the examiner machine, as shown here.

2. Select Network from the View drop-down list.
3. Create a new node using an IP address or hostname within the network view. Then click OK.

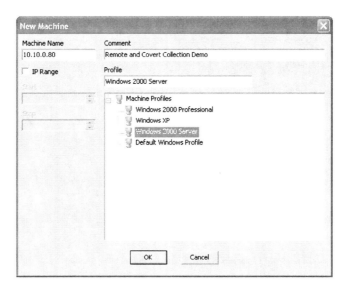

4. Click the New button, which will create a new case from which you can work.

5. A new window appears, as shown next, where you can select the appropriate security role. (EnCase uses granular role-based permissions that let an organization clearly define what actions the examiner can perform and to whom. Roles are defined by the administrator during setup of EnCase Enterprise. The roles are a collection of investigative powers that are granted to an authorized examiner. Each examiner must be assigned a role before he or she can conduct any type of investigation.) After you select a role and click Next, the New Case dialog will appear.

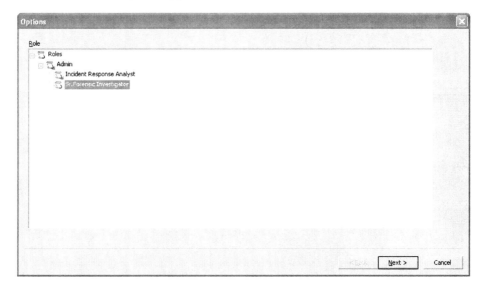

6. In the Case Options dialog, shown next, add the appropriate information for the new case and click Finish.

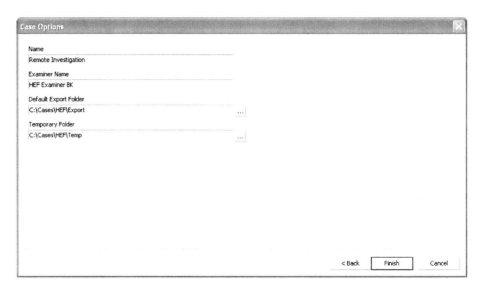

7. At the top of the EnCase Enterprise window, click the Add Device button, as shown here:

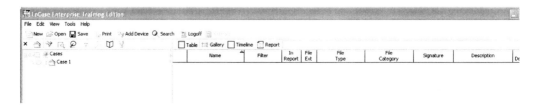

8. In the Add Device window, shown in Figure 5-1, select the appropriate node under Enterprise and then click Next.

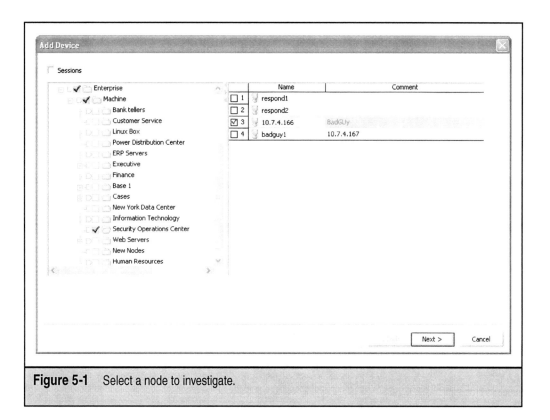

Figure 5-1   Select a node to investigate.

EnCase will display both physical drives and logical partitions or volumes. In most cases, you will want to select and acquire the *physical* drive. As shown in Figure 5-2, two entries are available. The second entry indicates that the target system has one physical drive (drive 0) with 4,194,304 total sectors. The top entry indicates a single logical partition (Volume C) with 4,192,901 total sectors. Make your selection and click Next.

NOTE   When you remotely preview a computer's hard drive across the network, you are viewing all the data in a read-only forensic fashion without having to copy the entire drive contents before analyzing them.

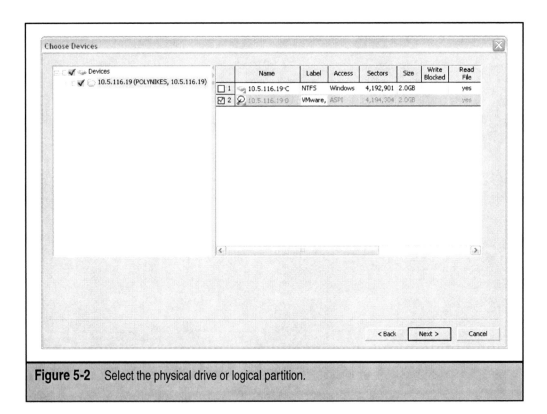

Figure 5-2   Select the physical drive or logical partition.

Once you've finished previewing the drive, as shown in Figure 5-3, you can perform a full forensic investigation of the remote system by analyzing the registry, carrying out keyword searches, performing file signature verification and hashing, carving data from the unallocated space, copying out deleted files, and many more operations.

NOTE   The true power of a remote investigation tool is clear. Instead of physically acquiring the drive to conduct a forensic analysis, you can use just a few clicks to access the data. The user of the target system will never know that an examiner is previewing and analyzing his or her machine. In the real world, this remote and covert approach can be invaluable. You do have to consider the network speed between you and your suspect, however, or it may take days to finish the drive imaging.

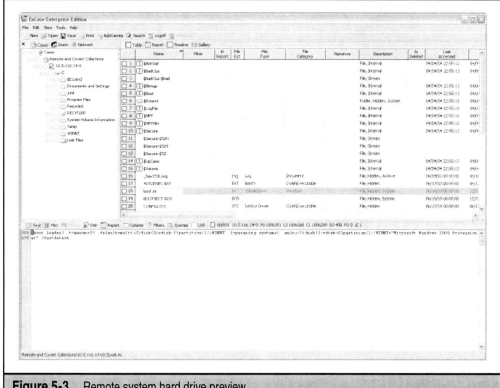

Figure 5-3 Remote system hard drive preview

Remote Analysis with ProDiscover

Before beginning your analysis, keep in mind that ProDiscover does not have encryption enabled by default, which means all analysis and collection traffic will be transferred in the clear until encryption is enabled. In addition, ProDiscover has no user permission system in place to prevent unauthorized examiners from carrying out investigations. Make sure the remote investigative technology deployed by your organization has been thoroughly tested and approved by the security organization.

To perform a remote analysis with ProDiscover, follow these steps:

1. Launch ProDiscover and create a new case by clicking open, as shown here:

2. Select Connect To from the ProDiscover toolbar.

3. In the pop-up window that appears, enter the hostname or IP address of the target machine, and then click the Connect button. You will then have access to the remote file system.

Once you're connected, you can carry out a forensic investigation of the remote system by viewing images and performing keyword searches and file hashing.

 As is the case with all forensic tools, training is critical to ensuring that the tool is used properly and that you understand how the technology works. You may have to defend your use of the tool and process if it becomes a material issue in a civil or criminal proceeding.

Remote Analysis with Paraben Enterprise

To perform a remote analysis with Paraben Enterprise, follow these steps:

1. Launch the P2EE Captain module.

2. In the Login dialog, log in to the Captain module, making sure that you specify the IP address for the P2EE proxy server that is visible to the computer you are going to inspect. Then click OK.

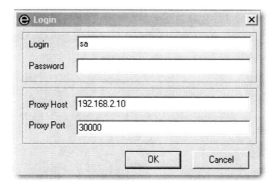

3. In the Explorer pane on the left side of the main screen, right-click Agent, and then choose Add Agent.

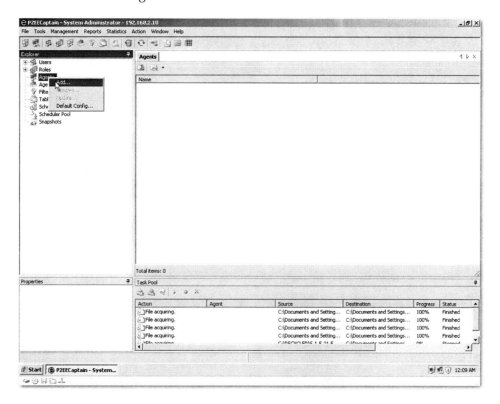

4. In the Agent Install window, type the IP address of the system to which you want to connect, and then click Scan.

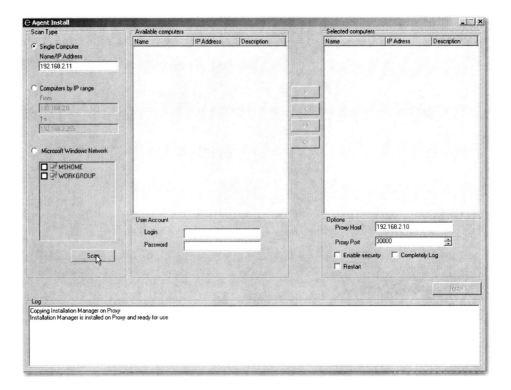

5. Enter either the network administrator login information or the local administrator login information for the system you chose.

6. Click the right arrow button to move the system from the Available Computers list to the Selected Computers list for agent deployment.

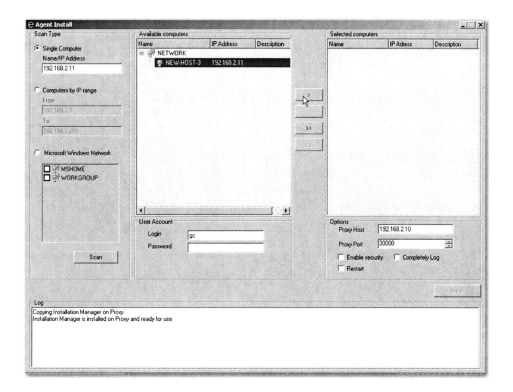

7. In the Options area, choose Enable Security to turn on security features, Completely Log if you want the install process logged for you to view, and Restart if you want to restart your computer when the process completes.

8. Click Install to deploy the agent.

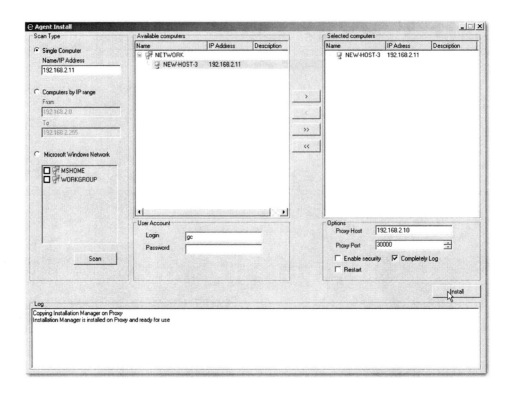

You can now view the registry, the drive contents, and the suspect's screen, and you can perform tasks in Paraben Enterprise.

Failing to Keep an Investigation Covert

Popularity:	5
Simplicity:	7
Impact:	10
Risk Rating:	**9**

Depending on the sensitivity of the case and the people involved, your ability to conduct a covert forensic investigation from a safe location is critical. Investigating a machine remotely means you no longer need to acquire the machine in the middle of the night (typically referred to as a *black bag job*) or escort the suspect away from his or her machine, causing a commotion among coworkers. Scenarios and issues that endanger a covert investigation include the following:

- Somebody discovers who is involved in the investigation and notifies co-conspirators, damaging the investigation.
- The subject discovers he or she is being investigated and destroys the evidence.

- The subject discovers he or she is being investigated, and when coworkers find out, employee morale is damaged.
- The subject discovers the investigation is taking place and modifies any inappropriate behavior, such as ceasing to perform fraudulent transactions.

Properly Performing Covert Investigations

EnCase, Paraben Enterprise, and ProDiscover give you the ability to carry out covert examinations without the subject discovering that he or she is being actively investigated. This capability is a key aspect of these technologies and if used correctly can determine the success or failure of the investigation. The following techniques and actions can help you ensure the success of a covert investigation:

- Minimize the number of simultaneous operations to minimize system resource usage. For example, don't perform a keyword search, file signature analysis, and hash analysis all at the same time.
- Give the remote investigative agent an operating system–friendly name such as *svchost.exe* and run it from the system directory, or in the case of Paraben Enterprise, choose Secure Mode.
- If your organization uses personal firewalls, make sure a standard policy is in place to allow inbound connections from the examiner's machine. Otherwise, the subject could be alerted by the firewall that somebody is trying to connect to his or her system.
- Ensure that the remote investigative agent does not leave any events in the event logs, because many savvy users check them regularly.
- Minimize the number of people who know about the investigation to reduce the risk of the subject finding out accidentally or intentionally that he or she is being investigated.
- To keep from alerting the subject, try to use an agent that runs as a system service each time the machine is started. That way, you aren't required to connect to the remote machine and start the service before beginning the examination.
- For sensitive cases, conduct the investigation during the evening when the suspect is most likely not at his or her machine.
- Time the investigation for periods when the subject expects a lot of hard drive activity, such as during regular antivirus scans or recent security vulnerability announcements.
- Search only the data that is relevant to the case. For instance, if you are looking for documents, narrow your search to specific areas and data types.

- Determine whether the target machine is a laptop or desktop machine. If the suspect is using a laptop, sustained hard drive activity can alert him or her to the investigation.

- Be patient and don't rush the investigation; if necessary, break it up into several phases.

REMOTE COLLECTIONS

Remote collections are changing the manner in which forensic investigators, compliance officers, human resource personnel, and other forensic practitioners are conducting computer- and network-based investigations. By remote collection, we mean acquiring a computer hard drive across the network in a forensically sound manner without having to be within physical proximity of the target media. Previously, we discussed remote investigations, which typically occur before you carry out a remote collection. In almost all cases, using remote tools such as EnCase Enterprise, Paraben Enterprise, and ProDiscover, you will first check for relevant artifacts and then begin collection if necessary. In Chapter 4, we covered methods and procedures for examining the evidence on-site. It's clear from the previous discussion in "Remote Investigations" that being able to investigate a system remotely without first acquiring it dramatically changes the way traditional investigations are conducted. If you need to acquire the machine for preservation or authentication purposes, you can accomplish this across the network using remote collection tools. The creation of these tools has reduced and simplified many of the challenges of collecting forensically sound evidence. You no longer have to travel to the target location, power down the machine (and potentially disrupt the business), or crack the computer case to collect media.

Sometimes, performing a remote collection is your only option. Here are a few examples:

- When you need to acquire a revenue-generating production server that can't be brought offline for any reason.

- When you're dealing with a large RAID server with many drives and complex configuration, in which case acquiring each individual drive and reassembling for analysis is an unreasonable option.

- If the machine is in a hostile environment, going on-site could be potentially dangerous.

- When critical evidence will be lost between the time an investigation is deemed necessary, and when the investigator can gain physical access to the computer.

To carry out a remote collection, the investigator needs to configure and deploy the appropriate software in advance. The tools discussed next have at least an examiner component that resides on the investigator's machine and an agent component that resides on the target machine. In the case of EnCase Enterprise, a third component is required for authentication purposes.

Remote Collection Tools

The collection options available to the examiner vary depending on the technology used to carry out the remote collection. No matter which tool you use, make sure the appropriate security controls are in place and that the tool works well over various network types, such as slower WAN (wide area network) connections.

 Remote collection tools can cause serious network problems if they are used incorrectly. It's important that you understand your network environment and plan accordingly. Unlike the remote analysis process that brings only a subset of the drive data across the network to the examiner, the acquisition process, in essence, brings the entire contents of the hard drive across the network. Remember that acquiring hard drive contents across a network is the same as copying a very large file, but in this case you're copying a forensic image. The amount of time it takes to collect a drive is typically a function of the available bandwidth and target machine resources and the amount of data on the remote machine's hard drive.

Remote Collection with EnCase

To perform remote collection with EnCase, follow these steps:

1. Log on to EnCase Enterprise Edition from the examiner machine.

2. Select Network from the View drop-down list.

3. Create a new node using an IP address or hostname within the network view, and then click OK.

4. Click the New button to create a new case.

5. Select the appropriate security role from the new window that appears. (These roles are described previously in "Remote Analysis with EnCase.") Then click Next.

6. In the Case Options dialog, enter the appropriate information for the new case, as shown here, and then click Finish.

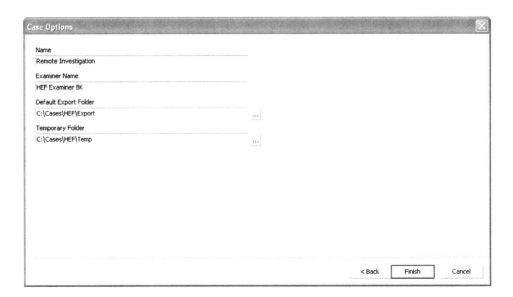

Several different methodologies are available for structuring your case information. It's important that you follow your organization's policies and procedures or what you learned from a forensic training program.

7. Click the Add Device button and select the node you are planning to acquire under the Enterprise section. Then click Next.

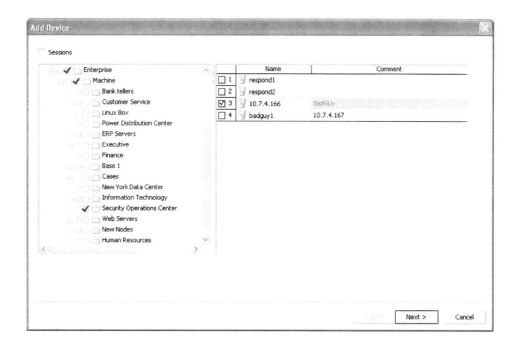

EnCase will display both physical drives and logical partitions or volumes. In most cases, you will want to select and acquire the *physical* drive. As shown earlier in Figure 5-2, two entries are available. The second entry indicates that the target system has one physical drive (drive 0) with 4,194,304 total sectors. The top entry indicates a single logical partition (Volume C) with 4,192,901 total sectors.

NOTE EnCase also offers the option of collecting the hard drive without previewing first. This lets the examiner begin a collection without having to read the file system first. To begin collecting without previewing first, right-click the Read File System box and invert the selection, as shown in the following dialog.

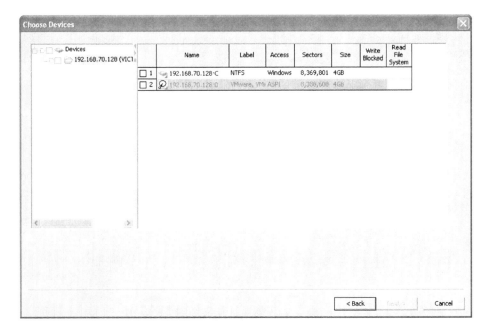

8. Make your selection and click Next.

9. After the preview is complete, highlight the physical or logical volume within EnCase that you plan to acquire. If you selected only the logical drive in the preceding step, the only option available is to acquire the logical volume.

10. Click the Acquire button, and the After Acquisition dialog box, shown here, will appear. If you simply want to acquire the drive, select the Do Not Add radio button and click Next.

11. In the Options window, enter all the relevant evidence and case information.

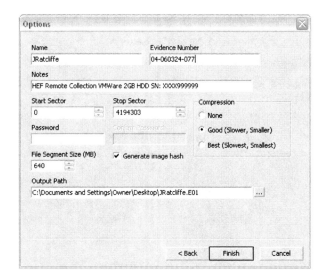

As you develop your organization's forensic procedures, keep in mind that many organizations stick to a common format for their naming of evidence files, one that ties in with their overall case management methodology.

12. Select the destination for the collected evidence. The size of the destination location should be at least equal to or greater than the size of the collected hard drive.

13. Select the appropriate compression radio button. The compression method you select will affect the speed of the acquisition and size of collected evidence. The fastest method for acquiring data is no compression because it does not require the processing overhead of compressing the data. The best method is the slowest because of the processing that needs to take place on the remote node to compress the data before transporting it back to the examiner's workstation.

14. Click the Finish button and the acquisition process will begin.

The amount of time it takes to collect data from the remote machine is tied to a number of variables such as overall available network bandwidth, amount of allocated and unallocated data on the drive, and available host resources.

Remote Collection with ProDiscover

To perform a remote collection with ProDiscover, follow these steps:

1. Launch ProDiscover and create a new case.

2. Choose Connect To from the toolbar.

3. In the pop-up window that appears, enter the hostname or IP address of target machine and then click Connect, as shown in Figure 5-4. You will then have access to the remote file system.

4. Choose Capture Image from the toolbar and the Capture Image dialog box will appear, as shown here:

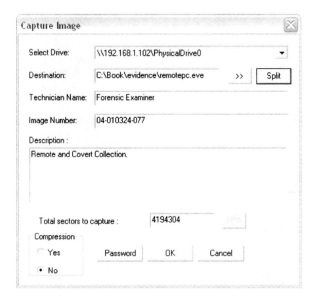

5. Specify which device you want to acquire from the Select Drive drop-down list.

6. Enter the appropriate evidence and case information.

7. Select a destination for the evidence.

8. Start the acquisition process by clicking OK.

Remote Collection with Paraben Enterprise

To perform a remote collection with Paraben Enterprise, follow these steps:

1. Launch the P2EE Captain module.

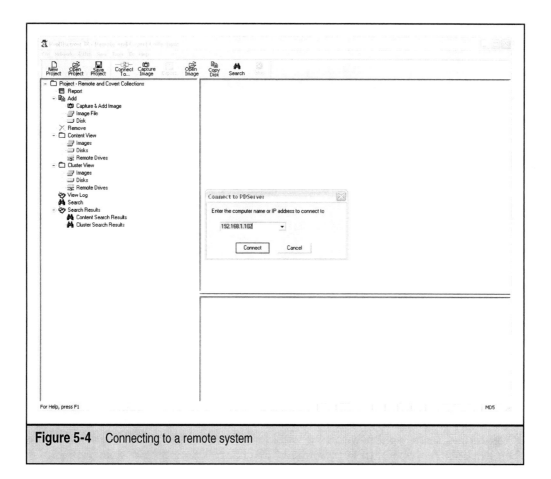

Figure 5-4 Connecting to a remote system

2. Select the agent name and choose the system you deployed earlier in the chapter.

3. Expand the agent tree in the left menu.

4. Click Storage.

5. Right-click the drive name and choose Acquire.

6. Choose the agent from which you will acquire data.

7. Select the physical drive if you want to create a forensic image.

8. Choose where you want to save the image and click OK.

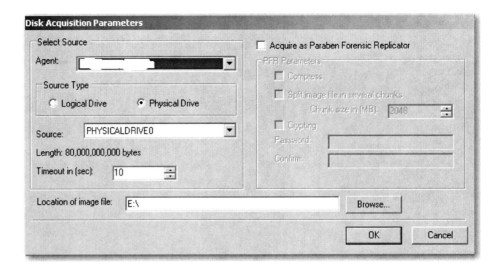

Carrying Out a Successful Covert Collection

Popularity:	8
Simplicity:	8
Impact:	9
Risk Rating:	7

Covert, or secret, collections occur without the knowledge of the target or others—
their existence is deliberately kept hidden. Covert acquisitions are possible but not in all
cases, especially during business hours. Unlike remote analyses, remote collections
potentially cause sustained hard drive activity and degrade performance on the remote
machine. With that in mind, use these techniques to ensure the success of a covert
collection:

- Perform remote collections in the evening when users are not working at their
  machines.
- Make sure company policy and culture require users to leave their machines
  turned on at all times as part of standard maintenance procedures.
- Collect at times when the suspect expects a lot of hard drive activity, such as
  during regular antivirus scans or recent security vulnerability announcements.
- Acquire only the media you need to support the investigation.
- Avoid acquiring laptops, if possible; their hard drives are slower and increased
  disk activity is apparent.

- Time your collection so it takes place when the suspect is going to be away from his or her desk for an extended period of time. Schedule an offsite meeting during the day and require that laptops remain in the office.

- Whenever possible, acquire the machine using a high-speed network connection; it will take much less time to acquire than it will on a slow WAN link.

CAUTION If the machine is shut down during the acquisition process, you must start over the acquisition. In some cases, this may add many hours to the collection process, but probably not nearly as many as would going on-site with needed equipment.

Challenging the Authenticity of Network-collected Evidence

The process of collecting evidence across the network is, in essence, similar to the process of acquiring the evidence while physically connected to the media. However, a number of differences can cause problems, depending on the audience and the approach you take to collect the evidence. Collecting evidence across the network is still a fairly new concept with regard to traditional forensic collection techniques. Although remote collection is not a widespread technique, it is growing in popularity as more and more organizations adopt technologies with remote collection capabilities.

Beyond the relative newness of the approach, a few other challenges are present. Successfully using remote collection tools requires that you understand multiple operating systems and network environments. Two of the biggest challenges arising from network collections are being unable to authenticate the original acquisition data and legacy forensic policy and procedures.

Countermeasure: Protecting Against Attacks to Network-collected Evidence

Although collecting evidence across the network poses a number of challenges, in a number of cases, evidence collected across the network has been used successfully for litigation purposes both in the corporate and law enforcement arenas. In addition, a number of methods can be used to overcome the challenges:

- Ensure that all investigators are highly trained and understand exactly what is going on during the collection process.

- Work from a defined, repeatable procedure. In many cases, cross examiners will go after the investigator's process, not necessarily the technology used.

- When you've completed collecting the media from across the network, have a trusted person on the remote end preserve the machine so it can be added into the formal evidence-collection process.

- Do your best to tie the collected evidence to the correct machine.

The Data Is Changing

To perform a remote network collection, the machine must be powered on and running. With the machine running, the data on the hard drive is, for the most part, changing constantly as the user or applications function normally.

 Applications such as EnCase Forensic Edition allow an investigator to acquire a machine via a crossover cable, which could be considered a network collection. To carry out of this type of collection, the investigator must be in close proximity and have physical access to the target machine. In the context of this chapter, we refer only to remote network collections.

When you begin a network collection, the tool typically starts collecting at the first sector of the media and keeps going until the last sector, unless otherwise specified. When the acquisition is complete, the examiner or the tool will generate an MD5 hash of the acquired data to authenticate it. In many cases, that MD5 hash is used so another examiner can compare the acquisition of the original media to your acquired version of the media. In the case of a network collection, you can't collect the media from a running system and expect to get the same MD5 hash as the original since the hard drive data will have changed due to normal operations when it is collected a second time. Forensically sound evidence collection is discussed in Chapter 4.

Policies and Procedures

The second issue arising from network collections is dealing with existing policy and procedures. Depending on the maturity of the organization, it might take some time to adopt new polices around acquiring media via a network collection mechanism versus the traditional method of physically connecting to the media to acquire it and take the original media with you.

 Remote network collections are growing in acceptance; however, it's a good idea to keep your legal group involved so they can support you in the event a matter does arise and the evidence is needed for litigation purposes.

ENCRYPTED VOLUMES OR DRIVES

A challenge faced by many forensic examiners is dealing with encrypted data. In some cases, subjects will use encryption technology for both legitimate and/or illegitimate purposes. Regardless, investigating encrypted data is typically difficult and sometimes an impossible problem to overcome.

With network-enabled analysis and collection tools such as EnCase Enterprise, it's now possible to overcome some of the challenges presented by encrypted volumes. Many encryption technologies make it easy to store and retrieve data from encrypted volumes of various sizes by mounting them as logical volumes on the host machine. For example, as shown in Figure 5-5, a mounted Stealth volume disk shows up as a logical drive on the host OS (we named the volume for demonstration purposes).

NOTE ProDiscover cannot perform mounted encrypted volumes.

When the encrypted volume is unmounted, you can no longer select it for investigation or collection. See Figure 5-6.

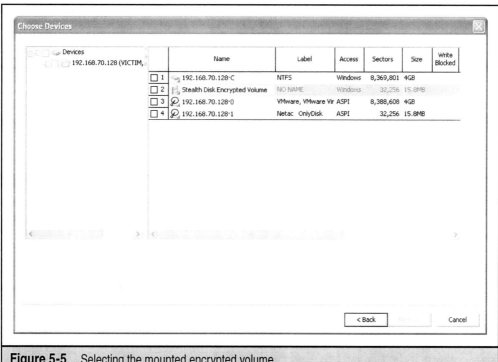

Figure 5-5 Selecting the mounted encrypted volume

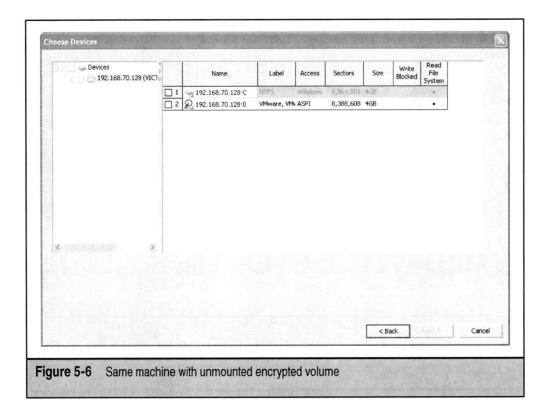

Figure 5-6 Same machine with unmounted encrypted volume

By investigating the volume that hosts the encrypted volume, you can most likely find the encrypted file by its extension. In Figure 5-7, you can see the file called HEF Volume.sdv. When we examine the specific file within EnCase, we see all the data is encrypted.

If the subject has his or her encrypted drive mounted, it's a fairly trivial task to analyze and acquire a remote machine's mounted encrypted volumes. Follow the same process described previously in the sections on investigating and collecting remote systems. You'll increase the odds of catching a suspect with his or her encrypted drives mounted by doing the following:

- Checking the last access times on the encrypted volume; this gives you an idea of when the suspect last used the volume.

- Understanding the characteristics of the encryption program. Find out if it mounts the volumes on startup and if an auto unmount feature is available.

NOTE During an investigation, look for encrypted files on the hard drive. Find one that is the same size as one of the mounted logical volumes on the remote machine; it is a good indication that the mounted volume is the encrypted one.

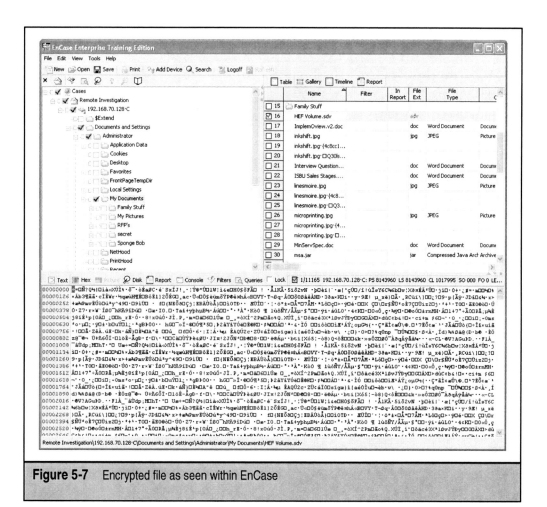

Figure 5-7   Encrypted file as seen within EnCase

USB THUMB DRIVES

Another challenge faced by many forensic examiners is dealing with external media such as USB thumb drives and FireWire IDE drives. These technologies are a great convenience but also a gigantic risk for corporations if not managed properly. Back in the day, it was pretty tough to smuggle lots of data out on floppy disks or on paper without drawing attention. In addition, you couldn't burn a CD on most corporate computers, so walking data out on CD was not common. Now that external storage is readily available and easy to use, corporations find their intellectual property being removed from the office on a regular basis through thumb drives.

In the past, if you suspected an employee of stealing intellectual property or keeping inappropriate material on a thumb drive, it was quite difficult to view the contents of the

USB device. And it was almost impossible to do it in a way that didn't modify any of the time data stamps on the external media. With remote analysis and collection tools, you can now analyze and collect these external storage devices covertly.

A good way to find out whether a person has been using a USB device is to check the registry. Go to HKEY_LOCAL_MACHINE\SYSTEM\CurrentControlSet\Enum\USBSTOR to learn what types of devices have been plugged into the system.

Figure 5-8 shows a machine with a USB storage device plugged in and initialized properly. These devices show up just like any other volume on the remote machine. At this point, you can connect to the volume and carry out a forensic investigation or remote collection without the suspect knowing.

Some USB thumb drives have a safety feature that hides part of the drive's available storage. When conducting an investigation that includes a USB thumb drive, you should keep in mind that it could be a secure USB device and you may not be seeing all the data. Identify the manufacture of the device and then identify whether it is indeed a secure USB device.

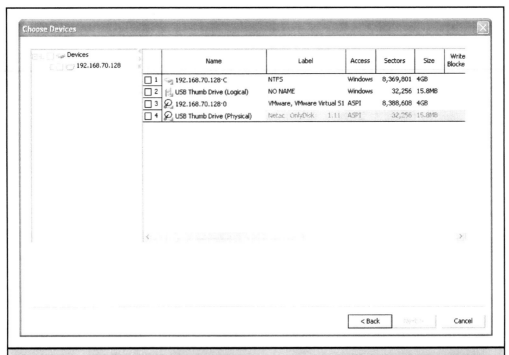

Figure 5-8   Selecting a physical or logical volume of a USB thumb drive within EnCase Enterprise

PART III

FORENSIC INVESTIGATION TECHNIQUES

CASE STUDY: ANALYZING THE DATA

ACME Services was greatly concerned. Before the investigation began, they had no way of knowing how long Charlie Blink had been compromising banking accounts and how he was getting the information. They did know at this point that Charlie was using key logging software. However, they didn't know the scope of his crimes.

Digging for Clues

Digging under the covers of the hard disk images, the real fun began. It wasn't long before the examination revealed the specific tools Charlie used. The analysis also exposed the Web sites he was visiting, including information on defeating the security settings on the computers he was using in manufacturer forums. We discovered that Charlie was working with a small gang to install a stealth key logging program on the company's computers, and he had manually visited the computers looking for bank account information. Later, Charlie's methodology and behavior became an indicator used to search other images quickly for subsequent activity, including the use of web-based e-mail to deliver the logged keystrokes to himself. Charlie had written programs that allowed him to sift through the keylogger's data quickly, finding only entries for which people were logging into banks. With his routine close to being automated, he enlisted the help of some friends to harvest his crop. The recovered date and time stamps of the recovered keystroke logs helped investigators tie the video surveillance cameras to the user at the computer, providing further evidence that the person leading this ring was in fact Charlie. Moreover, he had been capturing account information for more than two years in downtown New York City.

We're Not Done. Yet.

After Charlie was arrested, the judge released him on bail, and, as a dog returns to its vomit, so a fool repeats his folly. The story wasn't over. Our team wrote countermeasures to traverse the network and search for new instances of the key logging program. The software resurfaced on ACME Services' computers shortly after Mr. Blink was released on bail. Subsequent coordination with the video surveillance cameras clearly showed Charlie was at it again. Using a downloaded cracking tool, L0phtCrack, on one computer, Charlie discovered the new administrator password and installed the key logging software with administrative rights on several others. When we put a stop to the key logging software, he shifted to hardware keyloggers. These physically hide in the back of the computer, sitting between the keyboard connection and the PS-2 connector. Software could not discover these, but our continued investigation into the browsing habits and recovery of deleted files tipped us off as to what Charlie was trying to learn and how to get ahead of him by installing preventive measures he had not researched.

Finally

After careful examination and thorough researching, we had enough evidence for the US Attorney's Office to approach the judge and place Charlie Blink behind bars.

CHAPTER 6

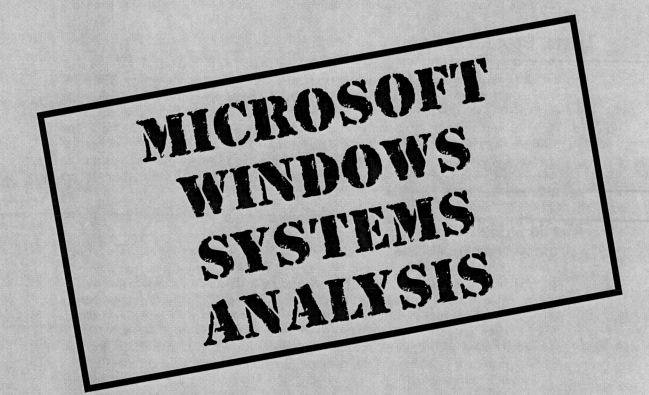

MICROSOFT
WINDOWS
SYSTEMS
ANALYSIS

The Microsoft Windows operating system contains an ample amount of opportunities for forensic recovery of deleted documents, user activities, and system artifacts. This chapter focuses on common tasks the forensic examiner will perform in an investigation of a Windows system, and specifically the file systems to which it writes our evidence. For each task, we will discuss the data you can expect to recover and the tools you can use to recover it. Each task is meant to stand on its own, so you can refer to this book as a reference when you are performing your investigation.

 This chapter does not offer an exclusive list of all possible forensic techniques for Windows operating and file systems, so this should not be your only source for forensic techniques.

WINDOWS FILE SYSTEMS

The Windows operating system has had two generations of file systems available to its users. The first file system, FAT (File Allocation Table), was used in earlier versions of the Windows/MS-DOS system and grew from a 12-bit file system called FAT12 to a 32-bit file system called FAT32. The second file system, NTFS, was introduced with Windows NT. Table 6-1 shows the Windows versions and the default file system present in each.

Master Boot Record

The first block of a drive is known as the MBR, or Master Boot Record. This record tells the BIOS where on the disk it should go next to continue booting the system. The MBR will point either to a boot loader that allows you to choose between installed operating systems or to the operating system on a partition. Most operating systems make use of the MBR, and all file systems we cover in this book are accessed through the MBR. The MBR points to partitions on the disk, and for each partition, a partition table informs the operating system of what type of file system is contained within it. If the partition table gets deleted, such as when someone deletes a partition with the fdisk utility, the partition still remains.

FAT File System

The FAT file system was used in MS-DOS and Windows 98 and earlier versions, though modern versions of FAT can still be found on external USB hard drives. FAT comes in three flavors—FAT12, FAT16, and FAT32—according to the amount of space that the file system could address in each partition. After Windows 98, some Windows Server versions had their boot partitions formatted in FAT and data partitions formatted in NTFS to allow for easy system recovery, since most boot disks cannot access NTFS file systems. Another offshoot introduced in Windows 95 was VFAT (Virtual File Allocation Table), which gave Windows the ability to use filenames longer than eight characters.

Common among all the FAT file systems is its structure on the physical disk. By knowing this structure, you can examine a disk and determine whether a FAT file system

Windows Version	Default File System	Practical Maximum Size	Notes
MS-DOS	FAT12	8MB	Disks could be formatted FAT12, 16, 32
Windows 3.1	FAT16	4GB	Disks could be formatted FAT12, 16, 32
Windows 95	FAT16	4GB	Disks could be formatted FAT12, 16, 32
Windows 98	FAT32	32GB	Disks could be formatted FAT12, 16, 32
Windows NT 3.5	NTFS	256TB	Disks could be formatted FAT or NTFS
Windows NT 4	NTFS	256TB	Disks could be formatted FAT or NTFS
Windows 2000	NTFS	256TB	Disks could be formatted FAT or NTFS
Windows XP	NTFS	256TB	Disks could be formatted FAT or NTFS
Windows Vista	NTFS	256TB	Disks should be formatted NTFS

Table 6-1   Default File Systems for Windows

existed on it and whether files and directories can be recovered from it, and you can even possibly recover a deleted FAT partition. The FAT structure begins with the boot block. A hard drive is laid out in a logical form for the BIOS to access. Figure 6-1 shows an example of how this physical disk layout looks in EnCase.

In the FAT file system, the namesake File Allocation Table describes clusters that are free for use, occupied, or bad. For occupied clusters, pointers in the FAT indicate whether they are linked to another cluster, and if they are, they indicate which cluster the system should go to next. Note that the FAT does not contain any information about the stored file—no filenames; attributes; modified, accessed, and created (MAC) times; or any other data about the file. The FAT simply informs the operating system of which clusters are free for use and which clusters to string together to read a file. The actual filenames, attributes, and MAC times are stored in the directory entries.

Directory entries are stored just like files on the disk but are linked to the FAT and noted as a special type of file entry in directory entries. These directories are linked from a parent directory, meaning that the directory layout is not defined in the FAT table but

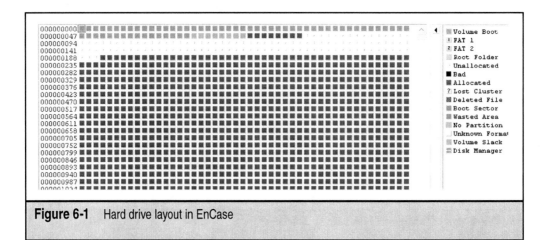

Figure 6-1   Hard drive layout in EnCase

is found as you traverse linked directories. The exception is the root directory, which is a special file whose space is allocated at the time of the file system creation, otherwise known as formatting. By accessing the root directory, you can access files and directories that are linked to it. Each directory contains the first cluster of a file or a directory and the file size of the file.

To read a file, the directory entry is accessed; the size is read and used to calculate how many clusters the file occupies. The first cluster number is read, and then the corresponding cluster marker in the FAT is accessed. If the file occupies more than one cluster, the first cluster marker in the FAT will contain the number of the second cluster, and the second cluster marker will contain the number of the third cluster, and so on until the last cluster marker is reached. The last cluster marker for the file contains "EOF" as an end of file marker. This string of clusters referenced in the FAT is read and the file is then strung together.

Since all FAT directories are written to the disk the same way as files, you can recover FAT directories as well as files. This is useful when portions of the disk have been overwritten or are physically damaged. Once a FAT directory entry has been recovered, the names of the files that were contained within it and their sizes and MAC times can be read. If the clusters to which the directory links still contain those files, you can access them as well.

NOTE   Remember that a FAT directory is just a special file entry; it exists on a FAT file system as a file entry but in terms of recovery exists just as a file.

You can recover a deleted FAT partition by finding the first sector of the partition and using your forensic tools to reconstruct it. For a FAT partition, the first sector, or the volume boot sector, of the file system will begin with ëX MSDOS or ëR MSWIN4.1 and end with hex characters 55 AA. For FAT32, a backup of the volume boot sector also is present, so if the volume boot sector is overwritten or physically damaged you can still recover the partition.

Recover FAT Partitions in EnCase

Here's how you can recover FAT partitions using EnCase:

1. Load your image in EnCase.

2. Create a new keyword: *MSWIN4.1*

3. Search the image for the keyword you just created.

4. View the hits in the disk view.

5. If the last four hexadecimal characters of the sector are 55 AA, right-click the sector in the disk view and choose Add Partition, as shown in Figure 6-2.

6. In the Add Partition dialog box, accept the defaults and click OK, as shown in Figure 6-3.

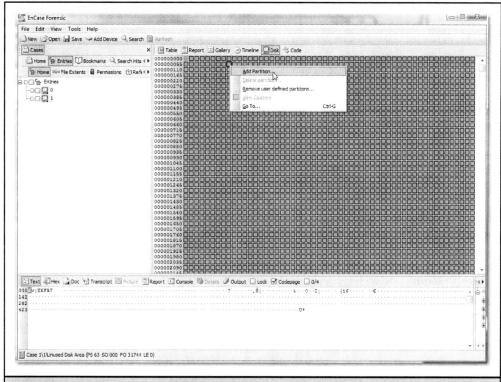

Figure 6-2 Adding a FAT partition in EnCase

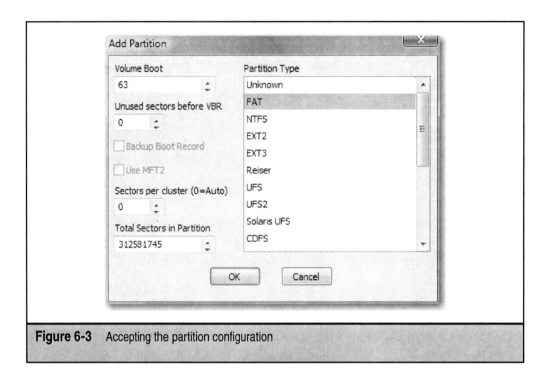

Figure 6-3   Accepting the partition configuration

Recover FAT Partitions in SMART

To recover FAT partitions using ASR Data's SMART, simply load your image into SMART. The program will scan the image and find the partitions itself.

NTFS

The NTFS file system, present in Windows NT and later versions, is a much more robust file system than FAT, as it allows for a multiple user environment with file-level permissions and ownership with much more security. Instead of using a FAT, NTFS uses a Master File Table (MFT) to keep track of the contents of the partition. For each entry in the MFT, a filename, attributes, and MAC time are stored, as well as other attributes accessed by the system when a user accesses a file. The list of available clusters exists in a special inode called $BITMAP$, which stores that information. One entry is made for every cluster on the disk, and a value indicates whether the cluster is free.

Like FAT32, NTFS keeps a backup of its file records in a backup MFT called $MFTMrr$. So if the MFT is overwritten or physically damaged, the backup can be read and you can still re-create the drive. However, you can no longer easily recover directories, as you can in FAT. Just as in FAT, an NTFS partition can be recovered if the partition entry is deleted. You will often encounter a system that has had its partition table wiped or the MFT quick-formatted. When this occurs, the backup MFT should still be in place, and you should still be able to recover the original data. The NTFS partition lies on the disk, just like FAT. In NTFS, the volume boot sector begins with ëR□NTFS and ends with the hex characters 55 AA.

Recover NTFS Partitions in EnCase

To recover NTFS partitions in EnCase, follow these instructions:

1. Create a new keyword: *NTFS*.

2. Search the image for the keyword you just created.

3. View the hits in the disk view.

4. If the last four hex characters of the sector are 55 AA, right-click the sector in the disk view and choose Add Partition, as shown in Figure 6-4.

5. In the Add Partition dialog box, accept the defaults and click OK, as shown in Figure 6-5.

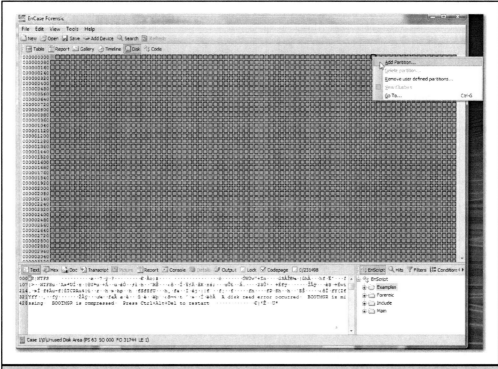

Figure 6-4   Adding a NTFS partition in EnCase

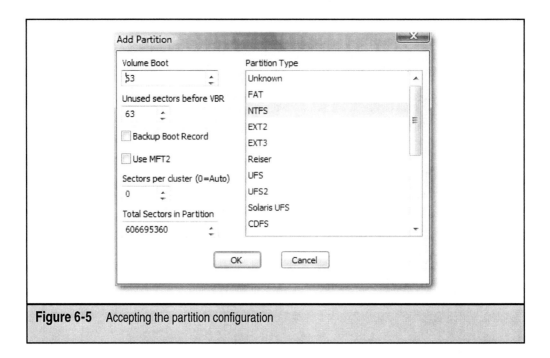

Figure 6-5 Accepting the partition configuration

Recover NTFS Partitions in SMART

To recover NTFS partitions using SMART, load your image into SMART, which will scan the image and find the file system itself.

RECOVERING DELETED FILES

Popularity:	*10*
Simplicity:	*10*
Impact:	*10*
Risk Rating:	*10*

One of the most common tasks requested in any investigation is to find and recover the files that have been deleted from the system. If you find mass deletions before your imaging occurred, this will often be a prime indicator of what the suspect was trying to hide.

Recovering deleted files with modern forensic tools is not an overly complex task, depending on the time frame between when the files were deleted and when they are being recovered. Most recovery tools allow you to view, examine, and recover many deleted items on a system.

Legal Briefs

If you're involved in a lawsuit, the judge may put forward a protective order, which allows the judge to state that nothing should be removed on identified systems. Protective orders are common in suits where electronic evidence is identified early in the case. With a protective order in place, there are real sanctions that can be put in place for even attempting to remove data from the system. If you are working on a system that is under a protective order, you should check to see when the last file was deleted to determine whether that order was violated.

NOTE   This note is especially for those unfamiliar with how the file system works. When we use the phrase *Deleted items* here, we are not referring to items in the Recycle Bin. Rather, we're referring to files that are marked as deleted or inactive by the file system and are no longer accessible to the user or the operating system, but that are still referenced through the FAT or MFT.

When file systems are designed, multiple factors are examined to determine what features should be implemented. For end-user systems, the top two priorities are usually speed and throughput. So when a deletion takes place, the software designer has two options: overwrite the data that existed on the disk and remove it from the disk, or mark it in the main allocation table as unused and move on to the next operation. Almost all file system designers choose the second option, because it takes less time to process. As a result, the data remains and only the pointer to it is lost. The good news for the forensic investigator is that we can recover possibly years' worth of deleted data because of this design.

Every file system marks a file as deleted in different ways. In Windows FAT file systems, the first character of the filename listed in the directory is marked with special hex characters E5, which is replaced by _ in most tools. These characters tell the operating system that the file is no longer in active use and that the clusters it occupies are available for reuse, as shown in Figure 6-6. In NTFS, the operating system will change an entry in the MFT to reflect this deletion. Specifically, when a user deletes a file, the operating system clears the IN_USE flag from the file's entry in the MFT.

Forensic tools automatically scan the MFT and FAT tables to show you the file system that exists on an image; locating any files that have been marked as deleted is part of that scan. The deleted filename, its attributes, and its data will continue to exist until the file is overwritten in part or in total while other actions are saved to disk. How soon overwriting occurs depends on three factors: the size of the disk, how far into the disk data has been written to, and how often large amounts of data are written to the disk. You may wonder why the size and location of data on the disk are important; since a disk allows for random access, why would we care about linear access? While it is true that you can access any part of the disk at any time, continually doing so takes time. Causing the user to wait for processing is considered bad, so designers try to keep this from occurring. This means that the operating system will attempt to write data out in a linear

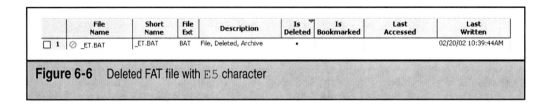

		File Name	Short Name	File Ext	Description	Is Deleted	Is Bookmarked	Last Accessed	Last Written
☐	1	⊘ _ET.BAT	_ET.BAT	BAT	File, Deleted, Archive	•			02/20/02 10:39:44AM

Figure 6-6   Deleted FAT file with E5 character

stream so that it can be read faster. If it cannot find a free cluster in its current position, it will skip forward in the disk to another free area.

Over time, the data deletions cause fragmentation of the disk. This is why Windows comes with a defragment utility (defrag) that scans the disks for the unallocated space left by deleted files and tries to put the still active files on the disk in a more linear form. However, until that defrag utility is run, the deleted data remains in its pristine state unless it is overwritten by another file. Even though a file is overwritten, fragments of the file may still exist, and the file's name and MAC times may still exist in the MFT or FAT directory entries. (We discuss recovering file fragments later in the chapter.) Basically, when the end of the disk is reached, data can no longer be written out in a linear fashion, so the operating system looks for locations to place new data. File allocation strategies actually change with file system revisions, and though this is not in fact how the file system operates, it's a good way to think about it; it can help you understand the three factors that make deleted files available for longer periods of time:

- **Disk size**   The larger the disk, the longer it will take for the operating system to reach the end of the disk and then go back to overwrite deleted files.

- **Disk position**   If the operating system is storing data at the beginning of the disk, it will take longer to reach the end of the disk; if the storage occurs farther down the storage line, it will reach the end more quickly.

- **Disk activity**   The more data written to the disk, the faster it will affect the other two factors.

Deleted Files

Popularity:	10
Simplicity:	10
Impact:	10
Risk Rating:	**10**

Deleting files is something that everyone knows how to do. If you as an investigator do not review the deleted files in a system, you could be missing out on important evidence, placing your investigation at risk of losing valuable information.

Recovering Deleted Files

When we talk about recovering deleted files, we are referring to taking a file that we know was marked as deleted or inactive in the file system and exporting that data out of the forensic environment for review with the application that created it. Although many tools can help you recover deleted files from a hard drive you directly attach to your system, forensic images require that sophisticated forensic tools be used to examine images. Most forensic software tools include built-in features for recovering deleted files.

Let's look at the steps you'll need to take with each tool to recover deleted files. Because the recovery process is the same for both FAT and NTFS file systems, they are treated as equals for the processes described here. If you were not using a modern forensic utility, the procedure could be much more manual and would involve many more steps.

Recovering Deleted Files in EnCase

Here's how to use EnCase to recover deleted files:

1. Load your image into EnCase.

2. Choose a deleted file (as identified in the Description column) and right-click the filename.

3. In the context menu, select Copy/Unerase, as shown in Figure 6-7.

File Name	Short Name	File Ext	Description	Is Deleted	Is Bookmarked	Last Accessed	Last Written
_ET.BAT	_ET.BAT	BAT	File, Deleted,				02/20/02 10:39:44AM
MSDOS.SYS	MSDOS.SYS	SYS	File, Invalid (	External Viewer	RET		04/23/99 10:22:00PM
COMMAND.COM	COMMAND.CO	COM	File, System,	Column	▶	07/31/01	06/20/01 04:23:40PM
DELTREE.EXE	DELTREE.EXE	EXE	File, Archive	Sort	▶	03/26/02	04/23/99 02:22:00PM
E100BPKT.COM	E100BPKT.CON	COM	File, Archive	Select/Deselect Row	Space	10/22/01	10/22/01 08:06:50AM
EDIT.COM	EDIT.COM	COM	File, Archive	Export...			04/23/99 10:22:00PM
EN.EXE	EN.EXE	EXE	File, Archive	Copy/Unerase...		03/26/02	03/26/02 10:06:16AM
FDISK.EXE	FDISK.EXE	EXE	File, Archive			03/26/02	04/23/99 02:22:00PM
FORMAT.COM	FORMAT.COM	COM	File, Archive			03/26/02	04/23/99 02:22:00PM
IO.SYS	IO.SYS	SYS	File, Hidden,	Bookmark Highlighted File... Ctrl-B		06/20/01	06/20/01 04:23:26PM
NET.BAT	NET.BAT	BAT	File, Archive				03/15/02 02:35:38PM
PACKET.TXT	PACKET.TXT	TXT	File, Archive	Set Filter		08/02/01	01/29/99 12:23:22PM
RTSPKT.COM	RTSPKT.COM	COM	File, Archive			06/20/01	06/25/00 09:10:00AM
SMCPKT.COM	SMCPKT.COM	COM	File, Archive	View File Structure		06/20/01	07/30/98 02:49:34PM
XCOPY.EXE	XCOPY.EXE	EXE	File, Archive			03/26/02	04/23/99 02:22:00PM

Figure 6-7   Selecting a file to recover in EnCase

4. Choose the Highlighted File option; for FAT file systems, you will pick the character that will replace the first character—the default is _. Remember that we lost the original character when the operating system replaced it with E5. Then click Next.

5. In the next dialog box, choose Logical File Only or Entire Physical File. Then click Next.

6. Indicate where you want to save the file and click Finish.

The file is now recovered and stored in the location you indicated in step 6.

Recovering Deleted Files in SMART

To recover a deleted file in SMART:

1. Load your image into SMART.

2. In the Active Case menu, right-click the partition in which you are interested.

3. Choose Filesystem | SMART | Study.

4. When the study completes, click File List.

5. Select a deleted file. A red X in the file icon next to the filename marks these files as deleted.

6. Right-click the deleted filename and choose Export Files, as shown in Figure 6-8.

7. Click Save Data To and choose where you want to store the data.

8. Click Export Files.

The file is now recovered at the location you selected in step 7.

Unallocated Data

Popularity:	*10*
Simplicity:	*10*
Impact:	*10*
Risk Rating:	*10*

After the file entry has been overwritten in FAT or NTFS, the clusters that contained the file's data become part of the unallocated space. The unallocated space is the group of clusters not in active use by any file; data within this space could have come from any file including the pagefile, and its file system MAC times are gone for good because you can no longer match the file's contents to its entry in the MFT or FAT. Good evidence often exists in unallocated space, and by not taking the time to find it, you could risk

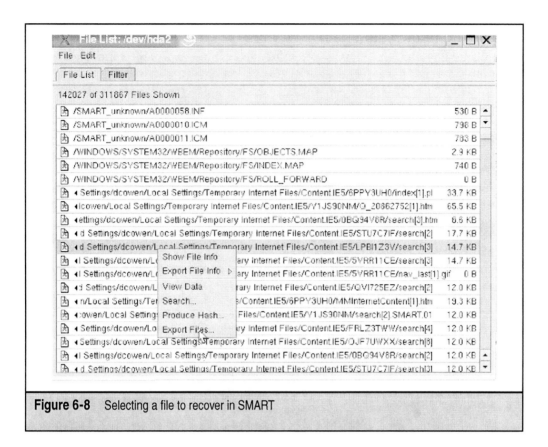

Figure 6-8 Selecting a file to recover in SMART

missing valuable data. Figure 6-9 shows how allocated and unallocated space looks on the disk.

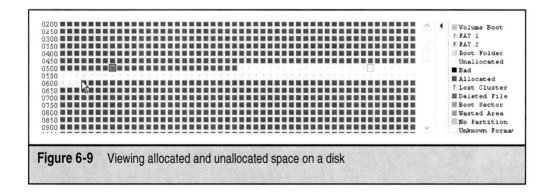

Figure 6-9 Viewing allocated and unallocated space on a disk

⊖ Recovering Unallocated Data

Since the unallocated space has no structure, you cannot expect an automated tool to show you a list of all of the files within it. Instead, you must decide what you are looking for to determine how you are to search or parse the unallocated space. Three major methods can be used for recovering data from the unallocated space: recovering complete files, recovering file fragments, and recovering slack space. As we venture into the unallocated data space, we also come into the portions of deleted data called *slack space*.

Recovering Complete Files

To recover complete files, you will need to know the header and footer for each file type you are seeking. This is a simple task for HTML documents, Microsoft Word documents, PDF documents, and other major structured file types; these documents have well-defined structures that contain plain ASCII or unique hexadecimal representations, leading to results with few false positives. This process lends itself to automation, and most recovery tools provide some ability to perform an automated recovery of complete files in the unallocated space.

Recovering Complete Files in EnCase   Using EnCase, you can either use EnScript or choose portions of unallocated space manually to export out of the image and back on to your local hard drive.

When using EnScript, you can either choose to write your own script or go to Guidance Software's Web site and choose an EnScript script from the EnScript library.

Here's how to run an EnScript to recover complete files:

1. Load your image into EnCase.
2. Depending on the EnCase version, do one of the following:
   - In version 3, click the EnScript button.
   - In version 4, click View Scripts.
   - In version 6, under Tools, click Case Processor, create a bookmark, and click Next.
3. Select the appropriate EnScript script you want to run; we recommend File Finder.
4. Click Run / Finish.

 Recovering files manually is covered in the sections "Recovering File Fragments in EnCase" and "Recovering File Fragments in SMART" a bit later in the chapter.

Recovering Complete Files in SMART   In SMART, you'll find it easier to use the extended features of the searching interface to write out any complete files it finds automatically. Here's how:

1. Load the image in SMART.

2. Right-click the image and choose Search.

3. Right-click the empty space where search terms are stored, and do one of the following:

   • Choose one of the file types from the Term Library to have SMART automatically fill in the header and footer of the document you are seeking.

   • Choose Add New Term and define your own header and footer.

4. Click Auto-Export.

5. Choose where you want to save files by typing in a prefix and extension, as shown in Figure 6-10.

6. Click Search, and as the search runs, the files will be recovered and stored in the location you defined in step 5.

Searching for Relevant Data in the Unallocated Space

You will need to search the entire disk to locate all relevant documents, logs, e-mails, and more in most of your cases. At times, though, you may want to find relevant data only in the unallocated space. To do so, you would search the unallocated space for keywords.

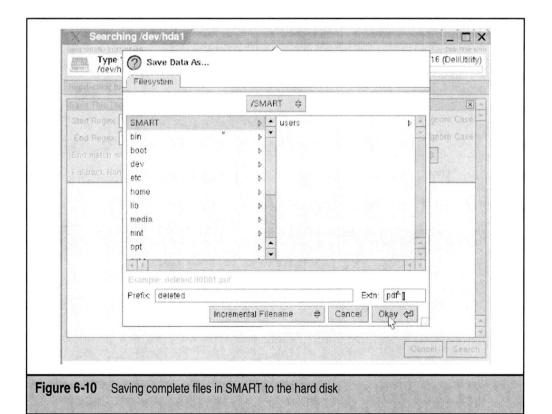

Figure 6-10   Saving complete files in SMART to the hard disk

This part of the process can be difficult because it's a manual process; no automated method can be used to tell the tool the context or file type of the relevant data that you seek. You will have to locate what appears to be relevant data and then export it out of the tool of your choice to begin reconstructing it for review.

Recovering File Fragments in EnCase   To recover file fragments manually in EnCase, do the following:

1. Create a new keyword, which will be the unique part of the header you are seeking.

2. Search for that keyword across the physical disk.

3. Review the hits and highlight the complete portions of the document that you would like to export out of EnCase.

4. Right-click the highlighted text and choose Export, as shown in Figure 6-11.

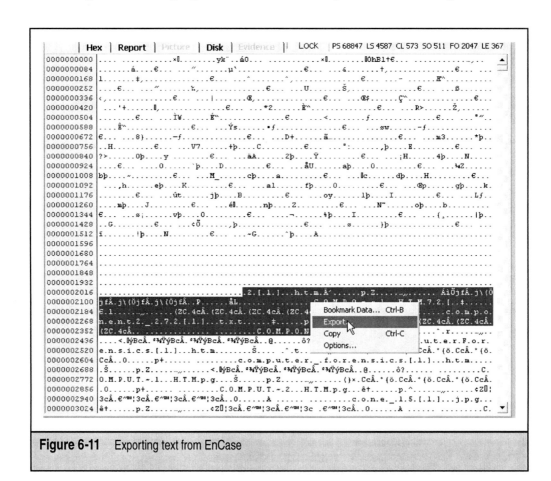

Figure 6-11   Exporting text from EnCase

5. In the Export View dialog box, choose the name of the file and the directory to which you want to write it, and then click OK, as shown in Figure 6-12.

The fragment now exists in the directory you chose.

Recovering File Fragments in SMART   To recover files manually in SMART, do the following:

1. Load your image in SMART.
2. Right-click Search.
3. Right-click the empty area in the Search box and choose Add New Term.
4. Enter the header of the type of document you are seeking.
5. Search the image.
6. Right-click a hit from the search and choose View Hit.
7. Highlight and then right-click the text you want to view.
8. Choose Selected Data | Export Data, as shown in Figure 6-13.
9. Click Save Data To and indicate where you want to save the data.
10. Click Export.

The data now exists in the directory you chose in step 9.

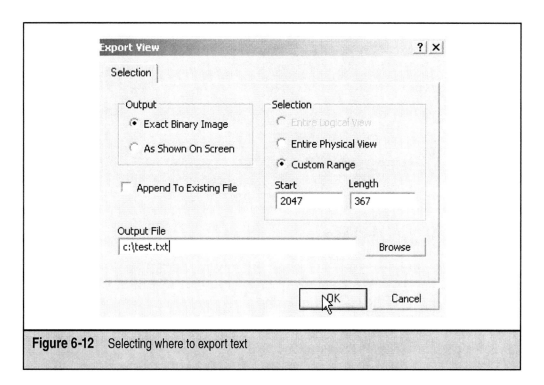

Figure 6-12   Selecting where to export text

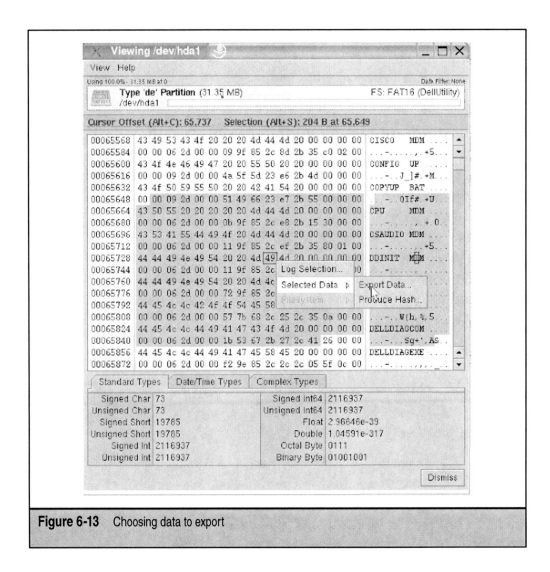

Figure 6-13   Choosing data to export

Parsing the Unallocated Space

Tools such as AccessData's Forensic Tool Kit (FTK) allow an investigator to take an entire image and try to identify all of the documents in the file system, including the unallocated space. If you want to search the entire disk many times over, tools such as FTK can help you build a full-text index. Full-text indexing allows you to build a binary tree–based dictionary of all the words that exist in an image, and you can search the entire image for those words in seconds. For more information on full-text indexing and more tools that can accomplish this task, refer to Chapter 10.

Limitations

Although data recovery methods mean that recovery is possible, recovering deleted data has its limitations. Not every system will produce results. This can be caused by a number of reasons:

- The system is newer and the user's data was copied to it, leaving the forensic remnants you are looking for on the older disk. When a file system is restored to another disk using a utility such as ghost, it does not by default bring the deleted files or unallocated space with it.

- A new hard drive could have been purchased and the data was copied to it.

- The system could have been reinstalled, meaning that the FATs would have been overwritten and only the unallocated space would contain the deleted data you are seeking. This prevents you from recovering all of the deleted documents.

- The user could have constantly run defragmentation tools. This would cause the earliest deleted data to be overwritten more quickly. This prevents you from recovering all the deleted documents.

Drive-Wiping

Popularity:	7
Simplicity:	8
Impact:	10
Risk Rating:	**8**

Another scenario, drive-wiping, involves overwriting every bit of the disk. Some tools in the market, such as PGP Wipe and BCWipe, allow a user to wipe out only the deleted, file slack, and unallocated portions of the disk. This type of wiping will eliminate most of the deleted and forensic data you are trying to recover. For a detailed review of wiping and all of the types of wiping you will encounter, refer to Chapter 9.

Detecting Wiping

Detecting when a disk has been wiped can be a manual task. You must check the image to determine the date back to which the deleted files extend and examine the unallocated space to see what data lies within it. Most wiping tools allow the user to choose the pattern that is used to write to the disk. Some tools will turn the entire unallocated space into 0's or the alphabet. Most modern wipers will employ a more randomized scheme, usually following the US Department of Defense (DOD) specifications for secure wiping. If actual recoverable text cannot be viewed in the unallocated space, and if the sectors tend to look exactly the same, you can be pretty sure that wiping has occurred.

In such a case, you should search the disk for wiping tools and review the user's Internet history for accesses to Web sites that discuss or provide wiping tools as well as the program files directory and the registry. Many partial wiping tools are available today that are advertised as "system cleaners" or "Internet evidence eliminators." These tools follow the same methodologies but are often not as thorough as a full disk wipe, as they are designed to target only certain files or locations and generally leave some evidence behind. Many evidence eliminator packages exist, and more are released every day; most of them share the same trait of any application in that they do not totally remove themselves upon being uninstalled. Finding them should be a matter of reviewing the programs installed on the system and reviewing the recently deleted files if your image was created soon after the program was uninstalled. Because the existence of a wiper is against policy at many companies today, you should check the relevant company's policies if you locate a wiper.

WINDOWS ARTIFACTS

Popularity:	10
Simplicity:	10
Impact:	10
Risk Rating:	**10**

In the process of using Windows, many files are created, deleted, modified, and accessed. Some of these patterns or specific types of changes are unique enough to allow us to say without doubt that a certain action has taken place. If you fail to determine whether or not these artifacts exist, you can wind up making incorrect conclusions or not being able to support your case argument. Windows artifacts can become key points in your investigations and often lead to the identification of key evidence. What we present here is not a comprehensive list of artifacts that can be covered in a Windows system, so make sure that you research other artifacts as you perform your own investigations.

Emptying the Recycle Bin

Popularity:	10
Simplicity:	10
Impact:	10
Risk Rating:	**10**

Most users empty the Recycle Bin often. Sometimes the files will wind up in the unallocated space, including much of the useful data you are hoping to find, such as the filename or where on the disk the file was stored.

Recovering INFO Records

Upon entering the Recycle Bin, a, INFO record (INFO2 for Windows 95 and later) is created for each file. The INFO record contains the path, the full filename, and the time when the file was deleted. Even after the Recycle Bin has been emptied, you can search for these INFO records to find all of the files that have been put in the bin. This is useful in cases in which certain named documents are alleged to have been misappropriated.

Recovering INFO Records in EnCase

Use the Info Record Finder EnScript that comes by default with EnCase to recover records.

Here's how to run an EnScript to recover INFO records:

1. Load your image into EnCase.
2. Depending on the EnCase version, do one of the following:
   - In version 3, click the EnScript button.
   - In version 4, click View Scripts.
   - In versions 5 and 6, click View and then EnScript.
3. Select the Info Record Finder script. In versions 5 and 6, choose the Case Processor and choose the appropriate options.
4. Click Run.

The results will be stored in your bookmarks.

Recovering INFO Records in SMART

In SMART, you must create a custom search term in the term library. You would do so by adding this hex string:

```
05 00 00 00 00 00 00 00 00 00 00 00 20 03
```

The hex string will match the header of any INFO2 record, which will contain one entry for every file placed in the Recycle Bin.

 ## Recovering Data from the Pagefile

Popularity:	10
Simplicity:	10
Impact:	10
Risk Rating:	**10**

The data that is created from processes that are active in memory do not exist in a structured file. Examples of data that is created by a running program includes the data created from copying a file from a floppy disk or a CD-ROM, or data created from loading a document from a removable hard drive. Instead of creating a structured file to store the data, it resides in memory.

 ## Understanding What Lies in the Page File

The page file, pagefile.sys, is a single file used by the system as additional memory. Within this single file is a free-form block of data much like the unallocated space, except that it holds data that was written to it as a form of secondary memory called *virtual memory*. You can think of virtual memory as a block of specialized, unallocated space that has no structure. Not only is the data unstructured, but much of it is actually raw data that we typically cannot reconstruct. With experience and effective keywords, you can begin to determine what possibly could have created the data you see within it and begin to identify things such as chat sessions, e-mails, and web pages.

Understanding the purpose of the page file is important, as many of the searches you perform in your investigation may show hits in it. Being able to view these hits and understand how they might have been created will help you determine whether a hit is something that came from a file access or whether it is a file that is being loaded into memory.

Here's an example of reconstruction of a page file that recovered the properties of an SSL certificate from a Web site that was visited:

```
"ldap:///CN=cert.io.fiosinc.com,CN=cert,CN=CDP,CN=Public%20Key%20Services,
CN=Services,CN=Configuration,DC=fiosinc,DC=com?certificateRevocationList?
base?objectclass=cRLDistributionPoint0@ >
```

Here's an example of the recovery of the name of a document opened in Microsoft Word:

```
SourceURL:file:///C:\Documents%20and%20Settings\dcowen\My%20Documents\
personal\book\forensics%20exposed\Content\chapter6\chapter6.doc"
```

 ## Printer Spools

Popularity:	10
Simplicity:	10
Impact:	10
Risk Rating:	10

Printing involves a spooling process that delays the data being sent to a printer. Print spooling is accomplished by creating temporary files that contain data to be printed and sufficient information to complete the print job. The two formats used to spool printing are RAW and EMF. Many times, documents that were deleted or accessed on external media will still exist in a printer spool file.

 ## Recovering Printed Documents

The spool files that Windows creates are stored in a file in the Windows system folder, which varies on the version of Windows you are using: \system32\spool\printers. The files that end with the extension .SPL are the image files—normally EMF, a Windows graphics file format. In Windows 95/98, you will find a .SPL file and a matching .SHD file that gives the name of the printer used, the name of the document, and the location of the temporary file that contains the image. If you find a printer spool, you can view its contents by loading it into an application that supports EMF.

In Windows 2000, you must search the disk for a file that has this header, in hexadecimal notation:

```
\x01\x00\x00\x00\x18\x17\x00
or
\x01\x00\x00\x00\xC4\x36\x00
```

In Windows XP, you must search the disk for a file that has this header, in hexadecimal notation:

```
\x01\x00\x00\x00\x5C\x01\x00
```

NOTE   If you are looking for printer spools on an NTFS file system, you may be out of luck. NTFS can create temporary files that are never committed to the disk and will not exist for later recovery.

 ## LNK Files

Popularity:	10
Simplicity:	10
Impact:	10
Risk Rating:	10

For most documents and programs opened on Windows 95 and later systems, a LNK, or link file, will be created. This file contains the path of the file and the type of storage on which it existed, such as hard drives, network drives, or floppy drives. It also contains the file's MAC times as well as the MAC times of its own that show when the LNK file was created. When you're trying to re-create a suspect's dealings with a document, as you would do when a suspect is accused of stealing a document, not reviewing LNK files can mean that you miss valuable evidence. For example, if a suspect accesses documents that were stored on external USB drives or on a CD-ROM, the only evidence left that shows where these files existed and how they were accessed is in the LNK file.

Recovering LNK Files

You will find LNK files in the active file system with the extension .LNK. Recovering all deleted LNK files in the unallocated space can be accomplished by searching the physical disk for the occurrence of the hex value 4C 00 00 00; this may turn up a large amount of false positive hits, however. Instead, it's better to search for the name of the file that is in question. Remember that the LNK files contain the filename in either ASCII or Unicode, depending on the version of Windows, so make sure you are searching for both encodings. In addition, most forensic tools today provide libraries and scripts to find LNK files in the unallocated space for you; try these utilities first.

 ASCII is an 8-bit computer representation of a character that almost all computing systems can easily represent and write. Unicode is an extended character set that can use 16 bits to represent a single character. Windows now uses Unicode at the system level, so some Windows files created by the operating system may exist in Unicode instead of ASCII.

 For a thorough review of LNK file information, check out "The Windows Shortcut File Format" at www .i2s-lab.com/Papers/The_Windows_Shortcut_File_Format.pdf.

 ## Removable USB Storage Devices

Popularity:	10
Simplicity:	10
Impact:	8
Risk Rating:	8

Identifying USB removable storage devices that were attached to a user's system is often necessary for many investigations, especially those dealing with theft of intellectual property. You can determine the date/time when a device was last attached to the system and obtain the device's vendor information such as make and model and other important values. These bits of evidence will be quite useful in aiding an investigation and in the device's recovery, if necessary.

 ## How to Identify a USB Storage Device

Whenever a USB storage device such as a CD ROM or ThumbDrive is attached to a Windows 2000 and later system, registry entries are created in the USBSTOR key located in the system registry. The first entry is the vendor key that contains the make, model, and revision information. The second entry is for the individual device itself; this keyname is located beneath the vendor key. Identical devices will appear under the same vendor key but will be identified by a different keyname. The keyname is generated by the Windows system and is unique. This unique name will stay the same between different windows systems.

```
HKEY_LOCAL_MACHINE\SYSTEM\CurrentControlSet\Enum\USBSTOR
\Disk&Ven_Kingston&Prod_DataTraveler_2.0&Rev_1.00e\
                        001000000000000000000297&0      (device1)
                        001000000000000000000358&0      (device2)
                        001000000000000000000390&0      (device3)
```

If the registry viewer you are using does not provide the Last Write Time for the device, you should be able to right-click and export the registry key out as a text file instead of a registry file to obtain it. Remember that you will need the Last Write Time for the device, not the one for the vendor key.

```
RegistryKey.txt
Key Name:      HKEY_LOCAL_MACHINE\SYSTEM\CurrentControlSet\Enum\USBSTOR\
Disk&Ven_Kingston&Prod_DataTraveler_2.0&Rev_1.00e\001000000000000000000297&0
\Device Parameters\MediaChangeNotification
Class Name:        <NO CLASS>
Last Write Time:   12/18/2008 - 7:33 AM
```

Identifying the Windows Version

Popularity:	10
Simplicity:	10
Impact:	8
Risk Rating:	8

In many investigations, you may find it necessary to learn which version of Windows is running on a suspect's system, because many version-specific features and forensic remnants exist in Windows that can be properly viewed only when the version is known. Making conclusions on Windows artifacts without knowing the version of Windows can lead to mistakes.

How to Identify the Windows Version

Identifying the Windows version involves examining the structure of the Windows directory and looking for the system's registry.

Version	Directory Path
Windows 98	\windows\system.dat
Windows NT	\winnt\system32\config\system
Windows XP	\windows\system32\config\system
Windows Vista	\windows\system32\config\system

You can gather information about which Windows version you have by viewing the CurrentVersion registry key with a registry viewer. Values such as the CurrentBuild, ProductName, and even the InstallDate are available here. Several free registry viewer tools are available on the Internet, as well as tools that convert the decimal value of the InstallDate to a date/time format if needed. Remember to take time-zone differences into account.

```
Registry Path:
HKEY_LOCAL_MACHINE\SOFTWARE\Microsoft\Windows NT\CurrentVersion
```

System Times

Popularity:	10
Simplicity:	10
Impact:	7
Risk Rating:	7

Discovering the last time a suspect shut down a system can be important in some cases. Specifically, if a suspect alleges not to have used the system during a specific period, or, in some cases, if a suspect is alleging that a system was in fact in active use, this information can help make a case. Checking system times can also help identify whether anyone else logged into the system after the suspect shut it down, or if an administrator or someone else tampered with the evidence. Trusting a suspect's word implicitly is not as reliable as checking out the system yourself.

Determining the Last Time a System Was Shut Down

In Windows 2000 and later, you can determine the last time the system was shut down by viewing the last written time of the registry hive key $$$PROTO.HIV.

You can also determine when the system was last shut down by examining the SysEvent log file in an event viewer. Sort the log by date/time and look for the last entry with the Event ID: 6006, which is an ID for shutdown.

```
Event Log Locations:
Windows 2000 and XP        \Windows\System32\Config
Windows Vista              \Windows\System32\winevt\Logs
```

The system registry also contains a Shutdown Time. The value is located within the following key: HKLM\SYSTEM\CurrentControlSet\Control\Windows. The binary value will need to be converted to a usable date/time format. Another method is to navigate to this same registry key, right-click it, and export it as a text file instead of a registry file. This way you can obtain the key's Last Write Time.

```
RegistryKey.txt
Key Name:       HKEY_LOCAL_MACHINE\SYSTEM\CurrentControlSet\Control\Windows
Class Name:     <NO CLASS>
Last Write Time:   12/17/2008 - 9:18 AM
```

For Windows 98 and earlier versions, you must rely on your own ability to determine whether the last dates of files being written to on the disk are feasible. This is a reliability issue, however, as file dates can be changed.

Determining the First Time a User Logged In

You can determine the first time a user logged into a system by viewing the creation date of the user's directory.

Version	User Directories
Windows 95	\windows\profiles
Windows 98	\windows\profiles
Windows NT 4.0	\documents and settings\
Windows 2000, XP	\documents and settings\
Windows Vista	\Users\

Determining the Last Time a User Logged Out

In Windows NT 4.0 and later, you can determine the last time a user logged out by viewing the modification date of the ntuser.dat file in the user's documents and settings directory. With Windows Vista, you would look in the Users directory instead of documents and settings directory.

Office Document Metadata

Popularity:	10
Simplicity:	10
Impact:	10
Risk Rating:	10

While Office is not part of Windows, it is the most common document creation application in use. Whenever an Office document is created, certain attributes and hidden data fields are placed in the document automatically. Many times, a suspect will delete a stolen Office document, and your ability to prove certain arguments, such as when or by whom it was created, can only be proven by data stored within the document itself.

Discovering the Properties of Deleted Office Documents

If you are able to recover an entire Office 97 or later document from the unallocated space, you can load the document into the Office application and view its properties. Or, if your forensic application supports it, such as EnCase, you can view the metadata within your forensic environment. Otherwise, if you can recover only a fragment of the original document, you will need to have access to utilities such as the OLE/COM Object Viewer from Microsoft to view the properties of the COM objects that the Office document contained. You will not always be able to recover the metadata from a fragment, but many times you will.

OleViewer.exe is included as part of Visual Studio and is located in the ..\tools\bin directory, or you can obtain a copy by downloading a Windows Resource Kit. Do an Internet search for "Windows Server 2003 Resource Kit Tools" or visit the following link: www.microsoft.com/downloads/details.aspx?familyid=9d467a69-57ff-4ae7-96ee-b18c4790cffd.

 ## Discovering the MAC Address of the System that Wrote a Word Document

Loading a Word document for any version of Office 97 and later (up to, but not including, Office XP) into a text editor that is not Word will show you the raw binary data in the document. Search that document for the keyword *PID_GUID*, and after some other data appears, you will see a bracket-enclosed piece of Unicode text:

```
{ 1 0 4 A 8 A 2 2 - 6 2 3 B - 1 1 D 4 - 8 8 D D - 0 0 D 0 B 7 1 B 0 4 C
4 }
```

The string 0 0 D 0 B 7 1 B 0 4 C 4 is the MAC (Media Access Control) or the hardware address MAC assigned to an Ethernet card. The Ethernet MAC is important to us because it allows us to tie the creation of a document to a particular user's system. This is powerful evidence in showing that a user was involved or directly responsible for some activity.

 ## Dr. Watson: Problems Reports and Solutions

Popularity:	10
Simplicity:	10
Impact:	6
Risk Rating:	8

Whenever a program crashes in Windows NT, 2000, or XP, the error handler called Dr. Watson creates a memory dump of the current system. If your case has at issue events that would have existed only in memory while the user experienced a crash, finding these files could provide valuable evidence.

In Windows Vista, Dr. Watson was replaced with the Problems Reports and Solutions Feature. See the following link for more information: http://technet.microsoft.com/en-us/library/cc709644.aspx.

Recovering a Memory Dump

A file called user.dmp, if it exists, contains a dump of the physical memory on the system. In Windows Vista you would look for the dump file at %SystemRoot%\MEMORY.DMP. Before you can work with the file, it must be converted, since it has null characters in between each character in the file. Once these null characters are removed, you can search the file to find any of the data you would hope to find in memory, such as Internet history, viewed file contents, opened files, and accessed processes.

Determining Programs a User Has Run (Windows 2000 and Later)

Popularity:	*10*
Simplicity:	*10*
Impact:	*8*
Risk Rating:	*8*

When a user executes a program or accesses certain types of files in Windows 2000 and later, a built-in Windows function records his or her actions. Often, when tools such as wipers, encryption programs, and other so-called anti-forensic tools are used, you will want to identify those tools. You should always check UserAssist keys to identify user actions and programs executed when they are of relevance to a case.

UserAssist

UserAssist is a feature of Windows 2000 and later that is not well documented or well understood by the public. It tracks the use of applications, shortcuts, and other items by frequency of use and time last used. It works like built-in spyware, because it captures the actions of a user until someone or something removes the entries from the registry or disables logging as with the Privacy feature in Windows Vista. UserAssist entries are encrypted, but lucky for us investigators, they are encrypted with ROT13! The following shows an example of what a UserAssist entry looks like encoded:

```
HRZR_EHACNGU:P:\CEBTEN~1\ZVPEBF~2\Bssvpr10\BHGYBBX.RKR
```

And here's a decoded UserAssist key:

```
UEME_RUNPATH:C:\PROGRA~1\MICROS~2\Office10\OUTLOOK.EXE
```

UserAssist keys can be found in the registry under HKEY_CURRENT_USER\ Software\Microsoft\Windows\CurrentVersion\Explorer\UserAssist.

In this registry key, you will find two subkeys, and within these are programs and web pages that the user has executed or visited. To recover UserAssist entries from the unallocated space, search for HRZR_, which is a static entry in all UserAssist entries.

 NOTE For more information about UserAssist, read "Understanding the UserAssist Registry Key" at www .accessdata.com/downloads/media/UserAssist%20Registry%20Key%209-8-08.pdf. Many free ROT13 converters are available on the Internet. To take a look at the UserAssist utility available for download, visit http://blog.didierstevens.com/programs/userassist. In addition, many forensic tools can view or search for ROT13 within their environments.

CHAPTER 7

LINUX ANALYSIS

In recent years, Linux has become the third most popular operating system, behind the Microsoft Windows platform and Apple's OS X. Linux users love its stability and the "close to the metal" feel they get from using it. The majority of scripted hacks and vulnerabilities are written to run under Linux, which means as an investigator you may spend a lot of time unwinding attacks that script kiddies and sophisticated hackers alike were trying to launch. Luckily, Linux is copiously documented, and you can easily find references on common attacks and procedures hackers use as well as how they try to cover their tracks. The other edge of the sword, however, is that a criminal can easily modify the OS to hide data, implement trap doors, and launch other kernel-space operations that are very difficult to unwind. Add to this the hundreds of arcane commands that exist, just waiting to be trojaned, and you can see why an investigation of a Linux system can be a daunting task.

THE LINUX FILE SYSTEM (EXT2 AND EXT3)

Much like Windows uses NTFS and FAT, Linux has its own file system structure. For older versions of Linux, data is stored on an ext2 format partition. Newer versions use ext3 or ext4, which is functionally identical to ext2 with the addition of journaling. (More on that later in the section "ext3/ext4 Structure.") As a practical matter, an ext file system also exists, but it's so old that it was deprecated about the time that Minux became Linux and is rare to find in use today. You may also run across other, more exotic, file systems, such as the encrypted file system (EFS), and those will be covered in more detail in Chapter 9. For now, we will focus on the ext2, ext3, and the Linux swap formats.

ext2 Structure

The layout of ext2 is heavily based upon UNIX file system concepts. The disk is divided into partitions that are subsections of the disk. These partitions are then further divided into groups, which are nothing more than partitions of the partition, and they help to break up the clustering. Each group contains a superblock, a group descriptor, a block bitmap, an inode bitmap, an inode table, and finally data blocks, in that order.

Superblock

The *superblock* stores all the metadata about the file system. Each group has its own superblock, and a master superblock stores the data about the entire file system. This block is vital to system operation since it is read when the file system is mounted. If this block becomes corrupted, the file system will no longer mount. If you think a system's superblock has been knocked out, you can re-create it, since Ext2fs utility stores a copy of the superblock in each group. When you run `Ext2fschk`, it checks for superblock consistency and repairs it if necessary.

Some versions of Linux, such as those that run on 68K platforms, use a byte-swapped file system to compensate for little-endian versus big-endian formats. Make sure you are aware of the type of platform you are working with.

Group Descriptors

The *group descriptor*, as its name suggests, contains information about the group. Within the group descriptor is the table of inodes and the allocation bitmaps for inodes and data blocks. This allocation bitmap is of huge importance to the investigator, since it tells the file system which blocks are used and which aren't. When a file is deleted, the allocation bitmap changes the state of the blocks used by the file to *unallocated*. This does not mean that the data in the blocks has been deleted. You can use the blocks along with the inode table to reconstruct a file that has supposedly been removed from the disk.

Inodes and File Structure

Files are represented by inodes, and directories are simple files that contain a list of entries and pointers to the files that can be found in said directory. To understand the inode structure, you can think of it as a sort of hierarchical chart. Each inode points to a set of data blocks that contain the data in the file. Fifteen pointers to data blocks are inside each inode. If you do the math, you will see that this is not a sufficient number of blocks for any reasonably sized file. Thus, only 13 blocks are used to hold data. If the file is bigger than 13 blocks, the 14th block is used to hold a pointer to a new "indirect block" that gives 13 more slots. If that still isn't enough, the 15th block is used to point to a "doubly indirect block" that stores pointers to other blocks that themselves have 15 slots. You can see how this gets confusing fast. Figure 7-1 may help to clarify the picture and shows you how the inodes link together in ext2.

If you do any substantive work with file recovery under Linux, understanding this inode structure inside and out is a must. Later in this chapter, when we talk about recovering data, we will look at how to use inodes to recover previously deleted files. As an aside, the linked structure of this system has some significant performance increases as well. Since the smaller files are so close to the inode root in the hierarchy, they are accessed more quickly than the larger files. As the following table shows, the majority of files on a disk are small enough to fit into this category.

File Size (bytes)	0–768	769–1.5K	1.5–3K	3–6K	6–12K	12K and up
Occurrence (%)	38.3	19.8	14.2	9.4	7.1	10.1
Cumulative (%)	38.3	58.1	72.3	81.7	89.8	99.9

As you may have guessed, the ext2 file system has inodes flying around all over the place. To consolidate all of this into one logical data structure, the inode table was created.

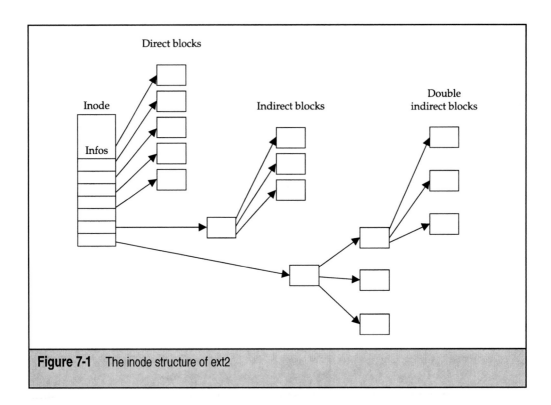

Figure 7-1 The inode structure of ext2

Directories

Using a system that requires the end user to refer to files by their inode numbers would be nearly impossible for the user. (Think about your daughter trying to access her school paper named 15332. Good luck remembering that.) As such, we need a way to tie a filename to an inode number. Enter the directory. As stated earlier, directories are nothing more than files that store pointers to the files contained in the directory. To clarify, take a look at Figure 7-2.

A special directory on the ext2 is /, the root directory, located at the top of the hierarchy. So that the hierarchy can be found when the system is rebooted and the file system remounted, the root directory node is stored in a constant location, namely the second inode. From this directory entry, the entire file system can be re-created. A subdirectory is nothing more than a link to the file that contains the directory entry for said subdirectory. Two special entries exist in each directory: . (a dot) and .. (two dots). These are the identity and previous pointers, respectively, and they are created when the directory is created and cannot be deleted.

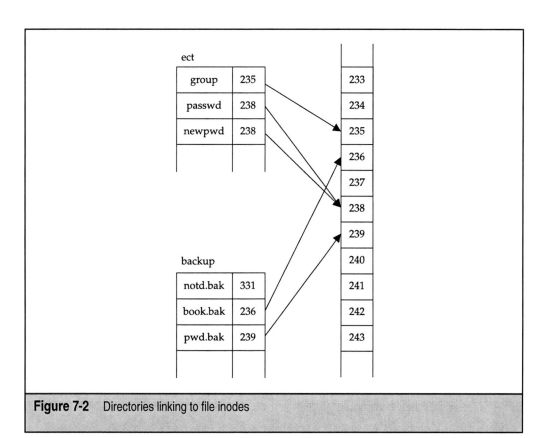

Figure 7-2   Directories linking to file inodes

ext3/ext4 Structure

The ext3/ext4 is commonly referred to as "ext2 + journaling." *Journaling* is a concept used to protect the structure of the files by changing the read/write process on the disk into an atomic transaction. This means that either all the data gets written to disk or none of it does. The majority of file system failures occur when a disk crashes midwrite and loses half of the information that it was writing to disk. To prevent this, a journaling OS uses an atomic write and has the file system first write to a buffer, or journal. Once in the journal, a transaction flag is set, which says the disk is in midwrite. After all the data has been successfully written to the disk, the transaction flag is cleared and the data is wiped from the journal. If something should happen midwrite, the next time the file system mounts, the system will see the transaction flag and recommit all the data in the journal, assuming that something happened in the process. This is important from a forensics standpoint: You should always check the journal to see whether something that was supposed to be written wasn't written. Conversely, by mounting one of these journaled file systems, you *will* change the disk, and any hashes you made of the disk will no longer be valid.

Linux Swap

Linux supports swaps in two forms: as a swap file or as a swap partition. If the swap is stored as a partition, the kernel uses the disk blocks to act as additional memory blocks for program usage (a memory paging system, to be semantically correct). This format is nothing more than an array of blocks. While this was never meant to be human-readable, it can be accessed with raw search tools that can search for keywords and binary sequences in the blocks themselves. This can be useful in memory and file-reconstruction.

LINUX ANALYSIS

Now that you have looked at the Linux file system, you can start doing some real investigation of user activity and tracking malicious activity. You have some theory under your belt, so let's take a look at a real file system to see how that theory translates into usage. We will use both SMART and an open source set of command-line tools (The Coroner's Toolkit, TCT), which when used together can perform a fairly comprehensive internal investigation and can act as a cross-validation. The open source tools require an image that is dd-compatible, meaning that it is a noncompressed, byte-for-byte copy of the partition. As with any investigation, you should always use some sort of case management tool such as SMART, and hash, hash, hash.

Finding File System Signatures

Popularity:	6
Simplicity:	8
Impact:	10
Risk Rating:	9

You may run into situations in which the disk appears to have been cleared of the partition table in an effort to destroy evidence. If you look at the disk with an editor and see that good information is still on the disk, chances are you can recover the data by finding the partition signatures and reconstructing the disk. Some tools can do this for you, but to complete the task in a forensically sound manner, you should use a tool like SMART to find the signatures and reconstruct the disk yourself. Remember that in ext2/ext3, everything is based on the superblock, so if you can find that, you can reconstruct the whole file system.

NOTE You can use several good utilities to find the partition information, such as findsuper and PartitionMagic. For more information, check out the Linux Documentation Project and its "Linux Ext2fs Undeletion mini-HOWTO" (www.tldp.org/HOWTO/Ext2fs-Undeletion.html), keeping in mind that they are not meant to be forensic tutorials.

The signature that you are looking for is 0xef53. Realize that you will get a bunch of false positives to go along with the true superblock. Also realize that backup copies of the superblock are stored all over the file system, so if the primary one is gone, you can still re-create it from a backup.

Locating and Recovering Deleted Files

Popularity:	6
Simplicity:	8
Impact:	10
Risk Rating:	9

The first thing that a suspect will do when she thinks she is in trouble is delete incriminating evidence. Searching for and recovering deleted files is a vital part of an investigation with Linux. The first place to start is the inode table, which is like a lookup table for the file system. When a file is deleted, it's respective inodes are marked as deleted and set as available for overwriting. If you can get to them before they are overwritten, you can reconstruct the files. If you want to use open source tools, the TASK toolkit has several command-line tools that can help. The tool fls can find files that have been deleted and help you get their inodes. Once you have the inodes, you use ICAT to pull out the file from the inode, if it still exists.

Recovering Files with SMART

SMART has great tools for performing analysis on ext2/ext3 file systems. It supports searching through unallocated space and finding deleted files. To find deleted files, mount the image read-only in SMART. Then right-click the image and choose Filesystem | SMART | Study. This will analyze the file system and find the deleted files.

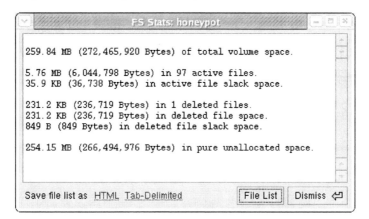

After the Study has completed, choose Filesystem | SMART and look at the file list, as shown next. Right-click the Filter tab and use the drop-down box to add a filter for active or deleted files. Select Deleted and click the Apply button.

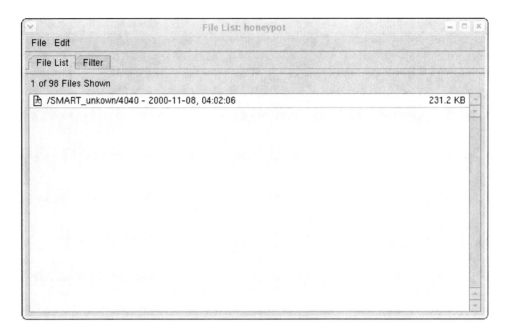

You can right-click the individual files to view them as text or graphics, to hash them, and to create reports for them. You can also export the file out so you can perform more analysis on it if you want. If you do this, make sure you hash when you export and hash during your analysis to show that the file hasn't been changed.

 ## Guidelines for Analyzing Deleted Files and Partitions

Working with deleted files can be a very tricky thing. Even if you do find information that you think is important, such as that shown in the preceding section, how do you know whether it actually ties the suspect to a crime? Make sure that you are thorough when performing this type of investigative work. Find and investigate all of the deleted files, and be prepared to justify every one of them in court. All the conventional rules for forensic investigation apply.

 ## Differences Among Linux Distributions

Popularity:	10
Simplicity:	9
Impact:	2
Risk Rating:	5

It's difficult these days to throw a rock and not hit two different Linux distributions. While all are based on the same Linux core, the supporting programs and file locations can vary widely. Once you determine what version of Linux the computer was running, you can adjust your investigation accordingly. The first place to look is in the /etc directory. Typically, you'll find a file such as redhat-release, debian-release, or redhat-version in this directory, which will indicate both the distribution and version of the install. Another file to check is /etc/issue, as most distributions place their information in this logon banner. Realize that these files are nonauthoritative and act only as a marker that points you in the right direction, not to a definitive answer.

If the answer cannot be found in one of these files, try looking in /var/log/dmesg or /var/log/messages. This is the startup log for the OS, and the distribution will typically announce itself in these logs. In addition, these files are not as obvious as those in /etc, and less sophisticated users will not be able to sanitize them easily. Once you know the distribution, you can make some inferences about the type of user that you are dealing with.

Ubuntu Linux   Ubuntu Linux has come on strong in the past few years and has gained a lot of ground in the distribution battle, with several reporting agencies stating that it's now the most popular distribution. A certification process exists for third-party utilities, and new releases of the operating system occur every six months. Ubuntu uses the Advanced Packaging Tool (APT) and the graphical front-end Synaptic to install new applications.

Red Hat/Fedora Linux   This is the most storied Linux distribution and typically the choice of those who are new to Linux. New programs are installed using the binary RPM (Red Hat Package Manager) distribution system, and a record of every program installed on the machine appears in the RPM database. Mandrake Linux is very similar in form and function to Red Hat.

Gentoo Linux   This distribution has made a lot of waves lately. The interesting thing about Gentoo is that everything is compiled for the machine on which it is being installed; nothing is done from a binary package. This can lead to epic installation times. The package manager for Gentoo is called portage/emerge and acts similarly to the BSD (Berkeley Software Distribution) ports system.

SUSE Linux   SUSE recently was acquired by Novell, and the company is in the process of porting all of its networking products to it. This means you may end up doing investigation on SUSE if you ever have to investigate a Novell network. The package manager for SUSE is YaST, which has capabilities similar to Red Hat's RPM system.

Debian Linux   Debian has traditionally been more of a developer's distribution. It has one of the best package management tools, APT, and the default installation is geared toward development tools and testing.

The Importance of Determining the Distribution

Each distribution has its own way of tracking and auditing user activity and system events. If you don't correctly identify which distribution is used early on, you will end up in the best case chasing your tail for unnecessary hours, and in the worst case missing evidence that can turn the outcome of a case. Spend the time to identify what you are dealing with and document your findings accordingly.

Tracking User Activity

Popularity:	8
Simplicity:	8
Impact:	8
Risk Rating:	**8**

The command interpreters for Linux are much more advanced than those used by Windows. From a forensics standpoint, this is a very good thing, because the two most popular interpreters, BASH and tcsh, leave audit trails for you to access that outline every command the user has run. Several other files are also unique to each shell that contain information we want to examine.

BASH

BASH is what you will most commonly run into on Linux systems. On the Linux platform, it is arguably the most advanced of the shells, with elaborate scripts and startup files that can do everything from give you the weather at the command prompt to color code your prompt based on machine name. The following table takes a look at the files that BASH uses and the purpose of each file. They can be found in the user's home directory.

Filename	Purpose
.bash_profile	Stores the commands that are run automatically when the shell is started. Commonly references a global file in the /etc/skel directory, so check that out.
.bash_history	The audit trail of the commands the user has run. The format is one command to a line with no time/date stamps.
.bash_logout	Like .bash_profile, the set of commands that are run when the shell exits. Many Linux installs ship with a global file in the /etc/skel directory.
.bashrc	Serves the same purpose as .bash_profile.

Tcsh

In our experience, tcsh is the shell of choice for people who learned on a platform other than Linux. The semantics are about the same between BASH and tcsh, with even the filenames being similar.

Filename	Purpose
.history	The audit trail of the commands the user has run. The format is one command to a line with no time/date stamps.
.logout/csh.logout	Like.bash_profile, the set of commands that are run when the shell exits. Many Linux installs ship with a global file in the /etc directory.
.tcshrc/.cshrc	Stores the commands that are run automatically when the shell is started. Commonly this references a global file in the /etc directory, so check that out.

Investigation Using Shells

Now that you have a frame of reference for the files we will be looking at, let's look at the common ways that suspects try to subvert this system. The most common way is simple deletion. If you go to the user's directory and these files aren't stored there, that should be a red flag. Either the suspect is using a shell from the 1980s, or he deleted the files. Time to fire up the deleted file recovery tool of choice and go to work. You will also commonly see that the suspect has created a link from the history file into the /dev/null special file. This is the kernel's version of a black hole. Things go in and nothing comes out. If you find this, you can do a check to determine whether you can get the prelinked file, but you may end up just trying to find another audit trail to follow.

Printer Activity

Popularity:	8
Simplicity:	8
Impact:	7
Risk Rating:	7

Determining what was printed can be extremely useful in espionage and IP cases. Linux has very stout printer auditing, derived from the older UNIX LPR daemons. If the distribution is newer, instead of using LPR, the CUPS daemon is used. LPR keeps a log in the /var/log directory named lpr.log and keeps the printer spools in /var/spool.

Look at these files to determine who printed what and when. If you determine that CUPS is installed, look in the directory /var/log/cups for the log files. In addition, if you can't find the logs, check in the /etc directory for the configuration files to see whether the logging has been moved.

 ## Finding Printed Documents

It's important that you locate both what was printed and who printed it. This can also serve as a tool for timeline reconstruction and as proof that a file was deleted. If you see that a file was printed and you can no longer find it in the file system, you now have a place to start when searching through deleted space.

 ## Mounting an Image

Popularity:	10
Simplicity:	8
Impact:	6
Risk Rating:	7

Using the mount command and the loop kernel module, you can mount drive images in Linux. This will allow you to work with the drive as a live file system. To do this, run this command:

```
[root@dhcppc3 mnt]# mount -r -o loop <image> <mount dir>
```

After this command is run, you can access the drive just as you would any other disk and run your favorite searching tools. The -r option requires some explanation—it forces the OS to mount the image as read-only. Never mount a forensic image where you can write to it. And always hash before you mount it and after you unmount it to show that you made no modifications to the data while it was mounted.

 ## Searching Unallocated Space with Lazarus

Popularity:	10
Simplicity:	8
Impact:	6
Risk Rating:	7

The Coroner's Toolkit (TCT) has a very useful tool called lazarus that attempts to re-create files from unallocated and deleted space. Be warned that this is not a fast process by any means. Simple extraction can take from hours to days, depending on the size, and the investigative time involved is also a consideration. Typically, you will want to run a tool such as unrm before you use lazarus, as unrm will extract only the deleted portions and significantly reduce the work lazarus has to do. Lazarus will then attempt to break the data into file types and blocks, and if you specify the −h option, it will actually create HTML that you can use to navigate around. Let's look at an example:

```
[root@dhcppc3 blocks]# unrm ../image.dd > output
[root@dhcppc3 test]# lazarus -h ../output
```

Running these commands creates the following files,

```
-rw-r--r--   1 root     root        206 May 22 22:36 output.frame.html
-rw-r--r--   1 root     root        158 May 22 22:39 output.html
-rw-r--r--   1 root     root       1472 May 22 22:36 output.menu.html
```

along with several subdirectories with the data files referenced in the HTML. If you take a look at the menu that lazarus creates, you'll see that it attempts to classify and color code the recovered data by file type.

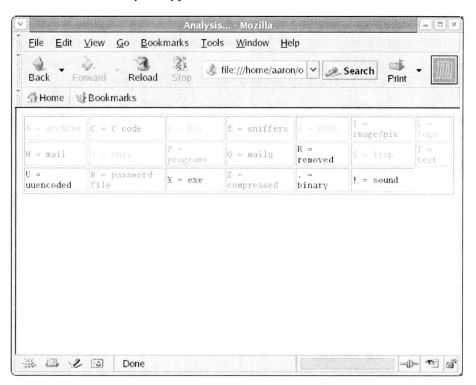

Analyzing the Swap Space

Popularity:	8
Simplicity:	8
Impact:	9
Risk Rating:	8

When the OS runs out of space in RAM, it will use the swap partition to store data temporarily. This can be a source of evidence and should always be examined when you are performing a Linux investigation. Pull the image of the swap partition in the same manner used to pull the other drive images. Once you have done that, you can treat it like a binary file. Remember that the Linux swap structure consists only of data blocks that represent blocks in memory that have been swapped out. Anything that can be stored in memory can end up in the swap file, including passwords, text files that were opened using editors, pictures, and so on. The downside to this structure is that you will very rarely find an entire file. Most of the time, since the blocks are not going to be allocated sequentially and nothing is tying the blocks together like an inode, you won't be able to pull an entire file. When you find information in the swap, make sure that you always explain what it is and how it fits into the context, and you should be OK.

Searching and Recovery

The ext2/ext3/ext4 file system and Linux in general offer suspects a multitude of ways to hide their tracks. Searching through an image and recovering the evidence is a very time-consuming and meticulous process. Always make sure that you approach this process in a methodical manner that is consistent with your process. Also, good search techniques can really speed up your investigation time. You will commonly find yourself going through gigabytes of unallocated or deleted space with little to no structure. This is the type of situation in which false positives can become your worst enemy. Take the time to learn how to search effectively, because it will save you a ton of time in the long run.

CHAPTER 8

MACINTOSH
ANALYSIS

Whether you're a forensic examiner who wants to use your Mac to perform forensic data analysis or an examiner who needs to create and/or analyze an image of a Macintosh computer's disk, this chapter is for you.

After nearly 20 years in the industry, I recently attended a computer forensics conference where the majority of presentations were running from Macs. I don't think there's been a day that I've gone out into the world without seeing an iPod or an iPhone in a long time.

Although today's Macintosh computers sport the "Intel Inside" sticker, Macs continue their tradition of being different. From a forensic analysis standpoint, there are still more similarities than differences between an Intel Mac and an Intel PC, but the two primary differences related to conducting meaningful forensics are the *partitioning scheme* and the *file system*.

Today's Macs use Guide Partition Table (GPT) to describe the layout of the boot volume. GPT is more extensible than earlier partitioning schemes and resolves several of the limitations inherent in the preceding implementation.

In addition to the new partitioning scheme, Apple has extensively enhanced the Hierarchical File System (HFS) volume format as well. Fortunately, Apple has a long history of doing things right. When the company introduced the newer HFS+ volume specification, it also introduced a "wrapper" that would allow older utilities to understand and respect newer file systems. When an HFS+ volume is presented to an older system that doesn't "understand" the HFS+ volume format, the user sees a file named "Where did all my files go?" The same kind of wrapper is used to describe a "protective MBR" so that GPT-unaware programs see a single, unknown partition that occupies the entire disk.

You can conduct a forensic examination of a Macintosh in a number of ways. As for the "best" way, that's a matter of opinion. From an analysis standpoint, you can look at Mac data using a Mac or any other platform. You'll learn about the pros and cons to each approach in this chapter.

One of the more valuable resources for a deeper understanding of the Mac OS is the Apple Developer Community. Despite its many differences when compared to other operating systems, the Mac OS is just another OS, and HFS is just another volume format when it comes down to it. The mantra "it's all just 1's and 0's" is a good chant to remember if you are tasked with examining a Macintosh for the first time.

THE EVOLUTION OF THE MAC OS

As with Microsoft Windows, Apple's operating and file systems have undergone a relentless and driving evolution. The major versions of the Mac OS (7, 8, 9, and X) have been increasingly more complex than earlier versions and have introduced many changes in the fundamental behavior of the operating system.

Mac OS X exemplifies this with the many differences between versions in the current major release cycle. The recent focus on the need for trustworthy computing, security concerns, and other initiatives and continued integration of the OS and the Internet has precipitated a paradigm shift not only of consumer awareness but for fundamental OS design as well.

Know Your Operating System

Popularity:	7
Simplicity:	7
Impact:	9
Risk:	8

Even a slight difference in the OS version, patch level, or update versus a "fresh install" can have a profound effect on the way your computer works, where and what data is stored, and what format is used for that data. Try this simple exercise at home:

1. Running Microsoft Windows XP, press CTRL-ALT-DEL to open the Task Manager window.

2. Click the Processes tab.

3. Start at the first item and ask yourself what it is and what it does. Also ask yourself how it may change the default behavior of the system and when it may not operate as intended. Repeat this process for each and every item in the list.

Remember that in court, questions like "Isn't it possible that…?" are fair game. Understanding your operating system is imperative. Since the chain is never stronger than the weakest link, an unknown and undocumented process running on a system does not avail you much and weakens your case. Clearly, you must be smart about how you approach, implement, and articulate your process and methodology in conducting a forensic investigation. Reducing the number of unknowns is a smart practice and a necessary part of your job.

It's Still Just 1's and 0's

From a technical standpoint, quite a few aspects of the Macintosh OS make it different from Windows or other operating systems. But let's review the similarities first, and then discuss the differences. Evidence collected from a Macintosh is no different from evidence collected from a PC, a Cray Supercomputer, or any other computer. It is digital evidence and is likely to exist in the same basic format and on the same types of media as any other digital evidence. The important concepts and attributes, such as chain of custody, quantifiable assurance of integrity, and preservation of best evidence, will still apply.

A Disk Is a Disk

Modern Macintosh computers generally use the same type of Serial ATA hard drives that are found in comparable PCs. An emerging trend is to use flash memory in lieu of rotating magnetic media. Although Apple has historically "branded" its OEM (original equipment manufacturer) hard disk drives, branding is an issue primarily when you're running an older Mac OS and utilities. While some versions of Apple disk utilities will work only on Apple-branded drives, for the most part, the physical devices are interchangeable; you could put a disk from a Mac into a PC and vice versa. The branding is based on the controller firmware and serves to identify Apple "authorized" hard disk drives.

Image Is Everything

Disk drives from an Apple computer can be removed and duplicated in any of the ways that work with disks from PCs: hardware duplication, software duplication, cloning—after all, it's just another disk at the device layer.

If you don't want to disassemble a laptop and remove the hard drive (and really, who does?), you could boot the Macintosh into FireWire disk mode. Most Macs that have onboard FireWire (IEEE 1394) allow you to hold down the T key during the boot process and place the computer into FireWire disk mode. When in this mode, the computer presents the internal primary master device as a FireWire device, similar to a Maxtor or other external IEEE 1394 hard disk drive.

You can connect the Mac to another machine via the FireWire cable and image, view, and search normally. Alternatively, you can create a bootable CD-ROM or thumb drive designed to bring up the system to a minimal state and image via the NIC card, USB, or FireWire ports. When you're imaging with a Windows computer, it cannot understand the HFS file system and thus will not be able to modify it; just don't initialize the disk.

Regardless of whether you use hardware or software, you should end up with, among other things, a *bit image copy*—a device clone or a segmented image that resides on a file system. You can use Windows tools, Linux/BSD tools, or Macintosh tools. (The Smart Acquisition Workshop (www.asrdata.com) is a user-friendly program that runs natively on Windows, Linux, and Macintosh.) Whatever tool you decide to use, you're ready to start looking at the data and answering some questions.

 Never boot a Macintosh that contains evidence unless you know exactly what you are doing. The "normal" boot process changes data.

LOOKING AT A MAC DISK OR IMAGE

As with other rotating magnetic media, Macs have a partition map that points to various partitions on the drive. *Partitions* are logically contiguous ranges of sectors or blocks. *Sectors* are currently defined as 512 bytes for most rotating magnetic disks and thumb or flash drives.

To help you better understand the Mac partitioning scheme, let's review a Windows Master Boot Record (MBR) and partition map, both located in logical sector 0 of the device.

A Windows MBR contains boot code, disk geometry information, and four buckets for primary partitions. Primary partitions can point to extended partitions, which give you four more buckets. Partitions within extended partitions may be conceptualized as belonging to the parent partition, which in turn belongs to the device. The device contains everything and describes how the disk is laid out right up front. The new Apple partitioning scheme (GUID Partition Table, or GPT) is much more flexible and extensible than Windows MBR partitioning.

When we refer to a physical device, such as the Serial ATA rotating magnetic disks like those found in Mac desktop and laptop computers, we need to define some terms and concepts. For this discussion, let's say that a device comprises n number of blocks, and that a block is a 512-byte sector on the device. If I have a 100 Gigabyte (107,374,182,400 bytes) hard drive, I have a disk with 209,715,200 sectors or blocks. Let's see how the blocks on disk are laid out.

The GUID Partition Table

The first block on an Apple-formatted GPT device is the *protective MBR*. According to Apple, "The protective MBR...defines a single partition entry that covers the entire area of the disk used by GPT structures and partitions. It is designed to prevent GPT-unaware programs from accidentally modifying a GPT disk. A GPT-unaware program sees the GPT disk as an MBR disk with a single, unknown partition. In a way, this is like the HFS wrapper around an HFS Plus disk."

The next block (LBA1) is the primary partition table header. Apple defines the *partition table header* as "a structure that defines various aspects of the disk, including a GUID to uniquely identify the disk, the starting block of the partition entry array, and the size of each partition entry in that array."

The 512-byte partition table header is laid out as follows:

Offset	Length	Contents
0	8 bytes	Signature ("EFI PART", 45 46 49 20 50 41 52 54)
8	4 bytes	Revision (for version 1.0, the value is 00 00 01 00)
12	4 bytes	Header size (in bytes, usually 5C 00 00 00 meaning 92 bytes)
16	4 bytes	CRC32 of header (0 to header size), with this field zeroed during calculation
20	4 bytes	Reserved, must be zero
24	8 bytes	Current LBA (location of this header copy)
32	8 bytes	Backup LBA (location of the other header copy)

Offset	Length	Contents
40	8 bytes	First usable LBA for partitions (primary partition table last LBA + 1)
48	8 bytes	Last usable LBA (secondary partition table first LBA − 1)
56	16 bytes	Disk GUID (also referred to as UUID on UNIX systems)
72	8 bytes	Partition entries starting LBA (always 2 in primary copy)
80	4 bytes	Number of partition entries
84	4 bytes	Size of a partition entry (usually 128 bytes)
88	4 bytes	CRC32 of partition array
92	*	Reserved, must be zeros for the rest of the block (420 bytes for a 512-byte LBA)

Partition Entry Array

This brings us to the partition entry array, starting at LBA2. The partition entry array is, as you might imagine, an array or list of all the partitions described in the partition table. GPT requires that the partition entry array be at least 16 KB. For a 512-byte block size, this is 32 blocks. The size of each entry is defined in the partition table header, and at the time this chapter was written is 128 bytes. This means that using the current default values, a GPT disk can contain and describe 128 partitions.

A typical 128-byte partition entry is laid out as shown in the following table:

Offset	Length	Contents
0	16 bytes	Partition type GUID
16	16 bytes	Unique partition GUID
32	8 bytes	First LBA (little-endian)
40	8 bytes	Last LBA (inclusive, usually odd)
48	8 bytes	Attribute flags (e.g., bit 60 denotes read-only)
56	72 bytes	Partition name (36 UTF-16LE code units)
128		Reserved (must be zero)

Bear in mind that block size and partition entry array size can, and probably will, change at some point in the future. Also remember that GPT is little-endian; that is, multi-byte quantities are stored with the least significant byte first.

The most common GPT partition types are defined in the GPT specification. Apple has defined a number of GUIDs to describe Apple-specific partition types, as shown in the next table:

Type	GUID	APM Equivalent
HFS [Plus]	48465300-0000-11AA-AA11-00306543ECAC	Apple_HFS
UFS	55465300-0000-11AA-AA11-00306543ECAC	Apple_UFS
Boot	426F6F74-0000-11AA-AA11-00306543ECAC	Apple_Boot
RAID	52414944-0000-11AA-AA11-00306543ECAC	Apple_RAID
Offline RAID	52414944-5F4F-11AA-AA11-00306543ECAC	Apple_RAID_Offline
Label	4C616265-6C00-11AA-AA11-00306543ECAC	Apple_Label

Note that the first three dash-delimited fields of the GUID are written to the disk in little-endian, and the last two fields are not.

Let's take a look at a GPT partitioned disk. Figure 8-1 shows SMART (www.asrdata .com/SMART/) looking at a GPT-formatted MacBook internal hard drive. The hard

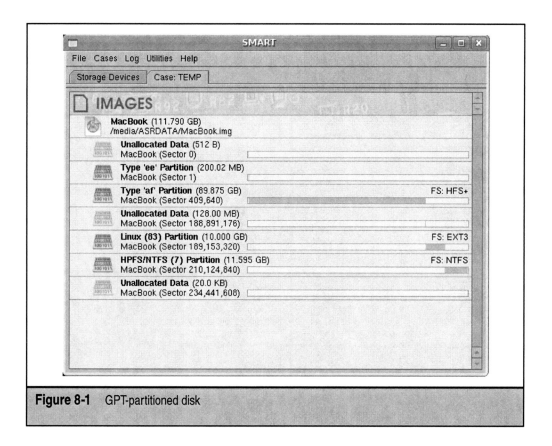

Figure 8-1 GPT-partitioned disk

drive is set up to triple-boot from either the Mac OS X installed in the HFS+ partition, Ubuntu Linux installed in the ext3 partition, or Windows XP installed in the NTFS partition.

The raw data that describes this structure is shown in Figure 8-2.

You can see that offset 32 for each entry specifies the starting LBA in little-endian format. This is more modern and straightforward compared with calculating and

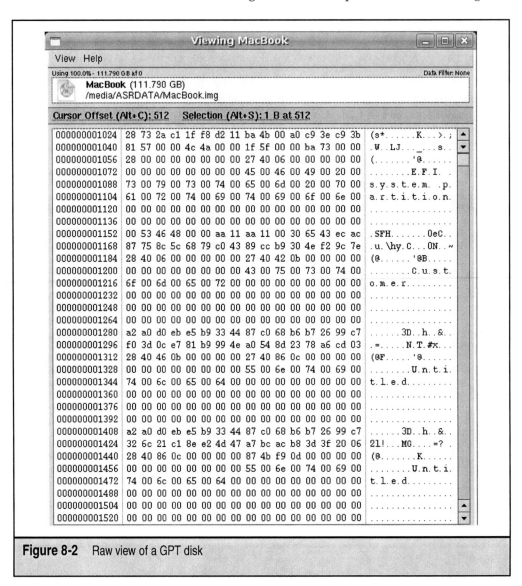

Figure 8-2   Raw view of a GPT disk

recording C:H:S values (cylinders:heads:sectors, which seem pretty silly when looking at solid state memory).

So now we know that the first block (LBA0) on an Apple-formatted GPT disk is the protective MBR, the second block (LBA1) contains the Primary GPT Partition table header, and that blocks 2–33 contain the partition table entry array.

The partitions that are set by Apple disk formatting utilities follow three simple rules, depending on the size of the device being partitioned. Apple defines disks in three ways—tiny, small, and big:

- **Tiny, less than 1GB**   Tiny disks are created with no reserved free space and no extra partitions; the partitions are laid out as the user specifies.

- **Small, 1–2GB**   Small disks are created with no extra partitions but have 128MB of free space at the end of each partition.

- **Big, larger than 2GB**   Big disks always have a 200MB Extensible Firmware Interface (EFI) system partition called the EFI System Partition (ESP) as the first partition on the disk, and they also have the 128MB of free space after each partition (not including the ESP partition).

Each partition is aligned to a 4KB boundary to accommodate the limitations of the HFS+ file system implementation on Mac OS X. Free space is left at the end of each partition to make it easier for future system software to manipulate the partition map in ways that cannot be anticipated at the moment.

The HFS File System

Thus far, we haven't even looked at a file system; it has all been partition information. Any discussion about HFS needs to include a discussion about B-trees (balanced or binary trees). These structures remain central to HFS and its variants.

A quick review of File Allocation Table (FAT)–based file systems will remind you that the file system has a *root* from which everything on the file system can be referenced via a *fully qualified path*. *Directories* are simply file entries that have a directory attribute set. File entries contain a pointer to a starting block and a length. Directory entries point to subdirectories. The FAT is an array of pointers. The values in the FAT are either pointers to clusters, EOF markers (that say "I am the last cluster in this chain"), or perhaps BAD, as in blocks that are mapped out by diagnostic programs.

It should be no surprise that the Macintosh file system is completely different. For one thing, no FAT is used in the HFS. The job of keeping track of the allocation blocks (clusters) allocated to a file is performed by the *allocation file*, a new structure introduced with HFS+ and similar to the volume bitmap in HFS: each allocation block is represented by 1 bit. A 0 (zero) means the block is free and a 1 means the block is in use. The main difference between the older HFS volume bitmap and the newer allocation file is that the allocation file is stored as a regular file; it does not occupy a special reserved space near the beginning of the volume as the older volume bitmap did. The allocation file can also change size and does not have to be stored contiguously within a volume. This more closely parallels the behavior of NTFS when it comes to file system internals.

The tree analogy is an extension of the notion that everything grows from the "root" of a file system. Trees are made up of *nodes*, logical groupings of information that are internal to the file system and contain records. *Records* contain data or pointers to data.

Different types of nodes appear on the tree: header nodes, index nodes, and leaf nodes. The leaf nodes give us information about files—their names, access times, and other attributes. Nodes are pointed to and/or linked together and may be conceptualized as layers. The header node is at the top, and under that are index nodes. Index nodes may point to other levels of index nodes or to leaf nodes.

You could say that the root node is at the top of the tree, at level 0. The root node contains pointers to B-tree header nodes, which in turn point to index nodes. Index nodes can point to other index nodes or to leaf nodes. The more files, folders, and stuff you have in your file system, the more levels you will have between the root node and the leaf nodes. In general, nodes that exist on the same level point to one another. These are called *FLINKS (forward links)* and *BLINKS (backward links)*, as shown in Figure 8-3.

When we go to the offset specified as the starting logical block address of a partition that contains an HFS+ file system, we see that the first two sectors of the volume are HFS *boot blocks*. These are identical to the boot blocks in an HFS volume and are part of the HFS wrapper.

Sector 2 of the partition contains the *volume header*. This is equivalent to the master directory block in an HFS volume. The volume header stores a wide variety of data about the volume itself, such as the size of allocation blocks, a time stamp that indicates when the volume was created, and the location of other volume structures such as the catalog file and extent overflow file. The volume header is always located in the same place.

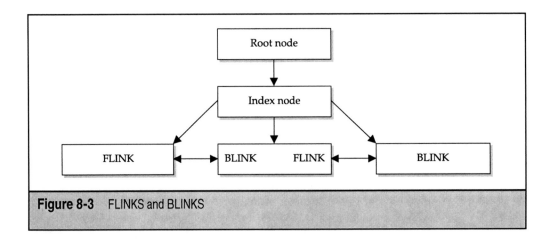

Figure 8-3 FLINKS and BLINKS

The layout of the Volume header is as follows:

Offset	Length	Value
0	2 bytes	`signature;`
2	2 bytes	`version;`
4	4 bytes	`attributes;`
8	4 bytes	`lastMountedVersion;`
12	4 bytes	`journalInfoBlock;`
16	4 bytes	`createDate;`
20	4 bytes	`modifyDate;`
24	4 bytes	`backupDate;`
28	4 bytes	`checkedDate;`
32	4 bytes	`fileCount;`
36	4 bytes	`folderCount;`
40	4 bytes	`blockSize;`
44	4 bytes	`totalBlocks;`
48	4 bytes	`freeBlocks;`
52	4 bytes	`nextAllocation;`
56	4 bytes	`rsrcClumpSize;`
60	4 bytes	`dataClumpSize;`
64	4 bytes	`nextCatalogID;`
68	4 bytes	`writeCount;`
72	8 bytes	`encodingsBitmap;`
80	4 bytes	`finderInfo[8];`
84	4 bytes	`allocationFile;`
88	4 bytes	`extentsFile;`
92	4 bytes	`catalogFile;`
96	4 bytes	`attributesFile;`
100	4 bytes	`startupFile;`

HFS+ dates are 32-bit values that represent the number of seconds since midnight, January 1, 1904, GMT. Earlier implementations used local time, not GMT. The exception is the creation date stored in the volume header. This field records local time, not GMT.

The *catalog file* is a branching tree data structure or (B*-tree) that contains records for all the files and directories stored in the volume. The HFS+ catalog file is similar to the HFS catalog file—the main differences being that records are larger to allow more fields and to allow for those fields to be larger (for example, to allow the longer 255-character Unicode filenames in HFS+). A record in the HFS catalog file is 512 bytes in size, and a record in the HFS+ catalog file is 4KB in Mac OS and 8KB in Mac OS X. Fields in HFS are of fixed size, and in HFS+, the size can vary depending on the actual size of the data they store.

The *extents overflow file* is another B*-tree that records the allocation blocks that are allocated to each file as extents. Each file record in the catalog file is capable of recording eight extents for each fork of a file; once those are used, extents are recorded in the extents overflow file. Bad blocks are also recorded as extents in the extents overflow file. The default size of an extent record in Mac OS is 1 KB and in Mac OS X is 4 KB.

The *attributes file* is a new B*-tree in HFS+ that does not have a corresponding structure in HFS. The attributes file can store three different types of 4KB records: *inline data attribute* records, *fork data attribute* records and *extension attribute* records. Inline data attribute records store small attributes that can fit within the record itself. Fork data attribute records contain references to a maximum of eight extents that can hold larger attributes. Extension attributes are used to extend a fork data attribute record when its eight extent records are already used.

The *startup file* is designed for non–Mac OS systems that don't have HFS or HFS+ support. It is similar to the boot blocks of an HFS volume. The second to last sector contains the *alternate volume header* equivalent to the alternate Master Directory Block of HFS. The last sector in the volume is reserved for use by Apple. It is used during the computer manufacturing process.

Unique Sequential File Identifiers

Every file system object in an HFS file system is assigned a unique, sequential file ID number when it is created. For a forensic examiner, this information is very useful, as the file with FILE ID 100 was created in the file system after the file with FILE ID 99, regardless of any date or time stamp information. The FILE ID attribute is relative to the file system you are examining. File ID numbers do *not* "go along with the file" when it is copied, downloaded, decompressed, and so on. The File ID number is one of the things that the HFS file system uses when organizing the B-tree.

DELETED FILES

On a FAT32 file system, files are "deleted" by replacing the first character of the filename with the hex byte E5. The file's clusters are flagged as "available," and the E5 entry in the directory still contains the (changed) name, attribute flags, date and time stamps, and logical size. On an NTFS system, the entry is "un-indexed" from the MFT. This is closer to what happens on an HFS or HFS+ volume. Let's take a look at a catalog B-tree leaf node containing file records (the lowest level of the tree), shown in Figure 8-4.

```
  Offset    0  1  2  3  4  5  6  7   8  9 10 11 12 13 14 15
00000000   00 00 04 60 00 00 04 5C  FF 01 00 03 00 00 14 00   ...`....\ÿ.......
00000016   00 00 0C A2 0E 57 69 6E  64 6F 77 73 20 39 38 2E   ...¢.Windows 98.
00000032   69 6D 67 00 02 00 00 00  72 6F 68 64 64 64 73 6B   img.....rohdddsk
00000048   80 00 00 00 00 00 00 00  00 00 00 0D 4D 00 00 00   |...........M...
00000064   00 00 00 00 00 00 00 00  00 00 02 14 00 06 9E 00   ..............|.
00000080   B4 37 A4 D4 B4 37 A4 D4  00 00 00 00 00 00 00 00   ´7¤Ô´7¤Ô........
00000096   00 00 00 00 00 00 00 00  00 00 00 00 00 00 00 00   ................
00000112   00 00 00 00 00 00 00 00  00 00 13 A7 00 01 00 00   ...........§....
00000128   00 00 00 00 00 00 00 00  00 00 0F 00 00 00 0C A2   ...............¢
00000144   09 57 69 70 65 20 49 6E  66 6F 02 00 00 00 41 50   .Wipe Info....AP
00000160   50 4C 50 4E 77 69 80 00  00 00 00 00 00 00 00 00   PLPNwi|.........
00000176   0D 4E 00 00 00 00 00 00  00 00 00 00 00 00 00 00   .N..............
00000192   02 06 00 06 9E 00 B4 9A  BB D6 B4 9A BB D6 00 00   ....|.´»Ö´»Ö..
00000208   00 00 00 00 00 00 00 00  00 00 00 00 00 00 00 00   ................
00000224   00 00 00 00 00 00 00 00  00 00 00 00 00 00 00 00   ................
00000240   13 A8 00 01 00 00 00 00  00 00 00 00 00 00 00 00   .¨..............
00000256   0E 00 00 00 0C A2 08 77  72 61 70 2E 67 69 66 00   .....¢.wrap.gif.
00000272   02 00 00 00 47 49 46 66  4A 56 57 52 80 00 00 00   ....GIFfJVWR|...
00000288   00 00 00 00 00 00 0D 4F  00 00 00 00 00 00 00 00   .......O........
00000304   00 00 00 00 00 00 02 DE  00 06 9E 00 B3 E5 92 9A   .......Þ..|.³å´|
00000320   B3 E5 92 9A 00 00 00 00  00 00 00 00 00 00 00 00   ³å´|............
00000336   00 00 00 00 00 00 00 00  00 00 00 00 00 00 00 00   ................
```

Figure 8-4 Tree leaf node data

Looking at the B-tree data, you can see filenames in plaintext, as well as information that you can identify as type and creator codes:

```
\x00 ulong    fLink    Forward link to next node on this level
\x04 ulong    bLink    Backwards link to previous node
\x08 uchar    nodeType FF=leaf node, 00=index node
              01=B-tree Header node, 02=2nd VBM
\x09 char     level    level of this node (1=leaf)
\x0A uint     numRecs  Number of records in this node
```

So looking at the first 12 bytes in Figure 8-4, you see the following:

- The forward link is 00 00 04 60 (Node 1120).
- The backward link is 00 00 04 5c (Node 1116).
- The node type is FF for a leaf node.
- The leaf node is at level 01 of the tree.
- Three records are contained in this node.

The three records in the example are leaf node entries for these files:

- Windows 98.img
- Wipe Info
- wrap.gif

So what happens if you delete the file Wipe Info? What changes would you observe in the node you are looking at? For one thing, offset \x0A (the number of records) would be decreased to 2. Slightly less obvious, the file records are arranged alphabetically within the node. Therefore, if you deleted the second file, Wipe Info in this example, the third entry would pop up in the stack of records tracked by the node. Think of it as the stack of plates at your favorite all-you-can-eat place. If you take the top plate off the stack, the second plate now becomes the first plate, and every plate underneath it shifts up the queue by one.

If you take the second plate off the stack, the first plate is still the first plate, but the second plate used to be the third plate. What this means to you is that the second entry (Wipe Info) is overwritten by the third entry (now the second entry). You would see that only two records were indexed in the node, Windows 98.img and wrap.gif, and you would see the original third entry as well as the "new" second entry. It might look like Figure 8-5.

```
Offset      0  1  2  3  4  5  6  7   8  9 10 11 12 13 14 15
00000000   00 00 04 60 00 00 04 5C  FF 01 00 03 00 00 14 00   ...`...\ÿ......
00000016   00 00 0C A2 0E 57 69 6E  64 6F 77 73 20 39 38 2E   ...¢.Windows 98.
00000032   69 6D 67 00 02 00 00 00  72 6F 68 64 64 64 73 6B   img.....rohdddsk
00000048   80 00 00 00 00 00 00 00  00 00 00 0D 4D 00 00 00   ¦..........M...
00000064   00 00 00 00 00 00 00 00  00 00 02 14 00 06 9E 00   ............¦.
00000080   B4 37 A4 D4 B4 37 A4 D4  00 00 00 00 00 00 00 00   ´7¤Ô´7¤Ô........
00000096   00 00 00 00 00 00 00 00  00 00 00 00 00 00 00 00   ................
00000112   00 00 00 00 00 00 00 00  00 00 13 A7 00 01 00 00   ...........S....
00000128   00 00 00 00 00 00 00 00  00 00 0F 00 00 00 0C A2   ................¢
00000144   0E 00 00 00 0C A2 08 77  72 61 70 2E 67 69 66 00   .....¢.wrap.gif.
00000160   02 00 00 00 47 49 46 66  4A 56 57 52 80 00 00 00   ....GIFfJVWR¦...
00000176   00 00 00 00 00 00 0D 4F  00 00 00 00 00 00 00 00   .......O........
00000192   00 00 00 00 00 00 02 DE  00 06 9E 00 B3 E5 92 9A   .......Þ..¦.³å´¦
00000208   B3 E5 92 9A 00 00 00 00  00 00 00 00 00 00 00 00   ³å´¦............
00000224   00 00 00 00 00 00 00 00  00 00 00 00 00 00 00 00   ................
00000240   13 A8 00 01 00 00 00 00  00 00 00 00 00 00 00 00   .¨..............
00000256   0E 00 00 00 0C A2 08 77  72 61 70 2E 67 69 66 00   .....¢.wrap.gif.
00000272   02 00 00 00 47 49 46 66  4A 56 57 52 80 00 00 00   ....GIFfJVWR¦...
00000288   00 00 00 00 00 00 0D 4F  00 00 00 00 00 00 00 00   .......O........
00000304   00 00 00 00 00 00 02 DE  00 06 9E 00 B3 E5 92 9A   .......Þ..¦.³å´¦
00000320   B3 E5 92 9A 00 00 00 00  00 00 00 00 00 00 00 00   ³å´¦............
00000336   00 00 00 00 00 00 00 00  00 00 00 00 00 00 00 00   ................
```

Figure 8-5   B-tree leaf node data showing node slack

However, not all is lost. Although the leaf node entry may be physically overwritten, other instances of the node data may still exist in unallocated space, in index nodes, and in nodes that have been removed from the tree at a higher level. If all the files in a node are deleted because their common parent (directory) has been deleted, it is not unusual to see "pruned" nodes with all of the records intact.

Within each file entry in the B-tree are numerous bit fields, pointers, keys, and data values that include important things like creation and modification dates, file ID numbers, locations for the data blocks that make up the file, and things like an icon's location and color. Apple's developer support and documentation are fairly comprehensive regarding these structures. The Apple Developer Tech Note 1150 and the reference "Inside Macintosh: Files" are great places to start digging deeper.

Recovering Deleted Files

If you are interested in recovering deleted files from an HFS or HFS+ file system, you can go about it in two primary ways. The first way is to aggregate the unallocated space and concatenate it, essentially creating one data stream comprising sequential (although not contiguous) unallocated clusters. This is relatively easy to do if you just invert (Boolean NOT) the bitmap that tells you which clusters are allocated and which ones are not. The second method of data recovery involves identifying file system metadata and mapping those entries to unallocated areas of the volume.

 NOTE Newer versions of the Mac OS allow files to be "shredded" or physically overwritten with the `rm  -P` option. If you see this in the bash_history file, it is safe to assume the locations referenced by the file at the time of its deletion have been overwritten.

Concatenating Unallocated Space

This method gives you everything marked as unallocated. No file system information is directly associated with the data—it's just a blob of data. This type of data is great if you are trying to recover data such as graphics, text, and other simple data formats. Fragmentation is eliminated, so if a deleted file were fragmented by an active file's allocation, the data taken together would be contiguous.

 # Large Ranges of Null or Other Wasted Space

Popularity:	7
Simplicity:	6
Impact:	8
Risk:	7

The aggregate of the unallocated space often consists of very large ranges of null or other wasted space. This can be a formatting pattern, a null, or some other repeating pattern. Depending on what you are looking for, filtering the blob can have many benefits. First, most grep implementations are line-based, so if you grep a blob of 2GB of null, grep will likely exhaust memory trying to buffer the first line. Since no line (just null) exists, memory is needlessly exhausted.

If you are looking for HTML or plaintext, you don't really need to know about nulls, and a side benefit is that if your term exists as a UTF-encoded term, stripping the nulls allows you to find it without the need for a Unicode search term. If you think about RFC822 headers, URLs, e-mail addresses, contact information, log entries, and other simple data types, you realize that you really need to concern yourself only with printable ASCII characters. Filtering the unallocated space (depending on what you are looking for) saves storage, time, effort, memory, and aggravation. This is called "normalizing" the data that you are working with. If the hex character \xFF doesn't appear in what you are looking for, then why copy and search it?

 ## Normalize Data

You have several friends here to help you—tr is your friend, strings is your friend, and SMART is your friend. Preprocessing (normalizing) the data before searching it for simple data constructs (when done correctly) allows more data to be searched fast using less memory and storage. Why wouldn't you do this?

While this is great for data recovery, you aren't helping much in a forensic analysis if all you can say is that the data exists in unallocated space. You want to be able to identify file attributes (name, date and time stamps, original location, and other info). For that, you need to use the second method of data recovery.

Scavenging for Unindexed Files and Pruned Nodes

Scavenging allocated leaf nodes for unindexed files and scavenging unallocated space for "pruned" index and leaf nodes is probably the best practical way to identify file system metadata and map those entries to unallocated areas of the volume.

Searching Unallocated Space for File Entries in Leaf Nodes

You could search unallocated space for file entries in leaf nodes. This presumes that you know what you are looking for, as in a filename or attribute data. When you don't have that, though, you need to search for the places that are likely to have what you want to find: leaf nodes in the B-tree. You could use a search term like this:

```
\xff\x01\x00
```

This expression means, "Since I don't know about the fLink and bLink, match any two double words (8 bytes) that are followed by \xff (leaf node), followed by \x01 (leaf level), followed by \x00 (index node)." You will probably never see a node with more than 255 descriptors in it. Of course, it helps if you know *what* you are looking for *and where* you are most likely to find it.

NOTE   The searched term \xff\x01\x00 is pretty loose and will likely generate hundreds, if not thousands, of false hits. Since you know that the data you are searching for is node header data, and you know it's offset within the node, you can search for hits that exhibit sector boundary alignment. Since all file system constructs are based on a sector, this will reduce your hits to those most likely to be responsive and independent of cluster or node size.

Whew. Let's take a moment and review. We've discussed devices, partitions, file systems, trees, and nodes—just scratching the surface of each. It's all important stuff, but way beyond the scope of this (or any single) chapter. Just like stacking matching bowls, you can see how these things relate to each other, as shown in Figure 8-6.

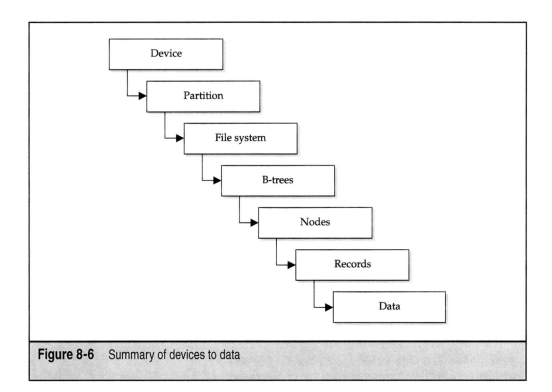

Figure 8-6   Summary of devices to data

A CLOSER LOOK AT MACINTOSH FILES

Now that we've taken a brief look at the file system structure, let's take a closer look at the files themselves. One of the things that make Macintosh files unique is the *resource fork*. Nowadays, file systems are more extensible and attributes can often be easily added, but it wasn't always this way. The Macintosh HFS filing system was one of the, if not the first, file systems to embrace the concept of a file comprising multiple streams of data. This is commonplace now in NTFS, but the concept's origins can be traced back to the Macintosh (as can the mouse, windows, task bars, and a great many other computer interface elements we see every day).

Archives

Relatively few major advances have occurred lately in compression technology. Compression algorithms are mature and reasonably well standardized. Years ago, StuffIt was the dominant Macintosh compression technology. With the Mac's interoperability enhancements, Mac-centric compression algorithms such as BinHex have fallen by the wayside in favor of zip, gzip, and tarball formats. This trend seems to be accelerating now that the Mac has more POSIX underpinnings.

Date and Time Stamps

The Mac never really had a Y2K crisis. At worst, it faces a year 2040 crisis. Over the years, the Mac OS and ROMs have used different "time zero" references and have stored date and time stamps in different formats. The original date and time utilities (introduced with the original Macintosh 128K computer in 1984) used a long word to store seconds, starting at midnight, January 1, 1904, Local Time. This approach allows the correct representation of dates up to 6:28:15 A.M. on February 6, 2040. The current date and time utilities, documented in *Inside Macintosh: Operating System Utilities* (http://developer .apple.com/documentation/mac/osutilities/OSUtilities-2.html), use a 64-bit signed value, which covers dates from 30,081 B.C. to 29,940 A.D.

E-mail

In stark contrast to the Windows experience, e-mail has remained much easier to analyze on Macintosh machines. Although PST files can be created and used to store e-mail on Macs, the native format for non-Microsoft MUAs (Mail User Agents) e-mail stores are plaintext. Remember that mail can exist in a wide variety of formats, including cached web pages (Yahoo!, Hotmail, and so on), PST files, mdir, mbox, and others.

The e-mail accounts for the Mac built-in mail client Mail are stored in /Users/*<user>*/ Library/Mail. The files named mbox contain the actual plaintext e-mail data, rfc822 data, and attachments. Attachments may be compressed in a variety of formats, including TAR, ZIP, GZ, BZ2, and graphics are typically encoded using base64 or UU-encoding. Programs like SMART may be used to carve individual messages and attachments automatically from mbox and newsgroup files.

/Users/*<user>*/Library/Caches/ contains recently cached images, movies, or other data viewed by Mail.app and Safari.app. The mail folder contains many subfolders (labeled 00–15) that appear to be recursive (of depth 3), but it is actually using a hash table (a programming technique used for efficiency). The Safari folder is the same, except it is of depth 2. The MS Internet cache is contained in a standard .waf file.

Graphics

The Mac has been known as a graphically intense machine since its introduction and still enjoys a stronghold in prepress, layout, and graphic design. Contemporary Macintosh operating systems support a myriad of graphics formats, although most often we see the "standard" graphics file formats (GIF and JPEG), particularly when they come from the Internet. The "endian-ness" of the processor doesn't affect the data format of the files. This is to say that even though memory and words are represented backward on a big-endian system, a GIF header will still be laid down on the disk in the same way, whether it is written to a FAT32 or HFS+ file system.

Web Browsing

Form follows function. Web browsing artifacts are similar to those found in the WinTel world. This is largely due to the standards in place for the various protocols that make the Internet work. HTTP is still a stateless protocol, cookies are still cookies, and HTML is still HTML. (In fact, this is far truer on the Mac compared to the Microsoft HTML implementation.)

/Users/*<user>*/Library/Safari contains the history files and bookmarks for the user. Also included is a folder of thumbnails named Icons. In Safari, when some Web sites are viewed, a thumbnail is displayed next to the URL that is relevant to the Web site being viewed (for example, Google uses its *g* logo, and CNN uses *cnn* in red on a white background).

/Users/*<user>*/Library/Cookies contains cookies of recently viewed Web sites. The cookies are stored in XML format. For more information about reviewing Web activity, see Chapter 12.

Resources

Resources are common objects whose templates are already defined elsewhere. A file's resource fork (stream) can contain anything but is supposed to contain data and customizations of common objects that are unique to the file. A good example is language localization: a program is written once, and all the dialog boxes have their text and buttons in English. To localize the program, all you need to do is edit the resources (the words displayed in menu bars, dialog boxes, and so on), so instead of being labeled *No*, the button would say *Nyet* (*No* in Russian) without having to recompile or rewrite the actual executable code.

Virtual Memory

Most every OS (and many applications) use a backing store, virtual memory, swap file (or slice or partition), or some other method of caching memory to disk. As with other forensic investigations, these artifacts may contain a wealth of pertinent information. Preprocessing or normalizing the data prior to searching for simple data constructs can save you time, disk memory, and storage.

The swap files are located in /var/vm. This is where passwords temporarily stored in memory could be written to disk.

System Log and Other System Files

/var/log/ contains a lot of information and is an extremely important file. Some of the information it contains includes serial numbers of removable media (thumb drives, SmartMedia, and so on) and some names of mounted media such as CDs and floppy disks.

/var/log/daily.out contains snapshots of mounted volume names and the dates they were mounted, as well as the used disk space on each of the mounted volumes.

/var/spool/cups contains files that hold information about documents recently printed. This includes the name of the document printed and the user who printed it.

/Library/Receipts is a folder containing system information about updates. This is useful in detecting whether a user had the latest system patches or security updates installed.

/Users/<user>/.bash_history contains recent terminal commands issued by the user. Look for rm -P commands, which mean that the user intentionally attempted to wipe data from a drive.

The var/vm folder contains another folder named app_profile. The files here that end with _names contain the names of applications that were recently opened. The files ending with _data contain temporary information useful to the applications in the _name documents.

/private/var/root/.bash_history contains recent terminal commands issued by the administrator. If this file exists, the user is probably familiar with Linux and should be considered to have at least an intermediate knowledge of OS X.

/Users/<user>/Library/Preferences/ contains preference files of programs installed on the computer. Even deleted programs will still have their preference files left behind if the program generated them. Inside the preferences folder are the following:

- com.apple.Preview.plist contains a list of recently viewed pictures and PDF documents.

- QuickTimeFavorites contains a list of recently viewed movies and the disk location of the movies.

/Users/<user>/Library/Logs/DiskUtility.log contains information about disks recently mounted using DiskUtility as well as disks erased or burned by this application.

MAC AS A FORENSICS PLATFORM

If you have the luxury (or budget) of getting a Mac, use it as a "base camp" for some exploration. A great way to start is to wipe a drive with null (this verifies the media as well as facilitates tighter compression); install the Mac OS of your choice; go through the initial first boot process using documented information for username, Internet settings, preferences, and so on; and then make a compressed image of the drive. This way, you can always return to a known state quickly and easily.

If you are using a Macintosh as your forensic platform of choice, you can minimize the possibility of an "Oops!" Whenever possible, use a hardware write-blocking device. Although not essential with a properly configured forensic acquisition and analysis platform and a well-trained examiner, you can think of write-blockers as airbags for your investigation. You wear a seatbelt, keep your eyes on the road, and hope you never see your airbag. You protect yourself by disabling disk arbitration and understanding the system configuration and behavior.

The Mac has been able to mount disk and file system images for quite some time. Numerous utilities let you mount images of CD-ROMs and many other types of file systems. Be aware that these files may contain a complete file system with many files, as well as their own slack space, deleted files, unallocated space, and directory structures. Type and creator codes of DIMG, DDSK, VMK, and IMG should be looked at very carefully, as should any very large file. Virtual PC provides hardware emulation and may mount and create disk images, as can Apple's Disk Copy.

Images of HFS, HFS+, many of the FAT flavors, and several other file systems may be mounted to this system for analysis. Setting the permissions of the underlying image file(s) to read-only should prevent any modifications to the data contained within the image. It is a common practice to embed the Cyclic Redundancy Check (CRC) or md5sum of the data into the image file's resource fork. This allows authentication information about the image to be integrated into the image without affecting the data (fork) of the image file.

CHAPTER 9

DEFEATING ANTI-FORENSIC TECHNIQUES

A n *anti-forensic technique* is any intentional or accidental change that can obscure, encrypt, or hide data from forensic tools. Very few anti-forensic techniques work the way a suspect might expect. Most suspects believe that by following the techniques illustrated in this chapter and in other publications, they can hide their tracks. Trying to do this, however, often merely helps the investigator know where to look for evidence. In fact, a suspect who tries to hide evidence can actually strengthen an investigator's success in uncovering it.

Most forensic examination tools used today tend not to trust data or view it in the same ways they did when computer forensics was a new field. For example, earlier versions of open source forensic tools could miss files and data due to logical coding errors. Most of the concepts discussed by most anti-forensic articles and covered in this chapter don't affect modern tools, but you should still be aware of them, because you could be expected to know this information in court. Plus, if you design or create your own forensic tools, you'll need to be aware of these issues.

OBSCURITY METHODS

An *obscurity method* is used by someone to try to obscure the true nature or meaning of some data, typically by changing its name or its contents. For our purposes, the term refers to a case in which someone has intentionally or accidentally changed the name or contents of a file, resulting in a file that will be either misinterpreted or disregarded in subsequent forensic analyses.

File Extension Renaming

Popularity:	5
Simplicity:	10
Impact:	5
Risk Rating:	**6**

Of all the types of obscurity methods encountered today, the most common and easiest to detect is *file extension renaming*. This can entail either renaming the entire filename or only the file extension to obscure which program can access it. Although you can now detect file renaming using a variety of automated techniques, you should be aware of its impact on your investigation, especially if you do not have time to run these tools (though you should do so in any investigation). If you are conducting an investigation and are asked to review documents of only a certain type, renamed files could cause you to overlook evidence contained in them.

File Signaturing

File signaturing allows you to determine what application has been used to create a file without regard to the file extension or filename. File signaturing compares some unique aspect of the file, typically the file's header and footer, to a database of signatures that relate to an extension. A *signature* in this case means a unique portion of data that exists in a certain file type that indicates which program can access it. For instance, a GIF image file always contains *GIF8* in the file header. Several tools can be used to determine a file's signature for you, and some of them are built into forensic tools.

> **NOTE** Renaming a filename or extension does not modify its contents, so file renaming or signaturing would not prevent a search from finding relevant data.

File Command

The UNIX `file` command will return the type of file according to its database of signatures. The database that `file` uses is called *magic* and is typically found in Linux at /usr/share. The most appealing feature of `file` is that the database is a plaintext file with standard delimiters. This allows the investigator to create and customize file signatures for investigations; thus, the database will grow as the investigator's cases do. To execute `file`, use the following:

```
# file top.jpg
top.jpg: JPEG image data, JFIF standard 1.02, aspect ratio, 100 x 100
```

As you can see, this execution of the `file` command on a JPEG image file returned information that not only tells you that the file is an image, but also provides the aspect ratio and the size of the image in pixels. Here, for example, we rename the file as *nothing. here* and rerun the `file` command, and the following occurs:

```
# mv top.jpg nothing.here
# file nothing.here
nothing.here: JPEG image data, JFIF standard 1.02, aspect ratio, 100 x 100
```

The name of the file had no bearing on the `file` command's ability to detect its true type. The `file` command is also available for Windows as part of the Cygwin package, which is found at www.cygwin.com.

EnCase

EnCase can detect file types and carry out file signature analysis to detect modified file types. After you load an image into EnCase, you can choose to validate the signatures on all of the files in the image when searching. To do so, click the search icon to open the Search dialog box, and then choose Verify File Signatures, as shown in Figure 9-1.

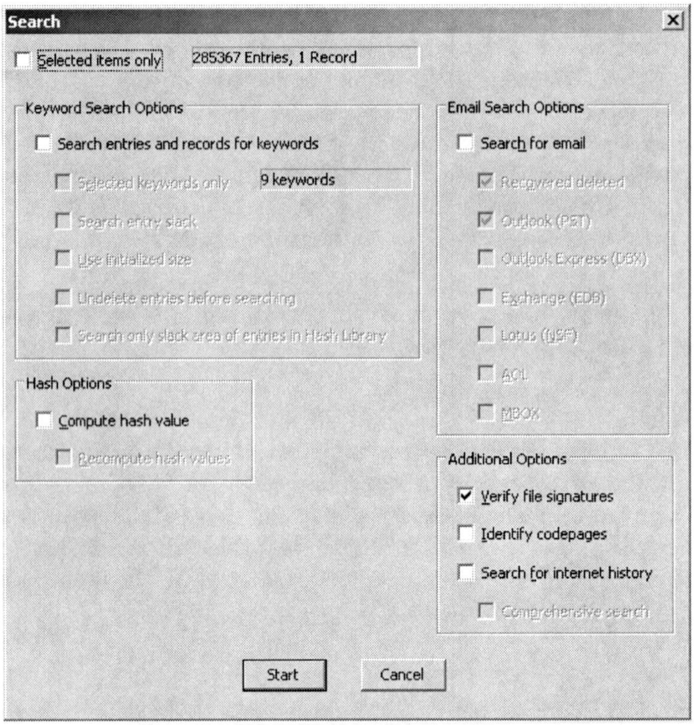

Figure 9-1   Choosing Verify File Signatures in EnCase

After the search is completed, the Signature column in the EnCase interface will be updated, as shown in Figure 9-2. If a file did not match its signature, this column would either read that it was mismatched or display the actual name of the file type, as shown in Figure 9-3.

Encoding Methods

Popularity:	5
Simplicity:	10
Impact:	10
Risk Rating:	8

Encoding means that a file's contents are changed in some way that can be easily reversed. Many times, a simple encoding mechanism called ROT13 is used. (ROT means *rotational* and *13* means the characters are rotated 13 times.) If someone were to run

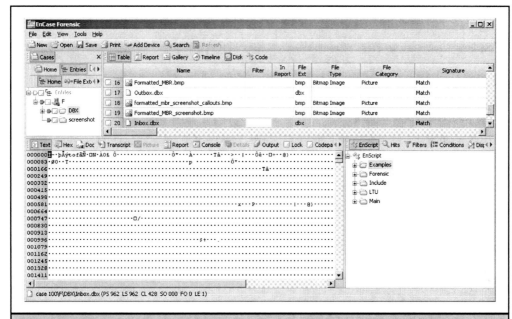

Figure 9-2   Viewing signatures in EnCase

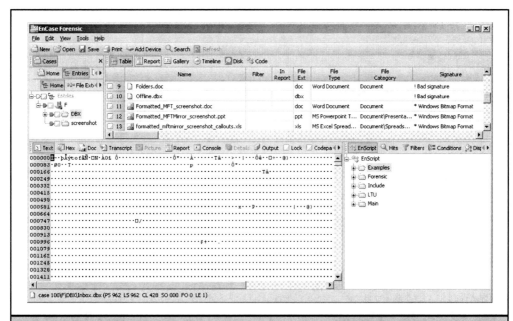

Figure 9-3   Viewing invalid signatures in EnCase

ROT13, the algorithm would take each character provided and replace it with a character 13 values in front of it. So, for example, an *A* would be replaced with an *N*. (*B* starts the count as element 1.) However, if you were to perform a search across encoded data, the search would not find the relevant data, as the expression the search was looking for would not decode ROT13 without being instructed to do so.

 ## Detecting Encoding

To detect that some kind of encoding has been used, such as ROT13, you would need to rely on file signaturing if the original extension remained on the filename. However, ROT13 and similar algorithms do not leave behind any standard signature, and no simple tool exists to detect its presence automatically. This doesn't mean, however, that detecting encoding cannot be accomplished. If a statistical analysis of the data were to occur with a ROT13 decoder, and the data was compared against the distribution of the English language, the distribution should be shown to be uniformly off by 13 places. ROT13 is especially popular for obscuring data contained in Windows registry keys.

> **NOTE**   You can find ROT13 decoders by searching for them on the Internet.

We have found that if backslashes (\), colons (:), or any other nonalphabetic characters appear in a file, a ROT13 decoder can help sort it out. ROT13 will rotate and replace alphabetic characters only; spaces, slashes, colons, and any other nonalphabetic symbols remain as is in the file after decoding. Although this will not help you in automatically decoding the data while searching across a disk, once you've found such data, you can subsequently search it.

> **NOTE**   Most people who are trying to hide data do not use ROT13; it is most commonly used to hide movie spoilers on Web pages and newsgroup postings. However, Microsoft has a long-standing "affair" with ROT13, so you should never assume that a ROT13 decoder won't be of help.

Compression Methods

Popularity:	10
Simplicity:	10
Impact:	10
Risk Rating:	**10**

Compression allows the content of a file to be reduced in size for storage and transmission. Compression algorithms analyze files to determine how the size of the file as it is stored can be reduced. This reduction is performed by analyzing the frequency of data in the file and applying an algorithm such as the deflation algorithms for gzip, PKZIP, and WinZip. It is not difficult to detect compressed files; however, most forensic tools do not permit direct access to compressed files during a search without some kind of prior interaction.

Accessing Compressed Files

Forensic tools provide a couple of options that can help you search within compressed data. You must handle compressed data differently from other data when searching and analyzing its contents. You cannot successfully search or analyze compressed data with a forensic tool until the data has been virtually uncompressed. The AccessData Forensic Toolkit (FTK) and EnCase both allow you to perform searches using this functionality. SMART and other systems require that you export these files out of the image, decompress them, and then search across them using separate tools.

Accessing Compressed Files with FTK

By default, the FTK opens and adds to its index the contents of any compressed files it finds on the image. In fact, if you are working with another forensic tool, such as SMART, which does not have the ability to virtually uncompress the files within the image, you can export that data for import into FTK, as it will allow you to perform searches.

Accessing Compressed Files with EnCase

Within EnCase, you can choose to mount a compressed file, as shown in Figure 9-4. *Mounting* here means that you are viewing the internal files within the compressed files. By mounting the compressed files, EnCase's search function will be able to search the files normally.

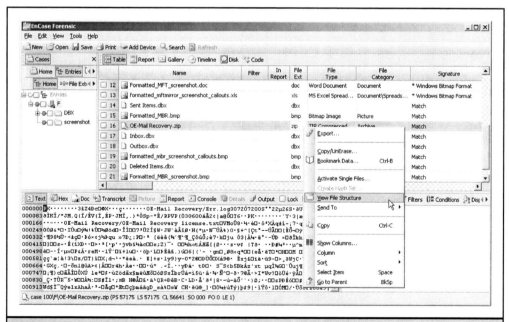

Figure 9-4 Mounting compressed files in EnCase

NTFS Alternate Data Streams

Popularity:	5
Simplicity:	3
Impact:	9
Risk Rating:	8

A popular topic that people like to bring up at anti-forensic talks is the *alternate data stream*, a secondary set of data that is attached to a single file within a NTFS file system. An alternate data stream is invisible to someone viewing the file through a Windows interface, such as Windows Explorer.

 **Searching Alternate Data Streams**

Most modern forensic tools can display alternate data streams. Specifically, FTK, EnCase, The Sleuth Kit, and SMART all detect alternate data streams and display them to the user when an NTFS image is provided. Even so, the presence of an alternate data stream does not prevent any tool that searches the physical disk from finding the data within the alternate data stream. An alternate data stream does, however, prevent you from detecting its existence on the disk without using a utility that can view its structure.

Slack Space

Popularity:	10
Simplicity:	10
Impact:	3
Risk Rating:	7

Slack space is a remnant of data that exists within a sector of data that has been overwritten. Specifically, slack space is the area of the sector that was not fully overwritten by a recent write to disk. Remember that sectors are fixed in their size, so, for example, if you wrote 3K of data to a 64K sector, the remaining 61K of data would not be reused. Instead, this unused sector space would still contain whatever data was written to it previously. Figure 9-5 shows a conceptual drawing of how slack space exists on the disk. While slack space is not a problem for any forensic tool that examines the physical disk itself, it is a problem if you are attempting to search a disk. If you were to search a disk using non-forensic utilities, you would miss all of the data in the slack space, while a forensic utility would allow you to see what is stored in the slack space and would even allow you to confine searches to it.

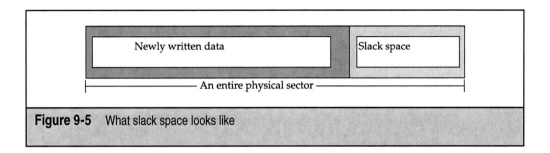

Figure 9-5   What slack space looks like

 ## Searching Slack Space

The answer to this dilemma is simply not to use standard search utilities in forensic investigations—that is, do attempt to search evidence using non-forensic tools and expect to re-create the data you would find using a forensic tool. All modern forensic tools examine the entire disk during searches and imaging and as such always capture and review the slack space.

PRIVACY MEASURES

Some of the recognized anti-forensic techniques are legitimate attempts to protect the privacy of the individual. Of course, this does not help us in our forensic examination of a system, so we need to be able to identify and access that protected information. In this section, we will address problems and solutions concerning privacy software, such as encryption, steganography, evidence eliminators, and disk wiping. We are not concerned here with spyware removers, pop-up blockers, or anti-spam tools, because these tools are meant to protect the privacy of information leaving a computer. We are interested in the privacy software that either protects or erases the data that exists on the disk.

Encryption

Only one true anti-forensic method will defeat forensic analysis of data other than wiping, and that is encryption. However, even encryption has its weaknesses depending on the type used. For data to be encrypted, it must first exist on the disk in its unencrypted form—normally. We say *normally* because it is possible for someone to download a document in memory and encrypt it in memory before the data even touches the disk, although this is very rare except in the cases of e-mail. Instead, most people choose to encrypt a file that already exists on a disk. This means the data could still be stored at three locations: in the original file on the disk if it is still present, in the contents of the deleted file in the unallocated and slack space, and in the original file in the swap or pagefile.

This section covers the two dominant types of encryption: symmetric and asymmetric. Note that technical detail on how encryption works and the methodologies behind it are beyond the scope of this book. What we will cover is how to identify the encrypted data and what tools you can use to break it.

Symmetric Key Encryption

Popularity:	5
Simplicity:	5
Impact:	10
Risk Rating:	6

Symmetric key encryption, in the most basic of terms, means that a symmetric key has been used to encrypt data: in other words, the same encryption key is used to encrypt and decrypt the data. Symmetric key encryption is only as strong as its key length and its ability to keep others from learning the key itself. If data is encrypted with a symmetric key, you will not be able to analyze or search its contents directly, and you will have to find some other method of identifying and accessing the data. In fact, you cannot determine whether data was encrypted with a symmetric algorithm unless you've identified it as such.

Identifying and Accessing Symmetric Key Encryption

You can identify symmetric key–encrypted files in two ways: either the file has an extension that is used by an encryption program to identify its files, or you will use a process known as *entropy testing*. Entropy testing is a process by which the randomness of the distribution of data within a file can be tested. The specific randomness can then be compared against a table of known algorithm randomness to identify whether a known algorithm has been used. This works well for all publicly known and documented encryption algorithms, because you can use them to document their randomness scale. However, if your suspect is using a new or nonpublic algorithm, an entropy test will not be able to identify the type of encryption used.

Identifying Symmetric Key Encryption with FTK

When any data is brought into FTK, you can run an entropy test on the data to determine whether it could be encrypted with a known algorithm. The Entropy Test option on the Evidence Processing screen, as shown in Figure 9-6, is displayed when evidence is added to FTK. After FTK has completed its indexing and analysis, encrypted files may be identified for you.

Accessing the Symmetric Key with the Password Recovery Toolkit

Accessing the symmetric key–encrypted data requires a tool that not only supports the algorithm but also provides the ability to do brute-force searching for the key. Although

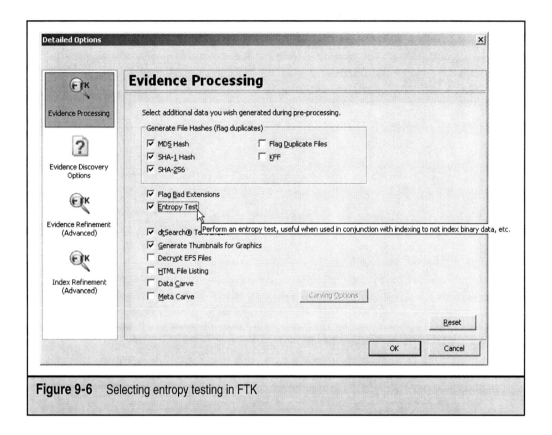

Figure 9-6   Selecting entropy testing in FTK

the original tool could be scripted against a list of keys of your own creation, several tools are available today to help you crack these encrypted files, such as AccessData's Password Recovery Toolkit (PRTK). While this is the not only tool available, we have used it successfully.

Here's how to crack a file with the PRTK:

1. Load the application.

2. From the main menu, choose Analyze | Select Files, as shown in Figure 9-7.

3. Select the files that have passwords you want to crack.

4. A Module Options screen, shown in Figure 9-8, appears, where you can select the password attacks that are available for the files you have selected. Some of these options have rather complicated instructions, but it is well worth your time to use as many attacks as possible to maximize your password cracking attempts. Click OK.

5. On the Select Profile screen shown in Figure 9-9, select one of the password profiles that customizes the dictionaries used and their order of use. Depending on what you know about the person who encrypted the files, careful selection

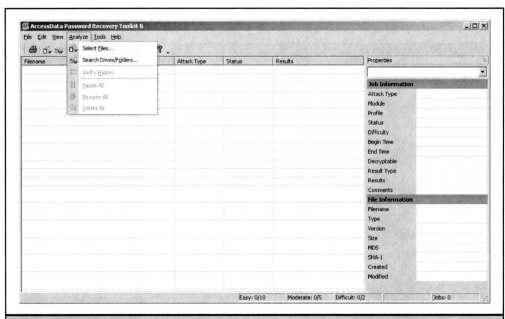

Figure 9-7   Selecting the files to crack

Figure 9-8   Viewing the status screen

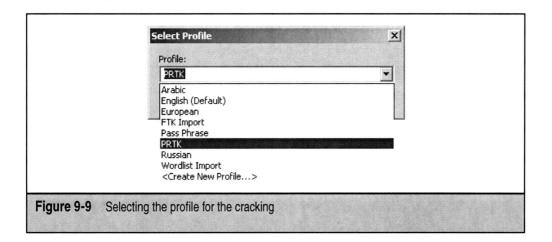

Figure 9-9   Selecting the profile for the cracking

of a profile can significantly affect your decryption time. For a more thorough explanation of profiles and dictionary selection, refer to the documentation provided with PRTK. Click OK to go back to the main screen.

After the password has been discovered, you will be notified of the fact. Then click the Open File button; for some types of files, you will have to enter the password to view the file in its application. For most file types, PRTK can automatically decrypt the file and save it to a location of your choosing, as shown in Figure 9-10.

Asymmetric Key Encryption

Popularity:	8
Simplicity:	8
Impact:	10
Risk Rating:	9

Asymmetric key encryption, in the most basic of terms, means that asymmetric keys have been used to encrypt data—in other words, one encryption key was used to encrypt and another was used to decrypt the data. Asymmetric key encryption is stronger than symmetric encryption because not only does the length of the key protect it, but the private key that is used to decrypt the data must be found before the data can be accessed. Having the public key—the key that is used to encrypt the data—will not allow you to access the original data. If data is encrypted with an asymmetric key, you will not be able to analyze or search the data contents; instead, you will have to find some other method of identifying and accessing the data.

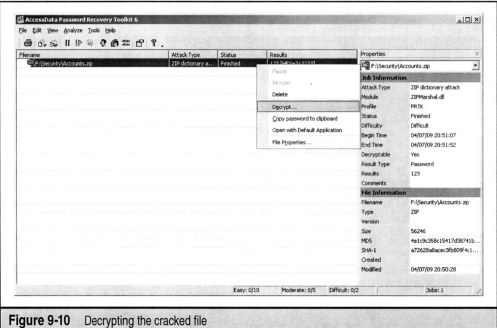

Figure 9-10   Decrypting the cracked file

Identifying and Accessing Asymmetric Key Encryption

You can identify asymmetric key–encrypted files in two ways: either the filename will have an extension such as .pgp that is used by an encryption program to identify its files, or you will have to use entropy testing, as discussed previously.

Identifying Asymmetric Key Encryption with FTK

When any data is brought into FTK, you can run an entropy test on the data to determine whether it could be encrypted with a known algorithm. Once FTK has completed its indexing and analysis, files that may have been encrypted will be identified.

Accessing the Asymmetric Key with the PRTK

Accessing the asymmetric key–encrypted data requires a tool that not only supports the algorithm but also provides the ability to brute-force the key. Although the original tool could be scripted against a list of keys of your own creation, ready-made tools, such as AccessData's PRTK, are available to help you. You should understand, though, that most asymmetric algorithms may require years of run time before the key can be determined. With a strong key, this can mean even hundreds of years. We can crack the passwords in the same way we did with symmetric encryption, except asymmetric keys take much, much longer to crack. AccessData's documentation states that it may take as long as

254 days to crack an asymmetric key, so before you try this method, be sure that you cannot recover data in any other way.

Distributed Network Attack

If you happen to have a few workstations that are sitting idle, AccessData's Distributed Network Attack (DNA) is ideal for password recovery. DNA works pretty much like PRTK, except it harnesses the processing power of multiple machines to decrypt passwords. A DNA server is installed on a network where machines running the DNA client can access it. A DNA Manager running on the DNA server assigns (aka distributes) small pieces of the searches to the DNA client machines on the network. By harnessing processing power this way, much faster decryption occurs. This setup is also ideal if you have a large amount of files to decrypt, but do not have the budget to send them out to a vendor for decryption.

Another bonus of using PRTK/DNA is that once it decrypts a file, it stores the password in a file called the Golden Dictionary. It then attempts to use those passwords first to decrypt other files before utilizing other attacks. This method is especially useful if a user set the same password for multiple files. To help increase the decryption speed, you can use FTK to export a full word index of an evidentiary image, and then import that index into PRTK/DNA. People frequently use phrases they use everyday as passwords since these are typically easier to remember. Using an index generated from a user's system significantly increases the likelihood and speed of finding a password.

The General Solution to Encryption

If you encounter encryption during a forensics examination, a simple and general solution is at hand: ask the suspect to supply the encryption key and the method by which he or she encrypted the data. Although this sounds simplistic and too good to be true, it often works. If you already have someone's data and he or she refuses to give up the encryption key, you can ask the court to order the person to produce the encryption key and the method used to encrypt the data. The person can, of course, refuse, but that will result in a contempt of court charge. The person will then be placed in a holding cell or have fines placed against him or her until the information is produced. This is how law enforcement normally deals with encryption.

● Steganography

Popularity:	3
Simplicity:	5
Impact:	10
Risk Rating:	6

Steganography is the ability to hide data inside another file. Using the steganography tools available today, suspects can even hide data inside JPEGs and audio files. When a sophisticated suspect is being investigated and remnants of a steganography tool exist, it would be very prudent of you to look for the existence of hidden data.

Detecting Steganography

Currently, we have used only one open-source tool to detect steganography with reliable results. Stegdetect (www.outguess.org/detection.php) allows you to inspect JPEG files for hidden data. Although other products are emerging on the market to deal with this problem, we have not used them so we cannot recommend them. The main commercial application that exists, Stego Suite by Wetstone (www.wetstonetech.com), is part of that list. In addition to these techniques, you can also search the system to determine whether steganography programs have been installed. However, we have yet to encounter steganography in a case, and it's hard to say when it will become a common forensics issue. Until then, though, keeping a steganography detection tool in your toolkit will allow you to perform a more thorough analysis when it is demanded.

Wiping

Popularity:	7
Simplicity:	5
Impact:	10
Risk Rating:	6

Wiping is a real problem when it's done correctly. It can be accomplished in many different ways, as you will see, but it shares some common aspects. For example, any data that has been truly wiped from the disk has been overwritten at least one time. Using the software tools that exist today, you cannot access any data that has been overwritten. You can determine whether wiping tools have been installed by reviewing the programs that exist and have existed on the disk, but you cannot bring that wiped data back.

Wiping a File

Popularity:	8
Simplicity:	7
Impact:	10
Risk Rating:	8

File wiping, also called *secure deletion*, is the most popular method and involves the removal of a file's data from the disk. File wiping will, in fact, overwrite the contents of the file as it existed on the disk, and upon completion of the wiping process that data is considered unrecoverable.

Detecting Wiping Activity

While it may be difficult or impossible to recover data that has been wiped, it is possible to determine whether wiping has occurred. One common trait of wiping is the existence of repeating characters over an entire file, the filename, slack space, and/or in unallocated space. The repeating character can be either the same character or a string of characters repeating over and over (such as *0123456789abcdefghijklmnopqrstufwxyz*). Some forensic software tools, such as EnCase, shown in Figure 9-11, come with a utility that will identify consecutive characters. These help in identifying consecutive sectors.

If you do find evidence of repeating characters, be sure that you verify when the operating was installed. It could be a new system build or a reinstalled operating system.

If you suspect wiping has occurred, check the registry (especially the UserAssist log) for any unusual programs that are installed or were run (see Figure 9-12). Even if a user has uninstalled the wiping utility, you may find evidence of it in the UserAssist log. Look for programs with atypical program names. Some wiping utilities delete themselves but also generate files of their own, such as temp or text files. Other wiping utilities clear the Master File Table (MFT) and generate several small files that appear to be deleted. Check

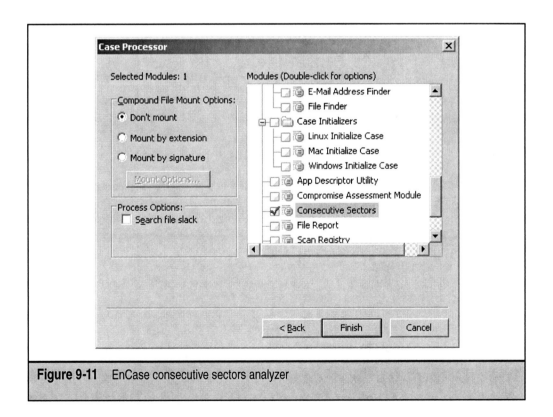

Figure 9-11   EnCase consecutive sectors analyzer

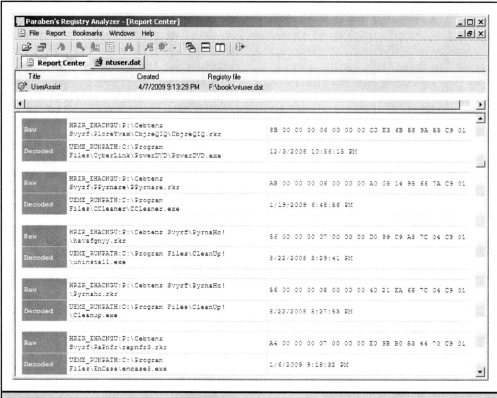

Figure 9-12 UserAssist log showing wiping tools

for unusual filenames and file extensions. Frequently, these temporary wiping files will have a consecutively ordered naming system such as BCW.001, where the number increases by 1 with each new file. These files also frequently have a uniform size, and there will be a lot of them, usually enough to fill the unallocated space completely. System restore points may also contain entries of wiping programs.

Another characteristic of wiping activity is the total lack of deleted files. Many wiping utilities will wipe deleted files. Of course, just because a system has no deleted files doesn't necessarily mean that wiping occurred, but when combined with other characteristics, it may point to wiping activity. If you find a program that you suspect is a wiping utility, you can test it by downloading it and installing it on an analysis machine. Run the program and then examine the machine for any forensic artifacts.

It is important that you keep an open mind and consider other possibilities before concluding that a drive was wiped. A user may have purchased a refurbished hard drive that was not completely wiped before it was purchased. Also note that some hard drive vendors use repeating characters in the formatting of their hard drives. In addition, some antivirus and security programs wipe files if they are unable to quarantine/clean them. It is up to you as the forensic examiner to eliminate these other possibilities before concluding a wipe has occurred. As you gain experience, you will recognize patterns of activity and be able to put the pieces together.

Recovering Remnants of Wiped Files

As stated, no silver bullet brings back this data. To recover a file that has been wiped, you can look in several places to determine whether at least parts and backups of previous copies of the file still exist. As a file is accessed, portions of it will be stored in various areas of the disk. You can look in the following locations for files that have been wiped:

- The pagefile or swap space if it was loaded into memory
- The MFT or FAT table to determine whether the file existed
- The NTFS journal if the data existed on an NTFS partition
- The slack space and unallocated space if it existed previously on the disk
- Any backups of the system

None of these solutions are bulletproof, but they can work. If you know part of the contents of a file, searching the physical disk for those contents could locate the file in any of these locations.

Wiping the Slack Space

Popularity:	4
Simplicity:	5
Impact:	3
Risk Rating:	4

Slack space wiping occurs in some of the more popular wipers. As discussed earlier, the slack space contains data from a file that was previously partially overwritten. Remember that slack space is simply unused space at the end of a fixed sector size, so a disk can be wiped of its slack space without modifying any of the data that is in use on the disk. When the slack space is wiped, the existing data is overwritten and can no longer be recovered.

Recovering Remnants of Files Stored in the Slack Space

To recover any files that existed in a wiped slack space, you can look in several places to determine whether the copies or backups of the data exist. As a file is accessed, portions of it will remain in areas of the disk. You can look in the following locations for data that was in the slack space:

- The pagefile or swap space if it was loaded into memory
- The MFT or FAT table to determine whether the file existed
- The NTFS journal if the data existed on an NTFS partition
- Any backups of the system

Again, none of these solutions are bulletproof. If you know part of the contents of a file, searching the physical disk for those contents could locate the data. Remember that data that existed in the slack space was already previously deleted, so the likelihood of recovery is low.

Wiping the Unallocated Space

Popularity:	7
Simplicity:	8
Impact:	10
Risk Rating:	8

Wiping the unallocated space takes a long time. Although unallocated space wipers are available, wiping the space can take an entire day. This is good news for us, because we rarely see a disk that has had its unallocated space wiped clean. However, if the unallocated space is wiped, the wiped data cannot be recovered.

Recovering Remnants of Data in the Unallocated Space

You can never fully recover the data that was stored in the unallocated space from the active portion of the disk because the unallocated space is too large. However, you can look in several places to determine whether some portion, copy, or backup of the data still exists:

- The NTFS journal if the data existed on an NTFS partition
- The MFT or FAT table to determine whether the file existed
- Any backups of the system

If you know part of the contents of a file, such as a specific phrase or name used in the file, searching the physical disk for those terms might locate the file in any of these locations. Remember that data that existed in the unallocated space was deleted previously, so the likelihood of recovery is low. Notice that we did not include the pagefile or swap space in our list of locations. This is because most wiping tools that wipe the unallocated space also overwrite the pagefile or swap space by filling the memory of the system. This will not *always* be the case, however, so make sure to check the pagefile and swap space as well.

Wiping a Disk

Popularity:	5
Simplicity:	7
Impact:	10
Risk Rating:	7

Of the available options for wiping, none is more detrimental to your investigation than a full disk wipe, which overwrites the entire physical disk. While it is obvious when the entire disk has been wiped, there is no way to recover the data.

Recovering Remnants of Data from Wiped Disks

Even though you cannot recover data that has been wiped from the disk, you can and should look for backups of the system itself. However, if you have received this disk in the course of a court investigation, you can have the judge either file sanctions against the person who has done this or order the person to produce any other data that may exist.

The filing for sanctions is important because it applies only if someone knowingly destroys evidence from any system that has been identified with a *protective order*—a document that a judge signs that states any evidence that exists on a system may not be deleted and must be preserved. Whether or not a preservation order exists, a judge will likely order an opposing party to produce more evidence if you can prove that some of the data provided was wiped. Also, many company policies prohibit the use of wipers on their property. As such, you should work with the company to determine whether such policies apply to this employee.

Reformatting the Drive/Reinstalling the Operating System

Popularity:	9
Simplicity:	7
Impact:	10
Risk Rating:	7

One of the most common information hiding methods we have found is reformatting the drive and reinstalling the OS. It's simple, it doesn't require any additional tools, and most people think that it deletes all the data that existed on the computer. As forensic examiners, however, we know better. The good news about this method is that unless a full format or a disk wipe was performed prior to the reformat, the data that existed from the previous installation can generally be found in the unallocated space. The unfortunate exception to this is the audit logs that may exist within the operating system. Typically these are placed on the disk first, so they are the first files to be overwritten when a new OS is installed. The other bad news about the reinstall is that the file system that existed previously is no longer intact, which means that the pointers to the file system are no longer there and you can't easily find the files. Think of it as a book with the pages ripped out and thrown in a pile. The examiner must search the pile, hoping to find the most important pages.

 ## Dealing with a Reformatted Drive

The first step in dealing with a reformatted drive is detecting it. Most modern operating systems keep some record of the install date. For instance, in Windows XP, this is a registry key and is generally the first place we look to determine whether a reinstall has occurred. Be careful, however, because sometimes just upgrading or refreshing the OS install can modify this date. As with all things in forensics, never rely on a single data point to draw a conclusion. You can also look to the metadata on the MFT itself to find the created date. Also, look at the creation date of the user accounts and registry files. These are generally created when a user is first created, which is often when the operating system was installed in its current state.

Once you have identified that the drive has been reformatted, finding the data that was once active on the drive is a less than straightforward process. As mentioned, the indexes used previously to access the data are no longer intact. This means that you must find alternative methods to locate the data, such as those that follow.

Keyword Searching

The most common and simplest way to find data in the unallocated space is to keyword search it with relevant terms. This is the analog of searching through each word on the pages to find sentences that are important. This is usually the first step that we use. The downside is that information recovered in this manner can be downright unwieldy. It is generally the raw code of the document in which it was stored and is not reader friendly. If you go this route, be prepared to allocate some serious time to formatting and cleaning up the results, and be prepared to have to explain to your nontechnical cohorts what exactly it is they are looking at and why it's important.

Recovering Folders

On several file systems, such as NTFS and FAT, the folder/directory information is stored separately from the file inode data. This means that even though the file records themselves are gone, you can still reconstruct the data from the folder files scattered throughout the disk. For example, on NTFS these files are known as $I30 files and can be carved out of the unallocated space just like any other file. While the exact contents vary from file system to file system, the general gist is these files contain the directory name and pointers to the files that are contained within that directory, as well as the relevant metadata such as modified, accessed, and created (MAC) times, in some cases.

Data Carving

Data carving is the black art of creating order out of chaos. The theory is you take a blob of electronic data, search it for file signatures that may indicate user-created documents and e-mail, and then "carve" that data out of the blob into the software's best guess of how the file used to look. A word of warning: When you go the data carving route, it will take a long time, and the results are going to be spotty at best. Nevertheless, we have had entire cases hinge upon documents that were located in the unallocated space and identified by data carving, so the returns can definitely be worth it.

It is best to leave data carving to a utility as opposed to trying some kind of manual process. With the exploding size of hard drives these days, it will take you years if you try to do it yourself. Our personal favorite utility is the data-carving functionality provided by Access Data's FTK. We understand that it is not always economically feasible to purchase a commercial tool, and some good open-source alternatives are out there. The grandfather of open-source carving is Lazarus, which was part of the original The Coroner's Toolkit (TCT) package. However, tools such as foremost and scalpel have since supplanted Lazarus as the options of choice for those involved in open-source investigations.

NOTE When deciding to go the data carving route, you should be aware of the specific type of file you are looking for and how it reacts to the carving process. For instance, we have had great luck with carving out images due to the extensive headers in the images, but much less luck with things such as Office documents and Personal Storage Table (PST) files due to the header structure and the sheer sizes of the files, which can end up scattered across the disk.

In summary, while a reformatted hard drive can be somewhat difficult to deal with, all hope is not lost. In fact, of all the various anti-forensic techniques, the potential for recovering data is most promising with this option. It may not be in the prettiest of formats, but generally you can find at least a small snippet of data here and there, an e-mail fragment, or even a prior UserAssist log in the unallocated space. And those snippets, combined with the fact that an attempt was made to hide the fact, can be an extremely powerful fact pattern. Just realize that you need to know exactly what you are doing, what your tools are doing, and how the individual data points link together, as you will get hammered on anything you find and present as evidence from the unallocated space.

CHAPTER 10

ENTERPRISE
STORAGE
ANALYSIS

Y̲ou can apply most of the tools and techniques covered so far in this book to any type of investigation. Despite their growing scope and complexity, most investigations scale well with the tools provided in other chapters. However, when you're forced to deal with terabytes of data with technology that was not designed for easy access from the desktop PC or laptop, you have to reevaluate your situation. This chapter defines how to deal with RAIDs (redundant array of inexpensive disks), SANs (storage area networks), tapes, and the large and expansive datasets that you will gather when dealing with a large investigation.

Many of the techniques discussed in this chapter also apply to electronic discovery. *Electronic discovery* relates to the collection, processing, review, and production of electronic documents in a lawsuit. Large datasets and wide ranges of system types are the rule, not the exception, in electronic discovery.

THE ENTERPRISE DATA UNIVERSE

Popularity:	10
Simplicity:	5
Impact:	10
Risk Rating:	**8**

First, let's define the enterprise environment. In this book, *enterprise environment* refers to all of the systems, servers, and data that make up a company's computing system. Most sets of data that are included in an enterprise scenario include *x*86-based servers (any operating system), non-*x*86 based servers, Network Attached Storage (NAS) systems, SAN systems, servers with RAIDs, tapes (lots of them), and hundreds to thousands of desktops and laptops. This list does not even include the portable devices now popular, such as PDAs, cell phones, and thumb drives, but those devices are covered in other chapters. Dealing with all of this data requires that you use tools that are made to handle searches of large quantities of data, so full-text indexing is also discussed here.

●ᐟ Working with RAID

Popularity:	10
Simplicity:	10
Impact:	10
Risk Rating:	**10**

RAID sets can be created by hardware or software such that either the hardware-based RAID controller creates and maintains the RAID set or the software does. A RAID allows several disks to be viewed by the operating system as a single disk. A RAID can pose a huge problem to an unprepared examiner, however, and most systems that use RAID are on server systems. This means that data stored on RAIDs is typically valuable, and the risk of modifying the RAID system can be harmful to its owner, as he or she would loose access to all of his/her data.

Unless configured as RAID 1, RAIDs will write data across all the disks that make up the RAID set. This means that you will have to image each disk in the RAID and keep the system powered down before you can allow the owner to access his or her data again. SAN and NAS systems, which are covered next, both use RAID.

Acquiring a RAID

Acquiring a RAID is similar to imaging other types of media, except that you need to be able to write down the disk's original sequence in the drive bays. If possible, you should also get the RAID configuration's settings stored within either the hardware card or the operating system. The system owner should be able to provide this information to you.

The information you need for the manual reconstruction of a RAID set is the RAID type, number of disks, stripe size or chunk size, and the order of the disks. This will allow the manual reconstruction of the RAID. Hardware RAID will have a supplemental bootup screen that shows where this information is available.

 Once you have acquired the RAID set, you can either reassemble it in Windows with Guidance Software's EnCase or within Linux using the raidtools set. It is difficult to replicate the hardware environment of the original RAID set. Additionally, re-creation using the original hardware could possibly overwrite the restored images in the process of initializing the RAID, resulting in high costs and potential failure.

Rebuilding RAIDs in EnCase

To rebuild a RAID in EnCase, you must select all of the RAID disks' images that you have created in EnCase when adding evidence to the case. EnCase will "automagically" recognize individual images that are part of a RAID set and attempt to reconstruct the RAID. The newly reconstructed RAID will then appear to you as a single disk.

Rebuilding RAIDs in Linux

To rebuild a RAID in Linux, you must have created each of the images with the dd utility. Once you have these images, you must mount them with the local loopback using the following command:

```
mount -o loop,ro /path/to/image /path/where/to/mount
```

Here, -o loop is for local loopback and ro is for read-only. If the mount was successful, you will have a read-only version of the image that will be treated as a disk on the Linux system. This means that you can use the raidtools program that comes with Linux to rebuild the RAID array. Since the RAID images are marked as read-only, you do not have to worry about raidtools or any other RAID toolkit overwriting or changing the image.

WORKING WITH NAS SYSTEMS

Popularity:	10
Simplicity:	10
Impact:	10
Risk Rating:	**10**

NAS allows remote systems to access disk sets created within them either as a network share or as a physical disk in the case of iSCSI (Internet SCSI). NAS systems are normally singular units that provide a large data volume as a single disk or a set of shares to a network. NAS systems can be as small as 200GB but can grow to several terabytes in size.

 ## Acquiring NAS

Unless the NAS you are working with supports iSCSI, you cannot make a direct connection to the NAS to create a true and correct image. Instead, you must shut down the NAS system and image each drive. This is not something to be taken lightly, as it could mean that you would have to shut down the NAS system for an entire day. Make sure that you plan ahead, and give the NAS owner time to prepare for the downtime.

Since the first edition of this book, some NAS systems such as NetApp have added a command shell that you can log into. If you are able to do this, mount a remote drive and use the dd syntax from Chapter 4 to image the NAS system to the network share you have mounted. You should increase the block size to make use of the network frame sizes and use the split command in case of a network error aborting your dd command.

 If you do not have to image a NAS system forensically, do not do it. Request a backup tape set instead.

WORKING WITH SAN SYSTEMS

Popularity:	10
Simplicity:	10
Impact:	10
Risk Rating:	10

SAN is a series of hard drives combined into different disk sets and available as physical disks to remote systems through some type of storage network, typically a fiber channel. SANs can be a potential nightmare to deal with in the field. A SAN is either a single system or a set of systems interconnected on a dedicated network, normally fiber, to create large sets of disks that can be assigned to specific servers or shared among multiple servers. A single SAN disk can span terabytes of data, which will quickly exceed the capacity of any single drive you put in front of it. Removing disks from a live SAN may cause the SAN to lose its index to data and cause the SAN owner to lose the data. So, if possible, do not remove the disks from the SAN itself.

 CAUTION If you do not have to image a SAN system forensically, do not do it. Request a backup tape set instead.

 ## Acquiring a SAN System

If you are required to make an image of a SAN network, you will need to gather some facts by asking the following questions:

- What type of network is connecting the SAN to the systems using it?
- On that network, are any ports free on the switch (fiber switch or Ethernet switch for iSCSI)?
- What type of adapter cards will you need? (Fiber adapter cards are not sold in stores, so make sure to ask this question early on.)

Next you need to do some research. Your best bet in creating an image of a dataset this large would be to bring a RAID set of your own on which to store all of this data. The only way to mount multi-terabyte volumes and acquire terabytes of data with high throughput—and without ever modifying the evidence—is to use a Linux system. If you use Windows to do this, the first thing Windows will do is *touch*—write to—the SAN disk. And, as you know, *modifying evidence is always a bad idea.*

Which distribution of Linux you choose to use depends on the adapter card you must install. Red Hat offers good support for adapter cards and is probably the best solution. Next, on most networks, the operational staff will have to add your system to its SAN so that you can do your job. Then you will have access to the SAN disks you need to image.

Make sure that any other system that could have access to the SAN is shut down; otherwise, the data can be modified as you collect it.

After you have completed all of this, your adapter card will provide mappings to SAN disks as SCSI devices. Use dd as you normally would, or use SMART. Hashing and verification will take some time, so plan on this taking at least a day to complete.

Many things can go wrong. We do not recommend that you attempt to image a SAN disk unless you are comfortable with the situation and are able to test all of your equipment beforehand. Remember that you don't want to harm what could be a million-dollar system.

WORKING WITH TAPES

Tapes, specifically backup tapes, come in a wide variety of flavors and have changed a great deal in the last decade. In fact, if you are given a tape that was written to more than five years ago, you may not be able to find a drive to read it. Tapes are slow and prone to breakage. Additionally, tapes are written with proprietary software in proprietary formats, and usually large sets make up a single backup. If you are doing any type of long-term work with an enterprise, you will encounter tapes. Your ability to work with those tapes and show competence doing so is important.

The current dominant tape formats, as of the year 2009, are Super Digital Linear Tape (DLT) and Linear Tape-Open (LTO). Many other formats, including 8mm, 4mm, quarter-inch cartridge (QIC), 16-track, and 32-track, among others, come in a large variety of formats themselves—including Advanced Intelligent Tape (AIT); Exabyte; IBM 3840; DLT 3000, 4000, 6000, 7000; SDLT1, SDLT220, SDLT320, SDLT600 and the value series DLT-VS; LTO1, LTO2, LTO3, LTO4; DDS-1, 2, 3, and 4; StorageTek, and more. You could spend lots of time and money trying to prepare to handle every type of tape media that exists. Instead, if you understand the basics of how tapes operate and how to interact with them, you will be well served in your efforts to deal with them.

If you receive more than 20 tapes to examine, you should look into getting a tape robot, also called an *autoloader*. It used to be that any type of tape robot was expensive and required large, complicated systems to work with, but this is no longer the case; the rapid change of tape technologies has created a large market for refurbished and used, low-priced tape robots. Most tape robots, and hopefully all tape robots you are required to handle, support a SCSI connection to your system. With the fall in prices of tape robots and the wide availability of SCSI components, a desktop system can quickly be adapted to handle any tape production. Your only concern, then, becomes how to store all of this data, a topic that is covered in Chapter 3.

Tapes have some inherit qualities that make forensic analysis easier: Almost all tapes have a write protect tab, meaning that upon setting the tab in the proper direction (this varies per tape), your drive will be unable to write to it. This is not a unique ability, but it means that you do not have to worry about tape write-blockers or modifying evidence on a tape while reading it. Before loading any tape, you should make sure to check the write-protect tab and set it properly.

Reading Tapes

Popularity:	10
Simplicity:	8
Impact:	10
Risk Rating:	**9**

When you are handed a tape, ask the following questions:

- Where did the tape come from?
- Who wrote the tape?
- What software wrote it?
- What type of drive wrote this tape?

While the model number on the tape can help you answer most of your drive-related questions, many times you cannot discover what software wrote the tape or even what is stored on it. If you cannot even determine what software wrote the data, let alone what is on the tape, the evidence becomes worthless and you cannot defend against its production to another party in a lawsuit. If this occurs, the opposing party can request to be given the tapes themselves in an attempt to access the data. The act of doing so can be seen as a "waiver of privilege." See Chapter 15 for details of privilege and evidence production.

Identifying Tapes

We have found it possible and beneficial to access the tape from its *raw device*—the actual path to the tape drive itself. This method lets you read data directly from the tape without having to use any translation or interpretation software in the middle. This can be done on Windows and UNIX systems.

Accessing Raw Tapes on Windows

Before accessing the raw tape drive in Windows, you should first install Cygwin, a free UNIX emulation environment for Windows, which is found at www.cygwin.com/.

UNIX utilities such as dd, covered in Chapter 4, were made to access tape devices and read the data out in blocks. Other utilities, such as type and more, will try to send the tape device control signals that it does not support, and your attempts to access the information will fail.

A plus side to accessing raw tape devices in Windows is that the Windows drivers automatically detect the block sizes of the tapes and any other tape-level settings, so you do not have to spend your time trying out different options.

After you have installed Cygwin, you can access the tape device by executing the following command:

```
dd if=/dev/st0 | less
```

Cygwin maps the standard Linux location of st0 or "standard tape 0" to the Windows physical, raw device \\.Tape0. This is the actual location the operating system uses to access the tape drive. The number at the end of st and Tape will grow to reflect each drive you attach to your system—so st1 = tape 1, st2 = tape 2, and so on. When the command has been successfully executed, abort it after the first screen of data has passed.

You may optionally choose to write out the data to a file by executing the following:

```
dd if=/dev/st0 > tape0
```

This command will write the tape's data out to a file called tape0. You are looking for data typically located in the first five lines of the file or screen. Most backup software identifies itself here with lines such as *arcserve*, *netbackup*, *tar*, and so on. If you are imaging one of the newer tape formats, make sure to pass on the sync option to dd or else the data speed of the tape output may cause dd to give an input/output error.

You can see a listing of all of the tape drives remapped for you by typing the following command:

```
mount
```

Accessing Raw Tapes on UNIX

Accessing the raw tape device under UNIX is actually the same as doing it in Windows using Cygwin. You use the same dd command with both operating systems. However, if you receive errors, you will have to attempt to guess the block size used to write to the tape. The easiest remedy to try is the following dd command:

```
dd if=/dev/st0 bs=0 > tape0
```

Setting bs, or block size, to 0 tells dd to detect the block size automatically. This usually solves the problem, but if it does not, you will need to install and use the MTX toolkit (available at http://mtx.opensource-sw.net/) to check the status of the tape drive. The MTX toolkit allows you to control attached tape robots manually and access tape devices at the raw SCSI level. Because no single solution to this problem exists, our recommendation would be to start at bs=64 and work your way up in powers of two.

If you are imaging one of the newer tape formats, make sure to pass on the `sync` option to `dd` or else the data speed of the tape output may cause `dd` to give an input/output error.

 NOTE If you are trying to acquire a modern tape, such as linear tape-open (LTO) or SDLT, you will need to pass in the `sync` option to `dd`:

```
dd if=/dev/st0 bs=0 conv=sync > tape0
```

Commercial Tools for Accessing Tapes

The only commercial tool for identifying and accessing tapes that we have used with good results is eMag Solutions' MediaMerge for PC (MM/PC), available at www .emaglink.com/MMPC.htm. MM/PC is one of few specialized tools available for accessing tapes in their raw form. This tool attempts to detect the tapes' format automatically and can read, extract, and—for some formats—catalog the contents of tapes without the original backup software that wrote the tapes.

MM/PC also lets you view the contents of a tape within a GUI environment. With the MM/PC environment, you can see the ASCII and hex values of the data on the tape and skip through the file records on the tape to view the type of data within it. MM/PC also offers a "forensic option" that allows you, if MM/PC supports the format, to inventory and capture the data on the tape without restoring the tape itself.

Preserving Tapes

Popularity:	*10*
Simplicity:	*10*
Impact:	*10*
Risk Rating:	*10*

You might think that a tape cannot be imaged, but this is not true. Using the dd tool, you can take an exact image of any tape that your tape drives can read. Imaging tapes can be useful when a tape has been reused multiple times in a backup. If older data on the tape was not overwritten—if the new backup did not completely overwrite the old— the older data can be restored by imaging the tape.

Imaging Tapes

The `dd` command can be used to image an entire tape, including every block that is readable on the tape. Use the following command:

```
dd if=/dev/nst0 bs=0 conv=noerror >> tape0.image
```

Note that `nst0` is used instead of `st0`. The device `nst0` means "non-rewinding." When you access `st0`, it will automatically rewind the tape before processing your request. Using `nst0`, you can continue to read into the tape with every consecutive execution of dd. To ensure that you have a complete image of the tape, you must execute the dd command multiple times to guarantee that you have hit the end of the tape and not just a blank file marker. A good rule of thumb is five end of tape error messages. This command is the same on Windows or UNIX systems.

Creating Too Much Evidence

Popularity:	*10*
Simplicity:	*10*
Impact:	*10*
Risk Rating:	**10**

One of the major misconceptions that exists when collecting large amounts of data from many systems is that forensic imaging is the only option available to you. Another larger and more damaging misconception is that forensic imaging is something that should be applied broadly and across any potentially relevant system.

Truth is, if you are collecting a large amount of data from a large number of systems, it is usually in support of some kind of legal action at the request of the court. When you are doing anything in support of a legal action, you must be aware of the ramifications of your decisions in court. In a nutshell, creating too much evidence is almost as bad as not preserving any at all. Why? Because when you create a forensic image without either a court order or the specific understanding that the system involved contains some amount of relevancy to the case, you remove several of the protections on which your legal counsel depends.

Specifically, you have lost your client's counsel most of his or her argument for "overly burdensome requests" that protects your client from having to spend exorbitant amounts of money to provide evidence to the court. For example, suppose you were approached in either an internal or external capacity to collect data from 100 users. If you decided on your own, without a request from counsel or the court, to incur the expense of creating forensic images of all 100 users' machines, you have basically cost your client unnecessary money, time, and possibly important defense tactics. If the opposing counsel were aware of the images' existence (and such information is normally discovered during depositions), the opposing counsel could make a motion for the court to order their production. Because your side would incur no additional costs in creating the images in response to the order, your counsel would have lost a major tactic in defending his or her side from overly broad evidence productions. (Evidence productions are discussed in detail in Chapter 15.)

Live File Collections

A *live file collection* is a fancy way of saying that you are copying, while preserving the MAC times of active files, to a central location for preservation, review, and production to opposing counsel. The MAC times of active files include Modification, Access, and

Creation or Change, depending on the operating system. *Active* files are known to the operating system and are not marked for deletion.

This obviously is not a technically difficult problem, but it is, however, a logistical and organizational problem. You need to discover where the relevant data exists, which users are relevant, which departments are relevant, which servers they use, and other similar information. After you have defined the scope of where your data lies, you need to deploy a tool that users can run to collect their own data or one that can access their systems over the network to allow the data to be copied.

Collecting Live Data from Windows Systems

Two tools that we have used to collect data in this fashion are Pixelab's XXCopy, found at www.xxcopy.com, and Microsoft's RoboCopy, available in the Windows resource kits. Pixelab provides a free version of XXCopy, while RoboCopy is available only as a free tool within the resource kit.

Preserving Files with XXCopy

XXCopy is a DOS-based tool that takes a large variety of command-line parameters for a wide range of results. We recommend the following syntax:

```
C:\xxcopy c: z: /s /h /tca /tcc /tcw
```

This would tell XXCopy to copy all of the files including all subdirectories, /s, and all hidden files, /h, from the c: drive to the z: drive. The switches /tca, /tcc, and /tcw tell XXCopy to preserve the access, creation, and modification times of the files. It does so by taking the original times from the source files and applying them to the destination files.

Preserving Files with Microsoft RoboCopy

RoboCopy, short for Robust File and Folder Copy, in the most recent version by default will preserve all of the modification, access, and creation times. The syntax for executing it is as follows:

```
C:\robocopy c: z: /e
```

This tells RoboCopy to copy all files from the c: drive to the z: drive for all subdirectories in c:.

FULL-TEXT INDEXING

When you encounter large datasets (such as those greater than 300 gigabytes), you may find yourself with a "needle in the haystack problem." The search features of most of the forensic and system tools we have discussed so far are not designed for continuous searches against large amounts of data. What you need is a way to take all of the data, which in some environments can grow to terabytes in size, and place it in some kind of search tree. The exact type of tree structure used varies by vendor.

Binary Search Trees

A binary search tree is a structure that allows your system to store dataset information in two *subtrees*, one left and one right. Data is sorted by key into one of the subtrees, and the key is used to determine in which subtree the search should continue. The search process continues to divide the information into two parts, narrowing the search to one part in sequence, until the sought item is found. The binary search tree enables you to search terabytes of data in seconds instead of hours or days.

The overall benefit is that you can search through any dataset of any size, the worst case being log base 2 n times, where n is the size of your data. This means that instead of searching through 500 gigabytes of data sequentially, you can find the specific words that make up your search in 39 steps, and you can search through 5 terabytes of data in 43 steps!

Compare this to the steps required to perform multiple sequential searches through the dataset: assuming we are examining 64k-byte blocks from a drive, it would take 7,812,500 steps to search 500 gigabytes of data completely and 78,125,000 steps to search through 5 terabytes of data completely. While the indexer must also perform these steps initially, for each subsequent search of the data it would only have to perform the log base 2 n searches.

This means you can search terabytes of data in seconds. Now you can perform all the searches requested without suggesting it will take a year and you'll call them when you're done. The general rule we follow is that if you plan to search the data only once, perform a linear search; if you plan to search it more than once, create a full text index using a binary search tree.

Missing Data When Indexing

Popularity:	10
Simplicity:	10
Impact:	10
Risk Rating:	10

As is often the case, you pay a price when using additional functionality, and in the case of indexing, the price is encoded files. When indexing, you must first create a *full-text index* of all of the data. This means that the indexer, the program that creates the index, must be able to distinguish words from your data to be included in the binary tree. While this is not a problem for source code, basic e-mail, and text files, it *is* a problem for Office documents, e-mail attachments, e-mail container files (such as Microsoft Outlook PST files), and any other file that is not made up of plain ASCII characters. You need to use an indexing program that will convert these file types for you, or you will have to convert the file types yourself. We will cover both types of indexing.

Glimpse

Glimpse is a free full-text indexing program that is packaged with a search interface called Webglimpse, available at www.webglimpse.org/. Glimpse will give you incredibly advanced indexing options such as merging indexes, appending and deleting files from indexes, and even using regular expressions against indexed data. Webglimpse even offers free and low-cost options for support. However, Glimpse does not automatically convert files for you. Glimpse expects that the files fed to the program will be in ASCII text form.

The Webglimpse package addresses the file-conversion challenge with a user-customizable listing of programs to call to convert your files. The Webglimpse Web site even provides links and instructions on how to convert the most popular file formats that users encounter. Adding file types and finding conversion utilities as well as testing their accuracy are up to you. Glimpse is not for the novice user, but with some experience and work, you'll find that Glimpse is a great free indexing system that will make quick work of your data searches.

Webglimpse acts like a familiar web search engine to search the data. In fact, Webglimpse was created primarily to allow for indexed searches of Web sites. The search interface will allow you to select and search across your indexes and will highlight the hits in an abstract of the file on the Web page that it returns. Anyone with a web browser can access the Webglimpse interface, and multiple users can search it at once. Also, Glimpse supports the ability to search the index directly from the command line, making for some great automation possibilities. Glimpse code must be compiled, but it can be compiled in either Linux or through Cygwin in Windows.

dtSearch

dtSearch leads the market of mid-range cost indexing systems and can be found at www.dtsearch.com. dtSearch has several configurations of its indexing system, including just the dtSearch engine for implementation into other products. dtSearch has support for the most popular data formats such as PST files, Office documents, and zip files and will create a full-text index of the data.

dtSearch allows you to search your indexes via a GUI. You pick the index you would like to search and enter in keywords, and then dtSearch will generate a list of files that match your query. Selecting a file will bring up a preview of it with the search strings highlighted within. dtSearch does not have a command-line interface and is available for Windows only. Another product, called the dtSearch engine, does support Linux as well as Windows.

AccessData's Forensic Toolkit

AccessData's Forensic Toolkit (FTK), found at www.accessdata.com, makes use of the dtSearch indexing engine. In addition to the standard file types supported by dtSearch, FTK offers internal conversions. FTK also allows you to index whole images: just feed FTK an image from Guidance Software's EnCase, ASR Data's SMART, or a dd image, and it will build a full-text index of all of the files and the unallocated space. When you are dealing with a large case, this can be a very useful feature that will quickly pay back its cost.

FTK allows you to search indexes through its GUI. You pick the index you want to search, enter in keywords, and FTK will generate a list of files that match your query. Selecting a file will bring up a preview of it with the search strings highlighted within them. FTK does not have a command-line interface and is available for Windows only.

 ## Paraben's Text Searcher

Paraben's Text Searcher, found at www.paraben-forensics.com, also makes use of the dtSearch indexing engine. Text Searcher allows you to search your indexes through its GUI. You pick the index you would like to search, enter keywords, and Text Searcher will generate a list of files that match your query. Selecting a file will open a preview of it with the search strings highlighted within. Text Searcher does not have a command-line interface and is available for Windows only.

 ## Verity

Verity, found at www.verity.com, is the 500-pound gorilla of indexers. Verity's product line of engines and enterprise-ready indexing systems do not come cheap, but they can handle the largest and most complex situations. Verity's product line is not a simple desktop-driven application that can be installed in an hour. Rather, the company's server systems require configuration and customization to create the results you desire. You may find few situations that demand a system as intensive as Verity, but in the event that you do, it is well worth the cost.

EnCase

EnCase, discussed throughout this book, has introduced full-text indexing of images as of version 6.

MAIL SERVERS

When dealing with the types of data and systems we describe in this chapter, it is only a matter of time before you have to deal with mail servers. Mail clients have data files designed to be accessed and have open interfaces to them, such as PST and NSF, with well-documented APIs and tools for using them. Mail servers, on the other hand, are designed to be accessed only by their own systems. Microsoft Exchange, Lotus Domino Mail Server (with Lotus Notes), Novell GroupWise, Netscape iPlanet, and others all contain proprietary methods for storing and accessing e-mail stored on the mail server.

Microsoft Exchange

Popularity:	*10*
Simplicity:	*10*
Impact:	*10*
Risk Rating:	*10*

Exchange servers keep their e-mail data in a file called priv.edb. The .edb, or exchange database format, is a Microsoft database with no known published structure. If you have the time, you can access the Microsoft Developers Network documents, located at http://msdn.microsoft.com, and try to reverse-engineer a solution yourself, but chances are you do not have that kind of time. Being able to search the .edb directly allows you to pull relevant e-mails from the current system and any backup of the system that may relate to your investigation.

Ontrack PowerControls

Ontrack PowerControls, available at www.ontrack.com/powercontrols/, is an excellent tool for accessing, searching, and extracting e-mails from an .edb. Not only will PowerControls allow you to access an .edb on the disk, but a licensed version of the software will also allow you to extract .edb files directly from tapes written by Veritas NetBackup, Veritas Backup Exec, Computer Associates BrightStor ARCserve, Legato NetWorker, IBM Tivoli, and NT Backup, the free backup utility that comes with Windows Server since Windows NT. PowerControls does the job well, while it is a bit more expensive than the other options. PowerControls has two limitations in the enterprise environment: the lack of automation capabilities and the inability to control tape robots while using the extract .edb tape tool in the extraction wizards.

Paraben's Network E-mail Examiner

On the commercial but lower cost end is Paraben's Network E-mail Examiner, or NEMX, available at www.paraben-forensics.com. NEMX will allow you to access, search, and extract messages from an .edb. However, it does not give you the tape-restoration abilities that are found in PowerControls. NEMX, like PowerControls, does not provide for any automation ability.

Recovery Manager for Exchange

Quest Software's Recovery Manager for Exchange, at www.quest.com/recovery-manager-for-exchange/, offers functionality that other tools in the market do not offer. While Recovery Manager for Exchange (RME) allows you to access, search, and extract messages from an .edb, it also allows the software to act as a virtual Exchange server. Why is this useful? If you are restoring Exchange servers from a set of tapes, which is typically the case when you are asked to do this type of work, you can point the backup software at the system with RME installed and running in emulation mode. In emulation mode, RME will take the restored data as if it were an Exchange server and write it to an .edb locally, where you can extract the messages. If you are dealing with a software package that will not allow you to restore an Exchange agent–based backup without restoring it to an Exchange server, the emulation mode is immensely useful. In addition, you can interoperate with the native backup software and take advantage of its abilities to use tape robots in automating the restoration using emulation capabilities.

 ## Microsoft Backup

If you are looking to make a backup of an exchange server and collect its data, Microsoft Backup is able to create a .bkf file that contains the running Exchange server's .edb. You can then extract it out as an .edb without Exchange and use it on the tools we mention here to access it.

 ## Microsoft Exchange Server

The final option you have is to install a new Microsoft Exchange Server, at www.microsoft.com/exchange/default.mspx, on a Windows server system. (MS Exchange will not install on Windows XP.) You can then re-create the configuration to emulate the name and domain of the original server. In doing so, you can either restore messages to the Exchange system using the backup software or you can have it access a restored .edb by loading the Exchange Server in what is called *recovery mode*. Recovery mode allows the Exchange Server to start up and access the .edb as it would normally, allowing you access to the messages within it. Exchange does not provide the ability to search across the text of mail in mailboxes, so you will have to export out each user's mailbox into a PST and search it afterward to determine whether it contains the evidence you're looking for. You can, however, search by sender, recipient, and date. This is by far the least preferred solution, and unless you already have licenses for Exchange, this is also likely the most expensive option.

 ## Lotus Domino Mail Server and Lotus Notes

Popularity:	6
Simplicity:	10
Impact:	10
Risk Rating:	8

IBM's Lotus Notes mail client has a corresponding mail server called Domino. Lotus Notes client and server both store their data in Notes Storage Facility (NSF) files. Lotus supports *real encryption*—the Lotus server and client use public key encryption algorithms that cannot be easily broken. Thankfully for us, the option to use encryption is not the default configuration. If you encounter an encrypted NSF, you should inform your client that the encrypted data might not be recoverable.

Network E-mail Examiner

NEMX will allow you to access, search, and extract messages from an NSF. NEMX, as stated earlier, does not provide for any automation ability.

Recovery Manager for Notes

Quest Software's Microsoft Exchange Email Recovery and Domino Recovery, found at http://wm.quest.com/, offers functionality that other tools in the market do not offer. It allows you to extract for NT Backup and other tape types to extract NSF files from tape to PST.

Domino Server

The other option is either to automate the Lotus Domino Mail Server through Lotus script or install a new Domino server and configure it as a recovery server to access the existing NSF.

Novell GroupWise

Popularity:	4
Simplicity:	10
Impact:	10
Risk Rating:	8

Novell's GroupWise mail server has been around for quite some time. However, there has never been an easy way to recover data from its local e-mail database. GroupWise is a closed architecture that by default stores all e-mail on the GroupWise server and allows you to archive e-mail off it to a local system. However, be aware that some systems are configured to delete e-mail messages automatically after a certain number of days, so make sure to examine the GroupWise server configuration before waiting to capture data.

Transend Migrator Forensic Edition

One of the few tools available to convert GroupWise data is Transend Migrator Forensic Edition, available at www.transend.com. Transend Migrator will allow the conversion of GroupWise data to a number of different formats so you can access the e-mail in one of the other tools we have covered in this book, such as AccessData's FTK. While Transend Migrator can connect to a GroupWise server to do the conversion, the GroupWise server must exist first for it to work. So in either case you are stuck installing a GroupWise server and recovering the previous mail database.

Network E-mail Examiner

Good news since the last edition of this book: NEMX now allows you to access, search, and extract messages from a GroupWise server. NEMX, as stated earlier, does not provide for any automation ability or tape extract abilities. If you keep the parent directory that contains NGWGUARD.DLL and the three directories ofmsg, ofuser, offiles underneath in a place accessible to NEMX, it can find and recover the messages and deleted messages from a GroupWise data store and export them to PST.

 ## Sun's iPlanet

Popularity:	5
Simplicity:	10
Impact:	10
Risk Rating:	**8**

Sun's iPlanet mail server is a UNIX-based mail system that shows its origins in its mail storage. The iPlanet system stores each individual message in a RFC-822–complaint e-mail format within a hive-like directory structure named after the user. This makes your life much easier as you do not have to worry about dealing with proprietary databases for accessing the messages.

 ## Searching RFC-822 and Decoding MIME

To access e-mail and attachments in an iPlanet server, you need some tools that can search RFC-822 and decode MIME. Paraben's E-mail Examiner and AccessData's FTK will allow you to do this. Using any search utility, you can access the text of the e-mails. For MIME encoding, you can also combine some open-source tools such as munpack to extract the attachments for further searching.

CHAPTER 11

E-MAIL ANALYSIS

Today's world functions on e-mail. E-mail is one of the fastest growing forms of communication and one of the most common means for transferring information about people, places, and activities. People will continue to use e-mail and the Internet to conduct business, legitimate or not. About 210 billion e-mails were sent each day in 2008, according to the Radicati Group (www.radicati.com/); that's 150 billon more e-mails per day than forecasted by IDC for 2006, and e-mail continues to grow by orders of magnitude each year. Nearly half of these e-mails contain personal information.

E-mail analysis today is one of the most common tasks in an investigation, with so much day-to-day business being conducted from e-mail and e-mail–enabled mobile devices. Personal and business information is being sent, received, and forwarded back and forth over mobile devices to traditional e-mail accounts.

This chapter discusses tools and techniques you can use to reconstruct client and web-based e-mail activities from the perspective of the local hard drive. (Enterprise server investigations are covered in Chapter 10, and cell phone and PDA investigations are covered in Chapter 13.) Although a single chapter can't cover every tool and technique available today, we do cover mainstream e-mail investigative techniques applicable for use in a corporate environment.

This chapter breaks up content into client-based and web-based e-mail. *Client-based* e-mail refers to programs installed on the client for reading e-mail, such as Outlook Express, Outlook, and generic UNIX readers. *Web-based* e-mail refers to online e-mail resources such as Yahoo!, Gmail, Hotmail, AOL, and Excite that are usually accessed through a browser.

Three key interesting components of an e-mail include the e-mail headers, text, and attachments. Additionally, other items useful to investigators can include message flags, certificates, or requested receipts for delivering or opening an e-mail.

FINDING E-MAIL ARTIFACTS

In the scenarios that follow, programs and techniques used to view e-mail data and extract relevant artifacts are discussed. If available, we discuss how to use professional products such as Paraben's E-mail Examiner, Paraben's Network E-mail Examiner, OutIndex, Guidance Software's EnCase, and Access Data's Forensic Toolkit (FTK). Other methods include using the native e-mail client or various tricks to get around simple controls. Remember that multiple tools and methods are available for searching and analyzing this data. Choose the tools and methods that best fit your needs.

Client- and web-based e-mail readers share much in common. Both can have e-mail headers, proofs of receipt, attachments, and more. Both generally follow the same rules as outlined in the RFCs (requests for comments). However, some differences are worth exploring, including the methods for viewing, location of evidence, and ease with which you can access and recover the evidence. We will get into more of this in each of the following sections.

CONVERTING E-MAIL FORMATS

In some instances you may need to convert e-mail from one format to another before you begin your investigation, or you may need to present e-mail results in a format that is easier for you or another party to analyze and review.

Transend Migrator (www.transend.com/) is a great tool for performing a number of e-mail tasks. Transend will allow you to convert EML, Text, mbox, and many other e-mail formats to Outlook PST format. The Forensic version of Transend will let you convert various e-mail formats to e-discovery and Compliance document management file formats such as PDF, TIFF, and HTML.

When dealing with OST files, you may need to repair a damaged OST or convert an Outlook OST file to PST format. Kernel for OST to PST Conversion by Nucleus Data Recovery (www.nucleustechnologies.com/exchange-ost-recovery.html) allows you to convert OST files to PST.

Paraben's Network E-mail Examiner may confuse you with the title being nearly identical to the Paraben E-mail Examiner, but these tools are entirely different. Network E-mail Examiner offers some rare and valuable features, such as the ability to convert mailboxes from Novell GroupWise, Lotus Notes, or EDB databases to Outlook PST, MSG, or EML. Network E-mail Examiner will also allow you to perform searches or browse the mailboxes in the NSF, DB, and EDBs.

OBTAINING WEB-BASED E-MAIL (WEBMAIL) FROM ONLINE SOURCES

In some scenarios, you may need to download webmail from Yahoo!, Gmail, or Hotmail. This can require multiple tools such as Outlook Express for Windows Live Mail (aka Hotmail) along with a Post Office Protocol/Internet Message Access Protocol (POP/IMAP) client such as Outlook or Thunderbird for Gmail and Yahoo!. In addition, getting the e-mail in the correct format may require some scripting experience.

You can download Gmail with a POP client by enabling POP on your Gmail account:

1. Click the Settings link.
2. Click the Forwarding and POP/IMAP tab.
3. Choose the Enable POP For All Mail option, and then click Save Changes.

Transend Migrator Forensic can simplify this task by grabbing Yahoo! e-mail in an easy three-step process:

1. In Transcend select POP Server from the Convert From drop-down box and Exchange/Outlook from the Convert To drop-down box. Then click Next.

2. Enter your username, POP server, and password. Then click Next.

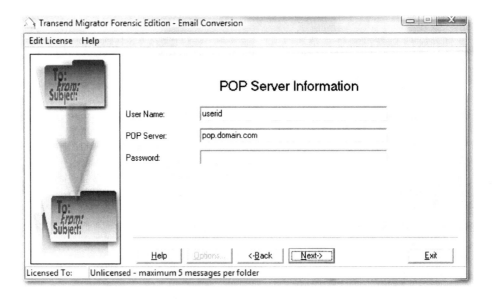

3. Enter a PST filename and password, if required, and then click Next.

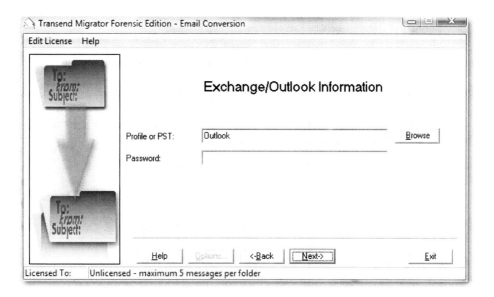

4. Select the folder you want and click Next.

5. Click Run.

CLIENT-BASED E-MAIL

Popularity:	10
Simplicity:	10
Impact:	8
Risk Rating:	**9**

Client-based e-mail includes programs such as Outlook and Outlook Express. Client e-mail is typically stored on the hard drive in an e-mail archive. This is important to know, as it increases the likelihood that you will find the information you need. Client-based e-mail is typically easier to work with than Internet-hosted mail in corporate environments because the e-mail exists on a company-owned asset. In the case of client-based e-mail, typically both the incoming and outgoing e-mails are recorded; this is not always the case for Internet-hosted e-mail.

An important point for overloaded corporate investigators is ease of access to the mail server. Investigators will have access either to the e-mail on the suspect's computer or the company-owned servers. Either way, this is much easier than demanding e-mail from an externally hosted e-mail provider. In many cases, the latter choice is not practical. (E-mail server investigations are covered in Chapter 10.)

Microsoft Outlook PST

Popularity:	10
Simplicity:	10
Impact:	8
Risk Rating:	9

Outlook, installed with the Microsoft Office suite, is the most popular e-mail client used in large corporations. It is also one of the most popular e-mail archive formats encountered in corporate investigations.

 ## PST (Microsoft Outlook) Examination Tools

The most well-known tools for reading Outlook files are Paraben's E-mail Examiner, Guidance Software's EnCase, Access Data's FTK, and Microsoft Outlook. For the open source advocates, a great tool is included in the libPST package.

Paraben's E-mail Examiner works by using a PST converter to translate the contents of the PST file into a generic UNIX mailbox format. The text file is then easily read and searched by E-mail Examiner. Paraben's product supports a large number of e-mail formats and is very fast in converting the PSTs. You can use EnCase by Guidance Software to open and search the contents of the PST directly. EnCase lets you use the same tool for e-mail that you use for locating other artifacts on the drive.

> **NOTE**   If you have EnCase and haven't updated to the latest version, you should do so. The newer versions have support for Outlook Compressible Encryption in searches.

FTK is also capable of searching through multiple mail files such as Outlook, Outlook Express, AOL, Netscape, Yahoo!, Earthlink, Eudora, Hotmail, and MSN e-mail. FTK provides an intuitive interface for reviewing large amounts of e-mail and will now identify and segregate webmail from other e-mail.

The open-source tool readPST from the libPST package is a project of SourceForge headed by Dave Smith. When you're done using readPST, you can use UniAccess to convert UNIX mail back into PST and other formats.

Examining Outlook Artifacts

Table 11-1 provides a helpful list of MS Outlook data and configuration files. Some of the folders have hidden attributes. You can change the Windows Explorer view to show hidden files by choosing Tools | Folder Options | View | Show Hidden Files And Folders.

Examining Artifacts with E-mail Examiner

E-mail Examiner (www.paraben-forensics.com/examiner.html) simplifies the complexity of the PST mail store by converting it into a generic mailbox format. Because of this

Data and Configuration Files	Location
Outlook data files (.PST)	*drive*:\Documents and Settings*<user>*\Local Settings\Application Data\Microsoft\Outlook
Offline folders file (.OST)	*drive*:\Documents and Settings*<user>*\Local Settings\Application Data\Microsoft\Outlook
Personal Address Book (.PAB)	*drive*:\Documents and Settings*<user>*\Local Settings\Application Data\Microsoft\Outlook
Offline Address Books (.OAB)	*drive*:\Documents and Settings*<user>*\Local Settings\Application Data\Microsoft\Outlook
Outlook contacts nicknames (.NK2)	*drive*:\Documents and Settings*<user>*\Application Data\Microsoft\Outlook
Rules (.RWZ)	*drive*:\Documents and Settings*<user>*\Application Data\Microsoft\Outlook. Note: If you use the rules import or export feature, the default location for .RWZ files is *drive*:\Documents and Settings*<user>*\My Documents
Signatures (.RTF, .TXT, .HTM)	*drive*:\Documents and Settings*<user>*\Application Data\Microsoft\Signatures
Dictionary (.DIC)	*drive*:\Documents and Settings*<user>*\Application Data\Microsoft\Proof
Message (.MSG, .HTM, .RTF)	*drive*:\Documents and Settings*<user>*\My Documents

Table 11-1 Summary of Microsoft Outlook Data Configuration Files

simplicity, the search capabilities are excellent. E-mail Examiner runs in a Windows environment and supports a wide variety of mail formats. Support for MS Outlook .PST files is available through Paraben's PST Converter, which is distributed with E-mail Examiner. This is similar to the conversion process used when converting AOL files. Here's how to do it:

1. Start the PST Converter.
2. Choose File | Import PST Files to open the PST Converter dialog box shown in Figure 11-1. If you do not see this command on the File menu, go to Program Files\Paraben Corporation\E-mail Examiner, and double-click pstconv.exe.
3. When the PST Converter dialog box opens, select the PST files to convert into a generic format by clicking Add Files.

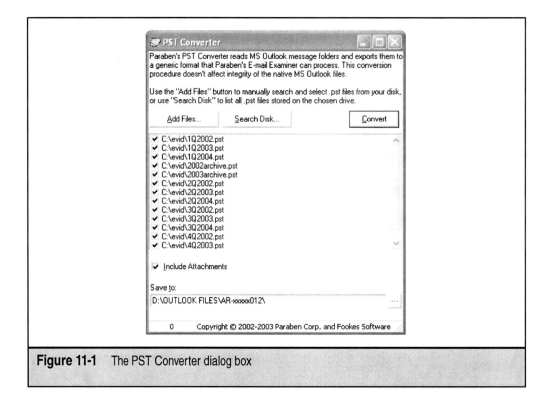

Figure 11-1   The PST Converter dialog box

4. Carefully select the destination directory, and then begin the conversion process by clicking Convert. When the process is completed (it may take some time for large PST files), the files will automatically appear in E-mail Examiner.

5. If you used the pstconv.exe utility and you need to open the e-mail later, choose File | Open Mailbox.

6. Select Files Of Type "Generic mail [*.*]" and find the folder in which you chose to store the converted files. When this is completed, you will find the e-mail located in the E-mail Examiner window, as shown in Figure 11-2.

If you typically have a large caseload with PST files, consider Paraben's text searcher, which is capable of searching through unique file types such as Outlook PST, PDF, and more.

Be aware that the searching options are robust and will require some learning to take advantage of all the features. Numerous options are available, and just about every view and feature is customizable to some degree. Ready reports are available for quickly producing statistical data based on variables such as word count and e-mail domains used. Options exist for extracting the attachments as well as extracting e-mails into EML and generic mailbox formats. Additional quick-reporting features of interest include the ability to extract all e-mail addresses and all originating servers into a single file.

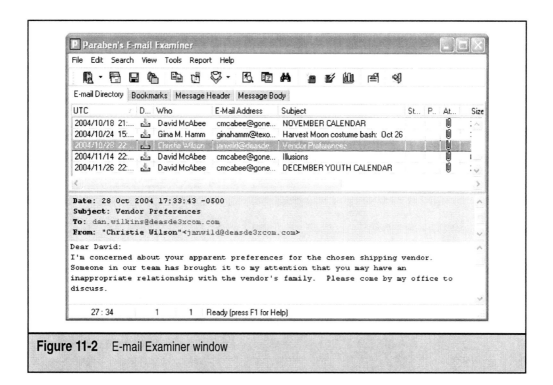

Figure 11-2   E-mail Examiner window

Examining Artifacts with EnCase

For the expert, EnCase's view of a PST and its Messaging Application Programming Interface (MAPI) objects proves valuable. Add the filtering, EnScript, and searching capabilities to this mix, and you have a powerful tool.

After collecting the evidence relevant to your case, consider using the readily available filters for locating different types of mail files. Simply select Filters in the bottom pane of the EnCase screen and double-click the filter you want to use. At this point, you can choose to mount and view the files within EnCase, or you can export them for use in other programs you prefer.

It's important that you remember that a PST is a binary file structure that is not interpreted correctly without your mounting the file inside of EnCase. Do this by right-clicking the PST of interest and choosing View File Structure. Then you can use the regular searching features inside EnCase.

In addition, EnCase lets you identify Outlook Compressible Encryption (OCE) files in unallocated space using CodePages. To identify OCE files in your search, you will need to configure the CodePage for OCE by each keyword you intend to include in your search. Here's how to do this:

1. Choose New Keyword.
2. Select Unicode.

3. Go to the CodePage tab.

4. Enable Outlook Compressible Encryption in the list; make sure that you select Unallocated Clusters in the directory tree for your evidence item before initiating the search.

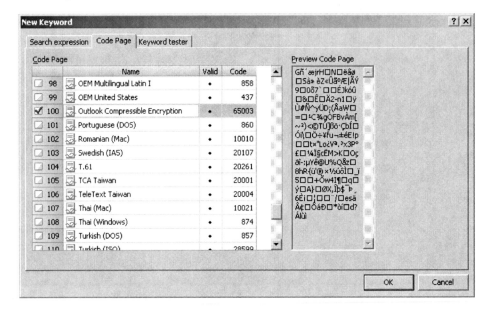

Figure 11-3 illustrates the selection for viewing the file structure and the filters available for quickly accessing PST files in your evidence. More features are available in the newer versions of EnCase, which continues to improve the experience with PST files.

Examining Artifacts with FTK

FTK is an excellent all-around tool for investigating e-mail files. Principle among its strongest features is its ability to create a full text index of large files. While this is time-consuming up front, you will save an enormous amount of time in large investigations in the long run. A good rule of thumb is that if you are going to search a file only one time, you don't necessarily have to index the file. If you are going to search the file more than five times, you need to consider the value of indexing the files. If you are going to search the file more than ten times, we would hope that you have indexed it already.

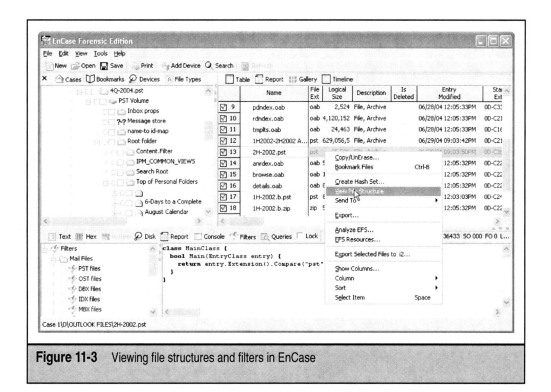

Figure 11-3   Viewing file structures and filters in EnCase

An advantage to using FTK is its ability to read PST and OST archives directly by accessing internal structures. The result is that e-mails are automatically indexed during the import process, making them easy to search quickly, especially across multiple mail stores. Keep in mind that FTK can also take EnCase images directly and create a full text index of the entire file. Figure 11-4 shows an example of the interface. Because there is no need to break down the PST, the e-mail is readily accessible right after you get the evidence imported.

Examining Artifacts with Outlook

If no other tools are available, you can use Microsoft Outlook to import and view PSTs. Here's how to do this:

1. Install and start Microsoft Outlook. When the prompt to create another mailbox appears, click No, and then click Continue.

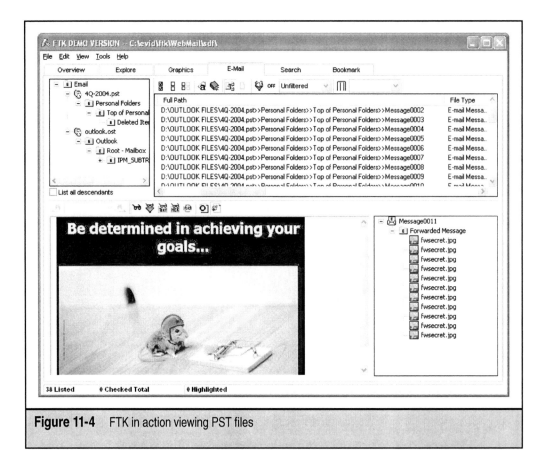

Figure 11-4   FTK in action viewing PST files

2. When Outlook opens, choose File | Data File Management | Add.

3. Select the correct file type and follow the prompts, as shown in Figure 11-5.

4. When you're done, you can use the familiar Outlook interface to search the PST as you would normally search any mail through Outlook.

Examining Artifacts with ReadPST (libPST Package)

ReadPST is a program made available as part of the libPST package, which is available from SourceForge at http://sourceforge.net/projects/ol2mbox/. Downloading the

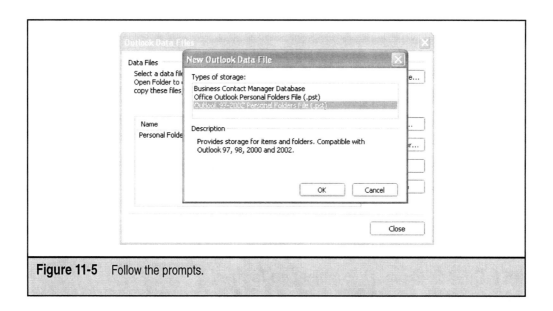

Figure 11-5   Follow the prompts.

libPST package and extracting it will place the contents of the package in the libpst directory on your hard drive. Enter that directory and execute the `make` command.

You can then execute the readPST program with the following options:

```
ReadPST v0.3.4 implementing LibPST v0.3.4
Usage: ./readpst [OPTIONS] {PST FILENAME}
OPTIONS:
        -h      - Help. This screen
        -k      - KMail. Output in kmail format
        -o      - Output Dir. Directory to write files to002
                  CWD is changed *after* opening pst file
        -r      - Recursive. Output in a recursive format
        -V      - Version. Display program version
        -w      - Overwrite any output mbox files
```

ReadPST will then convert the PST into RFC-compliant UNIX mail. You can access the extracted mail and attachments with any standard UNIX mail client. For example, to convert a PST into KDE mail format, you would execute this command:

```
./readpst -k mypst.pst
```

Microsoft Outlook Express

Popularity:	6
Simplicity:	10
Impact:	8
Risk Rating:	8

Outlook Express is a common e-mail and Internet news client. It is installed by default on a Windows-based operating system with Internet Explorer. Because it is readily available, some users choose to use it as their default e-mail client. Therefore, the forensic investigator must be prepared to reconstruct the e-mail generated from this program. Outlook Express stores e-mail in a database type file using a .DBX file extension that is similar to a PST file found in Outlook. Table 11-2 shows common data file locations.

DBX (Outlook Express) Examination Tools

A number of tools are capable of reading the Outlook Express DBX files, including the tools listed previously. The steps for importing and examining the data are nearly identical to those used with PST files in the "PST (Microsoft Outlook) Examination Tools" section with a few noted differences, which are outlined here.

Examining Artifacts with E-mail Examiner

E-mail Examiner reads Outlook Express files directly, and the same conversion process used for PSTs is not necessarily used for DBX files. You can import DBX files directly into E-mail Examiner, as shown in Figure 11-6.

Operating System	Location of Outlook Express Mail Storage
Windows 2000/XP/2003	C:\Documents and Settings*<local username>*\ Local Settings\Application Data\Identities\ *<unique lengthy string>*\Microsoft\Outlook Express
Windows NT	C:\winnt\profiles*<local username>*\Local Settings\ Application Data\Identities*<unique lengthy string>*\ Microsoft\Outlook Express
Windows 95/98/ME	C:\Windows\Application Data\Identities\ *<unique lengthy string>*\Microsoft\Outlook Express

Table 11-2   Summary of Mail Locations for Outlook Express

Figure 11-6 Using Paraben's E-mail Examiner to examine Outlook Express e-mail

Examining Artifacts with EnCase

EnCase requires that you right-click the files and choose the View File Structure command. Then filters and other search tools become available to help you with the investigation. Figure 11-7 shows a suspect's deleted e-mail folder. Notice that the e-mail is broken out under Deleted Items.dbx and listed as individual files named by e-mail subject. The file contents can be viewed by clicking the file.

Examining Artifacts with FTK

FTK's operational look and feel is the same for DBX files as it is for PST files. The index and search features are helpful across multiple and large e-mail data containers. Figure 11-8 illustrates how FTK handles Outlook Express e-mail.

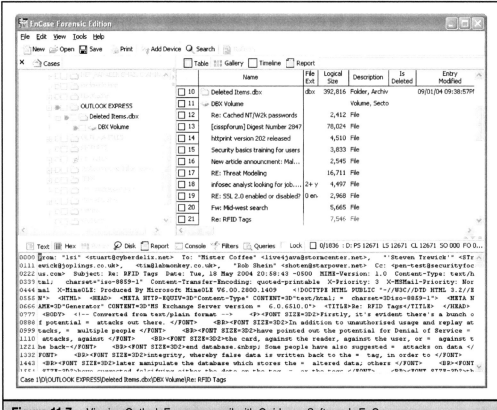

Figure 11-7   Viewing Outlook Express e-mail with Guidance Software's EnCase

Examining Artifacts Using Outlook Express

The process for importing files into Outlook Express is similar to that for importing data files into Microsoft Outlook. We assume that you understand how to perform this task on your own.

Using readDBX

Like its sister program libPST, libDBX contains a program called readDBX. This program, like readPST, allows an examiner to extract the contents of a DBX file into a RFC-compliant UNIX mail format. LibDBX can be found at http://sourceforge.net/projects/ol2mbox/. Downloading the libDBX package and extracting it will place the contents of the package in the libDBX directory. Enter that directory and execute the `make` command.

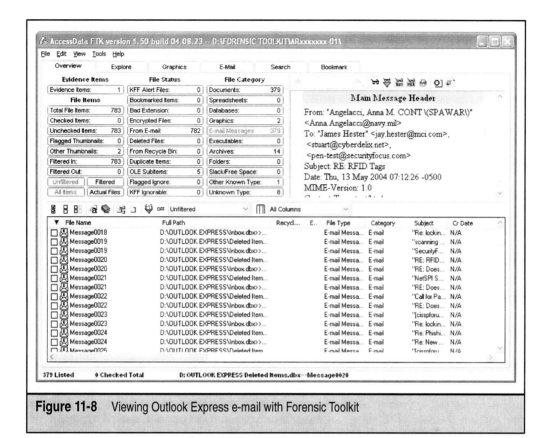

Figure 11-8   Viewing Outlook Express e-mail with Forensic Toolkit

You can then execute the readDBX program with the following options:

```
readdbx - Extract e-mails from MS Outlook Express 5.0 DBX files into mbox format.
File is taken from stdin unless -f is specified.
Output e-mails are written to stdout unless -o is specified

Usage: readdbx [OPTIONS]
Options:
        -h          display this help and exit
        -V          output version information and exit
        -f "file"   input DBX file
        -o "file"   file to write mbox format to
        -q          don't display extra information
```

ReadDBX will convert the DBX into RFC-compliant UNIX mail. You can access the extracted mail and attachments with any standard UNIX mail client. For example, to convert a PST into UNIX mail format, you would execute this command:

```
./readdbx -f mydbx.dbx -o mydbx
```

UNIX E-mail

Popularity:	8
Simplicity:	8
Impact:	8
Risk Rating:	**8**

UNIX mail is commonly used in many organizations, especially among engineering-oriented groups that are accustomed to using Linux and UNIX. With the increasing popularity and ease of use of the Linux desktop, the likelihood of encountering UNIX e-mail is growing.

UNIX Examination Tools

UNIX e-mail, unlike most Windows formats, does not normally contain binary information. Instead, the UNIX e-mail format follows and extends the RFCs and writes out its data as plain ASCII text. Attachments in UNIX mail, however, are encoded with MIME encoding, typically BASE64. This means that while you can search through the text of any e-mail with any standard search tool, you cannot search through the attachments without decoding all of the MIME information. Multiple variations of UNIX mail are available—such as KMail, Vm, and RMail—but they all share the same common characteristics.

Examining Artifacts with E-mail Examiner

E-mail Examiner reads UNIX mail files directly. You can import UNIX mail files directly into E-mail Examiner by choosing File | Open Mailbox and selecting the e-mail store. Another method of importing UNIX e-mail is to drag-and-drop it on the program window. The net result and view are the same as in the previous examples using Outlook and Outlook Express.

Examining Artifacts with EnCase

EnCase allows you to search through the text of any e-mail, but you cannot search through the attachments without decoding all of the MIME information.

Examining Artifacts with FTK

FTK's operational look and feel is the same for UNIX mail files as it is for other types of mail files. The indexing and searching features are still advantageous across multiple and large e-mail data containers.

Examining Artifacts with Grep

One of the beauties of UNIX e-mail is how easy it is to use regular grep expressions to search the mail store, because it's a simple text file. Regular grep expressions and searching techniques are covered in the Appendix of this book.

Netscape Navigator and Mozilla

Popularity:	5
Simplicity:	8
Impact:	8
Risk Rating:	7

Netscape Navigator and Mozilla are installed by default by their associated browser installations. These clients are not as popular as MS Outlook or UNIX, but they do exist in a number of organizations.

⊖ Netscape Navigator and Mozilla Examination Tools

Netscape Navigator and Mozilla have their own extensions of UNIX mail. Similar to UNIX mail, the Netscape and Mozilla files that constitute the e-mail folders are stored in a directory. All of the tools applicable to UNIX mail are applicable in the same way to Netscape Navigator and Mozilla. If you are dealing with these types of mail stores, review the section, "UNIX Examination Tools."

AOL

Popularity:	4
Simplicity:	9
Impact:	9
Risk Rating:	7

AOL is not typically used in corporate environments, but it is popular enough to cover here. If AOL is discovered, the impact can be quite high, because people are more likely to use this for their personal e-mail and let their guard down. Employees are more cautious with their work e-mail than with their play e-mail. It's also quite possible that workers will take their laptops home and check their AOL home accounts using their work machines.

It is important in this section to differentiate among AOL mail that remains on the AOL server, AOL mail archived on the local machine, and AOL mail that is accessed through a browser. In the following cases, we discuss the investigation of AOL's client storage archive.

⊖ AOL Examination Tools

AOL uses a proprietary format, and only a few tools can read AOL's PFC files. Three tools discussed briefly here are E-mail Examiner, EnCase, and FTK. Another tool that we do not discuss is Hot Pepper Technology's E-mail Detective (www.hotpepperinc.com/emd.html).

Examining Artifacts Using E-mail Examiner

Similar to the same process used by AOL for examining PST files, E-mail Examiner first converts AOL mail files into a generic mailbox format. Then do the following:

1. Begin the conversion process by starting the AOL Converter, shown in Figure 11-9.

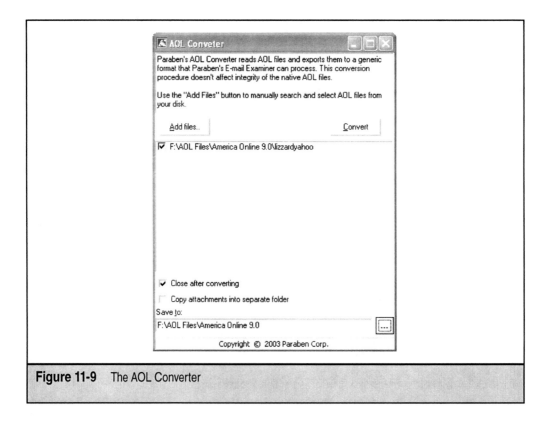

Figure 11-9 The AOL Converter

2. Choose File | Import AOL Files in E-mail Examiner. Choose the command to open the AOL Converter dialog box. If you do not see this command under the File menu, go to Program Files\Paraben Corporation\ E-mail Examiner and double-click AOLConverter.exe.

3. In the AOL Converter dialog box, select the AOL files and click Add Files to convert into a generic format.

4. Finally, carefully select the destination directory, and then begin the conversion process by clicking Convert.

5. When the process is completed (it may take some time for large AOL formats), you can view the e-mails in E-mail Examiner. Choose File | Open All E-mails.

6. Select Mailbox type Generic Mail (UNIX/mbox) and find the folder where you chose to output the files when you converted them. When this is completed, you will find the e-mail located in the E-mail Examiner window, as shown in Figure 11-10.

As with dealing with any other format using Paraben's tool, numerous options and ready reports are available. You can also extract e-mails into EML and generic mailbox formats.

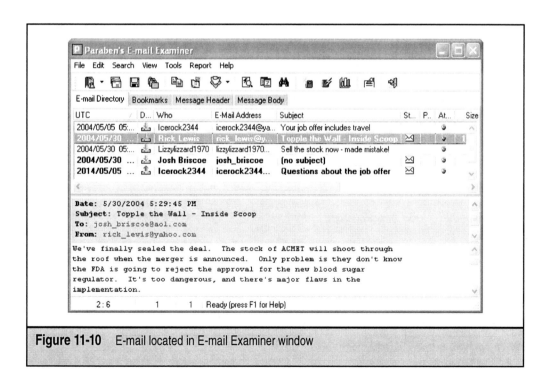

Figure 11-10   E-mail located in E-mail Examiner window

Examining Artifacts Using EnCase

You can use EnCase if you want to find the e-mail archives in their default location using the provided enscript Initialize Case. However, EnCase does not currently have the ability to decode the archive. If you are not using the scripts now, you can take advantage of a lot of additional functionality inside EnCase by choosing View | Scripts.

You should be aware of several limitations here. First, the initialize script searches only for the files in specific locations. Second, you need to export the files and use a third-party tool for analysis.

    Rather than using EnCase, we recommend that you use E-mail Examiner or FTK.

Examining Artifacts Using FTK

FTK's operational look and feel (Figure 11-11) holds the same continuity for AOL mail archives as it does for other types of mail archives. FTK is an easy-to-use tool that decodes the mail archive seamlessly, retrieving e-mail and other items of interest, such as the user's marked favorites.

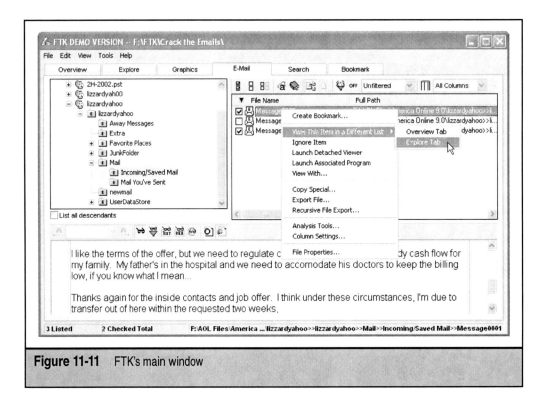

Figure 11-11   FTK's main window

Often, multiple mail types appear on a corporate user's computer. The ability of FTK to search, locate, and import multiple mail formats seamlessly is an asset. If you have a user with an Outlook PST and an AOL account, FTK does an excellent job of retrieving data across the different formats.

WEB-BASED E-MAIL

Web-based e-mail such as Yahoo! and Hotmail challenges investigators to find the e-mail on the computer, reconstruct activity, and identify users in ways that are different from client-based e-mail. Depending on the web mail service, where the e-mail is stored, how it is stored, and other factors, you may find nothing, the entire e-mail, or an e-mail remnant. And if that wasn't enough, all the major webmail providers now offer 5 or more gigabytes of storage, adding to the volume of e-mail that can be exchanged and stored with webmail providers.

> **NOTE** E-mail remnants are stored on a drive found on the media during analysis. Examples include previously deleted e-mails, web-based e-mail, and partially overwritten e-mails.

For example, web-based e-mail allows users to choose their own e-mail addresses. This makes it more difficult to identify users than with typical corporate e-mail systems. An address that doesn't definitely identify a user, such as Barney8237@yahoo.com, makes it difficult to identify a suspect. John.Smith@somecompany.com pretty much nails a user's identity.

Internet-Hosted Mail

Popularity:	8
Simplicity:	9
Impact:	7
Risk Rating:	8

Web-hosted e-mail is popular because a number of companies provide free e-mail services from the Internet. The impact to an investigation is high because the content of Internet mail is personal and reveals a lot about the user. Additionally, Internet mail requires credentials, providing further evidence that the user was at the computer during the time the e-mail was read—assuming you can somehow tie the user ID to the suspect. Even so, most users still believe that Internet mail is private and cannot be recovered.

In one recent case involving financial fraud, web-based e-mail was used to identify a single user from more than 200 workers who had shared access to a computer. The user was logging into his e-mail account to delete possible evidence. Using EnCase and a few scripts, we culled the webmail into a readable format. The result was a quick confession and subsequent dismissal.

It takes time and energy to get e-mail logs, attachments, and e-mails from hosted e-mail service providers. In some cases, this effort is definitely warranted. In others, or when you are searching for leads in a case, you will find additional methods useful for recovering cached e-mail. This isn't a perfect world, and at times these methods will not work. For example, if the suspect is using a privacy-friendly browser, you may have to resort to other evidence or consult the web e-mail hosting company to gather the necessary evidence.

NOTE   Today's browsers are increasingly more secure than their predecessors. Users are demanding privacy features and paying a premium for the luxury. Unfortunately, this creates a challenge for the investigator. For example, one browser encrypts the cache with Blowfish Encryption, does not use the registry, and does not use index.dat files. If that's not bad enough, all of the session data is securely wiped during and after the session is completed. When this occurs, you have moved from a technical problem to a people problem. You must now either confront your suspect to recover encryption keys or request subpoenas against the e-mail provider to allow you to view the suspect's e-mail logs.

Yahoo! E-mail

Popularity:	8
Simplicity:	10
Impact:	9
Risk Rating:	**9**

We know that end users are more likely to use web-hosted e-mail for personal business because they feel it's safer. Because of Yahoo!'s popularity and host of services, its webmail is common among end users as a way to handle personal business. The interface is simple, and with Yahoo!'s 100MB free space, there is plenty of room to store information.

Yahoo! Examination Tools

These techniques target recovering e-mails from the Internet cache. You can apply the same techniques to other Yahoo! services to recover information from Yahoo! Groups and other locales by re-creating the suspected event and studying the output.

Some key filenames of interest for Yahoo!-related mail include those beginning with *ShowFolder*, *ShowLetter*, *Compose*, and *Attachments*. They include the rendered HTML that was on the screen. It is possible to add the .HTM extension to these files and view them in your browser as the user would have seen them. However, in some cases you may have to remove the script that redirects you to the login page. The script exists to determine whether the session is still active. If this is the case, you can remove the script by editing the file in your chosen text editor.

ShowFolder   The ShowFolder file lists all of the suspect's folders on the left side of the screen when viewed in a web page. The body of the page contains e-mail subject lines with the alias of the person who sent the messages, message dates, and the sizes of the e-mails. This is a quick way to view the type of e-mail the user typically receives.

ShowLetter   The ShowLetter files contain the opened e-mail as seen by the user. Remember that the files are not binary or encoded files, and you can search them for strings using any tool you want.

Compose   The Compose files contain the e-mail to which the user is replying before any modification is done by the user. Additionally, another Compose file is present when the e-mail is sent as a confirmation that the e-mail was sent. This file contains the username and the name(s) of the intended recipient(s). Look for the information immediately following the hidden values:

```
input type=hidden name=<field name> value=
```

This is true for TO, CC, BCC, Subject, and 40 to 60 other fields, depending on the message. What's amazing, however, is that the entire text of the message is held as a hidden field. Look for the following text:

```
input type=hidden name=Body value=
```

In this particular sample, it looks something like this:

```
<input type=hidden name=Body value="&lt;DIV&gt;
&lt;DIV&gt;
&lt;DIV&gt;You&#39;re nuts!   There&#39;s no way we can get away with
this!   I&#39;m not going to join you in selling weapons
```

Attachments   The Attachments file contains the name of any attachments and the person or group of people for which the e-mail was intended. This file also contains all the same information as the compose field.

Examining Yahoo! E-mail Artifacts Using EnCase

EnCase does an excellent job of locating specific strings and ordering files. The search capabilities allow you to find files and e-mail remnants, but it will take time on large volumes. To find Yahoo! files, use the following grep expression for your search. You can export your findings or use an external viewer if you have one.

```
window.open\(\"http:\/\/mail.yahoo.com\", \"_top\"
```

One of the strengths of EnCase is the ease of ordering every file in the system by date, regardless of where the file resides in the hierarchical folder structure. We have used this feature to tie other computer-related events into a cohesive timeline rather quickly.

Examining Yahoo! E-mail Artifacts Using FTK

FTK is by far the fastest tool for searching through e-mail files. After acquiring and adding your evidence to FTK, select the Overview tab and then click the Documents button under File Category, as shown in Figure 11-12. FTK is smart enough to recognize these documents as HTML files and will render them as the suspect saw them on his or her computer. In the bottom pane, you can browse through documents until you find something of interest.

Remember, however, that much of the text does not show up here, but is actually in the source of the message as a hidden field. Right-click documents and use the viewer of your choice to see whether more information is contained in the source of the file.

Also remember the powerful indexed searching. If you are looking for something specific enough, you should start with those search terms and try to find corresponding e-mail messages.

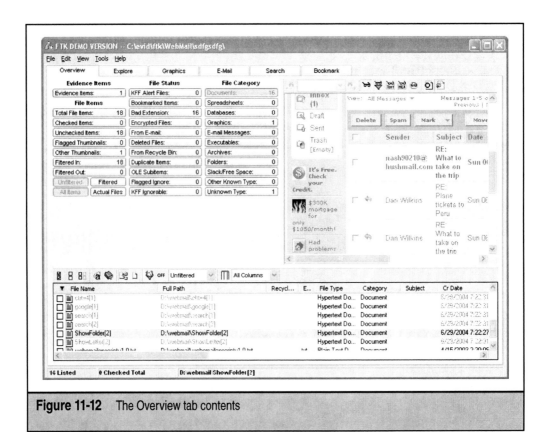

Figure 11-12 The Overview tab contents

Examining Yahoo! E-mail Artifacts Using Open Source Tools

Essentially, once you have the suspect's hard drive, you can find the location of the temporary Internet files. From there, carve out and manipulate the files of interest with the tools you're most comfortable using. This works because the files are not encoded. You can use any tool you want on the files, such as grep or strings.

Hotmail E-mail

Popularity:	*8*
Simplicity:	*10*
Impact:	*9*
Risk Rating:	*9*

As the popularity of this hosted service has grown, so has the use of Hotmail on corporate assets. Again, because of the usually personal nature of web-hosted e-mail, the impact and subsequent risk rating is high.

Hotmail Examination Tools

The tools and methods are the same as those of other types of e-mail, but the files are different for Hotmail. The files of interest are those beginning with *Hotmail*, *doaddress*, *getmsg*, *compose*, and *calendar*. When you're viewing the files in FTK, they will render as obviously Hotmail files and will have the e-mail data in the viewing window.

Here is a search expression to find Hotmail files:

```
/cgi-bin/dasp/E?N?/?hotmail_+#+.css\
```

Hushmail E-mail

Popularity:	*4*
Simplicity:	*7*
Impact:	*9*
Risk Rating:	*7*

Although it is still used less often than Yahoo! or Hotmail, Hushmail is growing in popularity. People value their privacy. Employees using Hushmail for personal communications may believe no one can gather any information about their e-mail activities. These employees tend to risk more in their communications.

Hushmail Examination Tools

What employees usually don't know is that Hushmail never promises client-side security, only security in transit and storage. Depending on how you want to approach the case, you can search for the individual files or use a low-level search for the specific strings. The files are titled beginning with *showMessagePane*. If you try to view the files as HTML files, you will miss most of the information that is buried in the message source.

To dig into the files or search for e-mail remnants, search for the e-mail field you want to find in this format:

```
hushAppletFrame.message.<e-mail field>
```

Figure 11-13 is a screenshot of EnCase being used to find the message inside the file by searching for hushAppletFrame.message and looking for the large splash of highlighted files. This allowed us to clue into the message body and other details rather quickly.

The following is from the source of an e-mail using Hushmail and helps illustrate the fields. Notice that the message body is located in the source, but if you render this in a browser, you will miss this information.

```
hushAppletFrame.message.from = "George Henderson
\<rockondude1999@yahoo.com\>";
hushAppletFrame.message.replyto
= "George Henderson \<rockondude1999@yahoo.com\>";

hushAppletFrame.message.to = "Dan Wilkins \<danwilkins1970@hotmail.com\>,
nash90210@hushmail.com";
hushAppletFrame.message.cc = "";
hushAppletFrame.message.bcc = "";
hushAppletFrame.message.date = "Sun, 27 Jun 2004 18:34:59 -0700";
hushAppletFrame.message.subject
= "RE: What to take on the trip";
hushAppletFrame.message.hushEncryption
= "";
hushAppletFrame.message.hushKeyblock
= "";
hushAppletFrame.message.body
"Yes - do that.\r\n\r\nDan Wilkins \<danwilkins1970@hotmail.com\>
wrote:Yeah, I agree. This too much money and too easy.
```

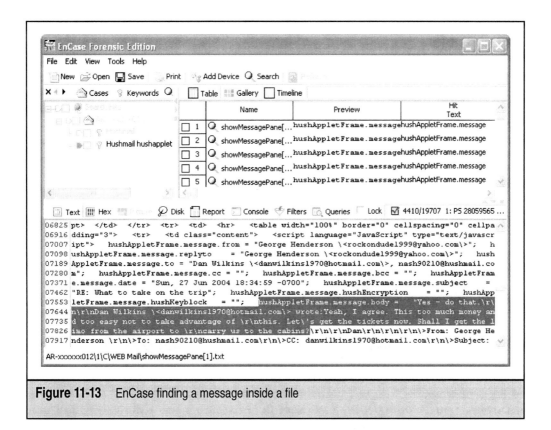

Figure 11-13   EnCase finding a message inside a file

INVESTIGATING E-MAIL HEADERS

E-mail headers contain general information including the e-mail addresses of who apparently authored the e-mail and the recipient of the e-mail. E-mail headers also contain routing information from the point of origin to the final destination. The servers assemble this information en route to the final destination and attach it to the top of the e-mail. Sometimes, depending on the client used and the e-mail servers, the information contained in the headers helps the examiner trace the origin of the e-mail back to the sender's computer or Internet connection. Other information found in headers includes the type of e-mail client used, the e-mail gateway used, and the names of e-mail attachments. This information is helpful to investigators because it helps tell the full story of what happened or points to other areas to investigate. The headers are constructed more or less uniformly across web-hosted and client-based e-mail.

E-mail Headers

Popularity:	10
Simplicity:	10
Impact:	5
Risk Rating:	8

The popularity and simplicity values of e-mail headers are high because e-mail programs automatically generate e-mail headers as part of RFC-822. Despite the ability to spoof e-mail headers, they are typically accurate in civil cases where it matters (spam aside). The impact to an investigation depends on the nature of the investigation. If e-mail is part of the crime, you must verify header information during your fact-finding routine. E-mail headers have influenced investigations by identifying the originating source of information, the type of computer the suspect may be using, and the completeness of a seizure, among other things.

In one recent example, federal authorities investigated a young man for creating an automatic key generator for a well-known piece of software. The expensive software suite normally sold for hundreds of thousands of US dollars, but the suspect advertised a key generator on his Web site for only $10. As part of the seizure, the authorities took the user's work computer and his home computers. The suspect verified that the authorities had seized all of the home computers.

Further investigation suggested the suspect withheld evidence from the legal seizure of his computers because of information contained in e-mail headers. The examiner discovered e-mails on the work asset sent from the user's home network. The e-mail headers contained information about an e-mail client program that was not on any of the computers seized from his home. The net result? The suspect must have used another computer from his home network to send e-mail, and this meant the suspect may have lied about the completeness of the seizure.

When the authorities confronted the suspect because of this find, he caved in and quickly confessed that he had one more computer in the house. This computer had the hard evidence that nailed him.

Examine E-mail Headers

E-mail headers reveal key information about the suspect's computer, the client used, and sometimes the approximate geographic location of the originating e-mail. When you find the e-mail headers, copy and paste them into your logs or text document of choice for easy viewing. This isn't to say that e-mail headers are completely trustworthy, because they can be spoofed. The only authoritative information included in a header is what is inserted by the routing servers. Now let's take a look at some e-mail headers.

E-mail Header Components

A typical e-mail header might look something like this:

```
From root  Mon Jan  6 04:02:16 2003
Return-Path: <root@fw>
Received: (from root@localhost)
        by fw (8.11.6/8.11.6) id h06A2FZ01645
        for root; Mon, 6 Jan 2003 04:02:15 -0600
Date: Mon, 6 Jan 2003 04:02:15 -0600
From: root <root@fw>
Message-Id: <200301061002.h06A2FZ01645@fw>
To: root@fw
Subject: LogWatch for fw
X-IMAPbase: 1010645096 1016
Status: RO
X-Status:
X-Keywords:
X-UID: 819.
```

From: From:, with a colon, identifies the sender of the message. Unfortunately, this is the easiest component to forge and hence the most unreliable.

From   From, without a colon, is distinctly different from the From: line in the mail user interface and is not actually part of the e-mail header. This line is often inserted by mail servers upon receiving the mail. This is especially common for UNIX mailers, which use this line to separate messages in a mail folder. This line can also be forged, but not always.

Reply-To: or Return-Path: This line contains the e-mail address for sending replies. This is an easy component to forge and is often not in the headers. In the world of spam, this line is helpful. This field is usually legitimate because spammers want to make money off their e-mail orders.

Sender: or X-Sender   The way this is supposed to work is that mail software inserts this line if the user modifies the From: line. However, most of the mailers ignore this rule, so this line is rarely present.

Message-ID: This is a unique string assigned by the mail system when the mail is created. This is more difficult to forge than the From line, but not impossible.

Received: These are the most reliable lines in the header and can be quite useful in identifying date/time approximations and geographic locations. They form a list of all sites through which the message traveled en route to the recipient. They are forgeable up to the point the message is inserted into the Internet on its way to the recipient. After this, they are authoritative and accurate.

Received: lines are added to the top of the headers as they pass through the mail servers. Therefore, they are read from bottom to top beginning with the server that first handled the e-mail and ending with the server that delivered it to the final recipient. The last (bottom) nonforged Received: line shows the likely starting point for the e-mail.

One easy way to identify fake Received: lines includes using nslookup to identify the purported sender. In the following example, mail.yahoo-store.com does not match the given IP address of 64.70.43.79, and instead reveals the message came from mx1.real-coupons.com. Some mail servers will do the reverse lookup for you, as illustrated here:

```
Received: from mail.yahoo-store.com (HELO mx1.real-coupons.com) (64.70.43.79)
by mta291.mail.scd.yahoo.com with SMTP; Tue, 25 May 2004 17:24:13 -0700
```

Other obvious things to check are the time stamps and IP addresses. If the time stamps between successive servers show a negative time, one of them is likely forged. The headers are also likely forged if the IP address contains a number greater than 255 or is an internal address such as 10.x.x.x, 192.169.x.x, 172.16.x.x, or 127.x.x.x.

E-mail Header Locations

E-mail header locations for popular mail programs are provided in Table 11-3. If you are working with another mainstream product or an esoteric mail reader, take a look at www.spamcop.net for information on how to find the e-mail headers.

E-mail Client	Location of E-mail Headers
Outlook	Open message and choose View	Options. Headers are in Internet Headers box.
Outlook Express	Select message and press CTRL-F3.
Pine	Press H to view headers. If they are not enabled, go to main menu, press (s)etup, then (c)onfig. Scroll down several lines to Enable-Full-Header-Cmd. Press ENTER. Press (E)xit and (Y)es to save changes. Then press H to display headers.
Netscape Navigator/ Communicator	Click yellow triangle to right of brief message headers to display full headers.
AOL Client	Open e-mail. Find Sent From The Internet (Details). Click Details.
Yahoo!	Open e-mail. Click Full Headers.
Hotmail	From main mail page, choose Options	Mail Display Settings. Select Advanced under Message Headers. Click OK and choose Mail tab to read e-mail with full headers displayed.

Table 11-3   Header Locations for Popular Mail Programs

CHAPTER 12

TRACKING USER ACTIVITY

Duringa forensics investigation, you'll spend most of your time reconstructing and tracing the actions that a suspect has taken. This can include web pages the suspect visited, documents he created, and other data he may have modified. Finding this evidence is only the first step in the process, however. You must be able to tie that evidence back to the suspect. What good is an incriminating Word document if you can't prove who wrote it?

Especially in the field of digital forensics, proving who was sitting at the keyboard and where documents originated is not a trivial task. Think back to the news reports of e-mail viruses running rampant. Most of these viruses took advantage of the Office macro language to spread automatically across the Internet. When the writers were caught, it was usually because authorities found some distinctive fingerprint in the code that pointed them to a suspect. For Office files, as will be discussed later in the chapter, this could be a Media Access Control (MAC) address, a unique identifier, or a timeline reconstructed from metadata. For web browsers, this involves investigating the history and using the cache files and cookies to reconstruct where a suspect went on the Internet and what he did while visiting those sites. The purpose of this chapter is to show you how to perform this digital sleuthing in a way that will stand up in court.

MICROSOFT OFFICE FORENSICS

Office has become ubiquitous in today's modern business world. As such, investigators frequently have to investigate incidents that involve Word documents. This can be trickier than it initially sounds. How do you prove that the suspect wrote the content in the document? How can you tie that document to a specific computer? What methods exist to subvert the Word user-tracking facilities and how can you tell when someone has tried to subvert tracking? With a bit of sound investigation and a couple of tricks, you can pull a surprising amount of information from Word documents, Excel spreadsheets, and other Office applications that can give you a clear picture of the timeline of events.

Since the release of Office 97, Microsoft Office has been notorious for storing a wealth of sensitive information about who authored the document. For example, if you are lucky enough to be working with a document that was modified with Track Changes turned on, you can pull a lot of data out of the document. The file stores who made modifications and all the content that was ever included in the document, even if it was deleted, plus information about the filenames and to whom the document was e-mailed. This can be incredibly useful in the process of re-creating a timeline.

NOTE Microsoft has released a utility called rdhtool.exe for Office 2003 that strips Office documents of all of this metadata. If you stumble onto a document that has no metadata at all, this tool may have been used to cover someone's tracks or as a matter of practice. Take this information in context and make note of the omission in your report.

E-mail Review

Popularity:	8
Simplicity:	6
Impact:	7
Risk Rating:	7

This first appeared in Office 2002 and can be incredibly useful in tying a specific user to a document. When you e-mail a document for review, you may see a dialog box like this when you open the document again:

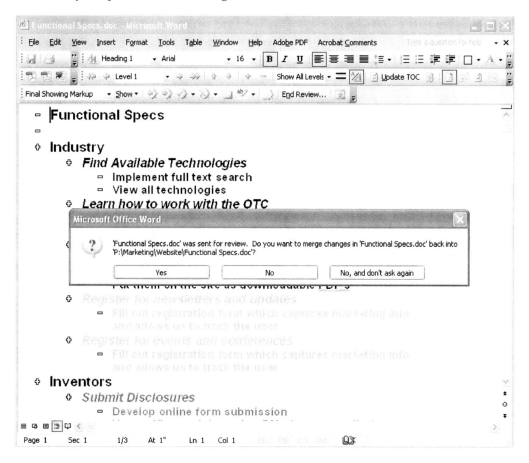

The sequence of events that causes this dialog to appear can provide some very important forensic data. Let's examine this process in detail. When you send an Office document for review in Outlook, several custom properties tags are placed into the metadata of the file. We show the five most important of these tags in the following table.

Tag Name	Format of Tag	Description
`_TentativeReviewCycleID`	Number	The unique ID of the revision of the document
`_ReviewCycleID`	Number	Often the same as `_TentativeReviewCycleID`, also a unique ID
`_EmailSubject`	Text	The subject of the e-mail message in which the document was sent
`_AuthorEmail`	Text	The e-mail address of the person who sent the document
`_AuthorEmailDisplayName`	Text	The display name (what shows up in Outlook) for the e-mail address

To view this data in any Office application, choose File | Properties, and then click the Custom tab. You will see a Properties dialog similar to that shown in Figure 12-1. As the figure shows, the information contained in custom tags is incredibly useful for tying a user to a document.

Let's turn our attention for a second to the tag `_ReviewCycleID`. As you can see from Figure 12-1, this is a number that appears to be some kind of identifier. In fact, it's the number that Office uses to determine whether it needs to merge changes back into an original document. So the next natural question is, Where does Office store the ID number outside the document for comparison? Actually, an old .ini-style file is placed in the user's Application Data folder, which stores all this information. The file is placed in *<User's Documents and Settings DIR>*\Application Data\Microsoft\Office. The file, depending on the version of Office, can be named either Adhoc.rcd or Review.rcd. Let's take a look at a snippet of the Review.rcd created for our file:

```
[DocSlots]
NextDoc=29
Doc22=3839962597
Doc24=1518299362
Doc26=1030839747
Doc28=4246392232
...
[4246392232]
Path=C:\Documents and Settings\Aaron Philipp\Desktop\Forensics Exposed\
Chapter 12 data\figure 2.doc
Slot=Doc28
Url=file:///C:\Documents%20and%20Settings\Aaron%20Philipp\Desktop\
Forensics%20Exposed\Chapter%2012%20data\figure%202.doc
```

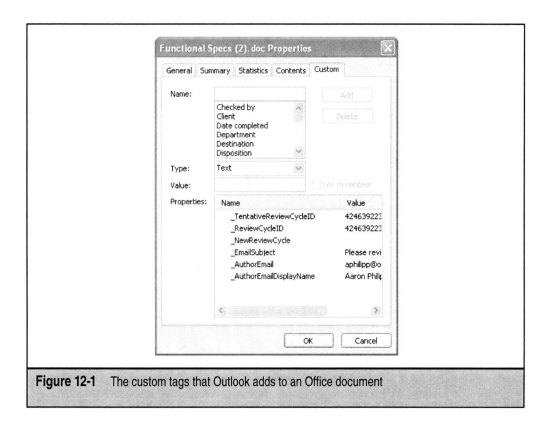

Figure 12-1   The custom tags that Outlook adds to an Office document

Recall from Figure 12-1 that the `_ReviewCycleID` property value for our document was 4246392232. As you can see in the snippet from Review.rcd, an entry for this document shows that it was in fact e-mailed from this machine by username Aaron Philipp. Not only that, but the e-mail address (property value `_AuthorEmail`) from which it was sent and the subject of the e-mail (property value `_EmailSubject`) are also displayed, so you should be able to go back through the Exchange server and dig up the message itself.

Recovering Undo Information

Popularity:	8
Simplicity:	6
Impact:	7
Risk Rating:	7

If a Word document is saved with Quick Save turned on, you can extract the undo information from the document. Look at the document shown in Figure 12-2. It seems to contain only one sentence.

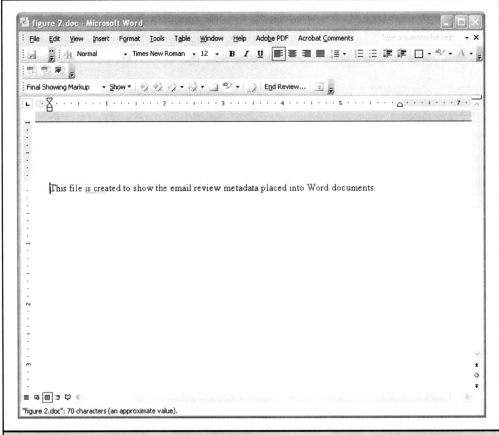

Figure 12-2 A Word document that has been modified and quick saved

First off, you need to understand why Quick Save exists. When a document gets big, it can be very time-consuming to save the document, tying up resources and basically slowing down the whole show. With Office's Auto Save feature, saving can become distracting and time-consuming while you are working. So Quick Save was created to save documents quickly and painlessly with minimum disruption to the user. It does this by not making changes to the body of the document; instead, it appends the changes, and information about where the changes appear goes at the end of the document. Once a certain file size is exceeded, the save goes back, incorporates all the changes into the main body of the document, and shrinks the file size back down. From a forensic investigation standpoint, this can be a great thing because data that a user *thinks* is deleted actually still exists in the document.

Let's go back to our example. If you open the file in a binary editor (I recommend XEmacs for non-forensics work), you can look for information that may have been "deleted" but not removed from the file. As you can see in Figure 12-3, a simple search of the document reveals information that appears as though it were still included in the document.

To confirm, we open Word and perform an undo to see what comes back. As you can see in Figure 12-4, the data deleted from the document in Figure 12-3 has been recovered.

This technique will work through multiple changes to the document and can actually go pretty far back in the revision history. You can typically find the data you are looking for using a keyword text search on the document with a tool such as EnCase or a binary editor, and then go back into Word to reconstruct the document.

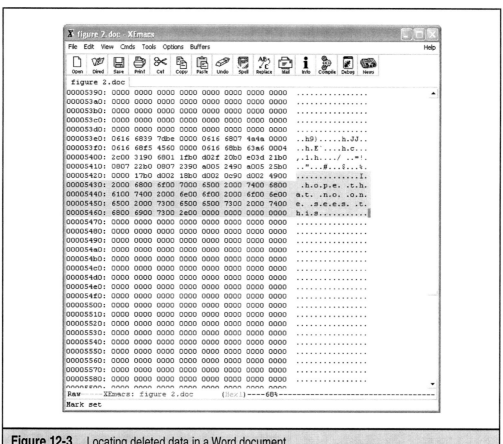

Figure 12-3   Locating deleted data in a Word document

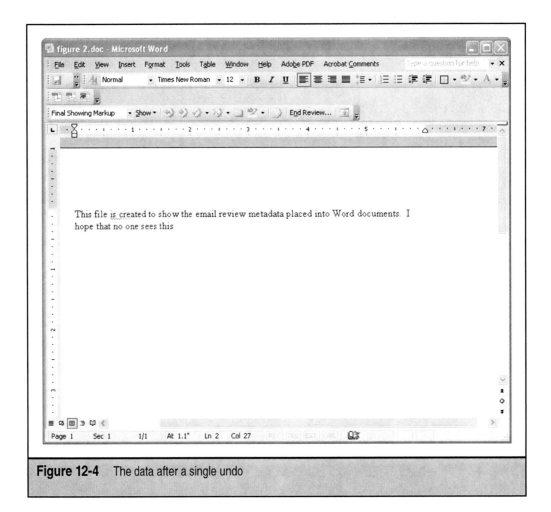

Figure 12-4   The data after a single undo

Word 97 MAC Address

Popularity:	8
Simplicity:	6
Impact:	7
Risk Rating:	7

If you are lucky enough to find a document that was created in Word 97, you can actually get the MAC address of the machine on which the document was created. A MAC address is like the fingerprint of a network card and is typically a number formatted like so: 00-09-5B-E6-24-5D. In the Word document, however, it's formatted a bit differently. Take a look at Figure 12-5, which shows the MAC address in the document itself.

To find the MAC address in a document, open the file in a binary editor and do a search for *PID*. This will bring up the entry.

Let's look at the PID-GUID for the Melissa virus document:

```
PID_GUID {572858EA-36DD-11D2-885F-004033E0078E}
```

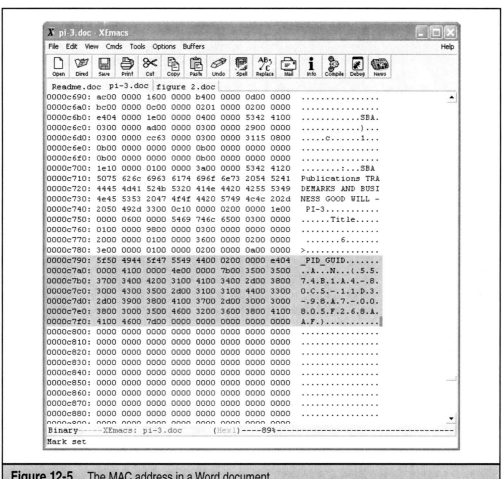

Figure 12-5   The MAC address in a Word document

If you look at the last chunk of data, *004033E0078E*, and break it down, you get *00-40-33-E0-07-8E*; this is clearly the MAC address of the machine on which the document was created. It must be stated, however, that this number can be modified and is nonauthoritative.

| **TIP** | You can check for a MAC address by looking at the first three pairs of numbers in the MAC address; this is the vendor ID. You can use any number of Internet database lookup sites to find out who owns that MAC address and who created the card. If you are certain that you know on what machine a document was created, you can use this information for cross validation purposes. If the vendor ID and the actual maker of the card do not match, that is a red flag that tampering has occurred. |

| **NOTE** | When opening an Office document, the program does a couple of very basic file size checks to make sure that nothing has been modified. If the document won't even open in Office, that should be a red flag that modification of metadata has occurred. |

Past Filenames

Popularity:	8
Simplicity:	6
Impact:	7
Risk Rating:	7

Older Office (pre-Office 2003) documents actually store every filename under which they have ever been saved in the file. This can be very handy if you are looking for directories to go after or network drives that may have been used, or if you need to subpoena removable media to conduct further investigation. The key to this technique is that the filenames are stored in Unicode instead of straight ASCII, so you need to use an application such as strings.exe from Systernals to extract the files. Running strings.exe with the −u argument will output only Unicode text strings from the document. Here's an example of running the strings program on a Word document:

```
Strings -u tester.doc
Strings v2.1
Copyright (C) 1999-2003 Mark Russinovich
Systems Internals - www.sysinternals.com
...
D:\mystuff\test.doc
...
Times New Roman
Root Entry
C:\draft.doc
```

As you can see, multiple filenames and paths are stored in the document. You can then use your image to trace back these files, and if they point to network shares, you can use this data as a reason to conduct further discovery during litigation.

Working with Office Documents

When you're working with Office documents, remember to be creative and always look beyond what you see when you open the document. You can pull a wealth of information from these documents if you know where to look for it. In fact, EnCase has built support for reading and searching the Unicode into the latest version to make this type of investigation easier. One caveat, however, is that the data is nonauthoritative by itself. If you base your court case solely upon this data, you are going to have a bad time. Use this information to corroborate evidence you've obtained from other sources or to develop new leads that you can follow. That said, a little bit of time with an Office document and a low-level editor can point you in the direction you need to go to investigate your case effectively.

TRACKING WEB USAGE

As an investigator, you will frequently find yourself reconstructing a user's web activity. Lucky for you, it seems as though everyone who decides to write a forensic tool writes it in a way that reads a browser's cookies and history. The process of going through the working files and reconstructing activity is actually pretty straightforward, and when properly validated it can be reasonably authoritative. To help you understand what we are going to be looking at, we'll discuss what kinds of records a web browser would keep that denotes user activity.

First, you have to look at what sites a user visited while using the browser. This information can be obtained from the history file, which stores information on every URL a user has loaded, going back for months. Even if a user has tried to cover her tracks by deleting the history, it may still be recoverable and useful in an investigation. Once you have the URLs that she has visited, you need a way to find out what she did while she was there. Conventionally, you can do this using two methods: by looking at the cookies for the site to determine user behavior or by reconstructing the web pages from the temporary Internet files. Let's look at how to conduct an investigation for the two most popular browsers: Internet Explorer and Firefox/Netscape.

Internet Explorer Forensics

Internet Explorer (IE) has been the default web browser for the Microsoft Windows platform since Windows 95. In fact, later versions of Windows have built IE to interact very closely with the operating system, opening some interesting paths for forensic investigation of activity. Covering your tracks in IE is a nontrivial task. Even if you delete the history using the IE facilities, it can still be recovered because of its close interaction with the OS.

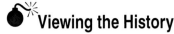 Viewing the History

Popularity:	8
Simplicity:	6
Impact:	10
Risk Rating:	9

The history utility in IE, shown in Figure 12-6, creates a convenient audit trail for what a user likes to do on the Internet. It can be used to show whether the user frequents certain types of sites, if she lands on a site inadvertently, and what she is doing when she visits a site. This information is useful in everything from policy violation cases all the way up to criminal activities.

NOTE EnCase comes with an EnScript feature that will automatically search the image for IE history and present it in a report format. If you use EnCase, this can greatly speed your investigation, although you should make sure you understand what the script does and how it does it.

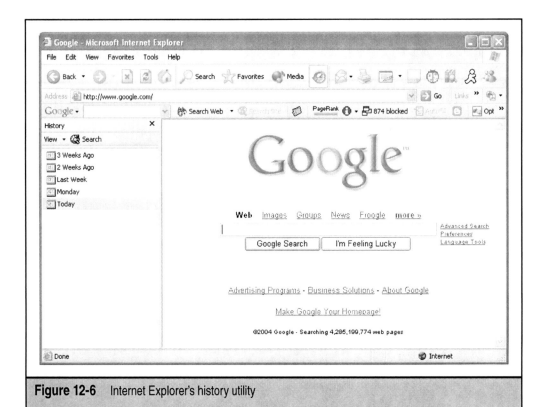

Figure 12-6   Internet Explorer's history utility

Filename	Description
C:\Documents and Settings\ <*username*>\Cookies\index.dat	The audit trail for the cookies that are installed on the system. Useful in locating cookies that are intentionally misnamed and obfuscated.
C:\Documents and Settings\ <*username*>\Local Settings\ History\History.IE5\index.dat	The history for the last calendar day that the browser was in use. Files older than one day roll into a separate folder.
C:\Documents and Settings\ <*username*>\Local Settings\ History\History.IE5\ MSHistXXXXXXXXXXX\ index.dat	Where the history data rolls to after it expires from the above index.dat. Each installation will have several of these directories, indicating yesterday, last week, two weeks ago, last month, and so on.
C:\Documents and Settings\ <*username*>\Local Settings\ Temporary Internet Files\ Content.IE5\index.dat	The audit trail for supporting files such as pictures and includes on the Web site. Look here to help reconstruct documents.
C:\Documents and Settings\<*username*>\ UserData\index.dat	This file holds information about automatic Windows accesses to the Internet, such as Windows update and other utilities.

Table 12-1   Breakdown of File Entries in Windows XP

Luckily, as long as you know where to look, you can use tons of tools to make this job easy. For the sake of demonstration, we will use a freeware command-line utility from Foundstone called Pasco. While completely devoid of any kind of flash or bells and whistles that other commercial products have, it gets the job done. It takes an index.dat file and converts the data into a tab-delimited format. Once you have that, you can import it into Excel and slice and dice it as you see fit. Then the fun begins. If you do a search for index.dat, you will find about five to ten entries. As you can quickly see from looking at any one of them, several different types of entries are included. Table 12-1 shows a breakdown of those that exist in Windows XP, their location, and what each one does.

If you are investigating an older version of Internet Explorer, here are some directories and file locations to look for that will hold the same information:

- C:\Windows\Cookies\index.dat
- C:\Windows\History\index.dat
- C:\Windows\History\MSHistXXXXXXXXXXXXXXXXX\index.dat

- C:\Windows\History\History.IE5\index.dat
- C:\Windows\History\History.IE5\MSHistXXXXXXXXXXXXXXXXXX\
  index.dat
- C:\Windows\Temporary Internet Files\index.dat (only in Internet Explorer 4.*x*)
- C:\Windows\Temporary Internet Files\Content.IE5\index.dat
- C:\Windows\UserData\index.dat
- C:\Windows\Profiles*<username>*\Cookies\index.dat
- C:\Windows\Profiles*<username>*\History\index.dat
- C:\Windows\Profiles*<username>*\History\
  MSHistXXXXXXXXXXXXXXXXXX\index.dat
- C:\Windows\Profiles*<username>*\History\History.IE5\index.dat
- C:\Windows\Profiles*<username>*\History\History.IE5\
  MSHistXXXXXXXXXXXXXXXXXX\index.dat
- C:\Windows\Profiles*<username>*\Temporary Internet Files\index.dat
- C:\Windows\Profiles*<username>*\Temporary Internet Files\Content.IE5\
  index.dat
- C:\Windows\Profiles*<username>*\UserData\index.dat

Now that you know where to look, let's examine how these interconnect and how you can use them to trace user activity. The first place you want to go is to the main history to locate what Web sites the user has visited. Here's a listing of the History.IE5 directory:

```
06/29/2004  01:22 PM              163,840 index.dat
06/14/2004  09:48 AM   <DIR>              MSHist012004060720040614
06/21/2004  09:05 AM   <DIR>              MSHist012004061420040621
06/28/2004  11:12 AM   <DIR>              MSHist012004062120040628
06/28/2004  11:12 AM   <DIR>              MSHist012004062820040629
06/29/2004  10:14 AM   <DIR>              MSHist012004062920040630
```

As you can see, five different directories start with *MSHist01* followed by a string of numbers. Let's decipher the sequence that MS uses for this structure.

The number *2004062820040629*, for example, looks pretty meaningless at first glance. If you break it up a bit, though, a pattern emerges: *2004-06-28* and *2004-06-29*. If you look at the created time, this suspicion is verified. This is how you tell what dates the directory holds. For our purposes, let's try to find an event that occurred on 2004-06-28, so we would use the index.dat in MSHist012004062120040628. You would go into the directory and actually extract the data from the file.

```
C:\Documents and Settings\<user>\Local Settings\History\History.IE5\MSHis
t012004062120040628>"C:\Documents and Settings\<user>\Desktop\Pasco\pasco
.exe" index.dat | more
```

```
History File: index.dat

TYPE,URL,MODIFIED TIME,ACCESS TIME,FILENAME,DIRECTORY,HTTP HEADERS
,URL,:2004062120040628: <user>@http://www.gnu.org/copyleft/gpl.html,Wed Jun 23
11:37:15 2004 ,Mon Jun 28 16:12:12 2004 ,URL  ,,URL
```

This is one line from the raw output of Pasco. As you can see, several fields are stored in the record. You need to determine what each one represents, as shown in Table 12-2.

For those who are unfamiliar with the command line, you can use the following command to dump the history into a text file that you can import into Excel:

```
Pasco <location of index.dat> > <output file>
```

Once you have created the text file and imported it into Excel, you should see something similar to the data shown in Figure 12-7.

From here, you can filter and sort the data to find the information relevant to the case. Most of the all-in-one forensics investigation tools have facilities for searching the history. That being the case, there is still something to be said for this method, because you can leverage the powerful searching and sorting features of a tool such as grep or Excel to help speed the investigation along, while still having a step-by-step process to show the court.

Field Name	Explanation
TYPE	The type of request that was made; usually a URL for a GET request.
URL	The actual URL requested along with the name of the user who requested it.
MODIFIED TIME	The time that the page was loaded into the history.
ACCESS TIME	The time that the history entry was last accessed. Through the course of normal operation, this will be the date of loading until the history file rolls back into an older directory; then it will be the date that the entry was added to the aged index.dat.
FILENAME	Used if redirection needs to occur; when a URL is requested, this will be URL.
DIRECTORY	The same thing as FILENAME but for the directory. Blank on a URL request.
HTTP HEADERS	Holds any headers that may have form data or whatnot for POST requests. Blank for URL requests.

Table 12-2   What Each Field Represents

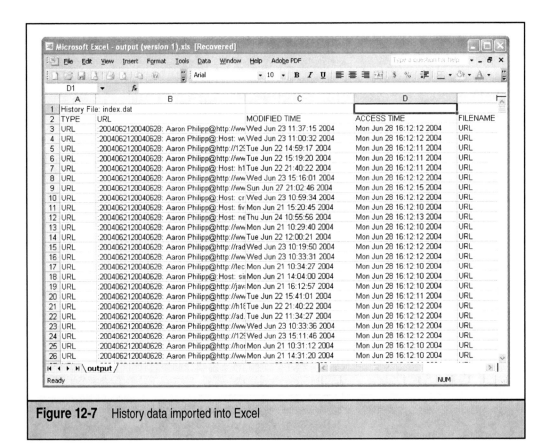

Figure 12-7 History data imported into Excel

Finding Information in Cookies

Popularity:	8
Simplicity:	6
Impact:	10
Risk Rating:	9

Cookies have become the predominant way for Web sites to store tracking information about their users. Every time you automatically log into a site, it remembers you and a cookie is involved. A cookie is a small text file earmarked with special data that is pertinent to a specific Web site. The information held in these cookies can be invaluable to forensics. Often, the cookie holds information about the username, the user's preferences, and the frequency with which the user visits the site. Like the history process, pulling information out of cookies is a straightforward process, but the devil is in the details. The first thing you want to do is investigate the history file in the C:\Documents and Settings\<*username*>\Cookies\ directory. This file is identical in structure to the main index.dat files, but instead of URLs, it stores the history of cookies. Here's a line of sample output:

```
TYPE,URL,MODIFIED TIME,ACCESS TIME,FILENAME,DIRECTORY,HTTP HEADERS
URL,Cookie:<user>@imrworldwide.com/cgi-bin,Sun Mar 21 05:25:33 2004 ,Thu
Jun 24 15:08:31 2004 ,<user>@cgi-bin[1].txt,,URL
```

The most notable aspect is the fact that the FILENAME field is populated with the name of the cookie as it's stored on the local hard disk. Notice as well that the filename of the cookie has nothing to do with the Web site from which it came. Some of the "shadier" Web sites will often name cookies to make it more difficult for you to discover that they are tracking you. This is why it's important to use the history file, because it will show you where the cookie originated and what server-side code produced it. Since the cookie history is identical in structure to the other histories, you can use the same techniques to search and find specific filenames of cookies.

Oftentimes, the mere existence of a cookie is enough to show that a user was visiting a site. But sometimes you'll need to delve deeper into the user activity and look inside the cookie itself. To do this, you can use a Foundstone tool called Galleta. It operates identically to the history tool used in the preceding section.

A cookie is nothing more than a data structure with a series of variable names and values. However, several fields of metadata are of interest and need explanation, as shown in the following table:

Field Name	Description
SITE	The name and URL of the cookie's Web site origin
VARIABLE	The name of the variable stored in the cookie
VALUE	The value stored inside the variable
CREATION TIME	The time the cookie was created, when the Web site was accessed
EXPIRE TIME	When the data inside the cookie expires; if a Web site pulls a cookie with expired data, it will expunge it and create a new one
FLAGS	Enumerates the flags set for each variable in the cookie; for a complete list of the flags, refer to the RFC on cookies

Here is a line created from the Galleta program run on a popular Web site, www .google.com:

```
C:\Documents and Settings\Admin\Cookies>"C:\Documents and Settings\
Admin\Desktop\galleta\galleta.exe" "admin@google[1].txt"
Cookie File: admin@google[1].txt

SITE      VARIABLE     VALUE     CREATION TIME    EXPIRE TIME     FLAGS
google.com/    PREF     ID=7757897559c7c13d:FF=4:TB=2:LD=en:NR=10:TM=1063258910:
LM=1076737164:S=VyefrLtaPC0FoJTZ         Sat Feb 14 05:39:23 2004       Sun Jan
17 19:14:07 2038       1536
```

Here you can see the variable `PREF` (presumably for user preferences) with a string value that Google accesses every time this browser goes to the home page. You can often look to the content inside the cookies to validate that a user spent time and actually logged into a Web site and didn't just land on it by accident. However, the existence of a cookie by itself isn't enough. Before you make statements regarding intent, make sure you empirically test how the cookie was created and what the values inside it can show you.

Reconstructing Activity from the Cache

Popularity:	8
Simplicity:	3
Impact:	10
Risk Rating:	**9**

To speed up Internet browsing, IE caches most of the pages you visit on your hard drive in case you want to go back. Good for forensics examiners, bad for suspects with something to hide. If you can navigate the maze that is the caching structure, you can re-create pages that the user saw and interacted with, including their forms data. There is a problem with caching Internet files, however. Think about what would happen if you cached everything under its original filename. The number of collisions in the cache would render the cache nearly useless (consider the number of pages named index.html, for example). As such, Microsoft has created a naming system that prevents that from occurring. In the cache directory, an index.dat file maps the pages on Web sites to files and directories in the cache.

The process for finding things in the cache is identical to the process for finding things in the history. Convert the index.dat to a readable format, slice and dice it to find the files that are important to the investigation, and then use the FILE and DIRECTORY fields to locate the files themselves. This time, the directory that we care about is C:\ Documents and Settings*Username*\Local Settings\Temporary Internet Files\ Content.IE5\.

Let's look at sample output from the index.dat file:

```
TYPE    URL     MODIFIED TIME   ACCESS TIME     FILENAME        DIRECTORY
HTTP HEADERS
URL     http://hp.msn.com/17/7M{T57_]6423LU+]0D]QKP.jpg Sat Jun 26 00:52:59 2004
        Mon Jun 28 22:01:05 2004        7M{T57_]6423LU+]0D]QKP[1].jpg   0PQLIJYD
        HTTP/1.1 200 OK  Content-Length: 2547  Content-Type: image/jpeg  ETag: "
6ee55ded175bc41:8b1"  P3P: CP="BUS CUR CONo FIN IVDo ONL OUR PHY SAMo TELo"
```

Let's try to make sense of this mess. First, notice that the original URL ties back to an MSN site. You can see a date when it was added to the cache and a date when it was last accessed. The areas where this differs from the history are the FILE, DIRECTORY, and HTTP HEADERS fields. The headers field can hold valuable information about the context in which the file was retrieved.

The two fields we care most about, however, are the FILE and DIRECTORY fields. These will locate the file in the cache for us. Take a look at the directory structure of the Content.IE5 directory:

```
06/29/2004  11:12 AM    <DIR>          .
06/29/2004  11:12 AM    <DIR>          ..
06/29/2004  10:17 PM    <DIR>          0PQLIJYD
06/30/2004  01:28 PM    <DIR>          S3LJ2IJT
06/30/2004  01:28 PM    <DIR>          UX7W5OVQ
02/12/2004  04:47 PM    <DIR>          W1OJKR87
02/12/2004  04:47 PM    <DIR>          WDQZGTMN
06/29/2004  10:17 PM    <DIR>          WLUFOTEF
06/30/2004  01:28 PM    <DIR>          YNMJAHUB
```

As you can see, several directories have very obscure names. However, if you look at the DIRECTORY field in the index.dat entry, it says *0PQLIJYD*, one of the directories in the hierarchy. If you go into that directory, you will find a file named 7M{T57_]6423LU+]0D] QKP[1].jpg, or the same value as the FILENAME field. You can repeat this step until all the files for a page including graphics and includes are located, allowing you to reconstruct completely the page that the user loaded and interacted with. The reconstruction process allows you to show pages as the user saw them and interacted with them by evaluating the base HTML documents and then resolving all the links.

Tips for Working with Internet Explorer

Working with IE can quickly get messy. The key to performing investigations on IE-related activities is to understand the overall scheme of how IE stores data. IE always uses an index.dat to serve as a lookup table to find the history, cache, and cookies for the username under which it's logged in. As long as you completely understand both the structure of the index.dat and the structure of the data to which it refers, you will be OK. If you try to perform investigations without fully understanding this scheme, you will get lost. Many tools automate this process to one level or another. But realize that even if you use an automated tool, if you are called to testify about the results, you must understand what the tool is doing. Don't fall into the temptation of using a graphical tool as a crutch.

Firefox/Mozilla Forensics

Firefox/Mozilla (Firefox from here out) is the primary browser used in open source circles. It was born out of Netscape's "crash-and-burn" back in 1998. It has been ported to every major operating system and is the Linux browser of choice. Its design focuses on cross-platform compatibility, so the information and metadata that you will be looking for is commonly kept in a file with an industry standard format as opposed to the IE way of doing things. This being said, you will have to deal with some interesting artifacts because the way it was developed (such as the history format) during your investigation.

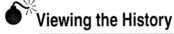

Viewing the History

Popularity:	8
Simplicity:	6
Impact:	10
Risk Rating:	**9**

The Mozilla history format (MORK) is an example of what happens when open source goes bad. MORK replaced the standard Berkeley database format (DBM), and no one really knows why. In fact, the format is listed as a bug on the Firefox development tracker.

Several free options are available for viewing the history, but the one we like the best is Red Cliff Web Historian. This will extract the history data and put it into plaintext or HTML. If you are working an investigation and must look forensically at the history file, you might also want to check out a tool called NetAnalysis, which we will use in the case study, to perform the searching. To become familiar with the format, however, let's look at the output from one of these tools. The location of the history file will vary based on operating system. In Windows, the file is located at C:\Documents and Settings*<user>*\ Application Data\Firefox\Profiles*<profile name>*\history.dat, and for UNIX/Linux it's in ~/ .Firefox/Profiles/*<profile name>*/history.dat. Now that you know where to look, let's see what we get:

```
1088622307      2       http://www.otc.utexas.edu/
1088622301      3       http://www.Firefox.org/start/
1088622301      3       http://www.Firefox.org/start/1.7/
```

As you can see, three columns of data are presented. The first column is the last access time in microseconds. The next column represents the number of times the URL has been accessed. This can be useful in showing that a user didn't just inadvertently end up on a Web site and was actually a repeat visitor. The third column is the URL that was accessed by the request. This is good for a cursory check of what a user was doing on a machine. A ton of information is included in the file that can help with an investigation. Unfortunately, because of the file format, you are going to have to learn to decipher it yourself or buy a tool that does it for you. Unless you have a degree in computer science or at least a strong background in linguistic computing, we recommend the latter. We have had good luck with the tool FireFox Forensics by Machor Software. It can automatically break out the profile data and user settings from these preference files.

Finding Information in Cookies

Popularity:	*8*
Simplicity:	*6*
Impact:	*10*
Risk Rating:	*9*

What Firefox lacks in a history file format it makes up for with cookies. All the client's cookies are stored in a central file, cookies.txt, which is in the profile directory. If you open it, you will notice that this file is human-readable and no special tools are required to view it. Let's look at a few lines of the file:

```
.amazon.com  TRUE /    FALSE 1089187200 session-id-time    1089187200
.amazon.com  TRUE /    FALSE 2082787201 ubid-main          430-1652529-3243032
.amazon.com  TRUE /    FALSE 1089187200 session-id          104-0716758-6083948
```

This is the cookie and variables for amazon.com, as you can see in the first column. The second value is the flag that says whether or not the cookie allows the POST command. The third column, a directory entry, tells the site for which URLs and sub-URLs the cookie is valid. The fourth value is the flag indicating whether the cookie is used on a secure (SSL/TLS) site. The end of the metadata information contains the expiration time of the cookie in milliseconds. Finally, the last two columns are the variable name and value. As you can see from the entry, this information can be useful because you can see that a session was created with Amazon, denoting a login.

> **NOTE** As of version 3 of Firefox, the browser now uses a SQLite database to store the cookies as well as other information. The best way that we have found to view these databases outside of forensic tools is through the use of SQLite Manager, a free add-on for Firefox. You can open the history file on another computer and export the results as a comma separated value (CSV) file.

Reconstructing Activity from the Cache

Popularity:	*8*
Simplicity:	*7*
Impact:	*10*
Risk Rating:	*9*

Cache browsing in Firefox is actually an easy process. If you can get hold of the cache directory in the profile, you can use Firefox to navigate it. Make sure that you make the cache read-only and that you properly hash everything before and after doing this, since you will be accessing the data with a non-forensics tool. That being said, fire up Firefox with the profile of the suspect. Then, in the browser bar, enter the URL **about:cache**, as shown in Figure 12-8.

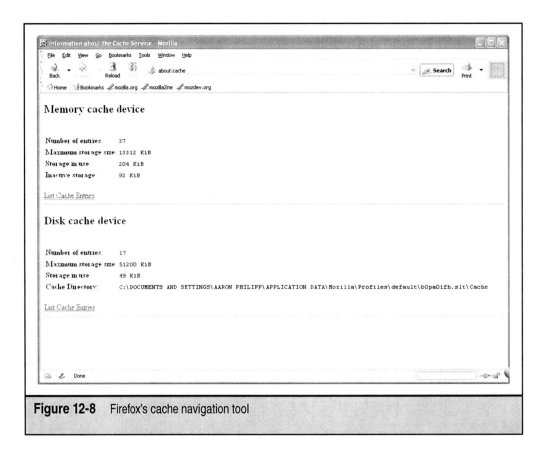

Figure 12-8 Firefox's cache navigation tool

You are concerned with the cache on the disk, so first ensure that the Cache Directory is set correctly and then click List Cache Entries. After you do this, you will see a listing of every file in the cache along with metadata, as shown in Figure 12-9.

If you need to drill down even more on a specific URL, you can click it to get more information, as shown in Figure 12-10.

As you can see in Figure 12-10, you are presented with everything you would want to know, and more, about the file. The most important part is the local filename, which tells you where to look on the file system to find the cached data. You can use this information to reconstruct entire pages with images and all includes.

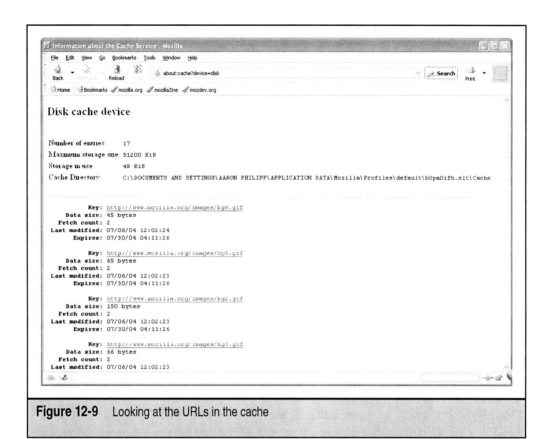

Figure 12-9   Looking at the URLs in the cache

Tips for Working with Firefox

History file aside, Firefox is much easier to work with during an investigation than Internet Explorer. Everything you need to look at is consolidated into one central location and the formatting is well documented. In addition, unlike IE, the location of the files stays relatively the same from operating system to operating system. The downfall of Firefox during an investigation, however, is the history file. If you are doing an investigation that you think may end up in court at some point, save yourself the worry and effort and purchase a tool that can decode the history file for you and present the data in a meaningful manner. As mentioned regarding IE forensics, however, do try and understand what you know and don't know about the format. Several good resources on the MORK format are available; read through these before you use a graphical tool.

Figure 12-10 Getting information about a specific URL

Case Study: Using NetAnalysis to Perform an Investigation

NetAnalysis is a graphical tool that makes investigation of web activity easy by pulling everything into one place. Let's look at how you can use this tool to do a complete web investigation.

This case involves an employee who is suspected of working with a competitor to leak corporate secrets via the competitor's Web site. The suspect was allegedly hacking into servers that contained secret information. We want to find out whether the user's web activity tells us anything about the hack. The user has Windows XP with Firefox/Mozilla as the browser.

Our first step is to check the history and determine whether he has accessed the competitor's site. After we have created a forensic copy of the user's web browser profile and are properly documented, we open the history in NetAnalysis, as shown next. We do this by choosing File | Open History.

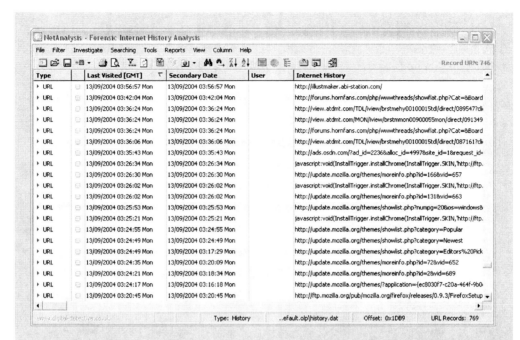

Once open, we can see exactly what our suspect has done. Let's see what he was searching for with Google. The best way to do this is by using a filter. Let's add one for searches we're looking for by choosing Investigate | Google Search Criteria. This will limit the history only to the queries made in Google.

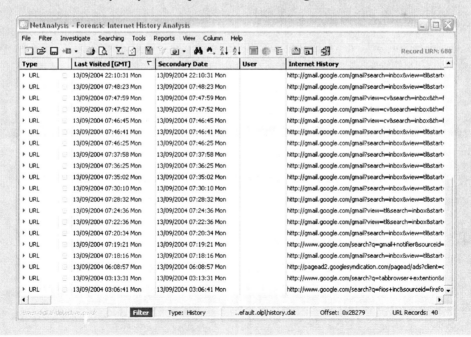

As you can see, the suspect used Google heavily (in fact, he even had a gmail account), as pretty much anyone who uses the Internet does. Let's search the queries that he made and see if he was trolling around for corporate secrets or passwords.

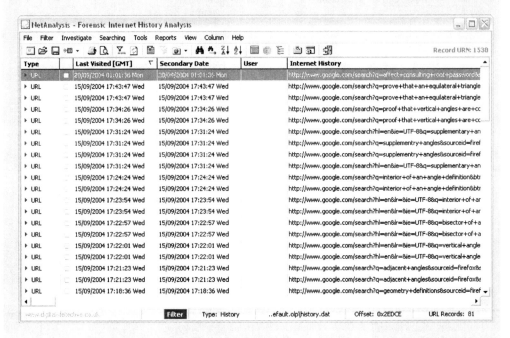

As you can see, he was definitely looking for things he shouldn't have been looking for with Google. This is a common pre-hack tactic to find out information about the company as well as passwords. Next, we follow proper forensic procedures to tag and bag the evidence and create our report for the higher ups.

OPERATING SYSTEM USER LOGS

The operating system on the computer can also be an effective tool in reconstructing user activities. While we discuss a few of these in depth in Chapters 6, 7, and 8, you should pay special attention to the UserAssist logs stored in Windows 2000, XP, and Vista. UserAssist can be immensely valuable in the timeline creation process.

UserAssist

UserAssist is a monitoring tool that tracks user activity: the programs a user accesses, double-clicks shortcuts, and performs other activities. The UserAssist key also maintains a count of these actions, as well as the last date and time a program was run by a user. It was first implemented in the Windows 2000 operating system.

Working with UserAssist

Popularity:	8
Simplicity:	7
Impact:	10
Risk Rating:	9

While UserAssist logging can be disabled, most casual computer users are not even aware that it is running. Because UserAssist is encrypted with ROT13, the average user wouldn't even know the UserAssist key if they saw it. ROT13 is a substitution cipher (also known as the Caesar cipher); it simply replaces a letter with another letter 13 places down the alphabet. While someone may easily figure out how to delete their Internet history, it never occurs to them to disable the UserAssist feature or to delete entries from the UserAssist key; thus the UserAssist log usually remains untouched and provides a history of user activity.

UserAssist is found under the following registry key in the NTUSER.DAT file:

```
HKEY_CURRENT_USER\Software\Microsoft\Windows\CurrentVersion\Explorer\UserAssist
```

The UserAssist key consists of two subkeys. One key is for the Active Desktop and the other is for the Internet toolbar. If the system in question uses Internet Explorer 7.0 installed, you will see a third subkey.

As you can see in Figure 12-11, each of the UserAssist subkeys contain the Count subkeys that contain a substantial amount of information. Figure 12-12 illustrates how one of these keys appears when the Registry Editor is used to view it.

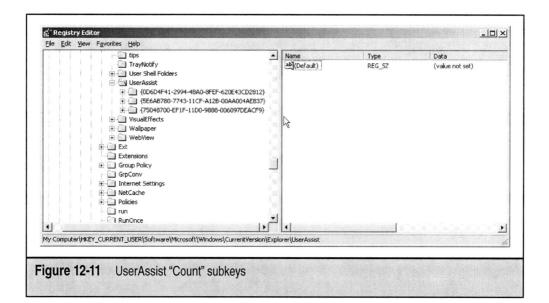

Figure 12-11   UserAssist "Count" subkeys

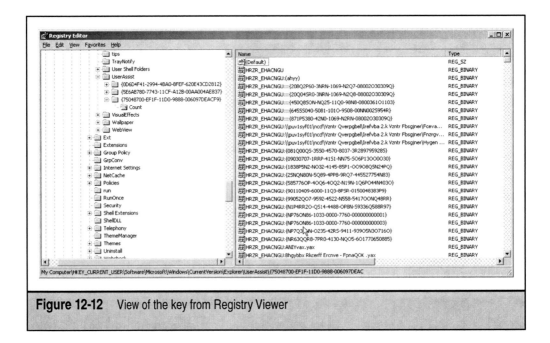

Figure 12-12   View of the key from Registry Viewer

Since Windows uses ROT13 to encrypt the data, the entries contained in the Count subkeys appear to be gibberish. However, several utilities can be used to decrypt them. One of them is Didier Stevens's UserAssist utility, which is free and available to download from his Web site at http://blog.didierstevens.com/programs/userassist/).

Figure 12-13 shows the UserAssist data decrypted. Many of the decrypted entries contain one of three tags: RUNPATH, RUNPIDL, and RUNCPL. Numerous other tags appear as well, but these three will be of the most interest to you as forensic examiner. RUNPATH is linked to when a user double-clicks an icon for an application (such as Word). RUNPIDL is related to the access of shortcuts or .lnk files. The Last Write date/time is updated every time a user performs a specific action. RUNCPL is associated with the execution of a Control Panel applet, such as Add/Remove Programs.

Figure 12-13   UserAssist data decrypted

Paraben's Registry Analyzer also decrypts ROT13 data. It shows both the raw (ROT13) data and the decrypted data, as illustrated in Figure 12-14. Using the ROT13 decryption, we can see, for example, that when HRZR_EHACNGU:NRKE.yax is decrypted, it is actually UEME_RUNPATH:AEXR.lnk.

NOTE   Microsoft has removed several UserAssist entries in the Vista rollout that were present in XP. Depending on what user activity you're looking for, it may be logged but could appear with a different tag, the entry may not contain the same specific information found in XP, or it may not be logged at all. You must verify whether or not you are examining a computer that has been upgraded from XP to Vista. If that is the case, you may see the old XP UserAssist entries as well as the Vista entries, so it's important to pay special attention when reviewing the UserAssist registry keys.

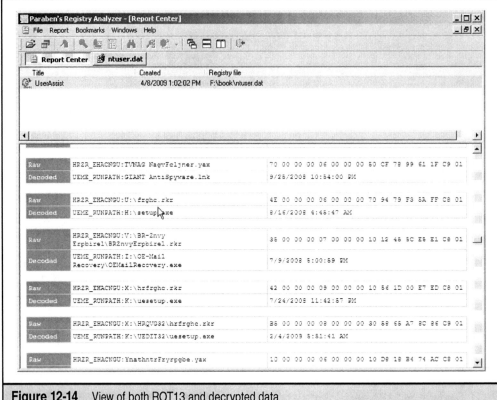

Figure 12-14 View of both ROT13 and decrypted data

Tips for UserAssist

As you can see, UserAssist contains a lot of useful information. It can help you find new artifacts of user activity or to support other evidence of user activity you may have already found.

CHAPTER 13

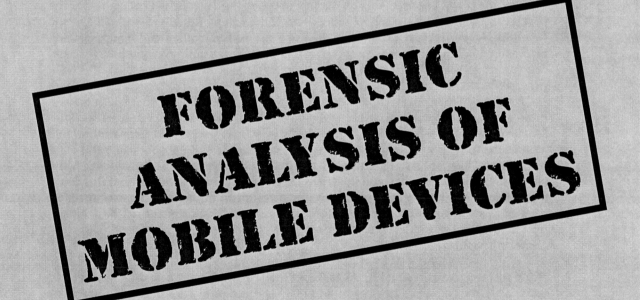

FORENSIC ANALYSIS OF MOBILE DEVICES

When I first wrote this chapter in 2004, little did I know how radically personal digital assistant (PDA) and cell phone technologies would evolve in a few short years—not only technically, but in our society and culture—as very real parts of our daily lives. In 2004, the concept of a combination cell phone/PDA was just really starting, and I thought I was on the cutting edge, because I had a Mobile Windows device that I could also use to place a call. Today, these combination devices have permeated our lives, and people are tied to them in ways they never thought possible. In the late 1990s, *The X Files* Agent Scully told Mulder he'd go catatonic if he went without his cell phone for 24 hours. Today, the same can be said of almost everyone I know.

In 2004, I thought it was insanely cool to be connected all the time. Today, one of my fondest wishes is to donate my PDA phone to David Letterman for the "What happens if you throw this off the top of the Ed Sullivan Theater" skit.

In 2006, when my son started junior high school, I got the cultural shock of my life. It was the first day of school and I was standing at the front door of the school, waiting to meet my sixth grader. The bell rang, doors opened, and a crowd of teenagers rushed by me. The memories started flooding back of my time at his age, and then I heard something I never heard back then. Almost at once, as if by some grand queue from the cosmos or one of those unexplained wonders of nature, like salmon possessed to swim upstream, *flip, flip, flip, flip, flip, flip, flip.* I looked back and saw swarms of school children flipping open their cell phones to check their voice mails or make that call home. As my son and I walked to the car, I noticed kids on the school buses, heads crouched over, texting. The next day I asked one of the school bus drivers if the texting thing was normal, and she said the kids even text their friends on the same bus instead of just standing up, walking over, and actually having a conversation with one another and building some interpersonal communication skills. Then it hit me, on a gut level, just how much these devices have truly permeated our society.

The reason I bring all this up isn't a form of self-therapy; rather, it's to make a point—to convey the concept in a way that will help you understand it on a gut level, as I did. Mobile devices are part of almost everyone's lives, and people feel very comfortable around them, which is nothing but good for investigators. Because when people are comfortable, they are truly themselves and they will let their defenses down. When people are comfortable, they will take risks they wouldn't normally take, and this could mean that you'll have good luck collecting relevant information from one of these devices. Cases in point: The gangster who killed a guy and took a picture of the deceased with his phone. The vandal who documented his actions using his phone and posted his crime on YouTube.

We've come a long way from the days of simple phones that let you make calls, or PDAs that simply maintained contacts, kept your schedule straight, and allowed you to take notes. Today, mobile devices provide wireless access to corporate e-mail servers, and they can surf the Web at broadband speeds, in color! They can also run database applications, create documents with embedded graphics, create spreadsheets, act as clients to terminal services, be cell phones, and, oh yeah, keep your contacts and schedule straight. Today's mobile devices really are computers in every sense of the word.

In 2004, only a handful of forensic tools had PDA and cell phone analysis capabilities. Today's forensic analyst has a wide range of options, from tools that are specifically designed to do nothing but acquire and analyze these devices, to tools that include this feature as part of a suite of functions.

In this chapter, we will describe several types mobile device collections, including Palm OS and Mobile Windows. We'll look at various tools and discuss their analyzing and reporting capabilities.

COLLECTING AND ANALYZING MOBILE DEVICE EVIDENCE

Before you can collect anything you must take physical custody of it, a topic that has already been covered in this book. Mobile devices are just like any other piece of electronic evidence and require all the same chain of custody, documentation, and proper handling procedures. However, you must meet additional requirements for PDAs that are not required for desktops, laptops, or servers.

The first requirement is power. Remember that, unlike other types of systems discussed in this book, some older mobile devices without nonvolatile (flash) memory store user-created files in RAM. The data on the ROM chip will survive if power is lost to the device, but data in RAM (that is, your evidence) will not survive. Therefore, you must ensure a constant supply of power to the device for as long as it's in your custody. A great many people have endured the collection process, stored these devices in their evidence lockers, and left them in there with no power for weeks, only to find out that the batteries are dead when they get around to the acquisition stage. "Boss, I've got some bad news…" and the conversation can go only downhill from there.

Next are the peripherals. It's important that you include entries in your collection checklists for the additional items you'll need when dealing with mobile devices, such as the following:

- Cradle
- Power supply
- Cables
- Secure digital cards
- Compact flash memory

Just as you must think about collecting CDs from a desk where you seize a PC, you must think about collecting the storage media that mobile devices use.

If collecting the cradle and power supply at the scene is not possible for whatever reason, you must keep in mind that you don't know exactly how long the device has been off the charger, and the device is running out of battery time. Therefore, you should include some mobile device peripherals as part of your standard deployment kit. If, however, you don't have the budget to build an inventory of cradles and power supplies, vendors such as Paraben distribute collection kits that have all the cables and other items you'll likely need.

If you are concerned about continued outside interaction with a mobile device, such as the remote deletion capabilities of a Blackberry device, you might consider obtaining a Paraben StrongHold Bag, an evidence bag that blocks all electronic signals from entering or exiting the device.

Collecting Evidence Using Device Seizure

Popularity:	10
Simplicity:	8
Impact:	10
Risk Rating:	9

In mid-2006, Paraben Corporation replaced the separate Device Seizure and Cell Seizure products that were documented in the first edition of this book with the new combined Device Seizure 1.0 product. The company realized that, with the converging technologies used for these types of devices, PDAs and cell phones no longer needed to be treated as separate entities. Device Seizure has evolved over the years and now supports a much broader group of devices than those highlighted in the first edition of this book. Today, the list includes the following:

- PDAs
- Smart phones
- Cell phones
- GPS receivers
- Subscriber Identity Module (SIM)/memory cards

The Device Seizure product was designed with the realization that consumers have choices regarding what kind of mobile device and carrier services they can buy. Think about how many different phone choices you have when you go to the phone store today versus the choices available in 2004. Because so many different types of devices are supported by this tool, and the fact that manufacturers process data and functions differently from device to device, accessing information will probably require that you use a specific plug-in to get the job done; in fact, some devices require the use of multiple plug-ins.

The following basic types of plug-ins are used by Device Seizure:

- **Logical plug-in** Acquires certain types of data, typically whole files and databases.
- **Physical plug-in** Contains all the data that is stored on the memory card.

For each type of device that's supported, a specific plug-in has been created, although some plug-ins can be used for several types of devices. Plug-ins are located in the plugins subfolder of the Device Seizure installation folder. Table 13-1 lists some available plug-ins and their purposes.

Plug-In	Purpose
BlackBerryImoport.dll	Import of Research In Motion (RIM) Blackberry backup files
BlackBerryPhysical.dll	Physical acquisition from RIM Blackberry devices
CardReaderLogical.dll	Logical acquisition from SIM card readers
CDMAPhysical.dll	Physical acquisition from Code Division Multiple Access (CDMA) cell phones
GarminGPSPhysical.dll	Physical acquisition from Garmin GPS devices
GPSLogical.dll	Logical acquisition from Garmin GPS devices
iDenLogical.dll	Logical acquisition from Motorola iDEN cell phones
iDenPhysical.dll	Physical acquisition from Motorola iDEN cell phones
iPhoneBackupImport.dll	Import of iPhone backup files
iPhoneLogical.dll	Logical acquisition of iPhone files
KyoceraCDMALogical.dll	Logical acquisition of Kyocera CDMA cell phones
LGCDMALogical.dll	Logical acquisition from LG CDMA cell phones
LGGSMLogical.dll	Logical acquisition from LG Global System for Mobile Communications (GSM) cell phones
MemoryCardPhysical.dll	Physical acquisition from card readers
MotorolaLogical.dll	Logical acquisition from Motorola cell phones
MotorolaPhysical.dll	Physical acquisition from Motorola cell phones
NokiaGSMLogical.dll	Logical acquisition from Nokia GSM cell phones
NokiaGSMPhysical.dll	Physical acquisition from Nokia GSM cell phones
NokiaTDMALogical.dll	Logical acquisition from Nokia Time Division Multiple Access (TDMA) cell phones

Table 13-1   Plug-ins for Mobile Device Data Acquisition

Plug-In	Purpose
PalmPhysical.dll	Physical acquisition from Palm devices
PsionLogical.dll	Logical acquisition from Psion devices
SamsungCDMALogical.dll	Logical acquisition Samsung CDMA cell phones
SamsungGSMLogical.dll	Logical acquisition from Samsung GSM cell phones
SamsungPhysical.dll	Physical acquisition Samsung GSM & CDMA cell phones
SiemensLogical.dll	Logical acquisition from Siemens cell phones
SiemensPhysical.dll	Physical acquisition from Siemens cell phones
SonyEricssonLogical.dll	Logical acquisition from Sony Ericsson cell phones
StickMotorola.dll	Import of the Motorola databases from CSI Stick
StickSamsung.dll	Import of the Samsung databases from CSI Stick
Symbian7X–8XLogical.dll	Logical acquisition Symbian 7.x.–8.x. smart phones
Symbian9xLogical.dll	Logical acquisition from Symbian 9.x. smart phones
Symbian60Logical.dll	Logical acquisition from Symbian 6.0. smart phones
Symbian61Logical.dll	Logical acquisition from Symbian 6.1. smart phones
SymbianPhysical.dll	Physical acquisition from Symbian smart phones
WindowsCE5.dll	Support library for working with Windows CE 5.x devices
WindowsCELogical.dll	Logical acquisition WindowsCE/PocketPC devices
WindowsCEPhysical.dll	Physical acquisition Windows Mobile 5.x–6.x devices

Table 13-1　Plug-ins for Mobile Device Data Acquisition *(continued)*

That's 37, and counting, that are available now, and more plug-ins are being created all the time. Although I originally intended to document each type and its proper acquisition method, I soon realized that would not be practical when the page count hit 50-plus and I wasn't even two-thirds of the way through my descriptions. Not wanting to bore you with too much information, I will instead review two common systems: Palm-based and Windows-based devices.

I want to take this opportunity to reiterate something that hopefully became painfully evident to you if you bothered to read the table of plug-ins, as it did me as I wrote it: You can use least 37 different methods, each with its own little nuances and procedures, to deal with an ever-growing number of mobile devices used by almost everyone on the planet. Consider a quick comparison: How many different methods can be used to acquire a hard drive? How many different things do you have to keep in mind to acquire a hard drive?

Acquisition of a Palm-based Device

Make sure the device is powered, is in the appropriate cradle, and is correctly connected to your acquisition system via either USB or a serial port. Then do the following:

1. Start Paraben's Device Seizure Acquisition Wizard by clicking the Data Acquisition button or by choosing Tools | Data Acquisition.
2. When the Acquisition Wizard appears, click the Next button.
3. In the list, select Palm OS Based Devices. Click Next.
4. Select Autodetect. Click Next.
5. Select the port to which your device is connected. Click Next.
6. Select the type of data you want to acquire. Click Next.

NOTE If you are acquiring a Palm-based device for the first time, it's strongly recommended that you select only Databases. If you do not choose this option, the device may become locked during the driver installation process before acquisition.

7. Define the additional parameters of data acquisition:

   - **Sort Images After Finish**   If this is checked, images from the acquired device will be added to the sorter automatically after the acquisition.

   - **Acquire Structure And Contents Of Files**   This checkbox appears for some types of PDAs and smart phones. If it is checked, all selected data will be acquired at once. Otherwise, only the structure of the data will be read.

8. To acquire a memory image, you need to put your device into console mode, also known as debug mode. To put the device in the console mode, do one of the following:

   - If the device has a graffiti area, write the following combination there: l..2 (a shortcut, with cursive lowercase L + dot + dot + 2). It should look like what's shown in Figure 13-1.

   - If the device is a Handspring Visor using a serial connection, instead of the l..2 command, write the shortcut l. (cursive lowercase L + dot), and then hold down the Up button while writing the number 2 (that is, l.2). Devices using a USB connection do not require this additional step.

- If the device has no graffiti area (which is the case with the Treo 650), use the special key combination, such as Search (shift)+Sync Mode, to put the device in console mode. Please note that this combination will depend on the model of your device, so check the documentation on the Web for the correct sequence if not specified here.

9. To acquire a logical image (databases), you need to put your device into the sync mode. Press the Sync button on the cradle or activate the sync mode through the screen dialog on the device.

If you're acquiring a Palm-based device for the first time, the driver installation for it begins at this time and may lock the device. If you're acquiring the databases and the device becomes locked, click Cancel. If acquiring memory and the device becomes locked, power cycle the device. If the data acquisition finishes correctly, you will see the last page of the data Acquisition Wizard. Click Finish.

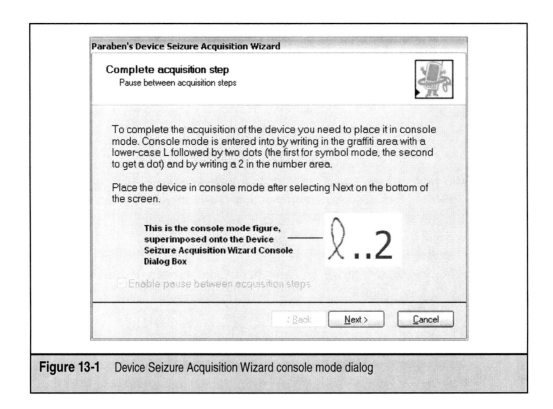

Figure 13-1   Device Seizure Acquisition Wizard console mode dialog

How you get the Palm-based device into debug mode depends on the particular generation of the device. In some of the newer models, the process involves holding the DOWN scroll button and performing a soft reset, while continuing to hold the DOWN scroll button for another 10 seconds. If you happen to be working on a model that slides open to reveal the reset button on the back, you've got some extra fun in store. You'll have to juggle the cradle, coordinate your finger on the DOWN scroll button, and stick a really small object in the reset hole without looking like a complete fool.

It is fairly easy to determine when the device is in debug mode based on the model. For older systems, you'll hear a long tone, followed by a shorter tone. Newer systems show a blinking square in the upper-left corner of the screen.

After the acquisition is complete, a .PDS file is created and you can begin the analysis portion of the process.

Acquisition of a Windows-based Device

Unlike with Palm-based systems, with Windows CE/Mobile Windows devices, Device Seizure does not load drivers to communicate with the system. Instead, it uses, and you will need to load, Microsoft ActiveSync to acquire the device. Before you begin acquisition, make sure the device is powered and correctly connected to your acquisition system using the Guest partnership.

 If you don't use the Guest partnership, you will start synchronizing the PDA with your acquisition system's own data, which is a bad thing.

1. Depending on the version of Windows CE/Mobile Windows loaded on the device you are acquiring, you will need to load the appropriate version of Microsoft ActiveSync:

   - Windows CE 3.0 and lower: ActiveSync 3.7
   - Windows CE 5.0 and higher: ActiveSync 4.5
   - Mobile Windows: Latest version

2. Connect the device to the acquisition system.

3. ActiveSync starts automatically. If it does not, start it manually.

4. Select a Guest Partnership, and click Next to finish.

To begin Data Acquisition, follow these steps:

1. Tap the Data Acquisition toolbar button or choose Tools | Data Acquisition in the Device Seizure interface to start data acquisition process.

2. The Device Seizure Acquisition Wizard will guide you through the process. Click Next.

3. In the drop-down pick list, select the model of the device to acquire and type of acquisition, physical or logical, and then click Next.

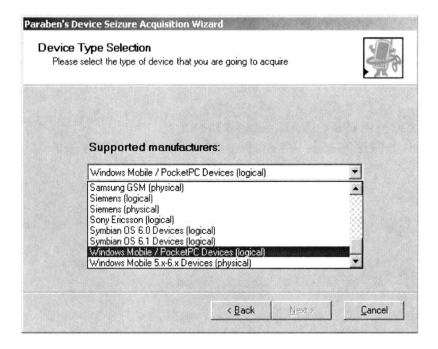

4. Select which data types you want to acquire from the device and click Next.

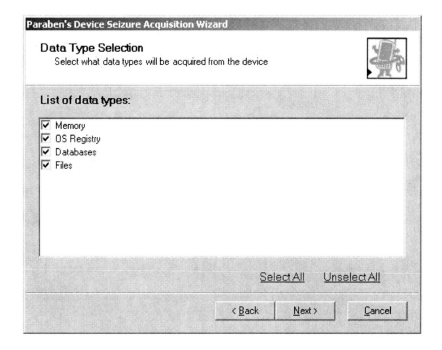

5. In the Summary of Your Selections dialog, as shown in Figure 13-2, you have one last chance to double-check the parameters for the acquisition. You'll see two checkboxes:

- **Fill the Sorter After Acquisition**   If checked, data from the acquired device will be added to the sorter automatically after acquisition.

- **Acquire Structure And Contents Of Files**   This checkbox is available only for some device types. If checked, all selected data will be acquired at once. If it's not checked, only the structure of the file system will be acquired and not the contents of the files.

NOTE   Another difference from a Palm OS acquisition is the device seizure client file, a 4K .DLL file that is placed on the device in the first available block of memory and removed at the end of the acquisition. Although the insertion of this file seems to violate one of the cornerstone rules of forensics, which is don't alter the original media, the architecture of a Windows CE/Mobile Windows device requires the use of this approach to obtain a copy of the physical memory.

To counter a possible argument that key files you might find during your analysis could have been altered as a result of the .DLL installation, you might want to do a logical file acquisition first. Since the .DLL is required only to obtain the physical memory, if you have a copy of the logical files with their corresponding MD5 hash values in a completely

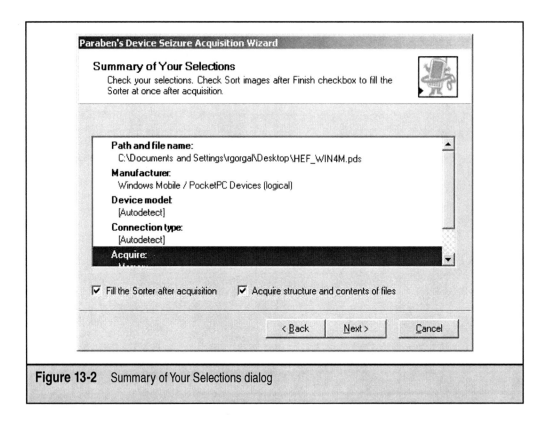

Figure 13-2   Summary of Your Selections dialog

separate Device Seizure image taken prior to the physical acquisition, you can compare those hash values. Armed with the MD5s prior to the installation of the .DLL, you'll be able to prove to a mathematical certainty that files found during the analysis were not altered.

Analysis of a Windows-based Device

The Device Seizure interface includes several panes, as shown in Figure 13-3:

- **Case pane**   Represents data stored in the case in a tree-view structure
- **Sorter pane**   Lets you sort case data by 12 different file types, such as images, documents, multimedia, and so on
- **Viewer pane**   Lets you view data in a Text Viewer, Hex Viewer, Image Viewer, and more
- **Properties pane**   Shows properties of specific files, MD5 hash codes, size, and so on
- **Attachments pane**   Shows files attached to the case
- **Bookmarks pane**   Lists all bookmarked items within the case
- **Search Results pane**   Lists results of searches performed

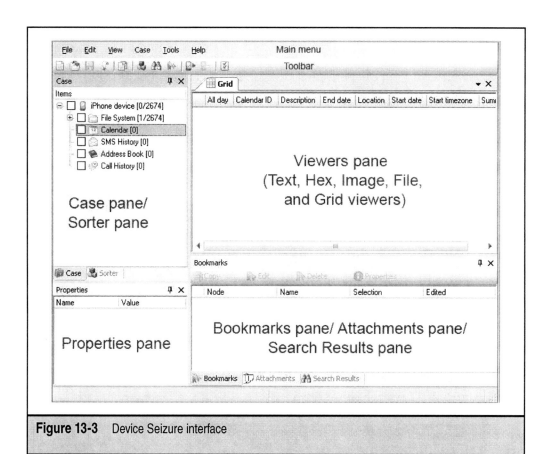

Figure 13-3   Device Seizure interface

As with other forensic tools, the real work gets done by searching.

To open the Find dialog box, do one of the following: choose Edit | Find, press CTRL-F, or click Find Data on the button bar.

The following options are available in the Find dialog to help you refine search results:

- **Search Text**   You can perform text string searches (including Boolean) across all the acquired data.

- **Match Whole Word**   Only the complete whole word will be returned—for example, a search on "stone" will not return "stones".

- **Match Case**   Defines whether to take capitalization into account—for example, a search on "stone" will not return "Stone".

- **Code Page**   Defines the encoding in which data will be searched—ASCII, UTF-8, and so on. You'll find available encodings defined by choosing Tools | Options | and then opening the Encodings tab. To add more encodings, click the ellipses (...) button to the right of the text field and check the necessary encodings.

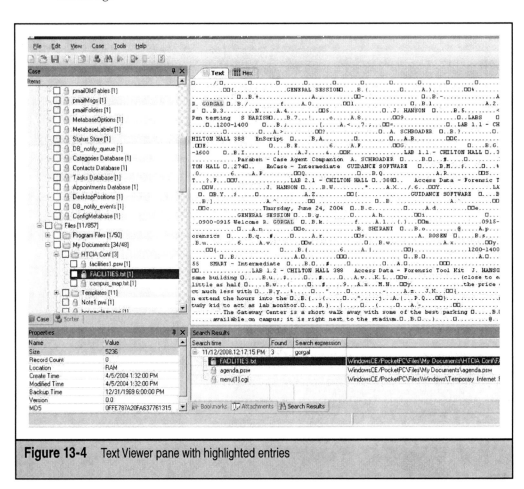

Figure 13-4   Text Viewer pane with highlighted entries

- **Locale** Defines the locale in which data will be searched. You'll find available encodings—such as en(English) or es(Spanish)—defined by choosing Tools | Options | and then opening the Locales tab. To add more locales, click the ellipses (...) button to the right of the text field and check the necessary locales.

Each row appearing in the Search Results pane represents a different file where the keyword is found, and each instance within the file is highlighted in the Text Viewer pane, as shown in Figure 13-4.

In addition to searching, you can also view files in a directory structure, as shown in Figure 13-5.

Analysis of a Palm-based Device

The naming conventions of Palm OS databases are straightforward and make it easy when you're performing analysis for the first time. For example, NetworkDB is where network connection information such as Internet service provider (ISP), type of connection, username, and so on, are stored. It's not difficult to guess what you're likely to find in ToDoDB, MemoDB, and AddressDB.

The Palm Operating System Emulator (POSE) allows the analyst to interact with and see the data as the original user did. The POSE interface displays a virtual device where you can select menus, open memos, access the calendar, and perform other tasks, as if you were working on a physical device.

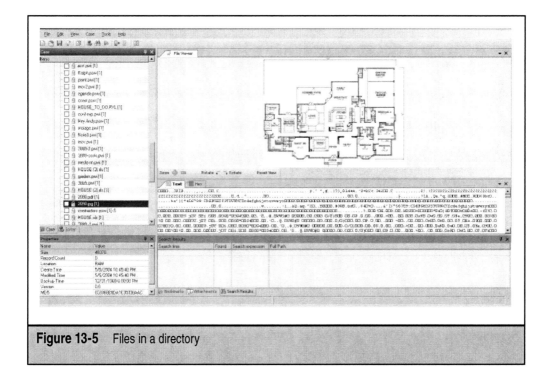

Figure 13-5 Files in a directory

The process of launching a POSE session is fairly straightforward and begins by exporting all the files from the Device Seizure image file:

1. Export the ROM binary node into the file. You should export the ROM binary node from the memory images but not the ROM folder from the databases.

2. Choose Tools | Palm Emulator.

3. In the Palm OS Emulator dialog, click New.

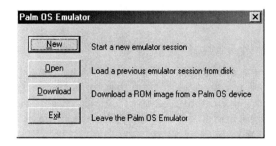

4. In the New Session dialog, choose Other from the ROM File drop-down list .

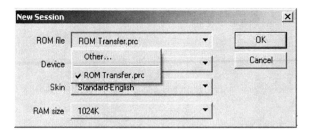

5. In the Choose ROM file dialog, select the appropriate ROM file.

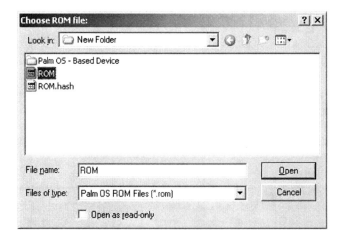

6. Click OK to run the Palm Emulator.

WindowsCE/Mobile Windows-based Devices vs. Palm Devices   Some of the differences between Palm and Windows device analysis stem from the differences in the architecture of the devices. If you choose to Acquire Registry, be prepared for the acquisition to take a long time; nevertheless, any good analyst knows the importance of being able to look at registry entries in any Windows-based system.

Other unique facets of Window CE/Mobile Windows analysis include the architecture itself. While Palm keeps everything in databases, Microsoft uses databases and files much like other versions of Windows, including dynamic link libraries (DLLs) and executable files.

If you acquire the memory, it can be searched like unallocated space in a Windows-based PC; however, complete files associated with any search results cannot be reconstructed.

Anyone who has done analysis of a Windows-based PC will be comfortable with a Windows CE/Mobile Windows analysis, so let's take a closer look at that.

Some older versions of Mobile Windows included installations of Terminal Services client, MSN Messenger, Pocket Internet Explorer, and Pocket versions of Microsoft Office applications, including Word, Excel, and Outlook. However, starting with version 5, the Terminal Services client is no longer included.

Even if you're comfortable analyzing Windows-based systems, you shouldn't expect Mobile Windows/Windows CE analysis to be a walk in the park. You'll find a list of Web sites visited in Index.dat, an Internet cache in the Temporary Internet Files folder, and a Cookies folder, and you'll able to analyze some of them in the same ways you did in other Windows environments. However, you won't find e-mail in a .PST file; instead you'll find it divided among different databases, including attachments that will be in pmailAttachments databases. In addition, e-mail-related folders will be maintained in the pmailFolders database with references therein to the actual folders that will use a naming convention of fldr[*NUMBER*]—such as fldr1013d4, for example. You won't find contacts in any .PST or .WAB files; instead you'll find that information in the Contacts Database, as shown in Figure 13-6.

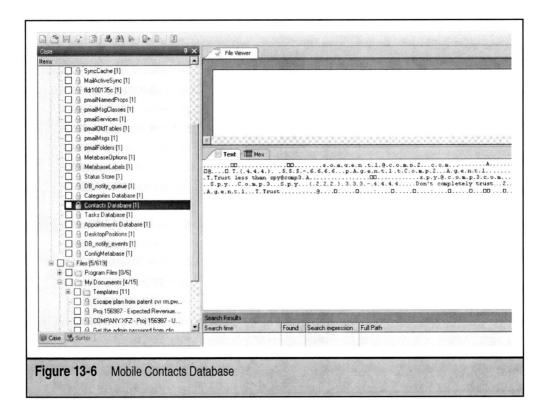

Figure 13-6 Mobile Contacts Database

You'll also have to contend with the fact that Word and Excel documents are converted to and from Mobile/Pocket Word and Mobile/Pocket Excel formats when the PDA is synched. Most Mobile/Pocket Word documents can be opened by MS Word without issue, but that's not the case for Mobile/Pocket Excel documents. In these cases, you'll need to take the exported .PXL document and convert it back to Excel format before you can view them outside of the PDA environment in MS Excel.

If you don't want to export files to look at them with the non-Mobile/Pocket versions for analysis purposes, the Device Seizure File Viewer pane will display the files adequately.

Bookmarking Data with Device Seizure

Bookmarking allows you to comment on part of the evidence you are reviewing. This allows you to quickly come back to that information when you need to continue your work, remember where you left off, or show the evidence to another person. You can bookmark data as you move through an investigation, which allows you to gather your findings and then proceed so when you finish you have the bigger picture in mind.

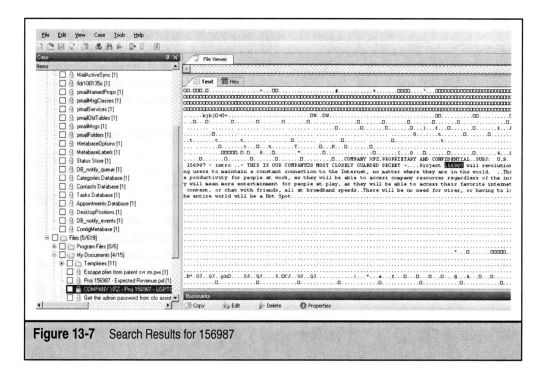

Figure 13-7   Search Results for 156987

As an example, searching the image based on the fictional project number 156987 has yielded one match, in a single .RTF document titled COMPANY XFZ – Project 156987 – USPTO – Intro Verbiage. That file was then bookmarked, as shown in Figure 13-7, in the Bookmarks pane, with the file contents displayed in the Text Viewer.

By right-clicking any bookmark, you can choose an option from the context menu to review, edit, or delete any bookmark. Figure 13-8 shows the Edit Bookmark dialog that appears if you select Edit from the context menu.

Running Associated Applications with Device Seizure

As with most other forensic tools, Device Seizure lets you view relevant files in their associated applications. It's always a plus to view files as they were meant to be displayed instead of in plaintext. Obviously, you can't view files of interest in their associated applications if those programs aren't loaded on your system, so the built-in viewer in Device Seizure can at least get you most of the way.

To launch an associated program, find a document of interest, right-click it, and choose Open With from the context menu. At this point, the default application associated with the file extension will open and display the file. If no association is found, you can choose the application from a list.

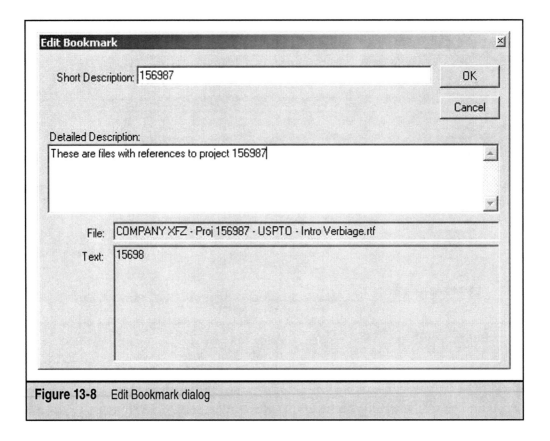

Figure 13-8   Edit Bookmark dialog

Exporting Files with Device Seizure

After reviewing some files, you may need to export copies of them from the image. To do so, in the Case pane, right-click the file and choose Export from the context menu. The file will be saved automatically to the Device Seizure folder.

Reporting with Device Seizure

Because it's never over until the paperwork is done, let's look at the Device Seizure reporting capabilities. Here's how to generate a report:

1. Click the Report icon on the toolbar, or choose File | Generate Report, to start the Device Seizure Report Wizard. Enter information about the case and yourself and click Next.

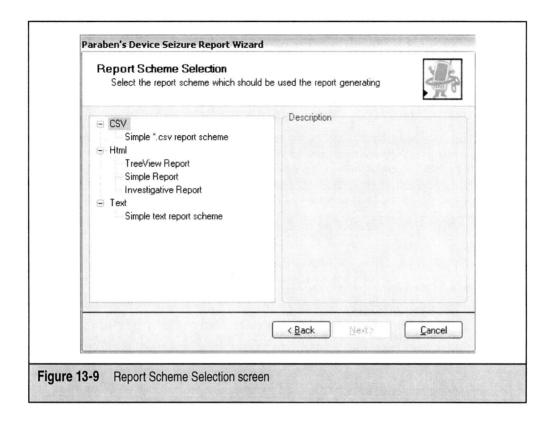

Figure 13-9   Report Scheme Selection screen

2. In the Report Scheme Selection screen, shown in Figure 13-9, select the format of the report from among the following options, and then click Next:

- CSV: Simple *.csv Report
- Text: Simple Text Report Scheme
- HTML:
  - TreeView Report
  - Simple Report
  - Investigative Report

The Investigative Report is specially designed for convenient printing of case data. It can include only the following information: case information, phone model information, phonebook/address book, SMS history, call logs, datebook/calendar, photos/images, unparsed data, and waypoints (for GPS).

3. In the Report Mode Selection and Options screen, shown in Figure 13-10, select the report mode from the drop-down list that offers the following options, and then click Next:

- **Entire Case**   All data (every file) from the image/case will be included in the report.

- **Selected Items Only**   Only checked items will be included in the report.

After you click Next, the report is generated. Since reports are generated in HTML or simple TXT formats, they can be modified with any HTML editor or imported into other applications to add a logo or verbiage such as confidentiality and handling instructions. Reports are automatically saved in the same directory as the case file.

Figures 13-11 and 13-12 illustrate the default Device Seizure reports in TXT and HTML formats.

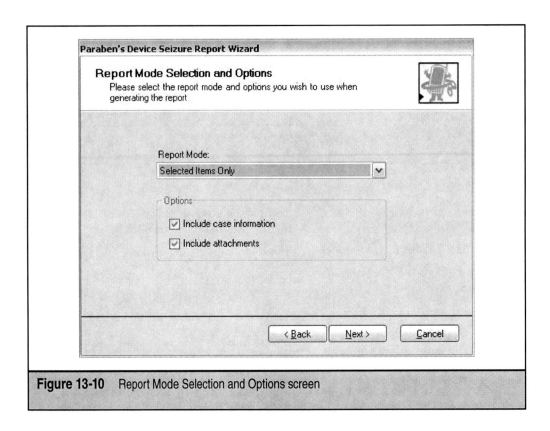

Figure 13-10   Report Mode Selection and Options screen

```
Paraben's Device Seizure Exported Case
-----------------------------------------
Case Information
=========================================
=========================================
WindowsCE/PocketPC
           -------------------------------
                PropertiesName | Value |
           -------------------------------
Vendor | PocketPC Vendor |
-
Device | PocketPC/WindowsCE Device |
-
File version | 7 |
-
Acquisition Time | 7/9/2004 2:02:40 PM |
-

=========================================
       FilesMy DocumentsHTCIA ConfFACILITIES.txt
-
ds.Text Files/FACILITIES.txt
   MD5 : E3271C2C5C56557DD4BE3C6338FC6E01   SHA1:
=========================================

=========================================
       2090.pdf
-
ds.Text Files/2090.pdf
   MD5 : 661CA7A7C334132A40DEDD637213D7C7   SHA1:
=========================================
```

Figure 13-11   Device Seizure report in TXT format

Figure 13-12   Device Seizure report in HTML format

◉ Analyzing Pocket/Mobile Outlook E-mail

Popularity:	10
Simplicity:	8
Impact:	10
Risk Rating:	9

As mentioned, with Mobile Windows devices, e-mail is not kept in a container file such as a .PST or .DBX file. Instead, Pocket/Mobile Outlook uses a combination of databases in which to store e-mail.

E-mails are kept in .MPB files, which are uniquely numbered and reside in the Windows | Messaging folder. Filenames look something like this: 0a0013438103102.mpb or 0e0011782810302.mpb. Opening these in Device Seizure will cause the internal File Viewer to open, and you will be able to see associated header information and text of the message.

Attachment information is kept in the pmailAttachs database. Pocket Outlook truncates long e-mails and doesn't download attachments unless the user goes back and marks the message for download. Then the remainder of the truncated body and any associated attachments will download and appear in the Text tab of the File Viewer, as shown in Figure 13-13. Pocket Outlook also stores Inbox, Outbox, Deleted Items, and other e-mail folders in separate files, which are identified in the pmailFolders file.

Here are some examples of the data contained within an e-mail file:

```
D.e.l.e.t.e.d. .I.t.e.m.s...f.l.d.r.1.0.0.1.9.7.c
D.e.l.e.t.e.d. .I.t.e.m.s...f.l.d.r.1.0.0.1.3.d.5
D.r.a.f.t.s...f.l.d.r.1.0.0.1.9.7.d
D.r.a.f.t.s...f.l.d.r.1.0.0.1.3.d.6
I.n.b.o.x...f.l.d.r.1.0.0.1.9.7.9
I.n.b.o.x...f.l.d.r.1.0.0.1.3.d.2
O.u.t.b.o.x...f.l.d.r.1.0.0.1.3.d.3
O.u.t.b.o.x...f.l.d.r.1.0.0.1.9.7
S.e.n.t. .I.t.e.m.s...f.l.d.r.1.0.0.1.9.7.b
S.e.n.t. .I.t.e.m.s...f.l.d.r.1.0.0.1.3.d
```

All you have to do is find the files and examine their contents to see information about the messages.

Finally, we cannot discuss e-mail analysis without including a discussion of Web-based e-mail. More and more people understand that company e-mail systems are monitored, and they believe their private webmail accounts leave behind no traces. However, that's not the case. Because you will find a Temporary Internet Files folder in a Mobile Windows device, as in other versions of the operating system, you can search across those files for copies of the HTML associated with webmail sessions. If any are found, accessing webmail is as easy as launching the associated web browser on your

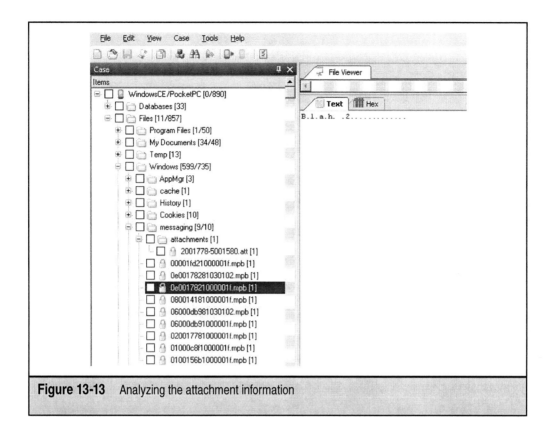

Figure 13-13   Analyzing the attachment information

system directly from Device Seizure, or copying and pasting the HTML to a text editor if you prefer.

You can also examine the Index.dat file or any cookies for references to webmail sites, as shown in Figure 13-14.

In addition to e-mail, MS Outlook keeps track of appointments and tasks, which is not a feature found in Pocket Outlook. Instead, Mobile Windows keeps track of that information in a set of databases not associated with the Pocket Outlook interface.

The database DB_notify_queue stores information for all timed activities that have not occurred, such as reminders, appointments, and so on, which are stored as well as the application associated with the event. Here are some examples.

This example was entered by my friend Richard when I let him borrow my PDA to "check his e-mail" as we passed the time waiting for *Spider-Man 2* to start at midnight on the day it opened:

```
C.A.L.E.N.D.A.R...E.X.E...R.i.c.h.a.r.d.s. .b.d.a.y..8.:.0.0. .A.M.-
.1.1.:.3.0. .P.M. .8./.3.0./.0.4. .(.B.u.y.
h.i.m..S.t.a.r.w.a.r.s..T.r.i.l.o.g.y..O.n..D.V.D.)...C.a.l.e.n.d.a.r.
.R.e.m.i.n.d.e.r...A.l.a.r.m.1...w.a.v.
```

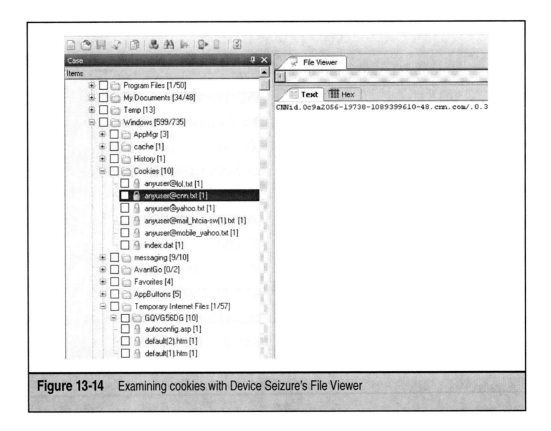

Figure 13-14 Examining cookies with Device Seizure's File Viewer

This was my alarm to make sure I got my wife, Carol, a birthday gift in 2008 (a few days *before* her birthday, by the way):

```
W.i.n.d.o.w.s.\.c.l.o.c.k...e.x.e...6.:.3.0. .A.M. . .7./.13./.0.8..Alarm...
A.l.a.r.m...A.l.a.r.m.1..C.A.L.N.O.T...E.X.E...A.p.p.R.u.n.A.t.T.i.m.e...A.p
.p.R.u.n.A.t..T.i.m.e...x.e...6.:.3.0. .A.M.  .7./.1.3./.0.8..
```

Investigating Terminal Services

Popularity:	6
Simplicity:	8
Impact:	8
Risk Rating:	7

Investigating possible use of the built-in Terminal Services Client in Mobile Windows is fairly limited to obtaining only the IP address and host name of any servers to which the software has attempted to connect. Because Terminal Services sessions are encrypted by default and the Terminal Services client does not keep a record of the session activities, there is no way to determine what specific actions were taken by a user during the Terminal Services session. However, determining whether a terminal server connection was made could be significant in any case.

You can search the registry for calls to rdpdr.dll, which should identify the host name of the terminal server and its associated license information.

Some people may underemphasize the importance of Terminal Services, but it is actually one of the most powerful features around, because it's a fully interactive session with the host system. In addition to examining the registry, you can look for an entry in Index.dat for \TSWeb; this is the default site created by the Windows 2000 Terminal Services Web interface. This allows the user to interact with a terminal server and conduct a session through Internet Explorer, and it does not require any client software to be installed. Although Pocket Internet Explorer cannot load the Active X control required to run Terminal Services Web Interface, any clues about user server connection attempts can prove valuable.

Investigating MSN Messenger

Popularity:	10
Simplicity:	8
Impact:	10
Risk Rating:	9

Investigating possible use of the built-in MSN Messenger client in Mobile Windows can also be done by searching the registry. The local client does not keep a session log; however, the registry does typically store text of the last session.

A typical Messenger session found in the registry will look something like this:

```
..M.S.N.M.e.s.s.e.n.g.e.r.S.e.r.v.i.c.e....I.d.e.n.t.i.t.y.N.a.m.e...S.P.Y.@
.C.o.m.p.3..c.o.m...S.P.Y.@.C.o.m.p.3...c.o.m. .(.E.-.m.a.i.l.
.A.d.d.r.e.s.s. .N.o.t. .V.e.r.i.f.i.e.d.)...M.S.N. .M.e.s.s.e.n.g.e.r.
S.e.r.v.i.c.e...P.r.e.s.e.t.M.s.g.s....*.I. .l.o.v.e. .m.y. .P.o.c.k.e.t.
.P.C.!..&.C.a.l.l. .m.e. .l.a.t.e.r...
..D.e.f.a.u.l.t…E.x.c.h.a.n...........M.S.N.S....P.a.s.s..U.s.e..P.U...<.C.o
.m.p.E.m.p.l.1.@.C.o.m.p.a.n.y...c.o.m..........M.S.G.S.....,.m.e.s.s.e.n.g
e.r...h.o.t.m.a.i.l...c.o.m..
```

This brief bit of data encompasses a complete session between our two fictional characters, Spy and CompEmpl1, which breaks down like this:

- Spy uses the PresetMsgs, which Microsoft refers to as My Text Messages in the user interface.

- The conversation consists of "I love my Pocket PC!" and "Call me later."

- The server that handled the session was messenger.hotmail.com.

Passwords and Other Security-related Stuff

Popularity:	10
Simplicity:	10
Impact:	10
Risk Rating:	**10**

Investigators must often contend with a suspect who protects his data, or at least tries to do so. Like most everything else in the forensics world, this can be good news and bad news. Typically, if you encounter an encrypted Microsoft Word or Excel document during a PC forensic case, either the suspect must give you the passwords or you must decrypt them yourself.

If the first option is unsuccessful or impossible, you can use one of many good tools to help you decrypt passwords. Luckily for you (at least for now), you don't have to contend with such issues with PDAs, because Pocket Word and Pocket Excel do not support passwords, and if you attempt to upload a password-protected Word or Excel file to a PDA, you'll get an error message.

That was the good news, and here's the bad. Just as third-party security applications exist for PCs, apps exist for PDAs. Obviously, they serve legitimate needs, but that doesn't make them any easier to love when you're trying to find data in a case. At the top of any list in this category has to be PGP Mobile. The name says it all: PGP (Pretty Good Privacy) is synonymous with security, and PGP Mobile has complete OpenPGP RFC 2440 compatibility, along with a feature set almost identical to PGP for the desktop. Previous versions of PGP Mobile supported both Palm OS and Windows, but the latest version operates only with Windows Mobile Pocket PC Phone Edition 5 and Windows Mobile Professional 6 environments.

Functionality in this software includes the following:

- E-mail encryption
- File encryption
- Clipboard decryption and verification
- Digital signatures
- Complete interoperability with all current PGP products
- PGP virtual disks
- PGP Zip–compatible with PGP Desktop clients for Windows and Mac OS X

As with other PGP products, the supported list of symmetric algorithms includes Advanced Encryption Standard (AES) up to 256-bit, International Data Encryption Algorithm (IDEA), Triple Data Encryption Standard (Triple DES), and CAST. Supported asymmetric algorithms include RSA up to 4096-bit, Diffie-Hellman, and Data Security Standard (DSS). It also supports both MD5 and SHA-1.

If you encounter files on a PDA that have been secured with PGP Mobile, as with its desktop cousins, you should just ignore them and keep on working, because there is nothing you can do with them at the present time.

In addition to PGP, Hushmail supports mobile devices with its Hushmail Mobile product. The Hushmail Mobile application works similar to regular Hushmail without being Java enabled. All the encryption operations take place on the Hushmail servers, and the connection between the servers and a mobile device is secured using Secure Sockets Layer (SSL) encryption.

To determine whether someone has been using Hushmail, you should examine the index.dat site for references to the hushmail.com Web site.

PASSWORD-PROTECTED WINDOWS DEVICES

Because ActiveSync is required for forensic examinations of a Mobile Windows device, you cannot bypass the Mobile Windows password scheme. When you attempt to connect to a password-protected Mobile Windows device, ActiveSync will prompt you for the device password.

Collecting PDA Evidence on a Palm OS Device Using EnCase

Popularity:	9
Simplicity:	8
Impact:	10
Risk Rating:	**9**

Another tool that can be used for acquisition and analysis of Palm-based devices is EnCase versions 3 and later. EnCase currently supports the following Palm models:

- Palm IIIx, IIIxe
- Palm V series
- Palm VII series
- Palm m series
- Up to Palm OS 3.5

If you've used EnCase to conduct forensics investigations in the past, or if you've read the preceding chapters in this book, you'll be familiar with what we're about to get into.

Acquisition

As with the previous acquisition example, make sure the Palm device is powered up, in the appropriate cradle, and correctly connected to your acquisition system via USB or a serial connection. If the Palm Desktop HotSync is installed on the acquisition system, it should be disabled.

Acquisition of a Palm device in EnCase starts by launching EnCase and putting the device into Console (aka Debug) mode by entering the appropriate characters in the graffiti area. Then do the following:

1. After the device is in Console mode, click the Add Device button.

2. Select Local and click Palm Pilot in the Add Device dialog, as shown next:

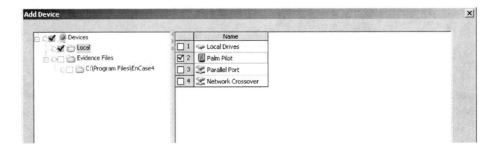

3. You will now be able to preview the contents of the device in the Cases tab, and you can navigate throughout the different files and/or apply search terms. If you then need to obtain a forensic image of the device, the process is the same as that with a hard disk.

4. Find the icon of the Palm device in the Cases tab, right-click, and choose Acquire from the context menu.

5. At this point, the wizard allows you to select a password, compression, and evidence file output path just as with any other media. Obviously, the time required to obtain the image will depend on the speed of your connection to the device, the amount of data, and your acquisition systems resources.

NOTE   Analysis and reporting of a Palm-based device in EnCase is the same as with any other media, as referenced in Chapter 6, so you won't have to read it all over again.

Collecting Cell Phone Evidence Using Device Seizure

Popularity:	8
Simplicity:	9
Impact:	10
Risk Rating:	9

In 2004, I started this section with "Although not conventionally thought of as a PDA by many people, the functionality of cell phones has increased so much over the years that it blurs the clear lines of definition. Yes, some integrated phone/PDAs are running on both the Palm and Mobile Windows platforms. However, most non-combination cell phones today come with many of the standard features that PDAs offer." In just five years, 2004 has become "the good old days." Today, the number of phones that don't include smart phone functionality is the distinct minority and getting smaller every year.

The latest version of Device Seizure allows you to acquire information from literally hundreds of models of cell phones. Currently, the following cell phone plug-ins are available:

- GSM SIM card (logical)
- LG CDMA (logical)
- LG GSM (logical)
- Motorola (logical) Web browser
- Motorola (physical)
- Motorola iDEN (logical)
- Motorola iDEN (physical)
- Nokia GSM (logical)
- Nokia GSM (physical)
- Nokia TDMA (logical)
- Samsung CDMA (logical)
- Samsung GSM (logical)
- Samsung GSM (physical)
- Siemens (logical)
- Siemens (physical)
- Sony Ericsson (logical) e-mail and text messaging

Before starting a phone analysis, remember this: The amount and the types of data that can be acquired depend on the type of the device being analyzed. Usually, the cell phone plug-ins in Device Seizure allow you to acquire the following data:

- SMS (text messaging) history, including deleted messages
- Phonebook, including data from both phone memory and SIM
- Calendar and To-Do list
- Text notes
- Voice notes
- Call history, including numbers dialed, received, and calls missed
- User-created files, such as multimedia, graphics, and music

Although modern cell phones and PDAs share many features, obvious differences exist in the underlying technologies used, and because of this you cannot think of a phone analysis in traditional forensic terms. One of the first major differences is that phone data storage is proprietary and based on the manufacturer, model, system, and other information.

SMS/EMS Data   SMS stands for Short Message Service, which to most of us translates to text messaging. Both incoming and outgoing SMS can be saved to the phone or SIM card. When the SMS is saved to the SIM card, it's encoded to Protocol Data Unit (PDU) format (a Global System for Mobile Communications [GSM]–specified documented format that is used to store the SMS on the SIM card). But when the SMS is saved to the phone, the format is defined by the firmware developers. That means that even the same models of phone can contain SMS messages that are encoded in different formats, and the format of the SMS depends on firmware that is installed on the phone. In the phone, the messages can be stored as one database file, in multiple files (each SMS message in a separate file), or in the EEPROM/user-data area of the NOR flash memory.

MMS Data   MMS stands for Multimedia Messaging Service, which to most of us means text messaging with pictures or videos. Because MMS messages can contain multimedia attachments along with a plaintext message, they are generally stored as files within the phone file system. MMS messages can be stored as solid files that contain both the message header (MIME encoded) and the message body and attachments. They can also be split into several files: header, body, and attachments.

Phonebook   The phonebook, like SMS, can be stored in the SIM card or in the phone. In the phone, it can be stored in one database or in the EEPROM/user-data area of the NOR flash memory. The data format is defined by the firmware developers.

Calendar and To-Do   Calendar and To-Do records may be stored as records in the database files (the format is defined by the firmware developers) or within an EEPROM/user-data area of the NOR flash memory.

Voice Records   The voice records format depends on the voice codec chip that is installed in the phone. For example, Samsung GSM phones contain a voice chip that encodes the voice into AdaptiveMultiRate (AMR) format. But the Samsung CDMA phones don't encode voice data. They record the data directly from the digital signal processor (DSP). The voice records can be stored as files or within an EEPROM/user-data area of the NOR flash memory.

Browser Bookmarks   The format depends on the browser used in the firmware. Some of the browsers can save the data to the file system, but, generally, bookmarks are saved to the EEPROM/user area of the NOR flash memory.

User-created Files   Most phones limit the user files to melodies, pictures, phone, and video files, but newer phones allow users to upload any type of file. Sound formats are usually MIDI, MMF (SMAF), AMR, MP3, WMA, WAV, and AAC. The standard picture/photos formats are JPEG, GIF, and BMP. The video formats are generally proprietary, but some phones encode video to the Motion JPEG or 3GP format. The video/photos encoding format depends on the camera chip used in the phone. Some of the phones store the pictures/video without any changes—that is, the file remains the same after it is uploaded to the phone. But some phones convert the uploaded files into proprietary formats to reduce the file size, and during the download process the files are converted back into the PC format.

Acquisition of Cell Phone Data

The first step in the acquisition is to make sure the phone is correctly connected to the system you will be using. As with PDAs, this means having the appropriate cable to attach the phone to your computer. If you don't have the cables that came with the phone you're working with, you can purchase cable kits from retailers and a Device Seizure cable kit from Paraben.

After the phone is connected to your system, you can start the acquisition using the same wizard discussed in the PDA portion of this chapter. The same interface and dialogs are used, so I won't waste space by inserting the same images. Refer back to the steps detailed in "Acquisition of a Windows-based Device," except select a phone, not a Windows PDA. Note that, depending on your selection in the Device Type Selection dialog, the options for what data can be acquired will change in the screen shown in Figure 13-15.

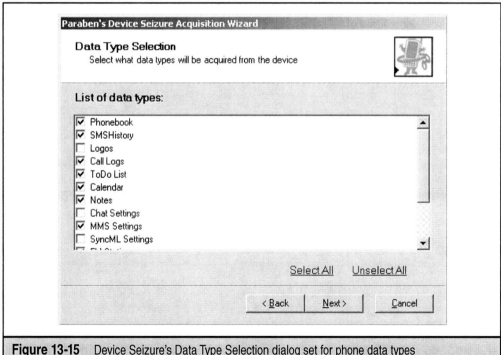

Figure 13-15   Device Seizure's Data Type Selection dialog set for phone data types

NOTE If you chose GSM SIM card as the manufacturer, only one option will appear in the Data Type Selection dialog.

Once the wizard completes, click the Acquire button to begin the process and wait for the acquisition to complete. (A lot of your time in computer forensics work will be spent waiting—don't let anyone tell you otherwise.) The end result will be a Device Seizure .PDS file.

Analysis of Cell Phone Data

After the .PDS is loaded, you will be able to see the data associated with the device, as shown in Figures 13-16 and 13-17. At this point, you can run keyword searches and bookmark findings for later inclusion in the final report.

To document your findings, you can access the reporting functions by choosing File | Report or by clicking the Report button on the button bar. The software will then

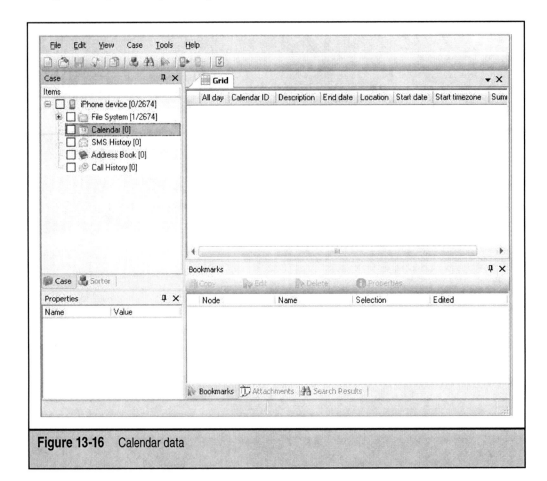

Figure 13-16 Calendar data

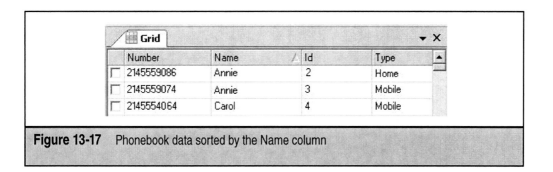

Figure 13-17   Phonebook data sorted by the Name column

prompt you for the report format options as discussed earlier in the chapter. After you've saved the file, it can be opened with an editor so that you can add a logo, handling and classification information, and other information.

Working with Earlier PDA Seizure or Cell Seizure Data Formats

If you have an older copy of either PDA or Cell Seizure that you've used to acquire a device, and you upgrade to Device Seizure, you will not be able to open older format files with it. You must first convert the older image and case formats to the current .PDS standard. Luckily, you can use a wizard that does it for you. To launch the converter, choose Tools | Case Converter. The wizard initiates and walks you through the process. First, as shown in Figure 13-18, select Browse to pick the location of the older case. Second, as shown in Figure 13-19, select the case file and click Open. Third, as shown in Figure 13-20, click Yes if you want to open the converted case.

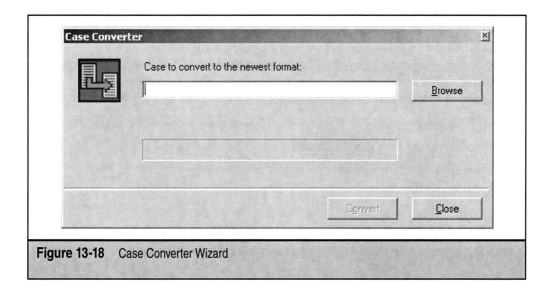

Figure 13-18   Case Converter Wizard

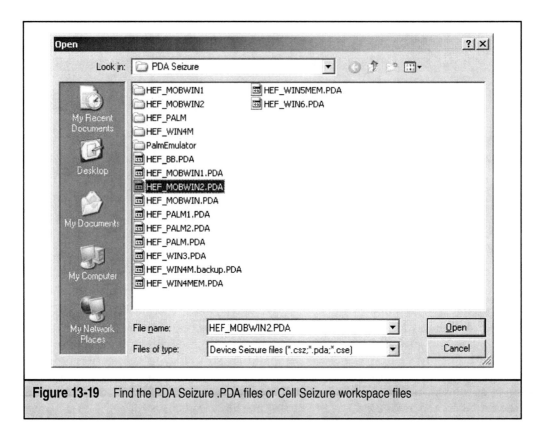

Figure 13-19 Find the PDA Seizure .PDA files or Cell Seizure workspace files

CONCLUSION

After reading this chapter, you should understand that PDAs and cell phones can offer a vast array of potential evidence in any investigation. Today these devices are more than just digital assistants—in many cases, they are high-tech diaries as well as a medium for transacting business. Some people spend more time with their PDAs than they do with their own children (a fact that no investigator should overlook).

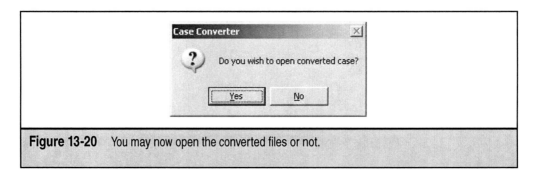

Figure 13-20 You may now open the converted files or not.

PART IV

PRESENTING YOUR FINDINGS

CASE STUDY: WRAPPING UP THE CASE

During and at the conclusion of the ACME Services case, we drafted several reports to counsel that were used to make decisions. With counsel's advisement, we produced reports and summaries of the evidence found for the US Attorney's Office and the US Secret Service. We did this so they could understand and re-create what we had found.

He Said, She Said...

Civil investigators need to understand what happens when the line is crossed and the findings become part of a criminal case. No one can testify to facts that were told to them by another party—this is considered hearsay—so the findings must be reproducible and verifiable by other investigators. We carefully document our procedures so other investigators can follow our steps and reproduce the results that we found. When another party re-creates our findings, they have first-party knowledge, which makes the evidence they recover admissible in court.

We carefully documented our methodologies and search terms to aid the US Secret Service so they could reproduce our findings. The Secret Service was then officially involved in a criminal case and had to have first-party knowledge of the investigation's findings so they could testify on the matter.

The US Attorney's Office then brought the suspect into court with the Secret Service acting as their witness. With a solid case in front of him, the judge revoked Charlie Blink's bail and placed him in custody pending trial. The trial was successful for the prosecution, and Blink was found guilty. Charlie Blink remains in prison today.

CHAPTER 14

DOCUMENTING THE INVESTIGATION

A fter you complete an investigation, you must deal with the most nontechnical part of the process, commonly viewed as the least entertaining part of the job: reporting. Reporting is, however, one of the most crucial parts of an investigation, because if you cannot clearly relate the facts of the matter to your audience, all of your hard work will be for naught.

READ ME

Your report is the one common tool that you and nontechnical people will use to discuss and understand your findings. Being able to write a clear, concise, and factual report is one of the more difficult aspects of the job for a technically oriented person, because your audience is usually not technical, so they will not understand all the terms and technology that you have employed in your investigation and may not be able to understand the impact of the "smoking gun" you found.

Such communication can be difficult. You must use care in your explanations to be sure that what you report can be understood and supported with evidence. If, for example, you tell someone what you know to be true based on the evidence you reviewed, you must make sure that your evidence proves what you say. Assumptions can lead to lawsuits for negligence or criminal complaints if your opinion is not based on hard, reliable evidence.

Events that can be reconstructed, re-created, or at least given credibility through some outside source are the only events you should represent as facts in a report. No matter how convinced you are of someone's intentions, motive, or guilt, it is your place as the forensic examiner to report only what the evidence tells you. You can offer your opinions during a conversation about the case, but you must not document these opinions in your report unless they can be based on facts. Your expert opinion is based on the facts you are able to ascertain from the evidence, not based on other assumptions. Documenting opinions that are not based on factual evidence can be used against you at a later time.

Different types of reports are used for different situations. The type of report you are asked to generate should indicate the magnitude of the work you are about to undertake. While an internal report to your manager may be informal and represent basic facts, an expert report to the court must be prepared with care and submitted only when you are confident with each fact and opinion you have put to page.

The reports discussed in this chapter are shown in Table 14-1.

In every kind of report, some specific items should be considered or included. Screenshots and any other illustration or visualization that you can provide are extremely helpful. Not all managers, attorneys, or judges are technically savvy and many have never before handled digital evidence. The more straightforward your evidence and the more support you give for evidence through visual representations and reconstruction, the more compelling your argument becomes.

Type of Report	Description
Internal reports	Reports whose intended audience is local counsel or your manager.
Affidavits	Reports whose intended audience is the court; such documents are signed in front of a notary and the statements within them are considered as legitimate as if they were sworn under oath.
Declarations	Reports whose intended audience is the court; these documents are not signed in front of a notary but are assumed to be factual.
Expert reports	Reports whose intended audience is the court; these documents are filed as a report of your findings to a judge upon being appointed an expert witness.

Table 14-1   Types of Reports

INTERNAL REPORT

The internal report is by far the most common report you will create. While the internal report is not a formal representation to the courts, it is a serious document. When you finish an internal report, it normally is first reviewed by your manager and then, if action is warranted, is passed on to your general counsel. The general counsel (your company's head internal attorney) may decide to take legal action against some person(s) depending on what you documented in your report.

Always explain every detail clearly to your attorney, whether he or she is internal to the company or from an outside firm, as the need to understand any legal assumptions or risks that may result from the evidence used for your report is paramount. All communication with the attorney and documents that you create at the direction of your attorney are held as attorney-client privilege. This means that whatever you tell your attorney is going to remain private and will not be presented to the opposing counsel as evidence. However, if legal action is undertaken, you may be asked to create a declaration or affidavit that restates your findings for the court. Anything you produce in these documents will be heavily scrutinized by the opposing counsel.

In some cases, you may be acting in a consultative role for the company. Many companies choose to hire outside consultants either to verify an internal investigation or to handle the investigation completely. The most common reason for hiring outside the company is that employees who perform the internal investigations can become fact witnesses. This means that the employees can be subpoenaed by the opposing counsel or by their own attorney to testify their first-person knowledge of events in front of a judge. This can be a risky endeavor, as an employee will always know more personal and nonrelevant information about a coworker, and this can be used by opposing counsel to claim a bias against the suspect.

When acting as a consultant, you should always follow the general principles of internal reporting: create clear, concise, and informal reports that explain in detail the matter at hand. Obviously, as a hired consultant, a higher expectation of quality and professionalism is expected, as this is hopefully the product of a well-paid and well-qualified consultant. As a consultant working at the direction of the attorneys, you also are covered by attorney-client privilege—any communication and work product created for the attorneys cannot be subpoenaed by the opposing counsel.

However, as a legal case enters the system, you may become what is known as an "expert consultant" or "expert witness." Be aware of an important and distinct difference between these rules. An expert consultant acts in an advisory role to the attorneys and is covered by attorney-client privilege. An expert witness does not have this privilege; all communication that is relevant to the case at hand, whether created during or before your appointment as an expert witness, is discoverable. This includes conversations of which you are a part or that you have overheard; e-mails you have sent, received, or been CC'd; and any reports you may have created. Make sure that you communicate to your attorney early and often about your role in any litigation to make sure that you both understand the impact of your report. While an early doubt expressed in a report may be clarified and reinforced at a later date, the documented existence of the doubt can be used against you by the opposing counsel.

Construction of an Internal Report

Some forensic tools such as ASR Data's SMART, Guidance Software's EnCase, Technology Pathways ProDiscover, Paraben's P2 suite, and AccessData's Forensic Tool Kit allow you to create reports. The reports generated by these tools are normally collections of bookmarked evidence that you have noted during your investigation, along with the structure of the disk in question, some information about the image itself (such as the MD5 hash), and any notes you might have created during your investigation. While this is valuable information and contains key evidence that will support your report, it should not be your end product.

Most internal reports begin with a statement describing the specific situation. Oftentimes, this is encompassed in an *executive summary*, a summary of the facts written at a high level that an executive from your company or your client should be able to read to ascertain what you have done. An executive summary might look something like this:

> *I, Ima Investigator, was asked to investigate Mr. Suspect by Ms. Supervisor in regard to Mr. Suspect's e-mail communications with competing companies. I was requested by Ms. Supervisor to create an image of Mr. Suspect's computer system on this date. The following report serves as a summary of my findings.*

The next section should provide a summary of your conclusions, called the *results section*. This should state what you were directed to do, what evidence you have found, and what subsequent requests were made. Remember that this will be the last part of your report that many people see and understand before you get into the "technical voodoo," so be sure that you make every point in this section that you plan to reinforce with evidence within the report itself. Here's an example of the results section:

After imaging the system of Mr. Suspect, I was instructed by Ms. Supervisor to identify and analyze all e-mails sent between Mr. Suspect and Mr. Ex-employee. Upon my reviewing the recovered e-mails, it is my opinion that Mr. Suspect has been supplying confidential information to Mr. Ex-employee and evidence of this can be found in section X of this report. Upon notification of this, Ms. Supervisor asked that further analysis be done to determine what other Internet-based activities Mr. Suspect had been involved in and what files were recently deleted. It is my opinion that Mr. Suspect is using company resources to distribute materials and send spam e-mails.

Following that section is the evidence you have recovered from the suspect's system. You should annotate each piece of evidence, explaining what it is and why you believe it to be of relevance. It is also recommended that you convert your report to a format such as Portable Document Format (PDF) or something similar so that you can be confident that your report will not be inadvertently modified as people review it and pass it to others.

Figures 14-1 and 14-2 show examples of the information that may be contained in an internal report. The information shown here is from a consultative perspective, but the exact same model can be applied to any internal report.

Final Report of Findings for
Acme Funds Inc.

Prepared by
David Cowen

Description: Investigation of Mr. Suspect
_____

Figure 14-1   The report cover page

1.1 Executive Summary

I was called into an investigation of the activities of Mr. Suspect on December 25, 2020. Investigators were briefed by Acme's head of investigations, Mr. Supervisor, on the suspected activities and asked to create an image of the suspect's computer system for analysis. This report serves as a final report of our findings in the matter.

1.2 Results

The initial request to investigators was to search for any access to prohibited web sites by Mr. Suspect and to determine if Mr. Suspect had misappropriated any of Acme's confidential materials.

With this search, investigators were successful in finding a series of e-mails that Mr. Suspect had sent to his personal Internet e-mail account that contained files marked as confidential. Evidence was also found that these e-mails were then forwarded to Mr. Ex Exployee at Emca.

During the search for Mr. Suspect's Internet history, investigators also discovered that Mr. Suspect spends most of his working hours running a marketing company and misuses company resources in distributing materials and sending spam e-mails from an internal company web server.

2.1 E-mails containing files received by Mr. Suspect

The e-mails included below are shown in chronological order.

2.1.1 Earliest e-mail 12/23/2020 11:57PM
Here Mr. Suspect is sending a file from his Acme account to a Mr. Ex Employee. The file in question is OurSpamPlan.doc.

Figure 14-2   An example internal report

DECLARATION

After you have written your initial report of an investigation and the attorneys decide to proceed with legal action, you will normally be asked to draft a *declaration*. Declarations are used by attorneys to support motions they present to the court. A *motion* can be just about any type of action that someone is requesting the court to take, such as motions to compel, temporary restraining orders, motions to dismiss, motions for summary judgment, motions for sanctions, or motions for expedited discovery. Your declaration would provide the technical merit for your attorney's argument.

A declaration differs from an internal report in that it is meant to be viewed and understood by a judge and opposing counsel. More so than in an internal report, you must ensure that all of your statements make sense to someone who does not have technical knowledge and that your conclusions are not lost in a maze of technical details. You should also be aware that the opposing counsel will base their arguments partly on the report you create; this means that any evidence you state and support will be examined and possibly attacked. Be prepared to defend any statement you have made, and realize that any evidence you reference could be requested or subpoenaed by the opposing counsel.

When the opposing counsel subpoenas some evidence, it means that they have gone to the judge and gotten a written order stating that whatever evidence they have referenced must now be produced in whatever manner the judge has granted them. Sometimes this means that an image will be handed over; other times it means that the original system will be produced to the opposing counsel and their expert will re-image the system and try to re-create your findings. If any of your conclusions were based on assumptions or any accidental access to the original evidence—and this can and will happen—and you did not state such in your declaration, the opposing counsel will challenge the evidence itself.

The same scenario plays both ways; if you are working for the defense and the plaintiff's expert has produced some evidence that shows signs of accidental or intentional tampering, you would most likely be asked to create a declaration stating this case. You must be careful, though, when moving toward these kinds of motions, as you never know all of what happened during the lifetime of the evidence. Make such suggestion to the attorneys only when you believe you have ample evidence to support your claims.

A declaration is also meant to be a factual statement. While you are not getting a notary to witness your signing of the document, as you would with an affidavit, you are still swearing to the fact that the statements you have written are true. This is important, because knowingly making false statements can bring serious repercussions such as perjury charges. Though making false statements in a declaration is probably not something you aspire to do, many attorneys who do not understand the details of the technology you are dealing with may ask you to reinterpret or more forcefully support a conclusion in a way that makes you feel less than comfortable. This is understandable, as the attorneys believe that your new conclusions may just be a point of view and not the actual factual representation that you and the opposing expert would understand. Remember that no matter who is paying you, you're signing your name on these documents, and you—not the attorneys—are liable for any false statements that are made.

Construction of a Declaration

Declarations have a very standard form regarding how they begin and end. It is what goes in the middle that lets you create a unique document. You should be sure to express your opinions in the matter, but remember to be as professional as possible. All declarations should begin with a statement similar to the following (the sections that you should fill in are underlined):

> I, _your name here_, declare as follows:
> I am a _your title_ with _your company_, _a description of what your company does._ _Your_

company has been retained by counsel for the plaintiffs/defense (name of the plaintiff/ defendant) in abc v. def, Civil Action No. some number (D. some state) to render an opinion regarding the possibility of what you where asked to do. The following contains my the opinion that you are planning to defend based upon my experience in the field and my knowledge of the current case.

The next section of a declaration is a primer on your background, stating what makes you qualified as an expert to make the opinions and conclusions you are about to state to the court. It should look something like the following, but it will be unique based on how you choose to represent yourself and your experience. The parts you should change or fill in are underlined.

My educational background is mainly technological/academic in nature, featuring more than some years of direct experience in the areas of what you have done and your job duties relating to this case or your investigation. I currently hold any certificates you might have. I am also an active member of any associations you may be a part of that have some bearing on your ability to be an expert. I have been trained in whatever and whoever has trained you in the areas relevant to the opinion you are making. If you are a consultant, you should name the company you work for and indicate your billing rate here.

After this, you should begin stating information on what you have been asked to base your opinion and on what you have reviewed in doing so. You should explain in layman's terms the technical aspects of whatever processes you have undertaken and discuss the evidence you have reviewed. This is important, as you can make opinions and conclusions based only on firsthand knowledge. Making a statement like "I was told by Ms. Jones that he arrived at work at 10 AM" would be considered hearsay. Be sure to ask for and review any documents or records that you will discuss in your declaration. You should also number your paragraphs so attorneys can easily reference them.

A declaration has no particular minimum or maximum page length requirements. If you can make all of your points and conclusions in one page, and it is understandable to a layman, that's fine. When you are done stating your opinions, you should end your declaration with a conclusion that covers all your opinions and conclusions about the matter and reaffirms your overall statement and support for the motion. An example of a conclusion is shown here:

After reviewing and analyzing all of the whatever evidence you reviewed in making your opinions, I am left with the opinion that whatever conclusion you have come to. Discuss the ramifications of what this opinion means to the motion at hand. In my opinion, state your overall conclusion and support for the motion.

An example of a declaration is shown in Figures 14-3 and 14-4. This declaration takes a more consultative perspective, but the same exact model can be applied to any declaration.

You do not have the same document modification concerns for a declaration after you have submitted it, since your signature must be in place on a printed document.

UNITED STATES DISTRICT COURT
SOUTHERN DISTRICT OF TEXAS,
HOUSTON DIVISION

ABC

        Plaintiff

    v.   Civil Action No._____

DEF

        Defendants

DECLARATION OF DAVID COWEN IN SUPPORT OF PLAINTIFF ABC
MOTION FOR SANCTIONS AGAINST DEFENDANT DEF

I, DAVID COWEN, declare as follows:

1.   I am a Senior Consultant with Fios, a computer consulting company that focuses on digital litigation support and forensic analysis. S3 Partners has been retained by counsel for the plaintiffs ("ABC") to render an opinion regarding the time and possibility of recovering relevant digital data from the Defendants' ("DEF") systems. I submit this declaration in support of Plaintiff ABC Motion for Sanctions Against Defendant DEF.

My educational background is technological in nature, featuring more than seven years of experience in the areas of integration, architecture, assessment, programming, forensic analysis and investigation. I currently hold the Certified Information Systems Security Professional certification from (ISC).˙ I have been trained in proper forensics practices by the High Tech Crime Investigators Association, Guidance Software, amongst others. I am an active member of the computer security community, including the High Technology Crime Investigators Association, where I frequently present and train on various forensic topics. I have managed, created, and worked with multiple forensics teams and associated forensic procedures. My experience spans a variety of environments ranging from high security military installations to large/small private sector companies. My billing rate as a senior consultant with FIOS is $sorry guys per hour.

DECLARATION OF DAVID COWEN IN SUPPORT OF PLAINTIFF ABC MOTION
FOR SANCTIONS AGAINST DEFENDANT DEF PAGE 1

Figure 14-3   Front page of a sample declaration

9. After reviewing and analyzing all of the seized evidence with the data first provided and then later discovered in subsequent searches, I am left with the opinion that evidence must exist in some form (i.e., on another system or storage media) that DEF has refused to produce to date. Without access to this additional evidence, we cannot determine the extent that DEF has infringed on ABC's intellectual property rights. In my opinion, DEF's expert has made significant misstatements and omissions to the court and has refused to deliver to the court those relevant documents ordered for production.

I declare under penalty of perjury that the foregoing is true and correct.

Dated: June 30, 2020
Dallas, Texas

_____

David Cowen

90037852.2doc

Figure 14-4 Last page of a sample declaration

However, you should carefully review any document that is put in front of you to sign, to make sure that no last-minute revisions were made that are inaccurate or that you cannot stand behind.

At the end of your declaration, you may want to add a glossary with a section name, such as "Definitions." Within this section, you should define any technical terms you have not explained in the declaration as well as any specific methodologies you followed. The glossary becomes a powerful tool for you in restricting the interpretability of your statements in that you can limit the scope and impact of particular technical terminology. This is very useful as you deal with opposing attorneys and experts who may be aggressive in trying to rebuke your otherwise factual declaration.

AFFIDAVIT

Affidavits are much like declarations, except that the paper affidavit documents require a notarized signature. Affidavits are viewed as "stronger" documents than declarations because of this signature, but the request for an affidavit or a declaration will be based on the court's needs, whether state or federal, and the type of motion you are supporting. Otherwise, an affidavit can be structured much like a declaration with the same rules applied.

EXPERT REPORT

Expert reports are the pinnacle of formal reports to a court. The expert report is your dissertation to the court on the matters at hand and your opinions regarding them. If you are being asked to create an expert report, it is because you have been deemed an expert witness by your attorney; you must readily adhere to the warning mentioned earlier in the chapter regarding such documentation.

While a declaration and an affidavit are made in support of a motion, an expert report stands alone as a document submitted to the courts. The expert report shows your abilities as an expert to state facts, explain details, and clearly support conclusions and opinions. Remember that as an expert, you have the ability and right to make opinions that are aggregated from the evidence you have reviewed, but you should do so carefully. Opposing counsel will have their own experts, possibly even one of the authors of this book, who will be scrutinizing every word of your report. If you have offered any opinions that are based mainly on speculation, they will be quickly opposed and refuted. Any opinion you can make based on reconstructed evidence and outside support will stand much better against the opposing onslaught.

It also works the other way, though. As the expert witness, you will review the opposing expert's opinion and will have the opportunity to respond by providing supplemental and rebuttal reports that address other documents that have been submitted to the court. This includes expert reports, declarations, affidavits, deposition testimony, and any other evidence that has been submitted to the court. Your expert report will also be used against you and the opposing expert when and if you are asked to testify before the courts.

When testifying, make sure that you make reference to your report and quote it when you can. Going back to your expert report allows you to reiterate your opinions to the judge and stand firm behind previous statements. Many attorneys will simply try to get you to restate your opinion in contrast to your report as a tactic to discredit you. Referring back to your report allows you to defend yourself and your opinions from attack.

When making any type of conclusion in your report, it is always a good idea to make use of an outside party's formal papers and reports. This is not considered hearsay, as you have personal knowledge of some published research paper or standard that is available for public use. This is especially true any time you are dealing with some kind of standard, whether it is a network protocol or a function of communication of a standardized service, such as HTTP. Making direct quotations and citing these public works enhances the credibility of your documentation.

You should also carefully research any public articles or presentations you have made in the past. Any public documents you have created in the past can be used against you if they pertain to the matter at hand. For instance, if at some point in the past you wrote an article about intrusion-detection systems and their inability to provide accurate reporting, you should be wary of making a statement in an expert report later stating that you believe the reports generated from the intrusion-detection system are always valid and factual.

Construction of an Expert Report

Expert reports can vary in their construction from expert to expert, but the form put forward here is fairly standard. You should begin the report with a cover page that states that this is your expert report in the following case. Next, the actual report begins. Expert reports are usually separated by sections that are numbered with Roman numerals. The first numbered section in this example is "I. Overview." The overview should state who you have been retained by, the matter name (the names of the entities suing each other), and what you were retained to do. An example overview follows:

> *I. OVERVIEW*
>
> *I have been retained by <u>ABC</u> in the matter styled <u>ABC v. DEF</u> to analyze the items seized from <u>DEF</u> during the court-ordered seizure of systems from <u>DEF</u>. This report sets forth my analysis and my expert opinions.*

The next section, entitled "II. Qualifications," is much like the qualifications section that you would write for a declaration. The following section, though, is unique to expert reports.

The next section is entitled "III. Prior Expert Witness Experience." In this section, you must list every case with which you have been involved and for which you have been declared the expert and provided a report. This is a very specific list, as it applies only when as an expert, you took some action in the suit. So if you were declared the expert in a lawsuit that then settled, you should not include that suit here, since you provided no actual services to the client. Unlike in the security world, where most client engagements are confidential and you cannot reveal the names of your clients, the legal world expects to see each case as soon as it is filed, as the lawsuit becomes public knowledge. While motions may be filed under seal, the overlying case will always be public record. This means that you cannot attempt to show some kind of expert experience without listing a public case that the court and opposing counsel can research and verify. Attempting to mislead or take out of context your role in a case would quickly lead to your removal as an expert in a case.

The qualifications section should resemble something like the following:

> *III. PRIOR EXPERT WITNESS EXPERIENCE*
>
> *I have previously been designated as testify expert witness in the following lawsuits:*
> *<u>XYZ v. 123 (Anytown District Court)</u>, <u>Bob v Jane (D. Anystate)</u>.*

The next sections are relatively straightforward; you must include a section stating your compensation for the work, if any, and what exactly you have reviewed in preparation for this report. The "Items Reviewed" section is important, because you are basically limiting yourself to these sources as potential evidence that you can quote from and show as support in your report. Make sure that you do not omit any evidence that you reviewed, as that will possibly create an argument without basis, which is an easy argument to refute.

The next section, "Analysis," is the bulk of the document, where you refer to your expert knowledge and the evidence you cited in the previous section to make your opinions and conclusions.

 It is important always to be a professional and to be as concise as possible. Remember that a judge will be reading your statements and needs to be able to understand all of the technical points to understand and uphold your point of view.

The last section is the "Conclusion" section. Much like declarations and affidavits, this is where you restate your conclusions and opinions and state their impacts on the matter at hand. In this section, you should quickly and concisely state your overall opinion and what harm you believe has occurred. Examples of an expert report are shown in Figures 14-5, 14-6, and 14-7.

Expert Report of
David L. Cowen

ABC v. DEF

Figure 14-5   The cover of an expert report

I. OVERVIEW

I have been retained by ABC in the matter styled ABC v. DEF. I have been retained to analyze the items seized from DEF and from the homes of the president and chief operating officer of DEF. This report sets forth my analysis and my expert opinions.

II. QUALIFICATIONS

My educational background is technological in nature. I have more than seven years of experience in the areas of integration, architecture, assessment, programming, forensic analysis and investigation. I currently hold the Certified Information Systems Security Professional certification from (ISC). I have been trained in proper forensics practices by the High Tech Crime Investigators Association, Guidance Software, amongst others.

I am also an active member of the computer security community, including the High Technology Crime Investigators Association. As a member of that community, I frequently present and train on various forensic topics. I have managed, created, and worked with multiple forensics teams and associated forensic procedures. My experience spans a variety of environments ranging from high security military installations to large/small private sector companies.

III. PRIOR EXPERT WITNESS EXPERIENCE

I have previously been designated as testifying expert witness in the following lawsuits: TXU v. Mosby (Dallas District Court), Trocciola v. Quris (D. Colo.), Measurement Computing v. National Instruments (D. Massachusetts), BMC v. Crabbyhacker (D. Texas). I also testified during this case at Temporary Restraining Order, Preliminary Injunction, and Sanctions Motion hearings.

IV. COMPENSATION

Sorry guys

V. ITEMS REVIEWED

I reviewed the following items to complete my analysis in this lawsuit:

a.   Items seized from DEF

VI. ANALYSIS

For purposes of this expert report, I have reviewed the evidence seized in this lawsuit to determine whether DEF is withholding evidence related to their development, sales, and distribution of the 123 program. As shown below, it is my expert opinion that

Figure 14-6   The first page of an expert report

DEF has withheld evidence in this lawsuit, such as the source code and executable for the latest version of 123 and evidence related to the development, sales and distribution of 123. As a result, DEF is currently free to continue to cause substantial and irreparable injury to ABC.

VII. CONCLUSION

After reviewing and analyzing all of the seized evidence with the data first provided and then later discovered in subsequent searches, it is my opinion that evidence must exist in some form (i.e., on another system or storage media) that DEF has withheld.

_____

David L. Cowen

September 19, 2020

Figure 14-7   The last page of an expert report

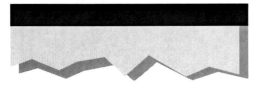

CHAPTER 15

THE JUSTICE SYSTEM

The global surge in the use of computers and electronic information over the past three decades has driven a proportionate demand for experts in the field of computer forensics. To this point, this book has focused on the best practices for a forensic expert to collect, analyze, and report findings based on electronic evidence. Where an investigation leads to a dispute between two parties, however—for instance, between an entity investigating a network breach and the perpetrator of that breach—the outcome of the dispute will often be decided by the courts. Whether the dispute is litigated in a civil or criminal court, and whether it is decided before a judge or a jury, it is imperative that you understand the role of electronic evidence and the use of computer forensics in the American justice system. This chapter provides a brief overview of our court system and explains how forensic evidence functions within it.

At bottom, "forensic science"—or "forensics" for short—applies principles from a wide array of sciences to provide answers to legal questions. "Forensic evidence," then, is simply evidence suitable for use in a court of law. Computer forensics is but one branch of forensic science that applies scientifically proven principles, accepted in the industry, to answer questions in a legal dispute over electronic evidence. The questions presented may range from what was found on a computer or storage device to how it arrived there, who placed it there, or what was done with it thereafter. The success of the forensic expert providing the answers will often depend on the legal admissibility of the physical evidence and the expert's direct testimony.

Modern computer forensics has exploded beyond its origins in the military and law enforcement and into the private sector. Highly trained and competent industry experts are frequently engaged by clients to investigate violations of criminal and civil law ranging from trade secret misappropriation to "cyber-hacking." While investigators with the US Department of Defense or branches of federal and state law enforcement agencies are well-educated in proper practices for presenting evidence in a court of law, private computer experts often lack formal training in collecting and presenting forensic evidence.

The best practices described in other chapters of this book for the preservation, analysis, and presentation of electronic evidence are of paramount concern for the forensic expert who is engaged by a private-sector client. We continue, then, with a basic description of the two distinct court systems—criminal and civil courts—and explain how the forensic consultant provides competent evidence in a trial.

THE CRIMINAL COURT SYSTEM

A criminal case generally begins when a complaint is lodged with a prosecutor in a specific state or federal jurisdiction. Each jurisdiction is governed by its own set of *substantive laws* and *procedural rules*. Federal crimes are governed in all federal courts by Title 18 of the US Code, as codified by Congress, and by the Federal Rules of Criminal Procedure promulgated by the US Supreme Court. Generally, the federal criminal statutes address conduct that extends beyond state borders or impacts a federally protected interest. State statutes likewise codify crimes that directly impact the persons of that state and are prosecuted under that state's own rules of procedure. While some states employ procedural rules modeled on the federal rules, other states' rules differ significantly.

Fundamental to the criminal justice system, however, is that the attorney who brings formal charges in any criminal case, whether a US attorney or a county prosecutor, represents the *government*—not the aggrieved party. Thus, while a private citizen can approach law enforcement or government attorneys to request a criminal investigation and formal charges, the decision whether to proceed with "pressing charges" is left to the government's attorneys. Once a complaint is lodged and prosecution begins, control over the prosecution and the evidence lies with the government. A complainant in a case involving a computer crime risks ceding control over his/her/their own data.

Importantly, while a private consultant is competent to forensically image and preserve a computer system and restore the original media to its prior uses, law enforcement in a criminal case must often seize the original media to establish the proper *chain of custody* and testify with first-hand knowledge regarding the preservation and analysis of the electronic evidence. A complaining party can lose control over the "crime scene"—which might include the party's own equipment, databases, or other critical systems. Though law enforcement today goes to great lengths to cooperate with the private sector, control over the evidence is fundamental to the prosecution's case. The decision whether to report a case for criminal prosecution or to pursue it privately through the civil courts, then, should not be taken lightly.

Equally important is that once a criminal case is commenced, the prosecution retains control, as the representative of the government, over whether to drop the charges. That is, even if the complainant and the accused reach an amicable settlement between them, the government is not obligated to halt criminal proceedings and might decide to press forward to a conviction. This independence can interfere with and even deter a private settlement of the dispute because the complainant cannot offer the accused finality without the government's consent.

At the heart of any complainant's decision to refer a case for prosecution, therefore, is its goal in resolving the underlying dispute. Some "crimes" are so damaging or egregious that criminal prosecution is the only appropriate remedy; others are better resolved through civil litigation or other private means. Even where the ultimate goal is to deter future criminal activity, a civil suit can provide that deterrence through publicity that is dictated and controlled by the plaintiff, not the government.

THE CIVIL JUSTICE SYSTEM

Civil courts resolve private controversies between individuals or entities. Far and away, civil courts are the better forum for an aggrieved private entity to address wrongs against it. Because civil lawsuits are initiated and controlled by private citizens—*plaintiffs*—litigants maintain their freedom to resolve and settle their disputes without governmental intrusion. While specific procedural rules govern "discovery"—the exchange of information about the dispute supplied by the litigants themselves—parties can agree through counsel on the volume, breadth, and format of the exchange to limit expense and reduce business interruption.

A civil suit proceeds in several phases:

1. Investigation of the underlying dispute

2. Commencing suit by filing a complaint or petition in the appropriate court

3. Discovery

4. Trial.

A brief description of each phase follows.

Phase One: Investigation

Prior to commencing suit, a private party and its counsel are obligated to investigate the core facts underlying a dispute to ensure that a good-faith basis exists for filing a complaint. For a computer forensics expert retained by a potential plaintiff, this phase is crucial to the ultimate success of the lawsuit. The expert should assess the perceived wrong, identify systems that contain potentially relevant data, and preserve those systems in a forensically sound manner while working with the client to ensure that relevant data is not lost or destroyed. An expert should also help the client to identify potential *custodians* of relevant evidence and offer advice on the best methods to gather data from the opposing party. While an expert may offer opinions during the investigation phase, these opinions are not typically written as formal opinions because they might change as information is discovered over time. It is imperative that a forensic expert remain objective during the investigation phase to provide the client with sound advice on how to proceed. An emphatic, conclusive opinion that later proves to be incorrect can have disastrous consequences for the client and the opposing party.

Phase Two: Commencing Suit

Once the initial investigation is completed and a party has assessed the merits of its case with its counsel, the attorneys file complaints (or petitions) that set forth the basic facts in the dispute and the legal claims against the defendant. In a trade-secrets case, for instance, the complaint will set forth in sufficient detail a description of the underlying trade secrets, the method of misappropriation of those secrets, and the specific laws violated by the defendant. The complaint will likely ask for monetary damages and, often, for *injunctive relief* requesting some form of restraint on the defendant's ability to cause further harm.

When a complaint is filed, it becomes public information. Documents included with the complaint or attached as evidence supporting a request for injunctive relief become public also—unless a party requests that the information be sealed and demonstrates a compelling need to keep sensitive information from the public.

After a plaintiff commences suit by filing a complaint and serving the defendant with process, the court becomes the arbiter of the lawsuit and presides over procedural disputes and the discovery process.

Phase Three: Discovery

In a case involving computer forensics, the formal "discovery" phase is often the most costly and time-consuming. Depending on the volume of data and the nature of the underlying dispute, an expert may be required to assist in the exchange of electronically stored information (ESI), review an opponent's computer systems, or direct counsel on the likely location of relevant evidence. That evidence may come in the form of deposition (pretrial) testimony, documents and ESI exchanged between the litigants or secured from third parties, interrogatories and responses, and informal interviews of persons with knowledge of relevant facts. The intent of the discovery phase is to provide the litigants with the building blocks for the prosecution or defense of their case—and it will often take many turns as opposing parties seek to secure information that supports their specific claims or defenses. For instance, a plaintiff alleging a trade-secret violation might request the analysis of a former employee's personal computer to determine whether the employee took confidential electronic files prior to departing. The expert might also direct counsel to obtain ESI from a third-party service provider such as Yahoo! or Hotmail if the defendant forwarded confidential material to a personal e-mail account. Each factual scenario presents its own unique problems—including claims of privacy, for instance, by the service provider or the defendant—and can lead to disputes and compromises between the litigants.

The discovery phase commences either at the filing of the lawsuit or shortly after the defendant answers the lawsuit—depending on the jurisdiction's procedural rules—and typically ends 30 to 60 days before the scheduled trial date. The timing and scope of discovery may be altered by agreement of the parties or upon request to the court.

The Federal Rules of Civil Procedure were amended effective December 1, 2006, to provide specifically for the preservation and exchange of ESI between litigants. The changes in the rules are an effort to reflect the change in times: In an electronic world, discovery rules governing the exchange of paper documents no longer fit the bill. The Federal Rules now provide defaults for the preservation and format of ESI production, the methods for requesting production, and safeguards for ensuring that privileged documents are not disclosed inadvertently. Many states have enacted similar procedural rules governing electronic discovery.

While requests for ESI and its exchange with party opponents are accomplished largely through counsel, a forensic consultant should be familiar with the basic concepts in order to advise a client's attorney on how best to procure evidence from an opponent in a manner and format that will be helpful to the case. Generally, a party will obtain ESI or identify the relevant computer systems of an opponent through requests for production, depositions, and interrogatories.

Requests for Production

A request for production asks the responding party to produce tangible items to the requesting party within 30 days of receipt of the request. Tangible items can be anything from a one-page document to all of the corporate e-mails related to the particular event in question. The production request must be in relation to the case and its scope will reflect that. However, in some cases, that scope can be extremely broad, as in anti-trust cases where almost any document might be considered relevant. In such cases, data produced could range in the terabytes. The lion's share of a forensics consultant's work will occur in relation to a request for production. Attorneys are quickly learning the value of electronic data and the secrets it holds. However, two types of documents do not have to be produced—privileged and nonrelevant documents.

Privileged Documents   Privilege means that a legal basis exists for the withholding of a document due to the nature of either its creation or to whom it was sent. For example, any document sent to an attorney or from an attorney or containing the attorney's thoughts on the matter at hand can be considered to be attorney work product and privileged. Likewise, correspondence between a client and his or her attorney can be considered privileged by virtue of the attorney-client privilege. Finally, and most importantly for the purposes of this chapter, correspondence between you, as the expert, and the attorney can be withheld as privileged under the attorney work product privilege. This privilege extends to agents of the attorney, such as nontestifying expert consultants who are involved in the preparation of the case. However, all privileged documents must be tracked in a privilege log, and their status as privileged may be challenged by the opposing party. It is up to the requesting party to challenge the designation of privileged. At that point, the responding party will provide a privilege log to the court, which will then review the documents privately, or in camera, and make a determination as to whether the privilege applies to the documents.

Nonrelevant Documents   Documents can be deemed nonrelevant by an attorney or the court. It is not a designation to be made by an expert. As an expert, you can render an opinion, but the actual act of declaring something nonrelevant is not your place. The responsibility of a production falls directly on an attorney and his or her client, so the ultimate decision must stay with them. A document is declared nonrelevant if the information contained within the document does not relate to the matter at hand.

Interrogatories

An interrogatory is similar to a request for production in that it is a tool used to learn new information. However, in an interrogatory, the requesting party is seeking answers and not tangible things. Using this discovery tool, counsel discovers the basis of the cause of the action, the names of the relevant witnesses, the names of the designated testifying experts, as well as any background information deemed to be relevant. For the purposes of computer forensics, this discovery tool has very little to do with your job.

Depositions

Depositions take place during the discovery phase of a trial. During this phase, both parties are seeking evidence that can bolster their cases. A deposition is a formal question-and-answer session in which the lawyers who retained your services and opposing counsel take turns asking you questions. The questions and their answers will be part of the official court record and will be on file in the court. All statements are recorded and transcribed by a court reporter that has obtained a court reporter certificate and transcribes all statements made during the deposition. In addition to a court reporter, the lawyers can ask that a videographer attend a deposition. Video is a powerful tool in that it allows the judge and jury to see, in a deponent's reluctance or slowness in responding, what a written transcription might miss.

For a period of time after deposition testimony, the deponent (the person whose deposition was taken) can correct the transcript before it is entered into the court record. Deponents can use this opportunity either to correct possible errors made by the court reporter, fill in answers that were not known at the time of the deposition, or add information to answers that were originally left incomplete. A deposition can take place at an attorney's office, your office, opposing counsel's office, or, in the very rare occasion, a courtroom. The location does not change the fact that you are making sworn testimony to the court. Transcription will begin when you "go on the record" and will stop any time counsel from either side requests that you "go off the record." When off the record, any statements made will not be transcribed, but they are still admissible in court.

Depositions begin with the swearing in of the witness to ensure that what is said during the deposition is considered testimony to the court and as such carries the burden of perjury. To commit perjury is to make false statements knowingly under oath, considered a felony that carries with it the penalty of imprisonment. During the deposition, counsel will take turns asking questions. The attorney requesting the deposition will begin and continue questioning until complete. The responding party may then ask questions of his or her own witness. Both parties will then have another chance to ask questions or end the deposition after the first round. The attorney representing you will have the opportunity to object to questions asked by opposing counsel. Be careful not to talk over the attorney's objections, and make certain that you do not answer the question before asking counsel for permission to answer. Opposing counsel will frequently look for ways to get confidential information from the witness. It is your attorney's job to keep that information from being shared, because of the privileged nature of the information. Always be careful of your statements, as they may contain privileged information. We will discuss more on privilege later in the chapter in the section "Expert Status."

Frequently, local or state rules mandate time limits on an individual's deposition. However, a deposition can last as little as 10 minutes or as long as five days—it simply depends on whether an agreement was reached between the parties regarding the length of depositions. In fact, for example, a deposition could last five days and then be put on hold. This means that the attorney can reopen the deposition at a later date because, as of today, the attorney does not believe that he or she has adequate information to ask you all of the relevant questions.

Phase Four: Trial

The trial phase is the final phase, wherein the fruits of the discovery are brought into the courtroom. At this point, testimony from the particular experts has already been elicited during depositions. The trial phase can take anywhere from one day to several months, and parties can agree to a trial by jury or judge. A typical trial consists of four phases: opening arguments, plaintiff's case, defendant's case, and then closing arguments. Expert testimony takes place during the presentation of the plaintiff's and defendant's cases.

Trial testimony takes place under oath in the courtroom in front of a judge and possibly a jury. Unlike deposition testimony, however, trial testimony allows for questions from a third party—the judge is allowed at any time to ask a question of the witness. Oftentimes, a judge will do this to get clarification on a topic or to determine your bias toward an opinion. There are no time limits. Testimony can last for anywhere from 10 minutes to five days. Like depositions, both parties will have an opportunity to ask questions.

EXPERT STATUS

In the preceding chapter, we talked about experts in the creation of reports. Specifically, we discussed what kind of reports should be created when you are deemed an expert for a certain capacity. You cannot simply deem yourself the expert; an expert must be retained by whatever attorney is litigating the case, and in some special cases by the court itself.

Expert Credentials

An expert witness, by definition, is a person who has more knowledge of some field than an ordinary person. What qualifies an expert is his or her ability to demonstrate his or her proficiency in his or her specialized area through statements and prior work history and training. No special class or certificate is necessary to become an expert. However, if challenged by the opposing party, the party presenting the witness must show to the court that the witness is a qualified expert in the field about which he or she is being asked to testify. This is typically demonstrated through a series of questions regarding the expert's educational and occupational history and previous cases for which the expert may have testified. The ultimate arbiter as to whether a witness qualifies as an expert is the presiding judge.

Nontestifying Expert Consultant

A nontestifying expert consultant is an expert who works for the attorney and whose work under advisement of the attorney is considered privileged. As an expert consultant, you will be asked to investigate and review confidential documents in the suit so that you can render an opinion to the attorney. You, at times, may also be asked to communicate with the chosen testifying expert witness to give specific information or evidence for his or her review. You may also be asked to write declarations and affidavits in support of some work you have done. Typically, nontestifying expert consultants are exempt from being deposed or called to testify, as they have not been designated as testifying experts. Their existence is usually shielded by counsel and nothing requires that a nontestifying witness be identified as a person with knowledge of relevant facts. As such, the nontestifying expert can conduct his or her work in complete anonymity. However, a nontestifying expert may be asked to testify if the party requesting the testimony can show the court that the witness has firsthand knowledge of the facts at issue. Since most consulting experts learn the facts of a case through the eyes of others, they are rarely required to testify.

Testifying Expert Witness

A testifying expert witness is an expert who is employed by the attorney to review evidence and render an independent opinion based on his or her expertise in the area. As stated in Chapter 14, no privilege is implied for any work or communication that an expert witness carries out in relation to a lawsuit. As a testifying expert witness, any document you are shown and conversation you overhear or are a part of is open for questioning. Also, any document you create—from an electronic document, to an e-mail, to a doodle on a napkin—is considered work product. Any work product you create can be requested for production by opposing counsel, so be aware of this when you are creating your notes. Attorneys will generally ask their testifying experts to refrain from drafting any notes that include legal conclusions or the work product of the attorney. Reports are not to be prepared until a specific request is issued from either counsel. At times, your opinion as an expert will harm the client's case. For that reason, your client may not want an expert report until it is specifically requested by opposing counsel. If it is not requested, counsel will likely try to de-designate you as an expert, not calling you to testify at deposition or trial.

Court-Appointed Expert

Sometimes a judge will appoint an expert to act as an independent expert for both parties. This happens often in criminal cases and smaller civil cases, where neither party has the knowledge or finances to find an expert on the subject. In addition, when a discovery dispute exists between the parties, a court will often designate an independent expert to look into the conflict and determine whether an alternative solution exists. As an expert for the court, all of the rules applied to an expert witness apply, but in addition you are required to be subjective as you are employed and paid by the court, not by either attorney.

Expert Interaction with the Court

As an expert representing a party, you cannot directly address the court or file motions stating your opinion. Instead, your ability to make written statements to the court is limited to affidavits and declarations in support of motions and expert reports such as those covered in Chapter 14. Other opportunities for you to make statements to the court do exist. Through testimony elicited by counsel for either party, you can state your opinion on the record at trial or at deposition. In addition, as previously discussed, if an expert report is prepared, it will likely be entered into the court record.

PART V

PUTTING IT ALL TOGETHER

CASE STUDY: NOW WHAT?

Even if you have a mastery of the technical fundamentals behind an investigation, it doesn't mean you have a clear picture of how to conduct an end-to-end investigation. Mr. Blink studies all the forensic techniques he can get his hands on. He knows the registry inside and out. Decrypting files? He's the expert. Disk wiped? Not a problem, as he is an expert with an electron microscope. In this case study, however, Mr. Blink learns that there's more to forensics than just knowing a few clever techniques.

Mr. Blink Becomes an Investigator

Mr. Blink is known around the company for his interest in forensics. He's always playing with various internals of the operating system, learning all the ins and outs. After an employee quit his job, Mr. Blink's manager tells the CTO that he thinks the ex-employee may have taken some files with him and sent some harassing e-mails to other employees on his way out. Knowing that Mr. Blink has an interest in the technical aspects of forensics, the CTO hands Mr. Blink the ex-employee's laptop and asks him to find out what happened.

Time to Understand the Business Issues

Quickly realizing that technical skill alone won't crack the case, Mr. Blink draws up some questions for the CTO: What are we looking for? What types of files do we think he took? What kind of evidence do you need to take this issue to the next step? How can I ensure that everything I do is within the law?

By understanding the type of investigation he is undertaking, and understanding what type of evidence is common in this investigation, as well as the facts unique to this matter, Mr. Blink cracks the case. He shows exactly how the files were copied off the computer, how the former employee sent the threatening e-mails from home, and exactly which USB devices the files were copied to and what happened to them after they left the company.

As stated in Part I, forensics is a process that involves business, legal, and technical issues. By understanding how these issues interplay in the specific type of case at hand, Mr. Blink has become the most effective forensic investigator he can be.

CHAPTER 16

IP THEFT

Computer forensics, including the tips and techniques described throughout this book, are becoming increasingly important in safeguarding company assets. Computer forensics specialists are routinely working hand-in-hand with Certified Fraud Examiners and other investigators to identify and recover assets that have been stolen or otherwise misappropriated, as well as in support of efforts to halt their illegal use.

In the digital age, intellectual assets, more often than physical assets, drive much of the economy. Increasing product innovation in the last decade has resulted in an explosion of new products and industries. Protecting the ideas behind these efforts is a critical part of today's corporate strategies and a critical component of today's IT professional. The growth of patent filings over the past decade is indicative of the increasing importance of intellectual property in our daily lives and to the businesses that provide the services and products to which we are now accustomed.

Intellectual assets (i.e., intellectual property) comes in many forms and can seem like an obscure and ill-defined concept. However, intellectual property has become the lifeblood of every new economy. Most things that are essential to our daily lives involve various intellectual property rights, including patents, copyrights, trademarks, or other trade secrets that help make one business more successful than another. From the clothes we wear and the cars we drive, to the foods and medicines we depend on to survive, intellectual property is all around us.

WHAT IS IP THEFT?

With the increased development of intellectual property over the past two decades, a new threat has arisen: intellectual property (IP) theft. Although IP theft is nothing new, the advent of the digital age has compounded the risks companies face from IP theft; it is now possible to fit hundreds of thousands of pages of electronic information onto something the size of a stick of gum. Whereas computer access was once limited to select employees within a corporation, today most employees have computers, or at least access to computers, including access to company networks. In addition, through the proliferation of e-mail, notebook computers, camera phones, Blackberrys, wireless communications, USBs and other portable storage devices, and CD and DVD burners, vast amounts of electronic information can be moved easily from one location to another with literally a push of a button. IP theft involves every industry, from health care to the energy sector, and information is at risk every day because employees can easily access, obtain, copy, and transport information.

As IP typically involves rights to the exclusive use of an invention, product, idea, or other creation through a patent, copyright, trademark, or other protective measure, it can be of significant value to its owner. Many companies and individuals jealously guard IP as it can be the key to their success. Musicians and record companies guard their music from unlawful reproduction through the Internet. Movie studios spend untold millions trying to guard their movie productions and prevent the unlawful copying and sale of movies on DVDs or other electronic media. While these are obvious examples, small companies can also have significant IP that needs protections, including customer lists, proprietary processes, and even marketing and advertising plans—any information that can be used as a business advantage. Since IP is valuable, it has become a target for theft, like other things of value.

Once IP is stolen, it is up to the IP owner to determine how, when, and what IP was stolen. IP theft can take many forms. From the copying (theft) of music and movie productions to the theft of technical design plans for the latest electronic gadget, IP theft involves stealing something of value that rightfully belongs to another.

Each company's IP is individual and unique, depending on the industry, the market, the company, and the individuals involved. Some IP is in the form of physical plans and drawings, some is in the form of software code, a list of customers, or an individual's ideas or know-how. The unlawful copying of a video, the illicit use of proprietary software code, the improper copying and distribution of a customer list, and the infringement on a company's or an individual's patent, copyright, or trademark are all forms of IP theft. The following types of IP theft are discussed in this chapter:

- Customer data
- Technology
- Trade secrets and other proprietary information

IP THEFT RAMIFICATIONS

While not all IP has clearly definable value, a significant proportion of the value of many companies today rests in their IP. As such, IP theft can have a detrimental impact on a company's success. As the digital age blossomed, companies began turning their attention to the value of their IP and in protecting that IP. At the same time, related IP theft and the accompanying investigations and litigation also increased proportionately. In many ways, the theft of customer data, technology, or other proprietary information may be difficult to measure because it may not have an immediate or direct impact on a company. Unlike the theft of cash or other physical assets, IP theft, as well as the results of IP theft, can be more difficult to see. Eventually, however, the loss of customers, the company's competitive position, and loss of profits can be unmistakable signs of stolen IP.

IP is typically a source, and sometimes the key, to a company's competitive advantage in the marketplace, and its ultimate success. Stolen IP can be used by a company's competitors to equalize the playing field or gain unfair advantage, or by former employees interested in establishing a foothold in the market through competing interests. The impact to the IP owner can be negligible, but it can be worth hundreds of millions to billions of dollars.

Loss of Customers

One the most common results of IP theft is loss of customers, as the IP owner may encounter new competition that did not previously exist, or, if a customer list was stolen, a competitor may use the list to woo customers away from the original company. Competing products may emerge, offering capabilities, functionality, and other features similar to those of the company whose IP was stolen. Often, and typically through the judicial process, it can be determined that the new competition, and the resulting loss of customers for the IP owner, was a direct result of the IP theft.

Manufacturing enterprises are particularly vulnerable to IP theft because of the significant amount of corporate secrets and know-how that can be involved in a manufacturing process. An undetected theft of IP related to manufacturing processes may give another company an advantage over time, yielding greater efficiencies in its operations and ability to compete more aggressively on price for the same customers.

Loss of Competitive Advantage

The ramifications from IP theft may not be direct or immediately noticeable. IP theft can result in a slow and gradual loss of competitive advantage. As a company's trade secrets are stolen and used by competing interests in the marketplace, a company may lose the competitive advantage it once held in its industry. Ultimately, a company's inability to compete effectively also results in the loss of customers and revenue, but the effects can be more gradual and difficult to ascertain, much more so than the direct loss of customers and revenue through pirated music or DVDs.

Unfortunately, as far as competitive advantage is concerned, the answer to the questions "What has value?" and "What needs protecting?" is the ubiquitous "It depends." What drives competitive advantage for a business can be veritable laundry list of contributions to the overall value and success of the business—from engineering designs, CAD drawings, and product development cycles on the manufacturing side, to customer lists, competitive analysis, and marketing analysis on the sales side.

Monetary Loss

Because IP typically has value, and the objective of IP theft is typically to capitalize on that value, IP theft can and often does result in a significant monetary loss to the original IP owner. As the digital age has grown, the abilities and means of individuals to steal valuable IP has increased as well. Although precise estimates are impossible to ascertain, the US Department of Commerce estimates that more than of $250 billion in IP is stolen from US companies each year.

While not all IP theft results in a monetary loss, and sometimes the monetary loss can be difficult to quantify, the intent of IP theft is typically no different than the intent in stealing physical assets (such as cash), and the objective is to rob the company of something that is considered valuable. Given this fact, many companies go to great lengths to protect their IP and are willing to expend significant sums in pursuit of those who have misappropriated or otherwise misused their IP. As evidenced in Figure 16-1, the number of patent-related lawsuits filed in federal courts in the U.S. over the past decade have increased substantially.

TYPES OF THEFT

When IP theft is suspected, the first step is to determine what IP is owned by the particular entity, how is it maintained, and what level of security exists to prevent unauthorized access to the IP as well as its misappropriation. While many companies believe that they understand what IP is most valuable in their organizations, in reality, most companies have not undertaken a detailed analysis of their IP and the relative contribution it provides to the company's overall success.

As mentioned, each company or entity is different, and IP can take many forms. Like most other aspects of business, as well as our personal lives, much of that IP has been converted to, maintained in, and stored in digital form. Whether it is valuable customer data, customer lists, proprietary designs, or other valuable information, it is likely held in some electronic format within the company. Any investigation must focus on what IP exists, how it is stored and/or protected, and who has access to it.

We describe three types of IP and recommend steps for securing and evaluating the computer and other electronic information when IP theft is suspected.

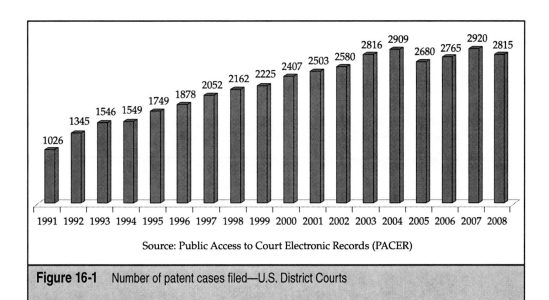

Source: Public Access to Court Electronic Records (PACER)

Figure 16-1   Number of patent cases filed—U.S. District Courts

 **Theft of Customer Data**

Popularity:	7
Simplicity:	9
Impact:	8
Risk Rating:	8

Customer data can take many forms—a hospital's patient records, a university's student records, or an electronic store's customer purchase records. This data typically contains confidential and proprietary information about individuals who have entrusted the company to keep the information protected. The information may include key attributes of a person's identify (such as Social Security number and date of birth) or information regarding bank account or credit card numbers. Some of the information may be of relatively little use to the perpetrators, but some information may put the individual customers at great risk. As such, the protection of customer data, and the apprehension of those who perpetrate the theft of IP, has garnered greater attention in recent years.

In addition, in recent years, the growth of outsourcing of various business functions to overseas entities that can provide the necessary support at a much cheaper cost creates greater risk for the loss of customer data. Outsourced business functions typically involve more data intensive and often customer- or employee-related aspects of the business. The outsourcing of business functions involving sensitive customer information presents greater opportunities for the misappropriation and misuse of that information as the outsourcing company typically has limited control over the security and data handling procedures of the outsourced company.

What to Understand

When a theft of customer data is confirmed or even suspected, standard protocols are recommended for identifying, reviewing, and evaluating the data in question to determine whether any of the information has been put at risk, and if so, to determine how the information was removed and by whom. As with the potential theft of most IP in electronic format, what you look for will depend on the type and format of the stolen information and how that information was maintained and secured.

You must determine whether the information was held in both electronic and hard-copy formats, and whether the theft could have been perpetrated by the straight copying and removal of the relevant IP. If the suspected IP theft appears to have occurred electronically, you must be familiar with the location, or locations, where the information was held. Was the information stolen from the hard-drive of a laptop computer? A portable storage device? Through direct interaction with the entity's internal network?

Next, you must get familiar with any security procedures that exist to protect the information, both to evaluate the relative risk of a perpetrator gaining access to the information and to narrow down the potential source of the theft. If the data's network location had secure or limited access, find out who had access and whether the security procedures could have been, or in fact were, overridden to gain access to the customer data in question.

Historically, most IP theft is committed by insiders. However, the definition of an "insider" has significantly expanded in recent years as the practices of customer, supplier and vendor portals, business partnering, and outsourcing have grown substantially. In addition, while "insider" used to mean the employee down the hall and five cubicles over, in reality, today's employees can include virtual as well as mobile employees who have access to all of the same corporate information and IP through dial-up connections, virtual private networks (VPNs), and web-based portals. Hence, the list of potential suspects and access points for the IP theft may be significantly greater than you might think.

What to Look For

The particular circumstances surrounding the customer data and suspected IP theft in question determines what you should look for in an investigation. Several aspects are common in the theft of customer data, however.

Access of Customer Data

Popularity:	5
Simplicity:	2
Impact:	9
Risk Rating:	6

Unlike other types of IP, customer data is usually stored in a central location. For most companies, this means some type of mainframe, database, or enterprise resource planning (ERP) system. These systems are great from a corporate standpoint because they centralize all the information in one place. They are also dangerous, because if access permissions are incorrectly applied, then someone who wants to access the information can reach it all in one place. These systems contain the crown jewels of the company's clientele—customer information for competitive advantage or identities for the purpose of ID theft.

Determining When and How Customer Information Is Accessed

When facing the theft of customer data, you must identify where the data was stored. If you are a third party conducting the investigation, discuss the matter with the CIO/CTO and find out who is the custodian of the information system. Map out the system with the IT staff and learn how employees access and use the system.

Even if you are familiar with a company's system, take the time to go through this process. Today's data management systems are so complex that almost every installation has its own nuances. Once you know the type of system you are dealing with, the access parameters granted to each employee, and how those employees access the system, you can begin your analysis.

We have identified three main types of systems: relational databases, mainframe systems, and ERP systems such as SAP. Each system requires some general considerations on your part, and each warrants further analysis.

Relational Databases Relational databases such as Microsoft SQL Server, MySQL, and Microsoft Access are the default selections for organizations that want to store customer data but do not want or need to spend huge amounts of money on more complicated solutions. Your first task, if the database allows it and the administrator has turned on logging, is to check the access logs to determine whether they can reveal access information. Logs can provide a surefire sign that something inappropriate has happened. Unfortunately, it is rare that you will be lucky enough to find exactly what you need in one place. In addition, many databases are set up with a default configuration, which means that access logging does not necessarily occur.

The good news about relational databases is that rarely can employees access data and remove it from the system without leaving a trace of their action. If you are dealing with a large-scale database such as a MS SQL database, most employees use some kind of intermediary file to copy data off the system. The key is to find that dump file. For instance, a tech savvy employee may use an SQL manager to dump the tables into a .sql file. This will allow her to go back later and reconstruct the database on a different machine. More commonly, however, is the creation of .csv or .tab files. These files are comma- and tab-separated, common formats used in data processing.

Typically, you will identify the type of database, find the common ways information is exported from the database, and then look for those types of files. For instance, to identify comma-separated files, you would run a search on the machine to look for filenames that end in .csv. Oftentimes, files such as .sql or .xml files will have file signatures that you can use to narrow down potentially relevant files. Also, don't forget to search by date range. If you know the timeframe when the data may have been copied from the computer, look for files created in that timeframe. The number of files created may be small enough that you can review each file to see what it contains.

Mainframe Systems Mainframe systems such as Tandem or DB2 are still in use all over the world. They have faithfully provided the information backbone for the largest companies and will continue to do so for a long time to come. Now for the bad news: Mainframes can be difficult systems to work with from an investigative standpoint. They are, at best, proprietary, arcane, and incompatible with about every modern forensic tool out there. If you are a mainframe forensics expert, you deserve congratulations, because your services will always be in demand. If you're not an expert, you may benefit from a few pointers to help you get the information you need.

First, find the custodian of the mainframe to learn how reports are run. Mainframe systems typically use a traditional dumb terminal architecture. Usually a VT100-type terminal software such as HyperTerminal is used to access the information. While the terminal software is great for accessing the system in adverse network conditions, it is not so good for running reports, so most of these mainframe systems have some secondary mechanism for running reports. Some have proprietary tools that are used to connect with the mainframe and can download comma separated value (CSV) or tab-delimited files. Others allow you to execute commands that can place reports on predesignated shared drives.

The good news about mainframes is that the access model is generally very rigid, and the logging is extensive. In addition, the reporting facility is usually something that an end user cannot change. The user can't, for instance, change the location of a saved report to hide it.

Once you understand exactly how the mainframe works and how it is accessed, you can use this information to find the relevant log entries and report files. Even if you can't find the report files—if they were deleted, for example—you can use the log entries to create a preliminary timeline and use that information to search the individual's computer for activity. More often than not, you will find some secondary and tertiary data points you can use to fill out the picture of what happened more completely.

ERP Systems   ERP systems are like a modern hybrid of the database and mainframe systems, with a dash of web server thrown in. These systems usually have a database backend that is not accessible to the user, so the user uses some type of web interface to access the system. This web interface uses the same kinds of input restrictions and access controls you'd see in a mainframe system, but with a few key differences. For instance, the reporting facilities on an ERP system are generally more flexible than those on a mainframe system. This offers convenience to the end user who may need to create many types of reports. This convenience, however, creates an issue for the investigator, because it means that he or she has no single place and report format to look for.

At the risk of sounding like a broken record, remember that if you need to investigate something involving one of these systems, talk to the custodian of the system first. Even if the ERP system is running on software you have used, some integration details can make the system totally different from what you have seen in the past. Typically, however, the reports generated by these systems are a bit more user-friendly than reports from a mainframe or relational database. This is good news for the investigator because it usually means that the filenames will be similar and you can use file header information as a search term to find a file on the hard drive.

In addition to accessing the server-side log files, you may be able to open a new avenue of audit, web browser history and cache, because these systems are web-based. Even if a suspect tries to cover his tracks by deleting a report after it has been copied, he may forget about the Internet history and cache. You can re-create these, as discussed in Chapter 9, to be the same web pages the user accessed. By using this data, you can often put together not only the data that was taken, but you can show the steps the individual used to access the data, showing that access was deliberate and not a result of an innocent mistake such as clicking the wrong button.

The Data Was Accessed. Now What?

After you've found the reports, correlated the logs, and reconstructed the dump files and internet cache, you may come to the unsettling conclusion that customer data was in fact accessed with the intent of copying it from the machine. If you do find these electronic reports, you'll need to determine if and how data was removed from the computer. These reports are considered proprietary information, and once you identify the files that contain information that can be copied, you can use the same techniques discussed in this chapter to determine how it was transmitted and where it was copied.

One last note before leaving the topic of dump files and reports. These files are digital evidence, just like anything else. Make sure that you have forensic copies of the data and that proper chain of custody is initiated. If the reports are stored on a file share, for instance, use a tool that will preserve the metadata, such as Robocopy, to make a copy of the files. When it's not possible to image or copy the data forensically, do the best you can to grab the records as they would be obtained in the normal course of business, and have the data custodian validate your process. If you have tape backups of the system, make sure you preserve the backups of the relevant timeframe until the matter has been resolved.

Technology

Popularity:	5
Simplicity:	8
Impact:	10
Risk Rating:	8

Businesses and individuals use technology to create competitive advantages relative to their competitors. Technology drives how we communicate (via e-mail, telecommunications, and so on); how we create, process, disseminate, and store information (in word processing documents, spreadsheets, graphical presentations, and so on); how we manage aspects of our businesses (such as accounting or inventory); and how efficiently we conduct business. Technology is also used to create distinct advantages in how we conduct business.

Through proprietary software code, computer programs, and specialized databases and spreadsheet applications, among other items, businesses use technology to create tailored and valuable tools that promote efficiency and enhance productivity; but these tools also create distinct competitive advantages, such as specialized software, pricing models, and so on. As with other forms of IP, technology often has significant value not only to the company, but to its competitors and others who may have similar uses for the technology in different applications.

What to Understand

When technology theft is suspected, as with most forms of IP theft, your first step as investigator is to understand in what form the technology exists. Unlike customer data and other types of IP that could be in hard-copy form, the technology in its electronic form has value to the company. In addition, whether source code, a web-based program, or a specialized computer application, the type of technology will dictate how it is maintained by the company, the locations of access points at which someone could have misappropriated the technology, and how it was misappropriated. For example, the theft of source code implies a level of sophistication that most employees within a typical company will typically not possess. In contrast, a specialized pricing model in spreadsheet format may be widely disseminated electronically throughout an organization, including multiple regions, cities, or countries. to various sales agents and others.

Unlike some forms of IP, technology theft is typically in electronic form, which means someone had to gain access to the technology, copy it to a computer hard drive or external or removable storage device, and possibly transmit it via e-mail or the Web—all of which leaves potential forensic evidence.

What to Look For

Finding source code/program theft is a topic worthy of an entire book (and, in fact, multiple books already exist). If you write code, read on. If you do not, you may want to defer this issue to someone who has experience with large-scale software and knows how to handle change-management systems and tools. That being said, here are a couple places to start.

Copying Source Code

Popularity:	7
Simplicity:	10
Impact:	10
Risk Rating:	9

The simplest way source code can be stolen is by cut-and-paste. A function, a module, or an entire routine can be cut from one program and copied into another. If you have a piece of software with hundreds of thousands of lines of code, finding bits of code cut and pasted into another program can be a daunting task. Thankfully, some developer tools that have been around for decades can help you out.

Finding Cuts-and-Pastes

Your first task is a simple filename and hash comparison. It's not uncommon for someone to copy code files verbatim and drop them into their own program. In fact, academic studies have found that a simple filename comparison can be used to find copied code in 60 percent of cases studied. This task is relatively simple: Create a hash set of the known source code and apply it to the code you want to check. If anything matches, you have found your source code. Then ensure that the matching files aren't public domain or compiler files, and you're set. If you don't get any custom matches, however, you will need to move on to the next step.

Performing Content Searches on Source Code   If the source code you are comparing is Java-based code, you are in luck. A tool called PMD is designed to find cut-and-pasted code in large-scale projects. You can download PMD at http://PMD.sourceforge.net. It is open source and free to use. Simply point it toward the two source trees and watch it go.

If the source code isn't Java-based, the situation gets trickier. We typically use the UNIX utilities CMP and DIFF. CMP is a standard UNIX utility that compares two files and will tell you if they are reasonably the same (as opposed to a hash, which will tell you whether they are bit-for-bit identical or not). CMP works well for complete files that may have been only slightly modified.

If the source code is embedded in other files, and you can't do a file-by-file analysis, then you have a tricky situation. Be prepared, because this will take time. The best way to review embedded source code is to use DIFF. While DIFF was written to determine differences in source code, you can also use it to review similarities. You can run DIFF in a myriad of ways in terms of what it looks for and what it outputs, but we generally suggest that you run it with defaults and then review the results for similarities.

NOTE   If you are running Windows and want to access the UNIX utilities, we recommend installing Cygwin on your computer. It will install a bash shell that you can use in a command-line environment to run these applications.

Comparing Without Source Code

Popularity:	7
Simplicity:	3
Impact:	6
Risk Rating:	5

If you don't have access to both source trees, your job gets quite a bit more difficult. First—and this sounds obvious—ask for the source code. If you can't get it or a suspected code thief refuses to give it to your client, you can still prove helpful by providing your client with enough evidentiary information to compel the other side to give you the code. By using screenshots and showing how layouts and/or other information are similar, you can construct a compelling argument for why it is reasonable to believe that some source code similarity exists.

Finding Similarity in the User Interface and Output

Although it will be difficult for you to say definitively that two programs are the same without access to the source code, you can still build a case. The key is to look for similarities. Study the user interface. Are controls laid out the same way? Is the input method similar? What about the size of the windows and text boxes? You can also look at the format and layout of the output. For instance, if the output is a CSV file with data points, how is the text file formatted and what columns are used? Look at the output for similarities with the original output. Do they both round to the same number of floating point decimals? Are the numbers sorted in a certain manner? What about the order of the columns? In general, find out the client program's "secret ingredient," and then look at how the program in question deals with some of the same issues. If you notice minor similarities, you may not have enough evidence to go on. But if you find occurrences such as output files that look exactly the same in both programs, or identical or nearly identical user interfaces, further investigation may be warranted.

Further Analysis   While you're reviewing source code, don't forget about the traditional methods of IP theft. The whole thing can get a lot easier if you can point definitively to an entire source tree being copied from a computer. It's important that you look not only at the source code itself, but at the computers on which it resided to determine whether the information was copied. (We discuss how to do this in greater detail in the next section.)

Trade Secrets and Other Proprietary Information

Popularity:	7
Simplicity:	8
Impact:	10
Risk Rating:	9

IP is typically categorized into various groups—patents, copyrights, trademarks, and trade secrets. These classifications coincide with those used by the US Patent and Trademark Office (USPTO) in describing and conveying certain rights to the respective IP owners—primarily the right to exclude others from the use and/or exploitation of the IP. Various types of patents can be obtained (such as utility, design, plant, animal), which cover a wide range of ideas and inventions, from tangible tools and machines, to things that are more intangible such as novel processes and designs. Copyrights cover the expression of an idea, but not necessarily the idea itself. The most common form of copyright is in association with literary or musical works. A trademark is generally a name, word, or symbol used by a business to market its goods.

In general, patents, copyrights, and trademarks provide their owners with the legal right to prevent anyone from using the technology or subject matter of the patent, copyrighted material, or trademark for a certain period of time, thereby guaranteeing the IP owner the exclusive right to reap whatever economic benefit or value may be associated with the IP. In addition, since they are typically already in the public domain (that is, a person can look up any patent with the USPTO or purchase a literary or musical work), patents are often misused or infringed upon, but they are rarely the subject of claims for theft or misappropriation. Patents, copyrights, and trademarks are not the only IP held by a company, however.

IP also incorporates a broader classification of intangible assets that provide value to a company. While patents, copyrights, and trademarks carry certain legal protections for their owners, of no less value and importance to a company are certain trade secrets or other propriety technology and information. Many of these types of IP may not share the same characteristics with patents, or they may simply be IP for which the owner chose not to seek a patent. Trade secrets encompass a broad range of things, and in some respects can be anything considered "secret" that gives the owner an economic advantage or benefit in its business—a unique process, design, or approach to a secret ingredient in the clam chowder at your favorite restaurant, for example. While your favorite restaurant may not have a patent on its clam chowder, the secret ingredient nonetheless has value to the restaurant because of the many customers who frequent the place to eat the famous soup.

The issuance of a patent, copyright, or trademark provides protection against the misuse of the IP from outsiders. Although it does not always prevent others from using the IP, it provides a legal framework for pursuing damages against those who do. Companies expend significant efforts in pursuing those who infringe upon their IP. However, companies likewise have the right to keep their trade secrets or other proprietary technology and know-how secret from their competitors or others who could use it to undermine their advantage and success in the marketplace.

Trade secrets come in many forms, from the secret recipe just described, to proprietary engineering or manufacturing processes, specialized software programs, customer lists or other collections of data such as customized databases of information, to the knowledge and skills of its top professionals. Because trade secrets take many forms, and may exist in various aspects of an organization, they can also be difficult to define, value, and protect. As a result, trade secrets are also the target and the subject of the most potential abuse and theft. While companies are typically paying attention to their most valuable patents, as well as the infringement or misuse of their copyrighted material or trademarks in the public domain, many of the various trade secrets that also contribute to a company's success are often left unguarded, and their misappropriation may go unnoticed for lengthy periods of time, if they're ever discovered.

What to Understand

Where a theft of trade secrets or other proprietary technology is suspected, you must first define the trade secret and/or proprietary technology in question and why it is believed that it may have been misappropriated. This can be one of the most difficult steps in an investigation, as trade secrets and know-how can cover a broad array information and technology.

You must define what exactly is believed to have been inappropriately taken. Is it tangible, such as software code, proprietary designs and drawings, a customer list, a compilation of data on the market, or the industry's/company's sales territories? Or is it more difficult to define, such as the general know-how related to the most efficient manufacturing process for a certain product. Or is it as simple as a copied recipe for clam chowder?

A clear understanding of what is suspected to have been misappropriated will help you define what efforts should be undertaken from a computer forensics perspective to investigate the possible theft. While customer data will usually be in the form of a large data set and, by necessity and convenience, will be in electronic format, not all trade secrets and other proprietary technology may be in electronic form. In some instances, a company's trade secrets may walk out the door in hard-copy form in someone's briefcase. However, it is more likely that some form of electronic media was used to gain access to the information stored on the company's network or in other electronic files, and either a copy of that information was created on disk or removable storage device, or it was transmitted electronically to outside parties via e-mail. Even the prized clam chowder recipe likely rests in an electronic file somewhere.

Next, you must understand where the information suspected of misappropriation may reside throughout an organization, both physically and electronically, and who in the organization may have had access to the information. You need to understand whether the information was potentially stolen from the hard-drive of a laptop computer or a portable storage device, through direct interaction with the entity's internal network, or even the potential scanning of hard-copy data to an electronic file.

Unlike customer data, which may reside in one specialized location, trade secrets and other proprietary technology may exist across various departments and divisions of a company with generalized access by numerous individuals. Many company trade secrets and other proprietary technology may not be protected as securely as you might expect. In fact, companies often do not realize the value of this IP and the need for security until after an incident has occurred. As such, the IP in question may be widely disseminated throughout an organization with available access via both a company's internal networks and individual user laptops. The information may also exist in hard-copy form in various locations.

How widely information is disseminated may pose challenges for an investigator if the list of potential perpetrators and access points cannot be sufficiently narrowed to justify the time and effort required to conduct a thorough investigation—in other words, if it could have been anyone. In such situations, other qualitative aspects may need to be evaluated by the investigative team, including identifying individuals who would have both the knowledge of the existence and potential value of the IP, as well as potential access to the information, and evaluating correlations with evidence of disgruntled or terminated employees. If a list of potential perpetrators, access points, and retrieval methods can be sufficiently narrowed, the computer forensic techniques can help tie these actions to an individual.

You must try to determine whether the information was stolen from the hard drive of a laptop computer, from a portable storage device, or through direct interaction with the entity's internal network. Then you need to understand what security procedures exist to protect the information, both to evaluate the relative risk of a perpetrator gaining access to the information and to narrow the potential source of the theft. If the network location of the data had secure or limited access, you need to know who had access, as well as whether the security procedures could have been, or in fact were, overridden to gain access to the data in question.

What to Look For

What to look for, as well as when to look, when a trade secret or proprietary technology is suspected of being misappropriated depends on what the IP is, how widely it is disseminated throughout the organization and in what form, and whether the suspected perpetrator, access points, and retrieval methods can be sufficiently narrowed to justify a wide-scale investigation. However, you can look for several definite patterns relative to the theft of trade secrets and other proprietary technology, and these provide good starting points for conducting an initial investigation. Nine times out of ten, you will be handed a computer and told, "We don't know what they took or how they took it, but we believe this person has taken data with them that they shouldn't have." In such situations, we like to start by determining what, if anything, was copied from the computer and when it happened. This information, coupled with a review of the data that was copied, is usually enough to frame the rest of what you are going to do in the investigation.

Look for Evidence of Copying   By definition, theft of proprietary data requires that copying or moving occurs. When you don't know what was taken, in what form it was taken, and when it was taken, you have to start by determining how it was taken. In modern operating systems, audit trails can be traced for most of the major methods used to get data off a computer. Use of a thumb drive leaves artifacts in the system files. Burning a CD leaves remnants in system directories. Using webmail leaves markers in the Internet history. Even printing leaves a trail in the print spooler. Knowing the different ways that data can leave the system and how to look at what was copied and where it was copied to is absolutely vital in these investigations.

Burning a CD/DVD

Popularity:	7
Simplicity:	10
Impact:	8
Risk Rating:	6

Most modern operating systems have the ability to burn a CD built into the packaged OS. Generally, as is the case with Mac OS X and Windows, you can drag-and-drop files onto the CD/DVD drive icon and the system will take care of the rest. Because of this ease of use, this is one of the primary ways used by individuals to copy information from a computer. The good news is that the burning process is generally a compilation feature, which means that files are dragged and dropped over a period of time and then later burned. An intermediary location is used to store the data to be burned to the CD, and that means you have a place you can audit if or when a CD was burned and you can determine what was placed on that disc.

Determining that a CD Was Burned

The methods you use to determine that a CD was burned varies from computer to computer and even user to user. For instance, some users drag-and-drop the files onto the CD icon and are done with it. Others will use third-party applications, such as NERO or Roxio's offerings, to burn the CDs. Each application has its own artifacts that you can try to detect, as well as its own stepwise process. Let's start with the Windows family of operating systems.

Operating System Burning (Drag-and-Drop)   This method is generally fairly easy to detect. Look for the CD Burning folder under the user's Documents and Settings\Application Data folder. When a user drags-and-drops a file or set of files to be burned, the files are placed in this directory as a temporary location. Once the CD has been burned, the files are deleted from this folder. This is good news for a forensic analyst, however. If the computer hasn't been used much since the CD burning took place, the files will generally remain intact. Just use your favorite forensic recovery tool and undelete the files. If the files are still in the CD Burning folder, that can indicate that the person wanted to burn the files but for some reason didn't do it. Look at the data's size to determine whether the number and size of files were too large for optical media. In that case, check for other methods that may have been used to get the data to determine whether the individual used something like a thumb drive or external hard drive.

Third-party Utilities   The User Assist logs and prefetch area can be your best friends in determining whether a third-party burning utility was used. Look through the logs to see if an application was used to burn a CD/DVD. The entries in these logs will persist even if the user uninstalled the program itself after burning the media in an effort to hide his or her tracks. If you find evidence that a utility was run, you can look for two things: Generally, when a third-party utility is used to create a CD, a temporary ISO image is created to avoid issues with the burner overrunning the buffer. Since these images are generally in Joilet format, you can search for the file system signature of the Joilet file system and go from there. In addition, you can look at the files that may have been mass-accessed during the time the application was running. While this is not an end-all-be-all answer, it can definitely point you toward any files that may have been copied. Then look for link files to see if the newly burned disc was accessed in the computer, showing that the files that had been accessed on the computer were in fact existent on the newly burned CD/DVD.

Sending via E-mail

Popularity:	7
Simplicity:	10
Impact:	9
Risk Rating:	**8**

E-mail is commonly used to remove and disperse IP. This generally occurs in one of two ways: the information is either e-mailed to another account using corporate e-mail, or personal webmail such as Gmail is used to send the files. Detecting this method of theft, while somewhat straightforward, definitely has its own set of pitfalls.

Finding IP in E-mail

Most forensic tools allow you to take a corporate mail store, such as a Personal Storage Table (PST), and create a table showing all messages to and from various senders. Look through this table and identify e-mails that look like they were sent from the suspect employee to a personal e-mail address. If you know the approximate date range when the theft may have occurred, you can also block out the e-mails that way. Then review all e-mails that meet these criteria to see if they contain any files or appear to have been used to send files off the computer. Some telltale signs are the use of no subjects, small messages that have no other threads, or empty messages. In addition, obtaining the suspect's webmail addresses can make your job even easier.

If you find nothing worth investigating in the corporate mail, or even if do find something, you'll need to reconstruct the suspect's webmail. We have discussed the Internet cache and how it stores webmail in preceding chapters, and you can apply those techniques here. Look for active webmail cache files on the system, and reconstruct them as appropriate. Doing this will often not reveal all the messages sent from the computer, however. The cache is periodically cleared, depending on the browser, and the suspect may have purposely cleared the cache as a cleanup step somewhere along the line. In this case, you'll need to employ other techniques: search terms and file carving.

Using Search Terms to Find E-mail　One of the most effective ways to find e-mails that have been removed from the web cache is by using keywords. The party asking you to perform the search probably has an idea of what the suspect employee was working on. Ask for terms pertaining to these clients and topics. Find any personal e-mail addresses or screen names that you can on the system and add those as keywords as well. Compile a list of all these terms and keywords and search for them across the unallocated space. More often than not, you will find additional e-mails or e-mail fragments that once existed in the active space of the computer. Some of our cases have hinged on fragments the employee thought were lost. Be warned, however, that this is an arduous process with many false positives. In addition, the data you can carve out of the unallocated space is not going to be the prettiest or most readable. If you find things that are relevant to the issue at hand, you can spend some time beautifying the results, as long as you include the original in your report and note that you have modified its structure only for readability.

 ## Copying to a USB Drive

Popularity:	9
Simplicity:	10
Impact:	9
Risk Rating:	9

This is by far the most common method we have found for users wanting to copy large amounts of data off the computer. It's cheap and easy, and the average user believes that there is no way anyone could detect that it has occurred. Fortunately for the forensic examiner, and unfortunately for the person doing the copying, nothing could be further from the truth with most modern operating systems.

Determining Whether Files Were Copied to a USB Drive

First, you should take inventory of which thumb drives have been plugged into the computer. For this section, we will focus on Windows XP/Vista. The process is the same with other operating systems, except the places to look for the drives may be different from those discussed here.

As discussed in Chapter 6, the Windows system registry stores the key USBSTOR, which contains information about the USB devices that have been plugged into the computer. Take inventory of this key. Look at the last modified time on the key, as this will generally be the last time the device was plugged into the computer. Also, take note of the parentID prefix and the friendly name (you might also look for the instanceID). You can use these identifiers later to get hold of the actual drives. Your argument gets much stronger when you go from "We know you plugged a USB drive into the computer" to "We know you plugged a Lexar FireFly into the computer on March 5, 2009, at 4:19 P.M." Once you have a listing of the thumb drives used on the computer and the approximate timeframes, it's time to see if you can determine usage.

> **NOTE**   The parentID prefix for a drive is provided by the OS and can change with OS versions. A much better number to use is the instanceID, which is a serial number hard-coded into the device. If the USB drive has a serial number hard-coded, it will not change. This number can be generated by the system, too, if no serial number is hard-coded, but if it is system generated, the second digit in the device instanceID will be an ampersand (&).

Link File Analysis   When an office file is opened from a USB drive, a shortcut file is created on the system for it. This shortcut will live on even after the drive has been disconnected from the system. It will give you the name of the device on which the file resided, as well as the filename and modified, accessed, and created (MAC) times for the file. This can be extremely valuable in an IP theft investigation because it gives you a connection between a file that existed on the computer and the same file that potentially existed on an external thumb drive. At the very least, having the set of link files showing proprietary information being opened on the thumb drive can be cause enough to make the suspect produce the USB drive.

BagsMRU   The BagsMRU key stores a list of all directories and files that existed in an Explorer window when the window was resized. This can be hugely valuable because it lets you get the entire directory listing for a USB drive. If the user opened the drive in Explorer and then resized the window, the listing will be in the BagsMRU area. Like the link files, the BagsMRU records can be used to establish that proprietary files may have existed on a thumb drive. This can be enough evidence to compel the suspect to produce the actual USB drive.

Mass Access   We will start by saying that this method is a bit less reliable than the methods already mentioned. However, if you have the times the USB drive was plugged into the machine, you can review the MAC times for the files on the drive to see if any mass accesses occurred around that time. This can be an indication that the files were copied en masse to the thumb drive. Be very careful when relying solely upon mass access. Many, many things can affect the access times of a file. Always use another data point and correlate it to the mass access, as opposed to making a statement like, "These files were mass accessed; therefore, they were copied to the USB drive."

Matching Up the USB Drive   If you are given a USB device and are told that this is the device you noted as being plugged into the machine, you need to check a couple of things. First, make sure the friendly names match up. If you see that a Lexar was plugged in and you've been handed a Corsair, something's awry. Second, look at the parentID prefix. This prefix is unique to the drive itself and can be used to match up thumb drives across computers. There is a caveat, however. The parentID prefix will change across operating systems, so don't expect the parentID to be the same for a thumb drive when it's plugged into Windows XP versus Windows Vista. As mentioned, also check for the instanceID. In general, it will be a much more reliable way to match up a thumb drive used across computers.

Once you have in hand the USB drive you expected, it's time to see what was copied. Generally, you start by performing a hash analysis and comparing values with the user files on the computer. More often than not, if files were copied to the USB drive, the hash values will match. It's important that you realize, however, that the standard operating system copy may not be an exact bit-for-bit copy and may have different hash values. If this is the case, make sure you also look at the filenames, sizes, content, and MAC times to see if they are reasonably identical.

> **TIP**   Remember that most USB drives are formatted with FAT32 for compatibility. This means that the access field isn't an access time—instead, it is an access date. Keep this in mind when building the timeline of activity, as a file could have been accessed multiple times in the same day but the access date would stay the same.

 ## Covering Their Tracks

Popularity:	9
Simplicity:	10
Impact:	9
Risk Rating:	9

Frequently, after copying the files off the computer, a user will attempt to cover his or her tracks. The method used depends on how the data was copied. If webmail was involved, the user may clear the Internet cache and history and call it a day. Or the user may reinstall the operating system—a quick, uncomplicated way to remove audit trails. The user can also use third-party wiping and evidence-clearing utilities.

 Detecting Wiping

As discussed in Chapter 9, look for evidence of disk wiping, review the User Assist logs, and look for programs installed that are specifically designed to wipe data. Always remember to check the OS installation date. Sometimes finding evidence that the user attempted to remove the trail can be just as good as finding the evidence itself.

TYING IT TOGETHER

IP theft can have serious detrimental impacts on an organization. The theft of a single piece of software code or an engineering trade secret has been known to result in the erosion of a company's competitive advantage and its profitability to competitors who have benefited from the ill-gotten IP. Likewise, the misappropriation of customer data can undermine confidence in a company's ability to protect customers' sensitive information, and can expose the company to significant liability to the extent the customer data is used for other illicit purposes. While identifying what was taken, as well as the source and extent of the IP theft, is critical to safeguarding the assets of the company, these are only half the battle. The other half is in the manner in which the investigation is conducted, how the evidence is collected, whether sufficient evidence has been identified to infer intent, in estimating and attempting to mitigate potential damages to the company, and in working with management, outside counsel, and others in seeking retribution and restitution from the perpetrators.

What Was Taken?

As mentioned earlier, you must first determine what IP was taken and by whom. However, of paramount importance to management and the company's ability to prevent the unauthorized use of the IP is to be able answer, with documented evidence, fundamental questions: "What?" "When?" "Where?" "How?" "By whom?"

Circumstantial evidence rarely persuades law enforcement or the courts to take action against individuals accused of IP theft, much less other kinds of theft. Parts I through IV in this book outline the recommended computer forensic techniques and procedures in preparing for an incident, collecting evidence, conducting the investigation, and in presenting your findings. Poorly or sloppily gathered evidence and/or presentation of your findings will undermine the level of confidence outside parties will place in the evidence in determining whether a theft in fact occurred. Likewise, incomplete evidence or unanswered questions may leave the company exposed if additional IP was taken, involving other individuals, and by different means.

While it is often difficult to ascertain, with any degree of certainty, the extent of an incident and all those involved, undertaking efforts to address the fundamental questions will ensure the company's ability to respond appropriately to the actual and potential threats posed by the IP theft. As described, understanding *what* was taken is the first question. However, understanding *when* is also important, as it may provide some insight into the exact content of the IP theft and what aspects of the business are at risk. It also may help define the extent of the potential damages to the company, as well as assist in the risk assessment regarding whether the misappropriated information could have been used or disseminated by the parties involved. *Where* IP was taken from may also be important both in eliminating additional involvement in illicit activities and in assisting the company in identifying where added security efforts may be required. Understanding the *how* also provides valuable information as to whether additional security efforts may be warranted.

Looking at Intent

Equally important to questions of what, when, where, how, and by whom is the *why*. Why was the IP taken? It is not uncommon for individuals to copy proprietary information to aid in their day-to-day responsibilities. Individuals often copy information to a computer hard-drive or removable storage device so that the information is portable and can be used while traveling or working at home. In fact, a number of the larger reported thefts of customer data involve individuals who did not directly perpetrate the theft, but instead made it possible by the unauthorized copying of information and the subsequent loss or theft of a laptop or theft through an insecure wireless or home computing network. These individuals were not guilty of theft, only poor judgment and the potential violation of corporate policies. However, the ramifications and potential damage to the corporation are the same.

Was the IP theft intentional or inadvertent? Did the accused unknowingly copy proprietary information, did she copy the IP with innocent intentions, or was it taken with the intent to do harm to the company or to benefit the individual or another enterprise? Intent becomes a critical component for law enforcement and the courts in evaluating whether the company has been damaged and to what extent the perpetrators may be required to provide restitution, as well as whether they face potential criminal action.

Estimating Damages

Of immediate concern in most IP theft situations is to plug the leak, and then contain the potential damage. Once the floodwaters have subsided and the relevant parties have been notified and engaged to assist in the investigation, the attention of higher-ups quickly turns to "what was the damage?" or more appropriately "what could the potential damage be?" While critical efforts are focused on identifying the source of potential theft, determining the extent of the IP that may have been taken, and how the potential theft was carried out, are also of concern. These efforts reveal the impact the stolen information could have or is having on the company and help you and the company determine how to mitigate both the potential for, as well as ongoing, losses to the company.

An initial assessment of potential damages should be made by relevant parties to the investigation, including corporate management, general counsel if one exists, outside counsel, and outside consultants. In certain instances, as in the case of customer data, response plans will need to be developed and implemented to minimize the risk to the company's customers from the loss of customer-specific data. Other immediate actions may be taken to halt the further dissemination of information in the case of the theft of technology or PI. In certain instances, the IP theft may pose a risk to other information or technology, and appropriate planning may need to take place to address various contingencies.

Often a theft is not identified until long after it occurs, when the company has little recourse in mitigating the potential damage. In such situations, the objectives focus on preventing further unauthorized use of the IP through injunctive relief, as well as through criminal and civil remedies via law enforcement and the courts, respectively. Available remedies differ depending on whether they are granted through court-ordered restitution and penalties in criminal matters or claims for damages in civil lawsuits. Remedies also differ depending on the type of IP and whether the issue and remedy pursued is governed by federal or state laws.

In most cases, damages are based on the economic detriment suffered by the IP owner. Most often, the measurement of economic detriment is based on a determination of the company's lost profits or the loss of business resulting from the loss of the company's competitive advantage that was associated with the stolen IP. In certain situations, the economic benefit derived by the perpetrator is allowed to serve as evidence of the estimated damages to the IP owner. In each case, estimating damages as a result of IP theft can be difficult. Whereas the value of IP, as well as various other intangible assets, is typically difficult to quantify, estimating the value of damages resulting from IP theft is also difficult to quantify. In such situations, companies often rely on the expertise of outside consultants including economists, accountants, and others with specialized knowledge and experience in valuing IP and in estimating damages.

Working with Higher-Ups

Any question involving potential IP theft will undoubtedly draw the attention of management, including likely senior management and the firm's in-house and outside counsel. The seriousness and potential damage to the company that could result from IP theft will escalate any investigative effort to include various parties in upper management, possibly the board of directors, and the firm's inside and outside counsel. You must recognize and be sensitive to the different priorities and perspectives each group may place on various aspects of the investigative process.

While as an IT specialist, your primary focus will likely be on the computer forensics aspects of the investigation, and the subject matter of this book, other parties may have different priorities, which may be no less important to the company's resolution of the matter. Upper management initially may be more concerned with understanding where the company's system of internal controls broke down (How did this happen? Has it happened before? How do we prevent it from happening again?), rather than the systematic approach of collecting, documenting, and evaluating potential evidence.

However, both are critical components in the overall investigation of IP theft and in designing and implementing additional security and controls to limit potential future occurrences. The IT professional needs to be sensitive to the various priorities of parties involved in the matter and be prepared to allocate the necessary time and resources to evaluating various elements and/or ramifications of the theft at the same time.

Working with Outside Counsel

Given the seriousness of the ramifications from IP theft, it is not unusual for outside counsel to be brought in to assist in evaluating avenues for potential recourse that are available to the company. Often, outside counsel will be asked to take over, or initiate, the internal investigation to ensure that adequate evidence gathering and documentation procedures are used so as to not to impair the company's potential causes of action against the perpetrators of the theft, as well as to enhance the potential recovery of the stolen IP and potential damages for harm to the company. Depending on the nature and extent of the IP theft, outside counsel may also seek to employ the services of various specialized consultants, including outside computer forensic specialists, licensed private investigators, forensic accountants, and public relations specialists, among others.

As with upper management, the outside counsel's primary concerns initially may be different from those of the IT administrator charged internally with uncovering the details of the suspected theft. Outside counsel likely will be more interested in protecting the company and pursuing legal action against the perpetrators. (How do we mitigate the risk to the company? How do we recover the IP and hold those accountable for the theft? Has the company been damaged, and can we recover those damages through the company's insurance or through a lawsuit?)

CHAPTER 17

EMPLOYEE MISCONDUCT

While computer forensics is routinely integral parts of investigations into allegations of fraud, IP theft, and other forms of corporate malfeasance or corruption, computer forensics is also used when various other forms of employee misconduct is suspected. Although not typically considered as serious as fraud or IP theft, employee misconduct can have serious, as well as potentially costly, ramifications for a company. From improper use of corporate assets to improper behavior in the workplace, employee misconduct results in lost productivity at least and at most can put the company at significant risk of potential lawsuits from a variety of employment-related issues.

As it has with embezzlement, IP theft, securities fraud, and other forms of potential wrongdoing in the corporate environment, the digital age has opened various new avenues and ways for employees to misuse corporate assets, invade the privacy of others, obtain unauthorized corporate information, or otherwise violate a host of corporate policies. Corporate policies related to many aspects of employee conduct have been standardized for many years, guided in part by labor laws, as well as trends in employment related issues. Many of these policies comprise an "employee handbook" that can be fairly standard from one corporation to another. However, corporations have been required to adopt a whole new set of policies during the past decade to address the various aspects and misuse or improper use of technology that has become part of the daily business environment.

Computer forensics can be a valuable tool when employee misconduct is suspected. However, the inappropriate use, timing, or absence of discretion when such techniques are targeted against an employee or group of employees can also result in significant, and sometimes unwarranted, discord among the employees in question, as well as among a company's wider employee population. The tools and techniques described throughout this chapter may be viewed by some as invasive and inappropriate in certain settings, especially where such investigative tools are in contrast to the established guidelines and culture established by the company. As such, while such techniques can often be beneficial to addressing questions and concerns surrounding employee conduct, you must take care to ensure that such efforts are within the framework of the company's policies and have the support of the various company departments (such as human resources) where such concerns might be expressed.

WHAT IS EMPLOYEE MISCONDUCT?

Employee misconduct can be defined as an employee action that violates a company's stated policies or agreements between an employer and an employee, or a former employee. It includes conduct that may be perceived as detrimental to the company or that may pose some risk or exposure to the company.

In its broadest sense, employee misconduct could also include the types of involved in relation to IP theft, as well as other types of improper conduct described in subsequent chapters (Chapters 18 and 19), including conduct in violation of the general laws and accepted industry norms and practices. However, for purposes of this chapter and the described computer forensic tools and techniques described here, we are limiting employee misconduct to the violation or abuse of various corporate policies and procedures, many of which may also be based in various federal and state laws including employment law. Such policies and procedures are generally defined in a corporation's employee handbook or other compilation of a company's personnel policies and procedures, to the extent they exist, as well as a corporation's code of conduct and ethics.

These policies, procedures, and codes of conduct and ethics may address the following:

- Code of business standards and code of ethics
- Usurpation of corporate opportunity
- Time and expense recording
- Travel, entertainment, and expense reimbursement policies
- Appropriate use of corporate resources (such as computers)
- Use of corporate licensed software
- E-mail and Internet access and usage

RAMIFICATIONS

As described, employee misconduct covers a wide array of behavior and activity that may be in violation of a corporation's explicit or implied code of conduct or other corporate policies and procedures, as well as activities considered unlawful under applicable laws or otherwise deemed inappropriate. The ramifications can also cover a wide array of potential harm to the corporation, from lost productivity, efficiency, and a disruptive work environment, to significant and costly lawsuits against the corporation and potential monetary loss.

Disruptive Work Environment

Corporations devise and implement policies and handbooks regarding business conduct and ethics in the workplace that provide guidance on acceptable and unacceptable behaviors to promote a healthy, stable, and productive work environment where employees can operate efficiently and effectively without undue distraction or interference. These policies and procedures are also implemented to safeguard a corporation's assets, which includes its employees, and to protect the corporation and its employees from unlawful or otherwise inappropriate activity that may put the corporation and its employees at risk.

At a minimum, employee misconduct has a negative impact on a corporation's work environment and the productivity of employees immediately affected by that conduct. Whether it's inappropriate workplace behavior or improper use of corporate resources, a prohibited activity typically effects the work habits and operating efficiency of the employee(s) in question, and it often extends beyond the employee(s) directly involved to those around him (such as those within the same work group or department, and potentially involving both superiors and/or subordinates). Harassment and discrimination almost always have a negative impact on the employee or employees that are the target of improper behavior. However, it often extends beyond that group to those who witness the behavior. Inefficiency, missed work time, mistrust, compromised relationships, and ineffective allocation and use of resources can all be products of employee misconduct.

Investigations by Authorities

If employee misconduct is not only in violation of corporate codes, policies and/or procedures, but is alleged to be potentially unlawful, the activity can subject employees and the corporation to potential investigation by outside authorities. Unlawful activities can fall under the jurisdiction of a variety of local, state, and federal authorities. As an example, both employment discrimination and harassment in the workplace, which is considered a form or discrimination, are addressed by a number of federal laws prohibiting job discrimination (such as the Federal Equal Employment Opportunity [EEO] Laws). These laws fall under the oversight of the US Equal Employment Opportunity Commission (EEOC). A claim arising against an employer for violation of one of the EEO laws can lead to an investigation by the EEOC and sometimes a lawsuit against the employer. However, many states and municipalities also have anti-discrimination laws as well as agencies responsible for enforcing those laws with the capability to conduct investigations when claims arise.

Other potential illicit activities by employees may also be in violation of state and/or federal laws and can thereby lead to potential investigations by outside authorities. Certain activities may be investigated by local law enforcement officials, including local district attorneys, while others may garner the attention of a state's attorney general or even the Federal Bureau of Investigation (FBI) and its respective investigative capabilities. Examples of activities that could receive the attention of attorneys general or the FBI include the improper use of corporate resources (such as computers and the Internet) to commit cybercrime such software piracy, unlawful computer intrusions, or the exploitation of children through child pornography. While some of the described employee misconduct may involve the improper conduct of just one employee, the existence of the activity on corporate premises or the inappropriate use of corporate assets could subject the corporation to investigation as well as potential lawsuits.

Lawsuits Against an Employer

Harassment, as well as other forms of discrimination, software piracy, and the improper use of corporate e-mail and the Internet, among others, can all have a significant impact to the corporation as well as the employee engaged in the improper behavior or act. While the inappropriate conduct may be limited to one individual, questions will often be raised as to the workplace established by the corporation and whether appropriate safeguards (such as policies, procedures, and codes of conduct and ethics) were in place to discourage such conduct and to protect other employees from the negative effects of such conduct. Often the corporation itself will be targeted in lawsuits involving employee misconduct, citing the corporation's failure to provide a workplace consistent with that required by the respective applicable laws and guidelines.

As with any lawsuit, lawsuits involving allegations of employee misconduct can be significantly costly to the corporation, even if the corporation ultimately prevails, as attorneys fees, outside consultants, and expert fees can be very costly to a corporation if not recoverable through the litigation. Likewise, similar to investigations of employee misconduct, lawsuits can be extremely disruptive to a corporation's work environment and often require substantial time and efforts of various employees to respond to written requests for information and participate in interviews and depositions by various parties throughout the litigation process.

Monetary Loss

While many types of activities prohibited by employee handbooks and business codes of conduct and ethics do not translate into direct monetary losses to a corporation, indirectly they can lead to significant disruptions in the work environment and inefficiencies that over time can have significant impact on a corporation's bottom line. Lost productivity due to personal e-mail and Internet usage while at work can be substantial when measured across an entire corporation. Likewise, other forms of employee misconduct such as discrimination can also have a significant impact on productivity as employees spend significant time engaged in, or focused upon, the conduct in question. Nationwide, it is estimated that corporations lose hundreds of billions of dollars annually due to lost productivity from these distractions and disruptions, as well as others.

In addition, corporations spend billions each year implementing systems and procedures to prevent and/or identify such conduct and disruptions. Many corporations monitor e-mail and Internet usage for both improper content, including the prevention and detection of potential IP theft, and lost productivity due to excessive usage. While the Internet has provided limitless access to useful information to enhance an individual's productivity and success in their profession, it also can provide limitless distractions. Whether it be due to conducting personal business (such as paying bills), shopping, or pursuing personal interests (such as sports or travel), or figuring out what movies are playing tonight, it all results in lost work time that ultimately costs the corporation.

It is also not uncommon for employees to use corporate assets for personal gain, thereby depriving the corporation the use of those assets and the potential return on those assets. Sometimes individuals will use corporate assets to run side businesses. In other situations, individuals may use access to confidential information to identify, and at times usurp, opportunities for personal gain that rightfully belonged to the corporation.

In summary, most types of employee misconduct incur some cost and therefore potential monetary loss to the corporation. While many types of improper behavior in the workplace may be minor and difficult to quantify, over time these transgressions can result in a significant monetary impact to the corporation through disruptions in the work environment and the overall loss of productivity. While identifying and tracking such behavior is oftentimes complicated, as well as costly to the extent undertaken, in some situations the potential costs and risks to the corporation justify the need for the types of computer forensic techniques described in this book. A few examples of those situations are described in more detail in this chapter.

TYPES OF MISCONDUCT

Employee misconduct can encompass a wide-range of prohibited, inappropriate, and even illegal behavior or activity. The most common or well-known forms of employee misconduct involve the misuse of corporate assets, including both the inadvertent and the intentional, such as removal of corporate assets for personal consumption (theft of office supplies). Everyone, no doubt, has at some point left the office with a pen, a pad of paper, or other asset purchased by and belonging to the corporation. In addition, everyone has likely used a computer printer or copier for personal reasons such as printing birthday invitations or copying personal records such as bill payments or tax returns. Each may likely be in violation of a corporation's policies prohibiting the use of corporate assets for personal business. (Early in my career I remember a study conducted by a company where I was working that concluded the company had purchased enough rulers and staplers in the past year for everyone in the company to have in excess of three each.) While the misuse/theft of office supplies may be the most common, in the digital age, corporate usage policies have also extended to include and cover the use of computers, e-mail, and Internet, limiting their use to legitimate business purposes only.

Employee misconduct can also be rooted in employment law surrounding the protection of employees from unlawful discrimination or harassment. While most companies have internal policies and procedures regarding the treatment of other employees in the workplace, many of these policies and procedures are governed by state and federal employment laws that protect employees from employment discrimination based on race, color, religion, sex, or national origin. Other federal laws protect individuals from wage discrimination and discrimination based on age or disability. Discrimination under these practices also precludes employees from being harassed, retaliated against, or denied advancement or promotion based on an individual's race, color, religion, sex, age, and so on.

In addition to the types of employee misconduct that may result from actions of current employees in the workplace, other misconduct may arise out of an employee's or a former employee's failure to adhere to certain conditions outlined in agreements between the respective employee and the corporation. In many corporate settings, certain employees enter into employment agreements stating the specific terms and conditions of the individual's employment, as well as the obligations expected of both parties to the agreement. Often these employment agreements, and sometimes supplemental agreements, especially where professional services are involved (such as accounting, consulting, and so on), will include certain conditions upon an employee's termination or departure from the corporation. These agreements typically take the form of a non-compete and/or non-solicitation agreement, where the individual is precluded, for a certain period of time, from competing against the corporation, soliciting either the corporation's clients and/or employees, or both. As many corporations invest heavily and rely significantly on the skills and expertise of their employees, the loss of such skills to a competing interest could have a significant impact on the company's profitability and overall success. As such, violations of agreements between employers and employees often lead to disagreements and disputes between the parties that sometimes end up in litigation.

While many individual actions may have negligible impact to a corporation, certain practices, especially where practices are sustained and widespread, can pose significant threats and have serious detrimental impacts to a corporation's health, productivity, and profitability. In these situations, computer forensics has proven to be a valuable tool in uncovering inappropriate, as well as illicit, behavior and in quantifying the extent of the behavior and potential risk and exposure to the corporation.

In this chapter, we focus on three examples of employee misconduct that are both commonplace and have the potential to be disruptive and costly to a corporation:

- Violation of corporate usage policies
- Employment discrimination and harassment
- Violation of non-compete/non-solicitation agreements

Inappropriate Use of Corporate Resources

Popularity:	10
Simplicity:	8
Impact:	7
Risk Rating:	**8**

Corporate resources come in many forms, from pens and paper clips, to computers, access to the Internet, and intellectual property. As with any asset, the corporation has an interest in protecting its assets from theft and improper use. In the digital age, the improper use of computers and the Internet is common. As more and more employees have access to computers, e-mail, and the Internet in the workplace, companies are finding it more difficult to monitor and control the use of those privileges. The use of computers, e-mail, and the Internet have become instrumental, as well as routine, in the day-to-day lives of many in the workplace; however, that access typically comes with a certain level of professional responsibility—namely to limit their use for business purposes.

While infrequent use of e-mail and the Internet for personal reasons is common, as well as commonly accepted in the workplace, they can all be used for improper or illegal activity that puts the corporation at significant risk. Examples may include the unlawful copying and/or downloading of software, videos, or music; using computers to view, download, and/or share pornographic materials; conducting improper and illegal activity with the use of corporate computers such as hacking into other computers and Web sites or creating and transmitting computer viruses or spam related e-mail traffic; and the dissemination of confidential information regarding the corporate practices or financial results.

What to Understand

When individuals are suspected of misusing corporate resources, you first need to understand whether the suspected behavior or activity involves computers, e-mail, the Internet, or some combination of the three. Each asset or resource will have its own unique characteristics in how it is accessed, utilized, maintained and tracked, as well as potentially backed up within an organization. Understanding an individual's access (open and secure) to a computer or computers, the corporation's system of networks, e-mail (whether corporate or access to personal e-mail accounts), and the Internet, will help you define the population of potential sources of information that may need to be evaluated to discern the nature and extent of the alleged inappropriate use of corporate resources. In other words, you must determine what is the web of potential access to information, computers, and networks that may emanate from an individual suspected of misusing corporate information or resources.

Second, consider whether the computer, e-mail, and networks in question are suspected of being used as a tool in the alleged misconduct (such as to gather and disseminate confidential information), were themselves alleged to be misused (such as to run a side business or used to hack into other systems and networks), or may merely contain evidence of employee misconduct (such as e-mail evidence of harassment, or downloaded files with improper content).

Third, consider the general nature and/or purpose of the inquiry regarding an employee's conduct. Is the corporation primarily concerned with ensuring compliance with existing corporate policies and procedures, or does concern extend to investigating potential illegal activity or other conduct that could result in the termination of the employee?

Fourth, when investigating allegations of suspected employee misconduct, clearly understanding what policies, procedures, and other guidelines may exist regarding such behavior is important. The breadth and specificity of corporate policies and procedures regarding the use of corporate resources and information varies from company to company. However, what is more common is the lack of knowledge and education among employees and management as to the existence of certain policies and procedures, as well as clear understanding as to what types of behaviors may be in violation of those policies and procedures. When investigating allegations of suspected employee misconduct, you must understand what policies, procedures, and other guidelines exist regarding such behavior. In other words, you need to know specifically what you're looking for and why the company considers it inappropriate.

What to Look For

What to look for depends on the circumstances of the alleged misconduct, the potential corporate resources involved, the corporate policies and procedures and federal and state laws that govern behavior in the workplace, and the purpose for the inquiry.

Pirated/Malicious Installed Software

Popularity:	8
Simplicity:	9
Impact:	10
Risk Rating:	9

Software may have been have installed on the computer. If a suspect is pirating software or downloading movies illegally, for instance, chances are she has either a point-to-point (P2P) client installed or some type of torrent downloader. In addition, she may have installed encryption or wiping utilities to attempt to hide or cover her tracks. We have seen this a lot when things like pornography are involved. Taking accurate inventory of not only what is installed on the computer but also what has been installed on the computer can be paramount in these types of situations.

Taking Inventory of Software on a Computer

At first glance, this seems like this would be an easy task with modern operating systems such as Windows XP, where the installed software registers with the system and has entries in the registry. And while that may be true for 90 percent of the software out there, if you check only the relevant registry keys, you could miss software that either was uninstalled or was designed to be intentionally evasive. Let's take a look at some of the areas both inside and outside the registry where information about installed programs can be found.

The Program Files Directory   This task, though simple, is incredibly effective. Go into the Program Files folder (Applications on OS X and /usr/bin on UNIX) and take a look at what's there. If you have a date range for when the activity may have started and ended, look at the metadata and the deleted files from that timeframe in this directory and see what comes to light.

The SOFTWARE Registry File   In the Windows family of operating systems, installed software gets its own registry file, which is located with the rest of the registry in C:\Windows\system32\config\SOFTWARE (referenced as HKLM/Software in registry viewer). As new software is installed on the computer, whatever global settings the software needs to function are generally stored in this set of keys. Generally, each key under the root of SOFTWARE will relate to an installed program. If you use a forensic tool such as Access Data's Registry Viewer, you can also determine when the registry keys were created and last modified, giving you an idea of when the software was installed and potentially last run.

The Windows Installer Registry   Inside the SOFTWARE registry file is a key that tracks all programs that have been installed on the system. This key is used by the Add/Remove Programs Control Panel widget. Navigate to Microsoft\Windows\CurrentVersion\ Uninstall and you will see large number of subfolders, each named the unique ID of the software installed. Inside each subfolder is a display name key and large amounts of metadata that can assist with your timeline reconstruction process, including such things as Publisher, Installed Date, Install Source, and the Estimated Size of the software.

The User Assist Logs   We have discussed how to access the User Assist utility at length in earlier chapters. These logs come in handy in this case as well, as they can show program execution for software that may have been uninstalled or wiped from the computer. Take a look for any suspiciously named software or software executed around the dates of interest. If something catches your eye, cross-reference it with the other methods to find installed software to determine whether it is still on the machine. If it's not, make a note about and follow up later.

Prefetch Entries   As discussed in earlier chapters, any time an executable is run in Windows XP and later systems, a file is created for it in C:\Windows\Prefetch. These entries can be valuable because they are user-independent. No matter who runs the software, the prefetch file will always be placed in this directory, as opposed to having to repeat analysis for multiple users. However, this can be an issue on multi-user systems. Also, if malware or spyware executes software it will be registered here as well. While the prefetch files can be valuable investigative tools, make sure you have some other data points to cross-validate findings and don't rely solely on them to conclude that the user was executing malicious software.

MRU Entries and Link Files   Finally, take a look at the various most recently used (MRU) registry keys and the link files that may exist on the system. The MRUs can store information about document type associations as well as which programs have been manually run from the command line. Additionally, the link files can help to determine what files were accessed when and if programs had been used that were previously on the computer and are no longer there. For more information on how to parse out and what is contained in these link files, refer to Chapter 6.

Making Sense of it All

There are many different ways to determine what software was installed on a computer and where it may have lived. Once you have created the list and have the set of items that you think may be at issue (for instance you find encryption software, or shredder programs being run), it's time to step back and look at it in the context of the investigation. Does the software have a legitimate business purpose? Is there any way you can tie the activity of the software to the individual? What does the usage of the software mean in the larger context of the law and even the corporation's policies?

Using Corporate Resources for Personal Profit

Popularity:	7
Simplicity:	9
Impact:	10
Risk Rating:	9

Using corporate resources for personal gain is nothing new and still holds true in the digital age as well. While most corporations allow a certain amount of personal use on the corporate IT system, some will step over the line—from running a side business selling designer socks to running a directly competitive company at lower rates to siphon off business.

Finding Evidence of Personal Profit

While we dedicate an entire chapter to full-fledged embezzlement, here we'll show you how to go about finding evidence that corporate resources are being used for personal profit, such as running side businesses, and that are in violation of the employment agreement. Look for the following.

E-mails from Other Company E-mail Address   This sounds pretty straightforward, and, in general, it is. Suppose you notice that an employee named Tim is sending e-mails from his computer using Tim@MyOtherCompany.com. This is what we call in the industry a "clue." When looking for evidence of this kind of activity, always check all of the installed mail programs, as Tim may use Outlook for his company e-mail and Outlook Express for his other company's e-mail. Also, don't forget about webmail. With the adoption of services such as Google's corporate mail services, people are increasingly using webmail to access these types of corporate accounts.

Documents Associated with the Other Company   It's hard to do business without creating things like spreadsheets and Word documents. If the user has a company-issued laptop, it's not uncommon for him or her to use that laptop to create these documents and business files. If you are reviewing a computer, take a look at the user documents on that computer. If you don't feel comfortable reviewing the documents for relevancy, offer to burn a DVD with the documents for your legal counsel or other investigators. If you do find something that seems pertinent to the case, be sure to preserve all the metadata and file information, as this file could potentially be vital to the case down the road.

Review Corporate Files for Evidence of Solicitation   We will discuss this in more detail later in the chapter, but don't forget to perform keyword searches and review on the e-mails and documents that have been created for the original company. I am always shocked at how many people will solicit or offer alternative arrangements that cut the company out of the loop inside a corporate e-mail. The same is true with user-created files. I remember once seeing a spreadsheet of company customers in which the individual had marked those that he thought he could do business with on the side. A complete and thorough review is vital.

Employment Discrimination/Harassment

Popularity:	8
Simplicity:	9
Impact:	10
Risk Rating:	9

Federal EEO laws prohibit job discrimination. Various federal laws were passed in the United States, including Title VII of the Civil Rights Act of 1964, the Equal Pay Act of 1963 (EPA), the Age Discrimination Act in Employment Act of 1967 (ADEA), Title I and Title V of the Americans with Disabilities Act of 1990 (ADA), Sections 501 and 505 of the Rehabilitation Act of 1973, and the Civil Rights Act of 1991. All of these laws protect individuals in the workplace from unwarranted discrimination and harassment on the basis of race, color, religion, sex, national origin, disability, or age.

Discrimination can take many shapes and forms and impact employees in the workplace in a variety of ways, including in relation to hiring/firing, compensation, promotions, benefits, use of corporate facilities, and access to internal opportunities and training, among others. Title VII prohibits intentional discrimination, as well as practices that have the effect of discriminating against individuals because of their race, color, national origin, religion, or sex. The ADEA banned discrimination on the basis of age.

Harassment is a form of employment discrimination that violates Title VII and is defined as "any unwelcome conduct that is based on race, color, national origin, disability, and/or age." When the "unwelcome conduct" is offensive and enduring, it becomes a condition of continued employment, or it creates a work environment that could be considered intimidating, hostile, or abusive, the conduct can be deemed illegal.

While discrimination and harassment are typically carried out by individuals, corporations can be held liable for such practices if employers do not properly advise employees of their rights; if the corporation is using and/or allowing practices, policies, or procedures that promote such practices (such as hiring policies and practices); and if the corporation fails to provide a workplace and environment that is free from such practices, especially if they are aware of its existence.

The occurrence of such improper practices, especially the existence of a pattern of conduct or practice over a long period of time and involving more than one individual, can put the corporation at significant risk for employment-related lawsuits, as well as investigations and including legal actions by the EEOC. Understanding the nature of the alleged misconduct and assisting appropriate management and board-level personnel to evaluate and address the misconduct in a timely manner can significantly mitigate that risk and prolonged harm to both the corporation and the employee.

What to Understand

You need to understand the nature of the alleged conduct giving rise to the claims of discrimination or harassment. While certain types of employee misconduct may involve the use of the corporation's computers, networks, and e-mails, employment discrimination and harassment more often will involve direct interaction between individuals. It is important that you understand the breadth of conduct that may be involved and whether documentation may exist to support the allegations. Is the alleged inappropriate conduct physical in nature, or does it extend to e-mails, text messages, voice mails, and other forms of communication within the workplace? Is the alleged conduct primarily through personal interaction or does it extend into company-related matters such as job-performance reviews and evaluations, promotion considerations, compensation adjustments, reprimands, or other documented performance issues? While much of this information may be readily available to human resource personnel with the company, other information or evidence of misconduct may be hidden, with attempts made to destroy it, once allegations become public and/or lawsuits or investigations have been initiated.

Not dissimilar to other types of employee misconduct, employment discrimination and harassment usually involve a pattern of conduct over a period of time. Determine how long the alleged misconduct may have occurred to provide a framework for the breadth of information and time periods that may need to be evaluated for potential information.

Next, you must understand the working and reporting relationships of the individuals involved, as well as others in close proximity to the individuals (that is, same department, division, work group or location, and so on). Even if the pattern of alleged misconduct exists only between two individuals, it may be witnessed by many. The individuals involved, as well as the witnesses to the conduct, may communicate and/or document their concern and frustration about the conduct in e-mails or other forms or written communication. Likewise, the longer the period of time the improper conduct exists, the greater the likelihood that others will have witnessed the conduct, as well as commented on the conduct through e-mail and other forms of communication.

What to Look For

While employment discrimination and harassment may not typically involve many of the computer forensics tools and techniques outlined in this book, computer forensics may be of importance in uncovering and documenting this type of employee misconduct. The types of information that may require the use of computer forensics may vary widely depending on whether the allegations are specific to an individual or more broadly targeted at corporate-wide practices. However, while many practices may be initiated through personal interaction, the pattern of misconduct often extends and is supported by e-mail, text messages, and other forms of written communication, and attempts may be made to discard or erase such evidence once allegations become known. We have employed computer forensics in employment discrimination and harassment cases for the following examples.

Threatening/Discriminatory Messages

Popularity:	8
Simplicity:	10
Impact:	8
Risk Rating:	9

These cases generally hinge upon some type of messages that were sent to or from coworkers. These messages can take several forms: e-mails, IMs, text messages, or even entries on internal WIKIs or Facebook pages. Generally, if harassment is the issue, the person being harassed will be able to point you in the direction of the type of messages received. Discrimination can be a different story. If an employee or ex-employee claims discrimination, he may withhold the messages until the last possible moment as a legal maneuver. In these situations, it is vital that a forensic investigator assist with the complete searches and help to locate the messages that the party finds to be discriminatory. Let's look at several techniques to locate these types of messages.

E-mail Messages   Finding these types of messages usually involves performing some type of keyword search or individual review. If the e-mail universe is small, you can usually just do an e-mail–by–e-mail review. If it's large, you can first triage the e-mail in several ways. First, you can look at the senders and receivers. If you see known players in the situation, review all of their e-mail boxes, as one person may have deleted an e-mail another person kept. Second, work with management and counsel to create a set of keywords that relate to the situation and use those to winnow down the e-mail. Also, use a tool such as EnCase or LTU-Finder to identify whether any explicit messages were sent or received by an individual.

Instant Messages/Chat Logs   Use of IMs and chats is prevalent in corporations these days. If logged properly, such chats can be extremely helpful in illuminating what really happened. If you are the administrator and you know where and how the logs are kept, you can use this information to find what you need. If you are an outside party, you should ask several key questions: What type of IM is used company-wide? Could other methods have been used? Armed with this information, you have a place to start. If they log the chat conversations, you can request the logs for the custodians in question during the relevant time periods and review them. If there are no logs, your task is more complex. Look to the actual computers used by the people involved and determine whether any additional logs or history type files are on the machine that aren't on the server. If you find none, then your last resort is to search the page file and the unallocated space on the machine for them. This is where knowing the chat program used becomes vital. For instance, Yahoo! Messenger stores the chat logs in an encoded temporary file, even if the history is turned off. With Lotus Sametime, you can look to the page file and find fragments of chat logs, as long as the chat didn't occur too far back in the past.

Phone Logs/SMS Messages   More and more corporations are issuing and paying for always-on smartphones such as Blackberrys and iPhones. These devices can be virtual treasure troves for this type of investigation. For example, with a Blackberry, as we discuss in Chapter 13, you can recover all the phone logs, text messages, and even things such as "to do" lists. I've experienced situations in which supposed harassment was actually identified as being mutual after it was discovered through SMS messages and phone call logs on the Blackberry device that the two people involved had been having an affair that "went bad." If you get hold of the smartphone and it has been reset or wiped, look for archives or backups. For instance, if someone uses the Blackberry Desktop Manager software, the software will create an archive weekly in an .ipd file that contains everything stored on the Blackberry in plaintext. These are also great archives for finding deleted messages, as a user will frequently delete them from the Blackberry but the inbox still stores the archive.

Violation of Non-compete/Non-solicitation Agreements

Popularity:	7
Simplicity:	6
Impact:	10
Risk Rating:	**8**

When employees leave positions with their companies for other opportunities, they are often subject to various types of non-compete and non-solicitation agreements. This is especially prevalent in industries and positions in which employees are key assets of the corporation and are directly responsible for generating revenue for the corporation—such as partners at law firms, accounting firms, and consulting firms, or other professional services firms where the entity is essentially selling the services of an individual. However, such agreements are also common in sales-related positions for which an employee has established significant relationships with the company's clients or an employee possesses key knowledge of a company's competitive advantages (such as proprietary technology, informational databases, customer lists, and so on).

The general purpose and use of such agreements is fairly intuitive. Companies expend substantial sums in recruiting, training, developing, and supporting their employees, and in return they entrust their employees with access to critical information and clients that are instrumental to the company's ongoing success. When an employee leaves such a position, the company naturally wants to protect against the employee's use of that information to compete against it through another company or enterprise, as well as protect against the loss of information critical to its success. These types of agreements also limit or prevent departed employees from soliciting business from the same clients, as well as soliciting other employees with similar knowledge and skills from leaving and joining them in their new endeavor. While these types of agreements take many forms, in essence they all attempt to protect a company's competitiveness in the marketplace.

However, while these types of agreements are often fairly specific in their application, many departed employees intentionally, or inadvertently, violate the provisions of their agreements. Often the relative availability of customer lists, sales databases, and other proprietary information that could be critically important to an employee's new endeavor are too tempting to pass up. In other situations, the lines between what is considered an employee's personal files and information versus corporate-owned information are often ill-defined.

If an employee fails to abide by the terms of a non-compete and non-solicitation agreement, it's often the case that any "illegal" actions were contemplated before the employee left her company. Such employees often lay the groundwork for their competing interests before they leave, including initiating efforts to solicit customers, as well as employees, to their company or venture. The efforts to lay that groundwork are often evidenced throughout a company's electronic records and files, including efforts to copy and extract propriety customer lists, sales databases, and marketing materials; communications with customers and other employees; and efforts to develop business and sales plans for new ventures based on the framework of their existing company.

What to Understand

When an individual is suspected of violating the terms of a non-compete and/or non-solicitation agreement, your first step is to define and understand the actual terms of the agreement(s) in question and specifically to what activities or actions they apply in relation to what is suspected or alleged of the former employee. Often what is or is not covered under such agreements may need to be defined by an attorney, especially since such agreements are most often written by a company's lawyers. Understanding what activities are specifically prohibited may define the initial parameters for an internal review.

Second, you should understand what is suspected of the former employee to help you define what efforts should be undertaken from a computer forensics perspective to investigate the allegations. Do the allegations involve the simple appearance of a former employee's efforts to compete against or solicit customers, or do the allegations involve the employee's suspected use of corporate proprietary information in that effort? Often employees who violate, or intend to violate, non-compete and/or non-solicitation agreements also misappropriate proprietary company information to assist them in their efforts. Is the former employee simply in the marketplace advertising similar services or is the former employee advertising a similar product using a similar model, approach, and pricing structure, or suspected of using proprietary information (such as customer lists, sales databases) that may have been misappropriated from the company in his efforts? The answer to these questions can sometimes mean the difference between a violation of the former employee's agreement to not compete against the company and, a more significant concern, that the employee misappropriated proprietary corporate information in support of that effort.

Third, you must determine whether the alleged or suspected activity of the former employee involves, or appears to be endorsed by, the former employee's new company. Is the observed or suspected activity limited to the former employee or is there a concern that the former employee's new employer may be supporting or even encouraging such behavior? Such questions have larger legal implications for a company beyond just a former employee's violation of his employment agreement.

Finally, and more obviously, you must understand the timeframe of the alleged or suspected activity relative to the former employee's departure. Such employees may gradually drift back into an area of competition against the former employer and in soliciting the same customers, especially if the company's efforts to monitor and police the non-compete and/or non-solicitation agreement appear to be lax. The timing, and intensity, of a former employee's violation may provide an indication as to whether the intent existed prior to his departure and the likelihood as to whether forensic evidence may exist to document such violation. However, the rapid development of a competing interest, the loss of customers, or the loss of other competitive advantages may give an indication as to the planning and resources involved and the potential misappropriation of proprietary information required to accomplish this feat.

Many employees who leave one company to join another, or form their own company, leave with the intent of continuing to provide the same level of service to the same customer base as in their former job, often in violation of non-compete and non-solicitation agreements. Those that do also often start their planning and transition process while working at their former companies. They also often succumb to the temptation to use, and remove, proprietary information from their current employers to enhance the opportunities for success in their new ventures. That fact, combined with the ease of copying and removing (or e-mailing) proprietary electronic information including customer lists, sales databases, and marketing materials, raises significant concern for many companies in relation to critical employees who leave where non-compete and non-solicitation agreements exist.

What to Look For

What to look for, as well as what time period to review, largely depends on the allegations or suspected behavior involving the former employee and whether it is believed the former employee initiated his efforts to violate the applicable non-compete and non-solicitation agreements before his departure and the likelihood that other materials and proprietary information may have been taken to assist in that process. However, we have observed definite patterns and/or trails of evidence in relation to the violation of these agreements, and these patterns typically start at the company before the employee's departure, providing good starting points for conducting an initial investigation.

Theft of IP

Popularity:	9
Simplicity:	7
Impact:	10
Risk Rating:	9

It is very common to see violations of employment agreements and IP theft. As such, proving that an employment agreement has been violated is often more easily accomplished through demonstrating that the former employee is also guilty of IP theft. Generally, if an individual intends to walk out the door with her team, she will usually take customer lists and other proprietary information as well. From an organizational standpoint, this can pack a real one-two punch, as not only has company talent walked out the door, but they have taken the company secrets and information along with them.

 ## Detecting Theft of IP

We discussed IP theft in detail in Chapter 16. Everything there applies in this situation as well. Look for evidence of customer lists being accessed and data being downloaded from servers and other large data dumps. Find out how the employee copied the information off the computer, whether it was through burning a CD-ROM, using a USB drive, or e-mailing out files. Keep in mind that in situations when an entire team leaves a company, the person who commits the IP theft rarely seems to be the main individual. Usually it is someone else on the team, so it is important to identify who else was involved and employ the same IP theft investigation techniques to them as well as the main players.

 ## Who Is Involved?

Popularity:	9
Simplicity:	10
Impact:	7
Risk Rating:	9

Sometimes the violations of employment agreements occur in a vacuum, where one rogue employee is off doing his own thing. Often, however, this is not the case. It is important that you investigate who else may have been involved and what that person contributed.

 ## Determining the Scope

The first phase in determining who is involved is good, old-fashioned gumshoe work. Figure out who the person associated with, who were his friends, and who reported to him. As you are going through the computer of the individual under suspicion, look at who he e-mailed, both with corporate e-mail and in the webmail caches. If he communicated on a regular basis or if questionable content was sent to other employees at the company, you'd be prudent to take a look at their computers as well. I worked on a case in which a team leader took his team to a new company, along with his assistant. His assistant was dating the purchaser at the company they left, a connection that we didn't discover until late in the investigation. We couldn't figure out how they were getting the internal pricing and customer lists over to the new company until we took a look at the purchaser's computer and realized that the purchaser was actually sending the information to them. Understanding who was involved and how they all related to each other was vital in digging up this piece of information that broke the case wide open.

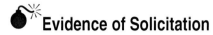Evidence of Solicitation

Popularity:	7
Simplicity:	9
Impact:	8
Risk Rating:	8

Determining the web of those involved is vital; so, too, is finding evidence that the employment agreement was actually broken. The key is to find the documents or other timeline events that can show that solicitation occurred. Meetings, phone calls, and e-mails can all be helpful. In one situation, we actually found an offer letter that stipulated that if the person successfully brought over his entire team, he'd get a bonus from the new company.

Finding the Evidence

While trying to find the evidence of solicitation, keep in mind what is needed to solicit someone. E-mails are the obvious first place to look. But don't forget to consider evidence beyond that as well. Look at calendar entries to determine whether any meetings were set up at the request of the alleged solicitor. If you have access to them, phone logs can also indicate who was talking to the new company before leaving the present firm. A thorough document review can be vital as well. After we found the offer letter mentioned above, the case was settled the next day.

Evidence of Improper Competition

Popularity:	9
Simplicity:	7
Impact:	8
Risk Rating:	8

Looking for violations of the non-compete can be a tricky thing. If you are fortunate, you'll find evidence of solicitation or IP theft on the computer. In such a case, you can use that evidence to get the computer and e-mails of the individual from the new company. Obtaining this data is vital in these types of investigations. Getting this data will also require the assistance of outside counsel and generally outside experts. Once you do get it, however, you can do a few things to find the pertinent evidence.

Finding Evidence of Improper Competition

After you have acquired the other company's computer, you will run all the same types of searches you ran on the original computer, but with some slight modifications. Generate a customer list from the company that may have been improperly approached.

Run these customer names as keyword searches across the hard drive, including unallocated space. More often than not, you will find keyword hits both in the allocated and unallocated space that are contained in e-mail fragments. The individual at the competing organization may feel "safer" by communicating with clients openly, thinking that the company he left won't be able to get hold of his communications. You may also find evidence in both e-mail and user documents that tie up loose ends from leads you find on the original company's network. For instance, in one case, an employee used code words for his meetings to avoid scrutiny. Once he got to the new company, he stopped using those terms, and it was easy for us to see that when he wrote "meet me about a personal issue," he actually meant "meet me so I can take your business with me to the new company."

Also, additional data can be helpful to see who he is still communicating with at the old company and what his future plans may be. In one situation, we actually found an Excel spreadsheet on the new company's network that contained a list of employees at the old company and the dates they would be transitioning to the new company, all without the old company's knowledge.

TYING IT TOGETHER

Employee misconduct encompasses a wide array of behavior by current and former employees that may be in violation of corporate policies and procedures, employment agreements, and/or federal and state employment laws. While companies endeavor to provide guidance to their employees through employee handbooks, by posting required federal and state regulations for employees in the workplace, and in monitoring various aspects of their employees' day-to-day responsibilities, employees can abuse and misuse the responsibility with which they are entrusted in myriad ways.

Employee misconduct can pose significant risks to the operational productivity and efficiency of a company's workforce, and it can expose the company to the risk of lawsuits and investigations in relation to employment discrimination and harassment matters. The misuse of corporate assets, as well as the conduct of former employees and their adherence to the terms of conditions of employment and severance agreements, can also cause disruptions and inefficiencies in the workplace and put a company at risk for the loss of customers, competitive advantages, and ultimately revenues and long-term profitability and success.

A company's objectives can be varied in responding to the various allegations of employee misconduct, depending on the nature of the allegation and the perceived risks to the company. In some situations, a company may want to ensure only that the behavior is identified and corrected. In others, a company's efforts may lead to termination of the employee or employees. In other situations, the company may seek restitution or legal remedies in court against the individual, especially when employment agreements have been violated or when assets or other proprietary information may have been misappropriated. In each instance, the company may need to rely on documented evidence of the misconduct and/or in appropriate behavior to support its arguments for change, termination, or legal recourse in the form of monetary damages.

While not all types of employee misconduct will involve computers, networks, and other electronic systems, the proliferation of the use of e-mail, text messaging, shared network drives, removable storage devices, and voice mail, among other systems, increases the likelihood that evidence of questioned conduct has been recorded, tracked, or memorized in some form by the employee in question or perhaps the employee's co-workers. Your ability to identify that evidence and the manner in which the evidence is collected can be important in working with management, outside counsel, and others to address the identified concerns, including efforts to mitigate the potential risks to the company.

What Is the Risk to the Company?

After the identification of potential misconduct by an employee, you need to determine the risk to the company. The greater the perceived risk, the greater the effort focused on identifying and collecting evidence to support some action by the company, whether it be in terminating an employee, seeking restitution, or filing a lawsuit. The perceived risk will likely dictate the required level of response and the relative importance of employing the computer forensic techniques outlined in this book.

You must attempt to define the level of perceived risk so that the relative response can be formulated, including the company's efforts to investigate the alleged misconduct. Regardless of the perceived risk, the computer forensic techniques and procedures defined here provide a strong framework for identifying, gathering, analyzing, and documenting evidence in relation to identified incidents. Often, single pieces of evidence can be the difference between an employee keeping her job or being terminated, whether post-termination benefits are paid, whether an individual's misuse of corporate assets was limited to personal pursuits or larger potential risks to the company, and whether the company is at risk for losing customers or other competitive advantage to a former employee and her new competing interest.

Poorly or sloppily gathered evidence and/or presentations of findings can undermine the level of confidence outside parties will place in the evidence in determining whether alleged conduct occurred or rises to a level of termination or other potential legal action. Likewise, incomplete evidence and unanswered questions may leave the company exposed if a broader pattern of misconduct existed or involved proprietary corporate information.

Looking at Intent

While the question of intent (that is, why something was done) is of paramount importance in relation to matters of IP theft, fraud, and other illicit activities, it can also be important in employee misconduct matters. In many cases, employee misconduct is driven by inappropriate behavior, personal biases, and prejudices in the workplace. In other cases, it is primarily the result of a lack of unawareness of corporate policies and procedures and federal and state laws. Misconduct can often be addressed through education and training or by termination of the employee in question. However, some employee misconduct is driven by motives for personal gain or with the intent of doing harm to the company. In these cases, understanding intent, as well as identifying and gathering evidence in support of intent, may be important in defining the scope and breadth of the investigation undertaken, as well as the potential recourse that can be sought from the employee through legal or other means.

Estimating Damages

Damages in relation to employee misconduct matters simply may be the loss of productivity and efficiency in the workplace resulting from the disruptions caused by the improper behavior. In many matters, the question of "damages" may not ever be raised, because the ability to quantify an amount resulting from the misconduct may be purely an academic exercise. However, in instances of wage or other types of employment discrimination, the damages sought by employees who have been the target of such discrimination may be significant. In addition, breaches of non-compete and non-solicitation agreements may also damage the company from lost customers or other business.

To the extent applicable, an assessment of potential damages may be relevant to the investigation, especially when decisions are being made by corporate management, outside counsel, and others in determining whether to pursue legal action, including how aggressively, against the alleged misconduct. Their ability to make an assessment of potential damages will often depend on the evidence in support of the misconduct, including how widespread or pervasive the conduct was, how specific the actions were, how long the conduct had been ongoing, and the potential risk to the company resulting from the disruptions, lost competitive advantage, or lawsuits.

Working with Higher-Ups

Depending on the severity of the conduct in question, as well as the perceived risk to the company, senior management and the firm's in-house and outside counsel may become involved in the investigation of any alleged employee misconduct. As with other types of investigations, you must recognize and be sensitive to the different priorities and perspectives each group may place on various aspects of the investigative process.

As an IT specialist, your primary focus will likely be on the computer forensics aspects of the investigation and the subject matter of this book. However, various other parties will have different priorities. An individual or department manager will no doubt question how pervasive the misconduct may have been and whether other employees were involved or affected. (Who else was involved or knew of the misconduct? How long has this been going on? How do we establish better communication to avoid this in the future?) In addition, concerns will likely be raised regarding the extent the misconduct, and whether it has, or potentially will in the future, affect the productivity of the department. A department manager may also be concerned with how to address the allegations efficiently while minimizing disruption to the department. An IT specialist may have a key role in assisting in management to address these questions. (Does e-mail or other electronic information support who else may have been involved and for how long? Can this be investigated discretely and limit further disruption?)

Upper management initially may be more concerned with understanding how to mitigate the effects of the misconduct, including how to minimize the perceived risks. (Is the company at risk for a lawsuit? Should the company consider filing a lawsuit? Does the identified misconduct warrant the involvement of law enforcement?) Upper management may also be concerned with how such behavior went unreported and whether the company adequately posted corporate policies, procedures, and federal and state law requirements regarding employment matters.

While the IT professional may be focused primarily on the systematic approach of collecting, documenting, and evaluating potential evidence, it is important to be sensitive to the various priorities of parties involved in the matter and be prepared to allocate the necessary time and resources to evaluating various elements and/or ramifications of the theft at the same time.

Working with Outside Counsel

Given the seriousness of the ramifications from certain types of employee misconduct, including the company's exposure to lawsuits, outside counsel may be brought in to assist in evaluating avenues for potential recourse that is available to the company. Often, outside counsel will be asked to take over, or initiate, the internal investigation to ensure that adequate evidence gathering and documentation procedures are used so as not to impair the company's potential causes of action against current or former employees, as well as to ensure that the company's interests are being adequately protected. As with upper management, the outside counsel's primary concerns initially may be different from those of the IT specialist charged internally with evaluating various aspects of the identified misconduct. Outside counsel likely will be more interested in protecting the company, evaluating the risk or the potential for lawsuits, and determining the proper legal action, if any, against the implicated employee.

CHAPTER 18

EMPLOYEE FRAUD

Fraud, corruption, embezzlement, white collar crime—we see these words more frequently in the newspaper and hear them more often discussed in the media each year. Since the late 1990s and the accounting scandals at Enron, WorldCom, HealthSouth, and many other companies, hardly a day passes in which an accounting scandal, option backdating allegation, investment Ponzi scheme, or other individual or corporate fraud is not in the local or national headlines. "White collar crime" has become an everyday term used for various types of financial fraud committed by respected employees, managers, and senior executives in the workplace.

Whether mention of an investigation by the Securities and Exchange Commission (SEC), the US Department of Justice (DOJ), a state attorney general, local law enforcement, or in a civil lawsuit brought by injured parties, various forms of fraud have been on the forefront of business news. In reality, fraud has existed in the workplace since the first business transaction or exchange that took place between two individuals. However, with the digital age and the broad access to electronic information inside and outside the workplace, various forms of fraud have taken on a new life as creative individuals have found more unique ways to deceive their companies, coworkers, customers, and others for personal gain—including some frauds of a staggering magnitude. But the digital age has also seen the development of new arsenal of technical tools and resources to combat and investigate potential fraud, including ways to identify, collect, and analyze evidence that previously did not exist.

The increase in fraud as well as their size and impact over the past several decades also has resulted in the emergence of respected organizations whose sole purpose is to facilitate the education and investigative capabilities of individuals to identify, investigate, and report on fraud, including organizations such as the Association of Certified Fraud Examiners and the National White Collar Crime Institute.

While individuals and corporations can commit fraud in a variety of ways, the next several chapters will focus on various broad areas of fraud that have been on the rise and that have become a serious concern for corporations, regulatory agencies, and the general public. This chapter will address of employee fraud or fraud committed by employees in the workplace. Chapter 19 focuses on corporate fraud, defined as fraud committed by corporations against their customers, shareholders, or others, where the corporation is the beneficiary or the instrument of fraud rather than the target. Chapter 20 discusses organized cyber crime. Chapter 21 covers consumer fraud.

WHAT IS EMPLOYEE FRAUD?

In the broadest sense, employee fraud is any fraud committed by an employee in the workplace that results in damage to his or her employer or company. The term "fraud" is used to describe a vast collective of improper and illegal activities conducted by individuals and companies. The term is often used with a modifier to define the type of fraud (such as vendor fraud, check fraud, billing fraud, and so on). In its simplest form, all fraud is essentially based in deception. Various legal definitions are used to describe fraud as containing certain elements, including 1) a misrepresentation, 2) of a material fact, 3) that is relied upon by some party, and 4) that results in harm or damage to that party. In other words, fraud essentially involves a lie (deception) regarding something important (material fact) that is believed by someone who ends up being harmed.

Employee fraud typically involves a situation in which an employee is intentionally and improperly enriching himself at the expense of his employer. Employee fraud includes the misuse or misappropriation of company assets, from the theft cash to complex billing schemes; embezzlement by senior management and executives; and various forms of corruption including conflicts of interest and the payment and/or receipt of illegal bribes or kickbacks.

RAMIFICATIONS

The ramifications of fraud can be costly and far-reaching to those involved. Almost all frauds involve some type of monetary damage to a company or an individual. Whether a simple theft of cash from the company or a multimillion-dollar false billing scheme, fraud committed by employees almost always involves money. However, the effects to the organization can go beyond just monetary damages and can include significant criminal investigations, civil lawsuits, and negative repercussions.

Monetary Loss

People dream up all sorts of ways to steal money from their employers, as well as ways to get money on the side (such as bribes and kickbacks), usually at the expense of their employers. The most common form of employee fraud occurs when someone simply pockets cash that may be sitting in a petty cash fund or that was collected from individuals at some event, such as a fundraiser, where cash transactions may be common. Other types of employee fraud involve more complex schemes to create fictitious companies or employees that do fictitious work but get paid in real dollars. Fraud can also involve the theft of materials or other assets. However, ultimately it all involves money that belongs to the company but that is being misappropriated (stolen) by the employee(s) in question.

Investigations by Authorities

Since fraud is generally illegal, the identification of a potential fraud may also necessitate the involvement of local law enforcement. Depending on the nature of the fraud, the individuals and/or companies involved, as well as the extent (size) of the fraud, various regulatory and investigative authorities may become involved. The most common types of employee fraud may involve the local district attorney or other local law enforcement. However, larger matters may rise to the level of the state attorney general or even the FBI and DOJ if so warranted.

Investigations of this type are usually focused on identifying the extent of the potential wrongdoing and in prosecuting the individuals responsible for that wrongdoing. Often the focus includes identifying the use and/or whereabouts of the misappropriated or embezzled funds and the potential for recovery through asset seizures or other forms of criminal penalties and restitution.

Criminal Penalties and Civil Lawsuits

At times, law enforcement may be successful in identifying and recovering certain amounts of the misappropriated or embezzled funds in question. Certain types of illegal activity also carry defined criminal penalties. In addition, prosecutors in criminal matters also have the authority to seek and request restitution for the victim. However, often a large part of the misappropriated funds have been expended or otherwise no longer exist. In other matters, the whereabouts of the funds may be effectively concealed through money-laundering or other efforts to hide assets. In such situations, as well as situations where criminal liability may be difficult to prove, it is not uncommon for companies to pursue remedies through civil lawsuits against the parties in question. These lawsuits will often involve some element of asset tracing to determine the ultimate disposition of the stolen funds or assets.

In summary, almost all types of employee fraud have some cost and therefore potential monetary loss to the corporation. While many types of employee fraud are small and involve individual acts of theft of cash or check fraud, others may be widespread involving collusion among various employees, outside vendors, and other parties that can reap millions in potential damages to a corporation if the theft goes undetected. Complex frauds can also be costly to corporations to support both internal and external investigative efforts, as well as potential efforts to recover misappropriated funds or other damages from the perpetrators through criminal and civil remedies.

TYPES OF EMPLOYEE FRAUD

The most common, or well-known, forms of employee fraud involve asset misappropriation, including embezzlement and various forms of corruption. However, many years ago, frauds committed by employees were more cash-based or involved fraudulent check writing and/or cashing. As depicted in the movie *Catch Me if You Can*, some of the more famous frauds of years past involved elaborate check fraud schemes. While cash and check fraud type schemes are still prevalent, employee fraud in today's business environment has become much more sophisticated along with the technological advancements of the digital age.

It would take much more than the pages in this chapter, or even this book, to adequately describe the many different ways individuals have devised over the years to commit fraud in the workplace. The creativity employed by individuals with regard to identifying ways to extract wealth is surprising. However, ultimately employee fraud comes down to various types of asset misappropriation, including embezzlement and larceny, and different forms of corruption.

Asset Misappropriation

Popularity:	8
Simplicity:	7
Impact:	8
Risk Rating:	8

Asset misappropriation is the broadest and most common form of employee fraud and includes the misappropriation of cash and other assets. Assets can be misappropriated from almost all aspects of a business. However, larger occurrences of fraud tend to occur predominantly in areas where individuals have access or control over cash or company processes and controls over payroll, expense reimbursement, accounts payable (paying vendors, suppliers, and others), and accounts receivable (the receipt or collection of payments/revenues from a company's customers).

Asset misappropriation can take the form of simple cash skimming type schemes by individual employees to complex frauds involving multiple employees, outside vendors, and other third-party accomplices. Common types include check fraud, including false, tampered with, or forged checks; fraudulent expense accounts; and manipulation of payroll practices, including the creation of ghost employees. More sophisticated frauds involve the establishment of fictitious companies to do fictitious work in return for payment. Each of these types of frauds involves falsified or fake documents and efforts by the parties involved to conceal the truth behind their actions, yet inevitably leave evidence behind for the trained fraud examiner, forensic accountant, and computer forensics specialist to find.

Embezzlement vs. Larceny

Embezzlement and larceny are both types of asset misappropriation, with the distinction being primarily one of whether the appropriated material was originally entrusted to the individual or not. Embezzlement is generally defined as the taking of something for one's own use where a violation of trust is involved. In other words, the accused was originally entrusted with the cash, funds, or other property that she subsequently converted or took for her own use. Larceny, on the other hand, could involve the same theft (of cash, funds, or other property), but by an individual who was not entrusted with the safekeeping of those assets. As such, while the misappropriation of assets is described throughout this chapter, remember that it involves various types of unlawful practices that encompass such things as embezzlement.

What to Understand

Often a company's first indication that it may be the victim of fraud will be through an anonymous tip or a whistleblower—someone who either has knowledge of the potential wrongdoing or who has become suspicious of the activities and/or personal lifestyle of a coworker. At times, a company, or an individual employee, may have circumstantial evidence about ongoing frauds including declining sales and profitability, unexplained expenses, and so on, but may fail to realize the connection between poorer financial performance and the reality that the corporation may be losing money from ongoing fraudulent activity.

When addressing whether computer forensics can be useful in evaluating the indicia or evidence of fraud, you must understand the basics about a typical fraud examination. One of the first areas to be evaluated by a fraud examiner or investigator will be the indicia of fraud (the questions and/or evidence that gave rise to the initial inquiry about an employee). This indicia may include financial and/or operational concerns, as well as matters that may be personal to the individual in question. Financial issues may involve questions around unusual payment practices, transactions, trends in expenditures, or unexplained financial results. Operational issues may relate to an individual's control over a certain business area (such as payroll), questionable internal controls, or other practices that may raise questions about an individual's actions (i.e., the opportunity to commit the fraud). In addition, people often first notice changes in the standard of living of a coworker, especially an employee who is believed to be on the same pay scale. New cars, expensive trips, and lavish personal expenditures (such as jewelry, electronics, and so on) often peak the natural curiosity, and even jealousy, in people who are quick to ask "How can they afford that?"

Next, a fraud examiner or investigator will analyze the various methods by which the suspected fraud could be committed, including identifying evidence that will be needed to evaluate the allegations. From a financial perspective, questions may center around the financial transactions believed to be at issue (such as payroll records, expense reports, fictitious invoices, and so on) and identifying the various parties that would necessarily have to be involved under different scenarios and the veracity or credibility of documents produced in support of those transactions. Questions will also be asked regarding the availability or opportunity to commit the fraud, and whether the employee(s) in question had control over a certain aspect of the business or areas of operations to accomplish the fraud without assistance. Internal controls, or the lack thereof, will also be questioned during this phase to evaluate what, if any, controls would needed to have been circumvented or avoided to accomplish the suspected fraud.

The third phase of the investigation typically involves gathering evidence to address the allegations and to evaluate the various theories developed as to the suspected fraudulent scheme. The computer forensic specialist will likely find his/her most significant involvement in the fraud investigation during this phase as evidence is sought to confirm or deny the allegations. The importance of the computer forensic specialist's role will likely depend on the extent of the fraud, as well as the potential cover-up. As described, by their nature frauds involve deception. The perfect fraud is said to be one where no evidence of wrongdoing exists. The authors of this book subscribe to the belief that there is always evidence; one only has to look in the right place to find it.

Efforts to conceal or cover up a fraud are usually evidenced somewhere, whether it is in falsified documents and records, fictitious invoices, correspondence or expense/payroll records, or disguised access to secure files. In addition, there is almost always a record of the perpetrator's actions, if even saved to a removable storage device or hard drive. Most people committing frauds have to keep track of what they're doing to avoid making mistakes. They, themselves, have to understand what is fake and what is real, and which transactions are legitimate and which ones are not.

Once the evidence is collected, the investigation's next phase involves the development of the case against the employee(s) involved. Often, identified evidence will give rise to serious concerns regarding the likelihood of the allegations, but will not be sufficient to fully establish the extent of the fraud, the period of time covered, or all the potential individuals involved. Sometimes it may be prudent to expand the scope of the investigation, while in other times experienced fraud examiners and investigators may seek to interview potential witnesses as well as the suspected perpetrators. Often, companies are more concerned with effecting proper controls to avoid future exposure to the fraud, rather than fully vetting the entire scope of the fraud committed. The internal investigation may be turned over to law enforcement to complete the remaining aspects of the investigation and to seek potential criminal penalties and restitution.

More than one issue often gives rise to concern, and each issue should be evaluated with regard to whether potential evidence may exist in areas where computer forensics could be of importance. Computer forensics may be instrumental in myriad ways while gathering evidence and conducting a fraud investigation including tracking access to secure networks and files, identifying supporting e-mail evidence, determining whether external files and/or storage devices have been used that may evidence the fraud, and evaluating whether documents have been altered or falsified, as well as when and by whom, to name a few.

What to Look For

By its nature, fraud is generally hidden as employees and corporations alike try to conceal their inappropriate actions. Computer forensics has become an integral tool used to uncover hidden, disguised, and concealed evidence to expose the actions for the fraud that it is.

What to look for depends on the circumstances surrounding the alleged fraud, the employee(s) and corporate department(s) involved, their respective access and controls around that access to the information required to perpetrate the fraud, and the use of computers and e-mail to commit the fraud, as well as other tangential elements that may be of importance. Examples of areas for review include the following.

Finding the Records of Embezzlement/Larceny

Popularity:	8
Simplicity:	7
Impact:	9
Risk Rating:	8

As discussed earlier, it's not uncommon for the individuals perpetrating the fraud to run a second set of books that keep track of everything they are doing. In general, this will be in addition to the proper set that is being obfuscated to make it look like everything is on the up-and-up. One of the vital roles that computer forensics plays in this type of investigation is assisting with the identification and location of the alternate ledgers. These can come in many forms: Excel spreadsheets, QuickBooks files, Act! databases, and so on. The key thing to remember here is that the fundamentals of computer forensics still apply.

 ## Where to Look for Records

When looking for these transaction logs, think like the fraudster. It's unlikely that the files or data you are looking for will be out there in plain sight. The suspected individual will have probably used some type of anti-forensic technique to hide the actual ledger. Let's look at a few cases and how to combat them.

Changing a Filename This is the most simple case. Instead of calling the ledger mysecondsetofbooks.xls, the individual renames the file pinkbunnies.jpg, with the hopes that whoever may be looking for the financials will pass right by this file, thinking it's a picture of bunnies. The way to combat this is via file signature analysis. One quick and easy way to do this is with the file command on your UNIX flavor of choice (or cygwin). However, the granularity of what types of files it can detect and differentiate leaves a bit to be desired. If you have access to a commercial forensics tool such as EnCase, you can use the file signature facilities in the software to perform this analysis quickly and easily.

Encrypting a File One of the most common ways these ledgers are hidden is by the use of encryption. The suspect knows the file is bad, and if the information inside the file gets out, he will be in a lot of trouble, so he takes steps to encrypt it. What method he actually uses varies based on the file type and the complexity of the user. Most people will just use the password-protection features of the software in which the file was created (for instance, applying a password to an Excel spreadsheet) and let that be it. Others may use more advanced forensic techniques. Using a tool such as Access Data's PRTK can be crucial not only in cracking the password but also in identifying the type of scheme that was used to encrypt it. There is also always the option of just asking for the password, but in my experience this rarely, if ever, works. Even if the higher-ups are OK with you asking for the password (which usually isn't the case, because they don't want to tip their hand that they know of the fraud), the person who knows the password generally "forgets" it around the time he finds out he is being investigated.

External Media The use of some type of secured thumb drive is very common in these cases, especially with the advent of the hardened, hardware-encrypted drives. A suspect will use these drives thinking that they are small and encrypted, and if it all comes crashing down he can throw it away or destroy it and no one will ever know the better. We have described in detail in other chapters how to identify that thumb drives are being used and how to locate what files may have been on them. Performing this same analysis, but this time with a focus on looking for accounting related files in the link files, temp files, and registry keys, can be an extremely fruitful path of investigation. This can also help determine who was involved, as it is not uncommon for these thumb drives to be passed around between the conspirators.

E-mails and Other Communications   This one is a bit of a long shot in these types of investigations, but you never know. Most individuals engaged in embezzlement/larceny are smart enough to keep their transgressions off of the corporate e-mail server. However, you may still be able to find some clues there, as well as in the personal webmail/e-mail of the individual and his smartphone records. Remember that you are not only looking for "caught red handed" type communications, but also patterns of communication that could indicate something deeper, as well as code words and other types of speech designed not to draw attention.

Finding Evidence of Check Fraud

Popularity:	8
Simplicity:	6
Impact:	8
Risk Rating:	7

Other than expense account fraud, check fraud still remains one of the most prevalent types of employee fraud out there. This typically entails an employee who gets hold of a check and modifies it in some way so that she can profit from it. This can mean changing dollar amounts, changing the payee name, or stealing new blank checks and filling them out. Oftentimes, they will scan the checks into the computer so that they can modify them and print out new, authentic-looking forged checks. This intermediary step is where computer forensics can play a role in detecting this type of check fraud.

Looking for the Counterfeit

Generally this type of fraud occurs in one of two ways: modification of an existing check or creation of a new check forged to look authentic. For the modification route, typically a tool such as Photoshop is used to modify the image of the check before it is printed. If the counterfeiter is creating a new check, a page layout tool such as Microsoft Word is used to lay out the fields so they match up with the paper check and to print the new check. Let's look at some of the various techniques you can use to find these forgeries.

Look for Pictures of the Check on the Computer   If the check is scanned into the computer to be modified, you may be able to locate both the before and after images on the computer. Do a search for all images on the computer (remember to do this on a file signature basis, as they may be trying to hide the files) and review by hand to see if you can find any images of the checks. Also, the individual may have deleted the images after the modification, so using a data-carving utility such as Scalpel or Access Data's FTK can be crucial here. Once you find the pictures, make sure you note the file metadata as well as the internal metadata (such as EXIF), as they can provide vital clues to who actually did the modification and what tools they used.

Find Documents That Lay Out the Check Forgery   If the individual stole blank checks to write out to herself, chances are that she won't just write out the check, but will attempt to print the information on the check so as to not attract attention. You can use this fact to your advantage and search for Word docs that contain the check layout. Make sure you also look at the temporary files and the unallocated space, as she may not have actually saved the file to the computer.

Look at the Printer Spool   If the check was laid out or modified on the computer, it was probably printed as well. Take a look at the various print spools for the operating system and see if a temporary file exists that contains the check data. Also, look for evidence that some other type of printer was used, such as a print to PDF or print to TIF type option. These options may have been used with some of the newer online check depositing services.

Tracing the Assets

Popularity:	8
Simplicity:	4
Impact:	8
Risk Rating:	7

Once you have identified that the embezzlement has occurred, the company will want to track the assets and figure out where they have gone. While this task falls primarily in the domain of forensic accountants, computer forensics can benefit and speed up this process in several ways.

What to Look For

You should understand or work with someone who understands how money flows through the organization and where the records are kept. If you are dealing with a large company, the assets will be handled through some kind of centralized system, such as a mainframe or enterprise resource planning (ERP) type system. Smaller companies generally use programs like QuickBooks to assist with the accounting. Also, if the company controls are lax enough, it is not uncommon for the fraudster to bypass these systems and interact with the bank accounts directly. Let's look at some various avenues for investigating where the assets came from and are going to.

Internet History   With the increasing popularity of online banking, this avenue of investigation can become a real boon. In smaller organizations with few controls over who has access to the money and what they can do with it, we are starting to see online banking as the point of fraud. The individual will log into the online banking site for the company, allocate some cash, and transfer it to a third-party bank under the guise of some type of invoice payment. In addition, he may also log into the recipient bank account to move the money around. All of these transactions can leave history in the Internet cache and cookies on the computer. This can be extremely helpful in reconstructing the bank accounts used and what funds were used to store what money.

Accounting Systems   This review will be conducted primarily by forensic accountants, but computer forensics can bring some things to the table in review of the financial accounting systems. First are the audit logs. One common tool used by embezzlers is to inflate the payout of an invoice or to back date the payout. With the requirements placed on larger companies in terms of financial reporting and compliance, these transactions are generally heavily logged and tracked. The typical flow of the investigation is that the accountants will flag a few transactions that look suspicious and ask for help regarding what can be identified about those transactions. For instance, look for the user who authorized the transaction, other types of transactions that follow the same pattern (payout to the same vendor, unusually round dollar amounts, and so on), and analyze the metadata around those. Take what the forensic accountants know and match that up to what the metadata says and see if any types of new patterns emerge.

Corruption

Popularity:	6
Simplicity:	5
Impact:	10
Risk Rating:	7

Corruption is another word used frequently with regard to individuals, corporations, and even governments. Corruption involves many activities that may be in violation of federal and state laws but may not necessarily involve the actual misappropriation of assets either through embezzlement or larceny, but still may result in economic loss and damage to a company through such things as undisclosed conflicts of interests, bribery, and kickbacks.

Conflicts of interest are generally described as any situation involving individuals with the authority to make decisions for a corporation, where a conflict may exist between the individual acting in the best interest of the corporation and acting in a manner in which the individual has a potential self-interest (the potential to receive a direct or indirect benefit). In its simplest form, if an individual has to decide what's best for the corporation versus what may be best for himself (for example, through a side or family business), a conflict of interest exists. Not all conflicts of interest are bad, nor are they illegal. In many situations, conflicts of interest are acknowledged and accepted as long as they are properly disclosed to the appropriate parties. However, conflicts of interest do give rise to opportunities for an individual to reward himself at the expense of the corporation, and in those situations, especially when undisclosed, a problem may exist.

Bribery and illegal kickbacks are probably the most common forms of corruption worldwide. While both continue to be prevalent in the United States, bribery and illegal kickbacks can be serious problems for businesses in developing countries around the world, so much so that the US government has adopted, and continues to enforce, efforts to identify, investigate, and prosecute businesses that engage in the bribery of officials around the world (the Foreign Corrupt Practices Act).

Bribery can range from a few dollars given to a *maître d'* for a better seat at a restaurant, to many millions of dollars when hundreds of millions to billions of dollars in business contracts may be at stake. Kickbacks, in some sense, are similar to bribery, yet they occur after the contract or action in question has already been approved. While bribery typically occurs prior to the award of a contract or receipt of business, kickback payments usually come from the business in question. Often, in exchange for steering business to a particular vendor, supplier, or other business entity, the individual may receive a kickback that could be a one-time payment or an ongoing payment in proportion to the amount of business referred (similar in nature to a commission).

What to Understand

The first question when corruption is suspected is whether the company is the victim or the perpetrator of corruption. Most often, corporations are the victims of corruption as various individuals take advantage of their positions within the corporation for personal gain, namely through conflicts of interests but also through the receipt of bribes and kickbacks for steering business one direction or another. However, corporations also commit bribery and pay kickbacks, especially where significant contracts or other potential business is involved. Whether the corporation is the victim or the perpetrator of alleged corruption significantly alters the dynamics of the potential sources of information and the services that could be rendered by a computer forensics specialist in uncovering fraud.

As described, the investigative process follows a fairly standard approach. However, it is important to understand that, by its nature, most corruption (that is, the transactions) occurs outside of the business in question. Unlike a misappropriation of assets where missing assets, falsified documents, and a trail of other evidence may likely exist for the fraud examiner or investigator to pursue, corruption may be far removed from the books and records of the company, especially when the company may be the victim. An individual receiving bribes or kickbacks for influencing certain decisions or steering business to a preferred client may never have to falsify a document or otherwise attempt to hide or conceal his efforts. These types of bribes and/or kickbacks may be paid directly to the employee with no evidence ever finding its way to the company's books and records.

Often, the initial, and sometimes the only, indicia of corruption may be a tip from a whistleblower, concerns expressed by a competing business interest, or an observed change in an individual's lifestyle and perceived standard of living (as previously described), especially where bribes and kickbacks may be involved. However, even when the process starts with a tip, computer forensics can be an important tool in identifying and collecting evidence of potential wrongdoing. Most individuals rarely keep their personal interests, or outside relationships, completely separate from their business responsibilities. Individuals often track personal records on corporate assets (i.e., their company-issued computer), as well as make and track contacts. Contacts are made through business e-mail, voice mail, calendar appointments, travel logs, and other means. Often perpetrators are lulled into complacency when they believe that no one is effectively watching.

In reality, everyone makes mistakes. Each of these areas may yield valuable evidence toward establishing an improper relationship between two parties—and sometimes that may be enough. Combined with other analytical information that investigators may obtain involving the hiring, contracting, or bid award practices of an individual, qualified fraud examiners and investigators may be able to make persuasive arguments about the potential for improper practices.

Where the company is suspected of being the perpetrator of fraud, including the payment of bribes of illegal kickbacks, the investigation may follow procedures similar to those used in relation to other types of employee fraud. Where bribes or kickbacks are suspected, the primary focus is to "follow the money." (Where did the money come from to pay the bribe or kickback? How is it reflected on the books and records of the company?) Often, the direct payment of a bribe or kickback may actually be in the books and records of the company, but disguised as some other payment or transaction. Or the questionable payment may have come from an off-book account or slush fund created and maintained by the company for that purpose. Such questions and avenues open up numerous possibilities for potential investigation as the efforts to create and maintain an off-book bank account or slush fund can often involve numerous falsified documents and/or fictitious transactions. Needless to say, an experienced fraud examiner or investigator may see numerous paths for review where computer forensic capabilities would prove valuable.

In summary, detecting and investigating corruption can be significantly more difficult than investigating other types of employee fraud, especially in situations where the company is the victim. Regardless, corruption follows the same basic principals as most fraud in that it involves a deception of some type, as well as efforts to conceal that deception, and transactions and payments that may ultimately be detrimental to the company. Armed with these basic facts, a trained fraud examiner or investigator with the assistance of computer forensics specialists can usually figure out where to start looking, and for what.

What to Look For

With respect to corruption, the types of information that may require the use of computer forensics can vary widely depending on whether the allegations are specific to an individual or more broadly targeted at corporate-wide practices, as well as whether the company is the victim or the alleged perpetrator. However, while we have noted that practices may be initiated through personal interaction, the pattern of corruption may often be supported by e-mail, voice mail, contact lists, and other electronic information, especially when someone believes she is not being watched.

Finding Communications Indicating Corruption

Popularity:	7
Simplicity:	9
Impact:	10
Risk Rating:	9

As discussed earlier, generally some type of communication will exist between the person paying the kickbacks and the group receiving them. Much past that overly broad statement, however, gets a lot more complicated. What methods did the person use to communicate with the payee? Were code words/terms used to describe the actual fraud? Who was involved, and was the person you have identified merely a middleman for a larger corruption cabal? Using phone records, e-mail, and other types of communication, you can put together a proper social network and show how all the actors interacted with each other. If you encounter communications that you think may be relevant or if you can't tell what they are discussing, you should run it by experts in the area you are looking for. For instance, an attorney versed in what constitutes a violation of the FCPA can take one look at an e-mail you may think is harmless and note five different violations of the law. As always, if you think you need extra help in deciphering what it all means, don't hesitate to bring in external assistance.

Building the Social Network

Multiple tools on the market today can show you who e-mailed whom and when. They create this pretty graph, with lines showing who e-mailed what to whom, with the thickness and color of the lines based upon things such as the volume of e-mails sent back and forth that are keyword responsive. Those types of graphs can be extremely helpful when people are not attempting to hide their communications. If they are attempting to hide what they are doing, these tools can fall flat on their faces. And, more often than not, in these corruption investigations the people involved are definitely trying to hide what they are doing. Let's look at some alternative ways to reconstruct this social network.

Look for Aliases This ties into the money laundering investigations we will discuss later in the book, but its important to mention here as well. Oftentimes the person asking for the bribe or kickback will use some type of alias to ask for the money, so as to distance himself from the transaction. These aliases often attempt to be as anonymous as possible, and the person will use free public web-based e-mail to communicate. Look for e-mails to and from these services (Yahoo!, Hotmail, Gmail—the "usual suspects") and have someone perform a content review. If it looks like the person is discussing things he has no business discussing over webmail with a random stranger, that's a clue that an alias could be in use. Mark the dates and times of these communications and match these up to when large business events occurred in the company. This may help to determine the context of why the parties were talking, and why increased communications occurred during those time periods.

Look for Personal E-mail   The individual you are investigating may also be using an alias. He may also be communicating through webmail because he thinks it is off the company's or regulatory body's radar. Make sure you do a thorough audit of not only what webmail exists on the machine, but also the various e-mail addresses and accounts that are used on the computer. Again, map these out onto the timeline so you can get the bigger picture of what may have been occurring at that point in time.

Cell Phone Records   The communications may not have occurred via e-mail at all. Grab the phone records from the cell phone using techniques discussed earlier in the book. Look for unusual area codes or country codes dialed. If an unusual number keeps popping up during time periods that are critical to the business, that can be a sign to investigate further. If you believe an outside organization was involved, look for country and area codes that track back to the company, as well as the exchange number. If the organization is large enough, it may have an entire exchange dedicated to it (the first three numbers of the seven-digit phone number), and this can be a huge clue that the individual is communicating with others inside the organization.

Voice Mails and Corporate Phone Records   If the company you are working with is on a modern PBX or voice-over-IP (VOIP) system, you should be able to recover the voice mail messages for the individual back to a certain point in time. Which point in time depends on the company's backup policy and how it retains the files in question. Normally these are stored in some type of proprietary WAV format, and the maker of the system can usually provide a utility to convert the file to a traditional WAV or PCM file. If a huge amount of voice mails are present, it may make sense to send them off to a transcriber to listen to them and transcribe them to text that you can search. Also, don't forget to pull the phone call logs from their phone and look at those in the same manner as the cell phone logs.

Calendar and Journal Entries   Look for cryptic calendar events that occur around company events. If the individual normally uses the full names and phone numbers of the people participating in a meeting, but you have found a meeting reminder for something to the effect of "meeting with RTL," that may indicate that the person doesn't want anyone to know who is RTL. This is why it's important to map out all this information on a timeline, as you can see who the person may have called, e-mailed, or otherwise communicated with when the meeting was set up, or immediately before or after the meeting.

Building the Network   Once you have completed all these tasks and have mapped out a timeline, certain key players and fact patterns will start to emerge. Who knew what when, who was involved at what times, and what role each person played will likely start to bubble up. With this information in hand, you can work with forensic accountants to expand the investigation to other individuals and start to look at the financial transactions that occurred around the communications. Using these facts in concert can help to elucidate who was involved, the mechanics of the fraud used, the extent of the corruption, and its effects on both the deals struck and society as a whole.

TYING IT TOGETHER

Of paramount importance in a fraud examination is the determination of who was involved, what they took, and whether or not anything can be recovered, as well as working with various authorities in that effort. However, investigating various forms of employee fraud is also as much about the "story" of how the fraudulent scheme was perpetrated as it is about what was taken and by whom. Being able to tell the story, often with small and circumstantial pieces of evidence, will help the fraud examiner or investigator effectively communicate to a prosecutor, regulatory authority, insurance company, and/or jury the nature and extent of the nature of the fraud, how it was able to have been perpetrated for so long, who else may have been involved, and the magnitude of the potential loss to the company.

What Is the Story?

Some types of employee fraud can be simple thefts of cash, which are easy to explain and understand. However, other types of fraud can be elaborate schemes in which individuals have circumvented internal controls, falsified documents, created fictitious companies, and otherwise avoided detection for years (often in collusion with others). In these instances, it is important to map the pieces of evidence together into a "story" of how the fraud was perpetrated, by whom, and how it has damaged the company. This is often accomplished through detailed timelines of activities and diagrams of interrelationships between parties who may have been acting in collusion to defraud the company. These timelines, diagrams, charts, and graphs often serve to show the connections and links between small, and often circumstantial, pieces of evidence to create a dynamic and compelling picture of the intricacies of the deception and fraud over time. Sometimes a single e-mail may be all that exists to connect two individuals, but it subsequently becomes clear that the "story" of the fraud could not have been accomplished without this connection because of its importance in being able to falsify certain documents or circumvent other internal controls.

Individual pieces of evidence can take on new meaning and significance when plugged into the overall picture of the fraudulent scheme. While this exercise is important for the pursuit of criminal or civil remedies with regard to the suspected employee(s), they are also important for the company in its efforts to enhance its systems of internal, and possibly external, controls to avoid falling victim to such frauds in the future. Companies often follow a significant fraud investigation with an in-depth evaluation of their internal controls and the corporate environment that allowed such abusive practices to take place. Whether changes in job functions, the implementation of job rotations, the creation of internal auditing functions, or the application of more sophisticated electronic checks and balances, companies often implement new policies and procedures to prevent future occurrences.

Estimating Losses

Various types of employee fraud can go undetected for years. However, it is rare that an individual initiates a massive fraud in collusion with others from the outset. Often the fraud starts with a single individual or transaction, sometimes by mistake, that subsequently goes undetected. As time passes, and the confidence of not being detected grows, the fraud may expand, become more refined, and may potentially increase in scope to include other areas of the business and sometimes other employees or parties outside of the company. This general observation is important because it helps you understand how to evaluate and estimate the potential losses to the company. Employees guilty of committing fraud seldom confess to everything. They often will confess only to what the fraud examiner or investigator has discovered. As such, the ability to identify fraudulent activity not just from the current period, but from historical periods as well, is important in establishing the period, and potential magnitude, of the losses to the company.

A computer forensics specialist can play an important role in assisting the fraud examiner or investigator in estimating the potential losses to the company. While sufficient evidence may have been identified to prove the existence of a fraud, evidence may be limited as to the scope of the fraud. Forensic evidence must be sought not only to uncover the fraudulent scheme, but to determine the length of the scheme and its extent or magnitude from one period to the next. Once a scheme has been uncovered and sufficient evidence identified to understand its nature, attention must be focused on expanding the search for evidence to enable an accurate estimate of the potential losses to the company. In other words, you need answers to the questions "How long has this been going on?" and "How much did they steal over the years?"

Working with Higher-Ups

As with other types of fraud, employee misconduct, and IP theft, a company's senior management, as well as in-house attorneys, will likely be involved in the investigation and efforts to address the failures in the company's internal controls, policies, and procedures that allowed the fraud to go undetected. Apart from wanting to understand the computer forensic techniques employed to search for and identify evidence, and the significance of the evidence identified, senior management also will likely have a keen interest in whether documents were falsified and how, whether individuals gained unauthorized access to key systems and how, and whether other internal controls were circumvented and how. The importance of these questions is obvious. As the fraud investigation evolves into a period of self-evaluation by the company, the computer forensics specialists may be called upon to provide assistance in strengthening the company's system of checks and balances to prevent similar occurrences in the future.

Working with Outside Counsel and Investigators

Various types of employee fraud, in addition to the termination of the employee(s) in question, will often involve either criminal proceedings, civil lawsuits, or both. Often outside counsel, forensic accountants, and specialized fraud examiners and investigators will be retained to assist in investigating the fraud and in estimating the losses to the company. As described, the information uncovered may be used in criminal proceedings against the employee(s) and others in question, as well as in support of civil lawsuits where the company may sue the individual(s) involved to recover additional funds. Sometimes what is required in one may be different than what is required in the other. While objectives are often aligned, at times the level of forensic evidence required to meet a certain criminal standard may be greater than that required to meet certain civil liability standards. As such, the computer forensic specialist may be called upon to provide support to various parties in their efforts on behalf of the company to bring matters to fruition, including expanding their efforts in various areas deemed necessary by the parties involved.

CHAPTER 19

CORPORATE FRAUD

The accounting, financial statements, and decisions of senior executives at many of the best-known companies in the world are being questioned every day. Since the corporate scandals at Enron, WorldCom, and HealthSouth in the late 1990s and the early part of this decade, accounting practices in the corporate world have been the subject of unprecedented public and regulatory scrutiny and litigation. Tough questions are routinely being asked by government and regulatory agencies, law enforcement, corporate shareholders, and the press. In 2006, a single article in the *Wall Street Journal* citing potential evidence that corporations may have backdated their stock option grants to senior executives and others launched a massive investigative effort by Securities and Exchange Commission (SEC) and internal investigative efforts by hundreds of corporations nationwide.

The pressure on boards of directors, corporate executives, accounting and auditing firms, bankers, and attorneys has never been greater. Shareholders, regulatory agencies, and others demand action when evidence of potential impropriety or fraud is first identified. The lessons learned over the past decade in relation to various long-standing corporate frauds is that they often involve very complex financial transactions, that participation can run deep into the organization and can involve various outside parties, and that the ultimate cost to the shareholders can reach into the millions and sometimes even the billions of dollars.

As the interdependence of today's global economies and the number and complexity of financial transactions between corporation's within those economies continues to grow, so do the instances of corporate fraud, with estimates of overall fraud-related losses reaching as high as the hundreds of billions of dollars. Many of the world's best-known companies routinely engage in complex cross-border financial transactions involving complex financial instruments and derivatives. While most of these transactions are governed by various accounting standards, SEC regulations, and currency exchange requirements, their complexity makes them difficult for any one party to evaluate and comprehend fully without in-depth analysis.

As instances of corporate fraud have increased over the years, so, too, have the numbers of experienced financial investigators and examiners, forensic accountants, data recovery and retrieval specialists, and computer forensics experts who bring the required experience and expertise in preventing, detecting, and investigating risks or threats to people, premises, and financial and intellectual assets.

Corporate fraud, like fraud perpetrated by the employees of a corporation, is nothing new. However, the growth in the number and the complexity of the financial transactions over the years has led to increased concern about the potential risk and exposure that shareholders and the general public may face when corporate fraud is suspected. The massive frauds of the late 1990s shook the foundations of the capital markets and many of the principals by which corporations were governed. In 2002, President Bush created the President's Corporate Fraud Task Force to restore public and investor confidence in America's corporations following the wave of major corporate scandals that had preceded it. The task force comprises representatives from various government agencies and is a cooperative effort focused on identifying, investigating, and prosecuting corporations and individuals for significant financial crimes. Since July 2002, the task force has accomplished more than 1300 convictions for corporate fraud, including nearly 400 CEOs, presidents, vice presidents, and CFOs.

WHAT IS CORPORATE FRAUD?

Corporate fraud is most typically defined as violations of various regulations and statutes by large, publicly traded (or private) corporations, and/or by their senior executives. Corporate fraud schemes are often characterized by their scope, complexity, and the magnitude of the negative economic consequences for communities, employees, lenders, investors, and financial markets. The President's Corporate Fraud Task Force defined corporate fraud as consisting of an array of significant financial crimes committed by commercial entities and directors, officers, professional advisors, and employees, including various types of accounting fraud, securities fraud, insider trading, antitrust and price fixing, and market manipulation, among others.

RAMIFICATIONS

The effects of the large corporate frauds over the past decade to shareholders, the financial markets, and the general public trust have been widespread and disastrous. From billions of dollars in losses by corporate employees, shareholders, and others to the advent of various new corporate regulations, the corporate landscape has forever changed...and changed dramatically.

Since the late 1990s, corporations of all types have come under greater scrutiny to protect against fraud and demonstrate their public accountability. The problems at many of the largest corporations highlighted by the highly-publicized scandals are not unique. As regulatory authorities, the media, and numerous lawsuits have pointed out in recent years, similar problems have been brought to light at a number of corporations, large and small, public and private, for-profit and tax-exempt. Some of these problems, including corporate scandals at the national level, were the impetus for increased regulation and oversight including the adoption of the Sarbanes-Oxley Act of 2002 (SBA) and enhanced disclosure requirements regarding the compensation of senior executives required by the SEC, as well as the referenced president's task force. The ramifications of these corporate frauds have touched every aspect of business in this country.

Impact to Shareholders and the Public

The Enron corporate fraud and scandal has come to symbolize the excesses and abuses in the corporate world during the economic boom of the 1990s and continuing into the present. Although Enron was one of the largest corporate frauds in American business history, and one of the first with such broad-reaching ramifications, there have been and continue to be numerous other corporate frauds exposed over the years. At the time of the publishing of the second edition of this book, the investment management company fraud perpetrated by Bernard Madoff has the potential of being as costly and devastating as even Enron in certain ways, although it will likely take years to unravel. It is also important to note that these scandals are not unique to American businesses, as massive corporate frauds have been perpetrated by corporations in other countries, as evidenced, in part, by the multibillion-dollar scandal at the Italian dairy and food company Parmalat SpA in 2003 and the current investigation into a billion-dollar fraud at Satyam, India's fourth largest company, which is currently being dubbed "India's Enron."

Each of these corporate frauds has had wide-reaching impacts because of the size of the corporations, the size of the fraud, the pubic visibility of the corporations in question, and the fact that the company and its executives were able to hide the frauds from the public for so long. At its peak in early 2001, Enron was the seventh largest company in the United States, with more than 20,000 employees and almost a billion dollars in net income. At the time, and because of its apparent success, Enron was believed to be one of the nation's best run companies. By year end, Enron was in bankruptcy with the value of its shares plummeting more than $60 billion, a significant portion of that owned by Enron employees through the company's 401(k) plan.

Investors and employees affected by the Enron matter lost billions. The repercussions also led to the demise of Enron, as well as its outside accounting firm, Arthur Andersen, resulting in tens of thousands of employees for both companies losing their jobs. Even more pronounced was the overall impact on investor confidence. How could so many have been fooled for so long? As the Enron fraud unraveled, the shakeup spread from industry to industry as hundreds, and perhaps thousands, of corporations undertook efforts to evaluate their own accounting practices, leading to an unprecedented level of corporations having to restate their financial earnings because of perceived financial and accounting shenanigans. Investor confidence plummeted as the integrity of the overall financial system was called into question, as well as the reliability of financial information at many of the best-known companies.

Regulatory Changes

Significant corporate frauds, especially those that have exploited a nuance or weakness in the accounting guidelines or other governmental regulations, often lead to new regulations. In addition, as the number and complexity of financial transactions including the use financial derivative type products continues to grow rapidly and change, we often observe the inadequacy of existing guidelines and regulations to account for, and regulate them, often necessitating new regulations.

As an example, the Enron and following scandals resulted in new legislation that reformed accounting practices and strengthened the ability of the SEC to investigate accounting fraud, including the passage of the Public Company Accounting Reform and Investor Protection Act in 2002, which created the Public Company Accounting Oversight Board (PCAOB), under the SEC's supervision, that was given the authority to set accounting standards and to investigate whether companies were conforming to the standards.

In addition, the adoption of the SOA required the management of public companies, both large and small, to assess and report on the effectiveness of internal controls over financial reporting annually. Even though not subject to the requirements of the SOA, many private entities also have availed themselves of many provisions that provide guidance as to best practices.

Corporate fraud scandals have ushered in a new era of corporate responsibility. Since the advent of the SOA and subsequent corporate governance recommendations, corporate boards of directors and executives have become subject to increasing scrutiny and expectations.

Investigations and Litigation

The identification or exposure of potential corporate fraud almost always leads to significant investigations by the regulatory agencies charged with overseeing that aspect of the corporation's business. Whether it's PCAOB and SEC investigations of accounting fraud and securities fraud, to investigations by the FBI of money laundering or the IRS of violations of the Internal Revenue Code, a host of agencies may need to launch investigations when significant corporate fraud is involved.

In addition to the various investigations of potential wrongdoing, litigation almost always follows. Most often, shareholders file suit against the corporation, its officers, and directors for past practices that have harmed the corporation and its shareholders. Other litigation may also result where outside parties (such as business partners, vendors, suppliers, and others) have been harmed through the illicit practices. While corporate fraud no doubt can be extremely costly to a corporation's employees and shareholders, the ensuing investigations and litigation can also have far-reaching impacts and costs on the day-to-day operations of the business as it moves forward.

TYPES OF CORPORATE FRAUD

Many types of corporate fraud are generally grouped by the principal regulating area, such as accounting fraud, securities fraud, and money laundering, as well as corporate fraud that is more targeted and well-defined to a specific practice or industry such as stock option backdating and mortgage fraud. While corporate fraud is often distinguished from other types of fraud by the significance of the financial crimes, as well as the repercussions to the corporation's shareholders, employees, and others, the lines can often be blurred between what we have defined as employee fraud and what is termed white-collar crime. In general, we distinguish corporate fraud from employee fraud, where the corporation itself is either the beneficiary or the instrument of the fraud rather than the target or victim as in employee fraud. That is not to say that corporate fraud is not ultimately detrimental to a corporation, but the artifice in which the fraud is perpetrated is different.

For purposes of this chapter, we focus on two areas of corporate fraud that have been, and continue to be, more prevalent in today's business environment: accounting fraud and securities fraud. While corporations have defrauded their customers, investors, business partners, and competitors over the years in various ways, the more prevalent methods involve manipulation of the corporation's accounting records and financial statements to alter reality regarding a company's true financial condition.

Accounting Fraud

Popularity:	7
Simplicity:	5
Impact:	9
Risk Rating:	8

The accounting and financial reporting of companies in the United States is generally governed by a set of widely agreed-upon rules and procedures that define how companies are to maintain their financial records and report their financial results and overall financial condition. These so-called generally accepted accounting principles (GAAP) are promulgated by the Financial Accounting Standards Board (FASB), with authority from the SEC. A company's compliance with GAAP is usually audited by an outside independent accounting firm that follow a set of generally accepted auditing standards (GAAS). The earlier referenced PCAOB was established, in part, to oversee and provide guidance to the auditors of public companies to maximize the protection of the interests of shareholders.

These standards lay out the fundamental means by which companies report the financial condition and period results of their business in their financial statements. One of the primary goals of having a set of accepted accounting principles is to provide a standardized approach for a company to reports its revenues and expenses, as well as its assets, liabilities, and the equity position of the company. This standardized approach is important to provide both a basis of comparison from one company to another and to enhance the confidence and reliance on the integrity of the financial markets and companies obtaining capital through those markets.

The term "accounting fraud" generally refers to a company's improper reporting of financial operations and results in violation of the applicable (GAAP) standards. While companies often make mistakes, the intentional misuse or misreporting of materially relevant financial information often gives rise to claims of accounting fraud. Accounting fraud typically involves efforts by a company to enhance or otherwise disguise their true performance, including overstating revenues, understating expenses, overstating the value of corporate assets, or understating the existence of liabilities—so-called "creative accounting."

Creative accounting is a typical euphemism for accounting irregularities and/or financial reporting practices at corporations that attempt to manage or manipulate their earnings through non-standard accounting practices and/or financial reporting, often to mislead the investment community and financial markets about their true economic performance. Most observed accounting irregularities typically involve some sort of earnings management or systematic misrepresentation of the true financial condition of a company. Such misrepresentation can have serious ramifications for the value of a company's publicly-traded shares (stock), its overall market capitalization, and its ongoing business activities that depend on the company's perceived financial condition, including its access to capital and the ability to pursue various acquisitions or joint ventures.

What to Understand

Accounting fraud is typically manifested through fraudulent financial reporting, which includes the manipulation or intentional misrepresentation of financial statements to distort the company's true economic condition. Often this involves the misrepresentation or omission of material events, transactions, or other information and the intentional misapplication of GAAP, both of which may be supported by the falsification of various types of underlying accounting and financial reporting support documentation. The main forms of accounting fraud involve various types of accounting irregularities or earnings management in the following areas:

- Creative accounting for acquisitions
- Overstatement of revenues through improper/aggressive revenue recognition
- Understatement of expenses or liabilities through inappropriate accruals and estimates
- Creating "cookie jar reserves" through improper estimates of potential costs
- Improper or lax financial reporting disclosures

What to Look For

As with most types of fraud, accounting fraud is often concealed to avoid detection by the company's outside auditors, investment analysts, and others. What to look for often depends on the type of accounting irregularity that is suspected (such as an overstatement of revenue or underreporting of expenses and liabilities). The questions may be specific to the facts and circumstances surrounding a specific acquisition, subsidiary, or special-purpose entity, or more broadly related to the firm's method for recognizing revenue or accruing for expenses. Regardless of the specific area, the types of computer forensic evidence sought during an investigation of accounting fraud may be similar. The questions asked are often the same:

- Who made the decision to account for something in a certain way?
- What level of research was performed in evaluating the proper accounting method?
- Did anyone object to the accounting or question its compliance with GAAP?
- Was the misrepresentation intentional or accidental?
- Was senior management involved in the decision or was it concealed from them?
- Was the company's outside auditor involved in the decision?

- Was any effort made to deceive senior management, outside auditors, or others?
- Was the misrepresentation material to the company's financial statements?
- Did the company benefit from the misrepresentation?

Let's take a look at several computer forensic techniques that we have found to be helpful in these situations.

Identifying Who Was Directing the Malfeasance

Popularity:	9
Simplicity:	7
Impact:	10
Risk Rating:	**9**

When dealing with accounting fraud, you must first identify who was involved. Was this the work of a few rogue accountants looking for ways to help the bottom line or a wider operation undertaken by the company management? Also, you can run into situations where the fraud appears to be contained to one branch or location, but in reality is taking place company-wide. Looking at the communication patterns of those involved can shed light on who knew what and when.

Tracking Communications

On the surface, this sounds like a fairly easy task. Go through the e-mails of the individuals you believe are involved in the fraud and see what turns up—that is until you think about the sheer volume of data this could entail. Hundreds to thousands of e-mails may have been sent to an executive at a large company in a single day. Sifting through all those communications to find the one or two needles in the haystack can be a real challenge (and a costly one at that). We have found the following techniques can be used to assist with the searching process.

Well-Chosen Keywords   Working with financial investigators or attorneys can really help in this process. You can use keywords to help winnow down the possible set of relevant e-mails. Once you have come up with these keywords, apply them to the e-mail set and see what bubbles up.

Date Range Filtering   Once you have a specific set of e-mails that you believe are responsive to the proper keywords, focus on the ones that occurred during accounting-relevant timeframes. For instance, look for e-mails between the auditors and executives during the period when quarterly results are coming out, as this is when these issues will be discussed.

Data Destruction

Popularity:	*8*
Simplicity:	*9*
Impact:	*10*
Risk Rating:	*9*

We often encounter data destruction in these types of investigations. Once the individuals responsible for the manipulation learn that they are being investigated, their first response is to attempt to hide their tracks. The type of data destruction that occurs in these investigations is actually a bit different from what we normally think of as data destruction or wiping. Instead of attempting to clear certain files or wipe the hard drive, the destruction usually focuses on less obvious selective deletion of e-mails and communications, or modifications of accounting templates.

Finding Evidence of Data Destruction

As stated, the type of data destruction that generally occurs in these investigations differs from that of other types of single hard drive analysis. Instead of wiping an entire Personal Storage Table (PST), the suspect may simply selectively delete an e-mail here and there. This can render the "broad stroke" methods of identifying wiping somewhat ineffective. Let's look at some things you can do.

Perform a Gap Analysis   Generally, individuals will follow somewhat regular e-mail patterns. They will generally send about the same number of e-mails per day on the weekdays over the course of a month, with some dips here and there. One of the techniques we use to determine whether anomalies occur in the e-mail that could be deletions is to look at the e-mail trends over the course of the investigation. For instance, if you do a month-by-month breakdown of the e-mail over the course of five years, and there are zero e-mails for the month of May 2005 when every other month has thousands, that is a key indicator that something happened in May 2005. The way we generally do this is twofold: If a full-blown investigation is underway and e-discovery tools are being used, a lot of them have facilities to run these types of reports. Otherwise, you can use a tool such as Transcend Migrator to dump the message header information into an Excel spreadsheet and create a pivot table that rolls up the e-mails by month.

Review the EDB Dumpsters   I have had entire cases hinge upon what was in the Exchange dumpster. We discussed this in more detail in earlier chapters, but it bears repeating here. If you are just getting into one of these investigations, have the dumpster turned on to a properly long time period (so that even deleted e-mails are retained) and periodically take a look using a tool such as Paraben NEMX to see what was attempted to be deleted. Even if you are looking in the past, the dumpster is typically turned on for seven days, so if you have weekly tape backups of the EDB files, you can get to the information by looking to the backups from the weeks you care about.

Compare Sender and Receiver Message Counts   If two individuals are of particular interest, take a look at both mailboxes for communications between them. While you would expect some small deviations here and there, as some people will delete messages more often than others, huge differences can be a sign that something fishy is going on.

Look for Minor Changes to Important Documents   I remember a case involving accounting fraud, when an issue came up with regard to the audit checklist. A critical item seemed to have been added after the fact to the checklist that wasn't applied when it would have mattered. The company, however, represented that the item had been there all along. Through the use of the revision number, created date, and modified date, we were able to show that the document had in fact been modified much later than identified by the company. This was confirmed when we pulled an old version of the document off of a backup tape from the relevant time period, and, as expected, the audit item wasn't there. Work with forensic accountants or counsel to determine which documents may be important and then take a look at them to determine when and how they were modified.

Securities Fraud

Popularity:	9
Simplicity:	6
Impact:	8
Risk Rating:	8

Trillions of dollars are invested in the stock market and various companies that seek investment capital through the issuance of securities (such as stocks, bonds, commodities, and so on) in the various markets in the United States and around the world. Those securities are routinely traded among individuals, corporations, and various other types of investors and investment vehicles. The value of the traded securities rises and falls along with the fortunes of those heavily invested in the stock market. Numerous laws and regulations are directed at protecting investors, securities traders, and the companies that seek capital in the public debt and equity markets. However, sometimes those rules are ignored or outright violated, which can lead to significant losses for those entities that have invested in the system and rely on its integrity.

Securities fraud is generally described as an act in violation of applicable securities laws and regulations where the intent is to manipulate or take advantage of the market, typically with respect to a company's stock price, through deliberate concealment or distortion of information, or through the use of material nonpublic information. Perpetrators of securities fraud may include stockbrokers, financial advisors, investment analysts, brokerage firms, and individual investors, but they often include corporations and their officers and directors. The most common forms of securities fraud include insider trading (trading the securities of particular entity with the information that is not available to the pubic); general financial reporting fraud (presenting false information on a company's financial statements, often in connection with accounting fraud as described); and stock manipulation schemes such as the backdating of employee stock options.

As described in relation to accounting fraud, companies will often conceal their true financial condition by hiding debts or beefing up revenues to appear more profitable or financially sound than they actually are, essentially by misleading both investors and shareholders.

Investing in the stock market and other securities is carefully regulated by rules and laws established for the protection of investors and the various parties involved. Securities issued by a corporation are governed primarily by the Securities and Exchange Commission (SEC). Violations of SEC rules and regulations can have serious consequences and lead to civil and criminal punishment. The SEC, as well as the National Association of Securities Dealers (NASD), can investigate securities fraud and impose civil fines against suspected individuals and corporations.

The Securities Act of 1933 (known as the "truth in securities" law) was established to "require that investors receive financial information and other significant information concerning securities being offered for public sale" and "prohibit deceit, misrepresentation, and other fraud in the sale of securities." The Securities Exchange Act of 1934 was established to empower the SEC with broad authority over the securities industry, including the power to "prohibit certain types of conduct" and to require "periodic reporting" by companies, all of which are aimed at protecting individual investors as well as the overall integrity of the system. However, not unlike other types of fraud, the various players in this arena have found myriad ways to circumvent or altogether violate the rules and regulations of the system and to take advantage of investment analysts, financial advisors, investors, and others for personal and corporate gain.

In addition, the Sarbanes-Oxley Act of 2002 added to the existing securities fraud statutes by further defining securities fraud to include "Whoever knowingly executes, or attempts to execute, a scheme or artifice (1) to defraud any person in connection with any security... or; (2) to obtain, by means of false or fraudulent pretenses, representations, promises, any money or property in connection with the purchase or sale of any security." Several of the more common means by which securities fraud is committed are discussed in the following sections.

Insider Trading

Popularity:	8
Simplicity:	10
Impact:	9
Risk Rating:	9

The term "insider trading" generally refers to the prohibited use of material, nonpublic information in the purchase and sale of securities. Typically, liability for insider trading typically falls upon so-called corporate insiders, such as officers, directors, and other key employees and shareholders—the ones most likely to have access to information that could influence the value or trading price of the company's underlying securities. Corporate insiders who possess material nonpublic information are required either to disclose what they know to the public or to refrain from trading on that information. However, the temptation to realize a profit through trading securities on information the public does not yet know is often too great.

What to Understand

Claims of insider trading are often investigated and prosecuted by the SEC. Abnormally high returns for one investor relative to those of other investors in the market can serve as a red flag to the SEC, which monitors stock trading across all capital markets, especially trades made by those identified as corporate insiders. An individual's sale of stock that occurs immediately preceding an announcement of bad news or the purchase of stock immediately preceding an announcement of good news will often raise questions as to the fortuitous timing of the transaction. Often, the players involved may not appear to be corporate insiders or directly linked to a corporate insider, especially with the existence of various brokers, traders, corporate entities, family limited partnerships, and so on, that could be trading the stock. However, when questions as to whether an individual or transaction may have benefited from insider information, experienced investigators and fraud examiners look for specific things.

First, they must understand the specifics of the stock purchase or sales transactions in question. With the exception of public filing requirements regarding stock transactions involving corporate insiders, only the SEC may have access to the daily trading activity in a particular stock. However, even general trends such as stock volatility, trading volume, increase in short-selling, and so on, may provide indicators of unusual activity in a company's stock before the announcement of certain confidential information. In addition, it is important to understand whether the event observed was a one-time occurrence or a pattern that has repeated at various points in time.

Second, investigations of this nature typically focus on one or more specific individuals. However, where the identity of persons potentially involved may not be known initially, the investigation may start with a broader population of those individuals who had access to the material non-public information. In any event, the investigation often begins with defining a population of potential insiders and their relationship to various outside parties that may have some involvement in the matter. The question of relationships often becomes key in linking outside parties with corporate insiders who divulged the information and are likely receiving some sort of benefit or kickback in return.

Third, it is important to understand who had relative access to the information. Sometimes information is limited to a small number of corporate insiders. In other situations, the circle of knowledge may be expanded to include not only corporate insiders, but outside attorneys, consultants, and others who may be providing service to the company, most likely under some sort of confidentiality or nondisclosure agreement. Questions often need to be asked relative to information access and security, whether the information is located on a secure network, and whether access to that network is tracked.

The appropriate steps to take will depend on the type of information suspected of being leaked to outside parties. It is not uncommon for individuals to use inside information in advance of quarterly or annual reports, especially where overly positive or negative news is concerned. Corporations typically have protocols for how such information is handled prior to the public disclosure, and the information is typically tightly controlled by a small group of individuals. Or the information in question may involve news related to a potential acquisition or significant legal issue, in which case various outside parties (such as attorneys, investment banks, and consultants) may also possess the material non-public information. This step of the investigative process begins with mapping the relative access to the information in question.

The next step often involves investigating whether the corporate insider who is suspected of being involved in insider trading or in facilitating the insider trading by an outside party may have benefited from the relationship. Very likely, this will be difficult to determine based on access only to corporate records. However, as with other types of fraud, it is surprising how often individuals use their corporate assets (such as computers, e-mail, voicemail, and so on) to conduct personal business, including business for which the individual may be a party to alleged fraudulent activity, such as insider trading.

The last couple of areas focus on the corporate insider's knowledge that he was divulging inside information and that it was being relied upon by an outside party in trading on that inside information. Corporate insiders are subject to non-public information throughout the course of their work. Not all non-public information is material. Often individuals lose track of, or fail to realize, the importance of certain information and the potential ramifications it may have on the company's stock price when made public. While the inadvertent disclosure of material non-public information may still have led to the improper trading by an outside party, the distinction may nonetheless be the difference between the corporate insider merely losing his job or going to prison.

What to Look For

What to look for depends on the corporation, the circumstances surrounding the suspected insider trading, and the extent of the individuals with knowledge of the non-public information. However, as with investigating certain types of fraud where the focus is to follow the money, insider trading in many respects is simply following the information—what was it, who knew it, how did it get out, and who used it?

When Did They Know the Information

Popularity:	9
Simplicity:	6
Impact:	10
Risk Rating:	8

In our experience, most insider trading investigations hinge upon when someone learned a piece of information. The most common way that this information is sent and received is by e-mail—perhaps an offhanded e-mail from a financial advisor to a client about movement in a company. As such, when confronted with the e-mail, the person accused of insider trading will generally state something to the effect of, "I didn't actually open the e-mail until after the trades were made." It will be your task as a forensic examiner to determine whether or not this is the truth.

When Was the E-mail Opened

The entire investigation can hinge on determining when the individual opened the e-mail. While this can be extremely difficult to determine, depending on what e-mail client is in use, with a little outside-the-box thinking you can find the information you need. Let's look at a few different ways to do this.

Webmail/Internet History   This method has obvious applications if you believe the e-mail was sent to a webmail account such as Yahoo!, Gmail, or Hotmail. However, I have often seen this history overlooked when corporate e-mail is involved. The thing to remember is that even if corporate e-mail is involved, the individual may still have used the webmail client (such as Outlook Web Access, or OWA) on his laptop or home computer. No matter what e-mail systems you are looking at, you should check the webmail just to be complete.

Having said that, let's discuss what exactly to look for. Generally, at the point when you are trying to determine when an e-mail was read, you know exactly which e-mail you are looking for (this would have been discovered earlier in the investigation). With that in mind, you can re-create the Internet cache and history to see if you can find the e-mail being opened. If you can, match it up with the date and time that it was first placed into the history/cache, as this will generally be the first time the e-mail was opened. If you can't find the exact e-mail, remember to look at the folder view web pages (such as the inbox page) where it shows the message subject and other information about the message. Generally, by looking at the URL status, you can tell whether the message has been read or not, and looking at how these indexes change over time (for instance, you can look at the index cached on Monday, versus the index cached on Wednesday) can help you narrow down exactly when the message was opened. You can sometimes get everything you need from the Internet history URL. Older versions of OWA would actually include the subject of the message in the URL and what action was requested (READ, FWD, Reply, and so on).

Exchange E-mail   When investigators hear Exchange, in my experience the first thing they head for are Personal Storage Tables (PSTs) and the Outlook metadata. However, the actual .edb file can be a treasure trove of information. Specifically, you should care about two pieces of metadata in the .edb with respect to this task—an is_read flag and a last_modified date and time for each message. When a message is placed in the .edb, the modified date is set to the date when it was placed in the container and the is_read flag is set to false. When an e-mail is opened, the is_read flag changes to true, which causes the last modified date and time to change to the time the flag changed. Don't rely on this date and time completely, however, as other things can change it as well. Take a look to see if the message has been replied to, moved, or forwarded. All these actions will change the last modified date. Still, this can be a great place to start, and if you can eliminate all other options on why the modified date changed, the is_read flag can be crucial.

Stock Option Backdating

Popularity:	7
Simplicity:	6
Impact:	8
Risk Rating:	7

Several articles by the *Wall Street Journal* in late 2005 and early 2006 raised serious questions regarding a number of apparently well-timed or fortuitous stock option grants to various corporate officers and directors of publicly traded companies. One of the articles, "The Perfect Payday," cited significant research and analysis performed by a University of Iowa professor, which purported that option grants to officers and directors and many large public companies could not have been random and likely were the result of efforts to time or "backdate" the option grants to days when the company's stock price was at a relative low.

Stock options give the recipients the right to buy stock at a preset price called the exercise or strike price. Often that price is set the day the options are granted, with the right to exercise that option (that is, buy the stock at that price) usually not vesting with the individual for a period of time (usually a year or more). Intuitively, the lower the exercise price, the lower the amount the individual has to pay to exercise that option and buy the stock. For example, an option with an exercise price of $10 versus one with $20 can be significantly more valuable if at the time the option is exercised the value of the stock was $30 per share (that is, it would be $10 more valuable). The reports referenced by the *Wall Street Journal* inferred that officers and directors at many of the companies in question had intentionally backdated option grants to periods when a company's stock price was low to reap the additional benefits from a rebound or rise in the stock price over time.

By the end of 2006, the SEC had launched several hundred formal and informal probes into the alleged stock option backdating, and hundreds, if not thousands, of other companies had launched their own internal investigations into past stock option granting practices. In addition to obvious concerns of potential fraud involved in purposely backdating option grants, especially where false statements or misrepresentations were made in support of the granting practices, many of these practices also violated the accounting practices at these companies, leading to the need to restate their financials and amend their financial disclosures for many years.

What to Understand

When investigating potential stock option backdating, you must understand the stock option grants in question. Stock options became a popular form of compensation and incentive compensation in the 1990s during the tech boom, as options offered companies a cheap alternative compensation to cash with the potential for significant reward if the company was successful and its stock price increased relative to the time it was granted. As such, many companies (especially in the high-tech industry) routinely granted stock options to new employees, to promoted employees in lieu of bonuses and raises, to directors for their service on the company's board as a reward for outstanding performance or to provide recognition for some achievement, or as a routine component of merit pay increases. As such, you need to understand whether all of the company's option grant practices are in question or just certain types (such as those to officers and directors).

Stock option grants are typically awarded pursuant to a defined stock option plan that has been approved by the company's board and its shareholders. The relevant stock option plan will generally describe the terms upon which options are to be granted, including often defining when the grant date occurs and how the exercise or strike price is determined on that grant date.

Stock option grants are generally approved by a company's board of directors. However, it is not uncommon for the board to delegate its authority to a committee of directors, usually the compensation committee, or even to management. With regard to the specific grant type (officer, director, new hire, and so on), it is important that you understand who had the authority to approve such grants.

In addition, certain types of stock option grants are discretionary and occur at random or infrequent intervals, while others are specifically planned to occur at certain points in time (such as the beginning of a quarter, last business day of the year, and so on). Obviously, option grants that have defined dates for being approved and granted preclude the idea of backdating to a more preferable date.

In summary, the key question with regard to the potential for backdated stock option grants is whether an individual or group of individuals determined that stock option grants were to be awarded on one date but decided to "look back" to a different date when the company's stock price was lower to provide some benefit to those who received the option grants. During the course of investigations into these matters, various other schemes or improper practices can be identified in addition to the simple question of backdating, but the primary questions remain: Were the options granted in accordance with the company's stock option plan? Was the grant date the date when all the required granting actions and approvals had been completed and the exercise price was known?

What to Look For

Start with any contemporaneous evidence that may exist surrounding the stock option granting and approval process. Stock option approvals are typically evidenced by board or compensation committee meeting minutes or other documents executed by directors and known as unanimous written consents (UWCs) that are used in between scheduled board and committee meetings. However, questions often exist as to the veracity of certain board minutes or other documented evidence of decisions when the timing of option grants appears fortuitous. In such situations, additional investigation with the assistance of computer forensics specialists is often required to identify the existence of various contemporaneous documents prepared in support of the option grants, including when the documents were prepared and by whom, if they were modified and when, and when they were sent to others for review and approval. In more egregious situations, concerns can be raised as to the falsification of documents to support a grant date different from the original. The following areas have required detailed review in a number of our stock option backdating investigations.

Detecting Modification of Documents

Popularity:	*9*
Simplicity:	*8*
Impact:	*9*
Risk Rating:	*9*

Computer forensics will be called upon in these investigations for one primary purpose: to determine whether the documentation and timing around stock option grants were on the up and up or if things were changed after the fact. The core skills needed to perform such an investigation are the same ones we have discussed throughout the book: Looking at the metadata, seeing how the file changed over time, and comparing versions to see what was added and removed.

What to Look For

Again, these are techniques that have been largely discussed previously. However, you have some advantages due to the scale and timeframe of these investigations. Generally these investigations span large periods of time, and you will have access to many years' worth of backup tapes. Since the files you will review are company records, more often than not they will be backed up on tape. Make sure that you not only perform the review on the document you are asked to look at, but also look to the backup tapes to see if the document exists on any earlier backups. For instance, if a grant was made in April 2004, and the tape backups show that the file changed size and content in June 2004, that can be a big indicator that backdating may have occurred. Create a report showing when the document was modified and what was taken out/added and work with the financial investigators to determine the importance. They can also help point you toward other supporting documents that may need to be reviewed as well, based upon the information you have provided.

CHAPTER 20

ORGANIZED
CYBER CRIME

Much has been made lately of identity theft, bot-nets, and good, old-fashioned malicious hacking. Increasing globalization and the spread of capitalism has brought about a new day in malicious hacking, where threats no longer involve the kid in the basement, but organized, multinational corporations and crime syndicates that have one goal in mind: to use technology to defraud the western society. Many books have been written on the art of incident response and how to investigate these attacks. The purpose of this chapter is not to reiterate what those books discuss, but to look at the issue from the perspective of a computer forensics examiner to see what additional information you can gather by adding proper computer forensic techniques to the arsenal of weapons used to combat malicious hackers. That being said, let's start with a historical perspective on where these groups came from and what kind of methods they typically use.

THE CHANGING LANDSCAPE OF HACKING

Most of us have heard the stereotype by now: Sitting in a dark room, the solitary, antisocial hacker is working away, the only light the dim glow of the monitor, quietly spending the nights breaking into your computer network. In the past, this stereotype rang true. However, with the changing global landscape and the advancement of the Internet into developing third-world countries, the solitary American hacker is becoming a wistful memory. Today's hacker has evolved into large, multinational corporations, based in emerging capitalist societies, whose bottom line depends upon the exploitation of American networks.

To understand what is driving this change, let's look at the example of the former Soviet Union. Under the former system of Soviet communism, bureaucracy and byzantine rules were the norm. This, combined with the lack of economic prosperity under this system, bred a culture in which it was acceptable to find ways to work around the system. This was further compounded by the fact that the best and brightest in the USSR were driven to science and mathematics.

When capitalism broke out, the counties that formed the Soviet Union went through the normal growing pains of emerging capitalist societies. Even for the most educated individuals, it was hard to find work that would pay the bills. Couple this economic desperation with a fundamental distrust of rules and regulations, and you get the seeds of the modern hacking culture. These educated, well-connected individuals realized that there was money to be made in the Western world, no matter the legal ramifications, and with good reason. More often than not, the countries in which they reside shield these companies.

There are many reasons for this. First, the governments are resource strapped and don't have the money to go after these types of command-and-control, brutally efficient corporations. Second, as a complication for the West, these governments do not go after hackers due to corruption or other more nefarious reasons. Somewhat replacing the cloak and dagger of times past, these organizations provide countries a level of deniability they've never before experienced.

The Russian Business Network

A primary example of this new type of organization is the Russian Business Network (RBN). On the surface, the RBN appears to be an Internet service provider (ISP) that hosts Web sites and e-mail accounts. However, a bit of digging reveals its intent to be a bit more nefarious. It serves as the launching point for everything from spam to coordinated cyber-military strikes against countries such as Estonia and Georgia. Using the railroad industry as an analogue, RBN is the Union Pacific of the cyber-crime industry. It supplies the underlying infrastructure that allows these crimes to take place, and it takes infrastructure fees from the spoils of fraud. This can be incredibly profitable, as shown by the estimated $150 million profit made from just one instance of crime documented by Verisign. Without knowing it, most of us have come across a RBN-based scheme. They are some of the most prevalent schemes on the Internet, ranging from nuisances to events that can destroy companies and worse, people's lives.

Infrastructure and Bot-Nets

RBN does have traditional network infrastructure, like a telecommunications company or ISP, where its power resides—but it doesn't have wires in the ground or a interconnected network of company-owned computers. The true power of the Internet lies in its distributed and decentralized nature, an idea not lost on the RBN. The RBN exerts its power through a bot-net that works like this: A user unknowingly downloads a piece of software to her computer. This software then "phones home" and turns a person's computer into what is known as a "zombie" or "slave computer." A zombie lives on the bot-net, awaiting further instructions, which can be anything from sending out spam e-mail, to hacking a network, to collecting proprietary information from the computer it lives on. RBN's bot-net, Storm, is thought to be the largest bot-net in the world. By some estimates, the Storm bot-net had taken over from 1 million to 50 million computers in September 2007. Through that September, it was estimated that Storm had sent more than 1.2 billion spam e-mails that were infected with the bot-net software, designed to infect other computers and turn them into zombies.

The complexity of the Storm bot-net does not reside just in its infection rate, size, and reach. It was designed with commercial viability in mind. Like any good network design, fault tolerance and survivability are key aspects of Storm. It can also be partitioned by task and volume. Clients pay for use of a specific section of the bot-net—say, 10,000 machines—with an option for custom design for a specific task. The admins of the bot-net then designate a unique encryption key that allows only that client to access that portion of the bot-net during their allotted time. Depending on the task, they then allow either the existing code to execute (such as sending out e-mails) or put together custom code packages (such as attacks on foreign governments) and deploy them to the network for execution.

Again, like a traditional ISP, uptime and the guarantee of service is vital to retaining customers. As such, the Storm bot-net is designed with uptime in mind. If a node goes down, another will pick up where it left off. It also has a sophisticated security mechanism. In our research, we have identified that the bot-net software is able to manipulate virus and malware scanners, the primary mechanism for detecting and removing the bot-net software. These scanners have a database of "electronic fingerprints" of nefarious software. The bot-net will change itself to hide from the scanner, and it will sabotage the scanner software itself to prevent detection. In addition, the bot-net software has the capability to know when someone is attempting reverse-engineer or remove it and will call for help. This help typically comes in the form of some kind of secondary external attack, such as a large scale Distributed Denial of Service (DDoS) or some type of hackback such as attempts at massive infection of internal networks. In addition to isolated attacks, the bot-net is constantly going after anti-spam services and sites designed to help bring it down.

All of this implies a network infrastructure that is incredibly powerful. By some estimates, this network is as powerful as some of the world's best supercomputers. The amount of bandwidth—the most valuable resource on the Internet—that this network is able to corral and use is staggering. Traditional companies and ISPs are limited by the connection of bandwidth to cost. The bigger the pipe, the higher the cost. Since Storm doesn't own any of the infrastructure, cost is of no concern. Locality is also an issue for ISPs. If you are serving clients in the United States who want their site accessed in Australia, you have to find a way to get the information to Australia. The bot-net has zombies all over the world, which allows for massive economies of scale and profit margins that are powerful enough to literally take entire countries off the Internet for periods of time.

The Russian-Estonian Conflict

In May 2007, a conflict erupted between Russia and Estonia as a result of Estonia's refusal to allow a Baltic oil pipeline to be built through Estonia to Germany. The Russian government launched an effort to destabilize the Estonian economy. In addition to using traditional methods such as cutting off supply lines and transportation routes, a new tactic was used: cyber warfare. Using bot-nets, hackers performed DOS attacks on the Estonian government, preventing Estonia from functioning normally and inhibiting the government's ability to respond to Russian-created propaganda. While there is speculation about indirect Russian government involvement in these attacks, a group of pro-Kremlin hackers in Moldova and Transnistria have claimed responsibility. Due to the legal status of Transnistria (it is not an Estonian-recognized country, so it is not bound to any mutual legal assistance treaties, a problem common in this part of the world), serious legal hurdles are involved in tracking down the individuals who were directly responsible for these attacks.

Effects on Western Companies

The impact on US companies from these organized hacker networks has been realized to some extent already. But it has the potential to get much worse. We are seeing the targets of these attacks shifting from the individual to the corporation, particularly companies with publicly traded stock. For instance, these bot-nets are being outfitted to send spam relating to a "pump-and-dump" scam. In this scam, after a penny stock is identified, the scammers use US brokerages to purchase shares of the stock at the penny value. Then an e-mail is crafted that extols (falsely, usually) the virtues of the stock. This e-mail is sent out using these massive spam networks to millions of e-mail accounts. And while most readers won't give pause to the e-mail when it arrives in their inbox, some will. They will then purchase the stock, raising the stock price. One or two people doing this won't have much effect. But this coordinated, worldwide transaction can falsely raise the stock price as much as 100 times in a matter of days. When the stock has reached the scammer's identified rate of return, the scammer then sells the stock and collects the money. This becomes damaging to the individuals who bought into the company and to the company itself. As the company settles to its fair market value stock price, individuals who bought in at 10 or 50 times are getting pennies back on the dollar—not to mention the damage to the reputation of the company. If you extrapolate this one example into the thousands of weekly pump-and-dump schemes, you can see the effect this can have on the markets at large.

TYPES OF HACKS AND THE ROLE OF COMPUTER FORENSICS

As stated at the beginning of this book, copious resources are out there, including some very good *Hacking Exposed* books on the topics of hacking and how to detect hackers. However, you can gain additional value by looking at these events from the perspective of a forensics investigator. Advanced computer forensics techniques, coupled with traditional incident response techniques, can add a dimension to what you can determine after something has occurred, and they can even help to prevent it from occurring in the first place. Let's take a look at several common hack methodologies and how computer forensics can supplement an investigation.

Bot/Remote Control Malware

Malware can be especially dangerous to corporate networks and information assurance. These types of bots can usually lie in wait, taking over a computer and waiting a set interval for instructions. Once activated, these bots can allow hackers to take complete control of the system and run amok on the network without having to deal with the firewall or other IDS/IPS type systems. Once one of these bots does become active and noticed, a whole slew of questions will follow: Who put this on the computer? How did it get there? How long has it been there? What else on the computer did it affect? Did it affect any other computers on the network? Let's look at some of these questions and how computer forensics can help provide answers.

Is Malware Even There?

Popularity:	8
Simplicity:	5
Impact:	10
Risk Rating:	8

One of the first questions to ask when you notice malware-type activity is this: Does malware even exist on the system? It's not uncommon for employees who are caught browsing Web sites outside of corporate policy to blame it on malware. Sometimes employees will actually use malware to cover up their hacking activities. If you have something to correlate and show that the malware exists, you have a starting place for where to look. If you don't, then just as with any other forensic investigation, you will want to start from the beginning, triage the data, and drill-down on things that look suspicious.

Finding Malware

Depending on the sophistication of the malware, the prospect of finding it can be fairly straightforward or somewhat difficult. We have identified a few places to start that can be very helpful in tracking down where the malware resides.

Registry Keys and Startup Files   Copious numbers of registry keys are on a Windows 2000 and later computer that can be used to initiate software when the computer is booted up or a user is logged on. These keys are a good first place to look for suspicious software. Several of these keys live in the individual user's registry hive, so if you find malware in one of these keys, you can then start to narrow down how the malware made its way onto the computer.

> **CAUTION**   It's important that you perform this analysis using a forensic registry viewer. If you use a tool such as regedit, it may not show registry keys that have null entries, and this is a common way that malware will attempt to hide itself from investigators.

Here are the locations to look for auto-running malware:

- Software registry files
    - Microsoft\Windows\CurrentVersion\RunServicesOnce
    - Microsoft\Windows\CurrentVersion\RunServices
    - Microsoft\Windows\CurrentVersion\RunOnce
    - Microsoft\Windows\CurrentVersion\RunOnceEx
    - Microsoft\Windows\CurrentVersion\Policies\Explorer\Run
    - Microsoft\Windows NT\CurrentVersion\Winlogon\Userinit

- Microsoft\Windows NT\CurrentVersion\Winlogon\Notify
- Microsoft\Windows\CurrentVersion\ShellServiceObjectDelayLoad
- Microsoft\Windows\CurrentVersion\Explorer\SharedTaskScheduler

- NTUSER.DAT registry files
  - Software\Microsoft\Windows\CurrentVersion\RunServicesOnce
  - Software\Microsoft\Windows\CurrentVersion\RunServices
  - Software\Microsoft\Windows\CurrentVersion\Run
  - Software\Microsoft\Windows\CurrentVersion\RunOnce
  - Software\Microsoft\Windows\CurrentVersion\Policies\Explorer\Run
  - Software\Microsoft\Windows NT\CurrentVersion\Windows\load

In addition to the registry keys, you should check several batch and startup files to see if any suspicious programs are started:

- c:\autoexec.bat
- c:\config.sys
- c:\windows\wininit.ini
- c:\windows\winstart.bat
- c:\windows\win.ini
- c:\windows\system.ini
- c:\windows\system\autoexec.nt
- c:\windows\system\config.nt

Virus Scanner Logs Many of the modern-day malware tools can change or modify the system's virus scanner in an effort to hide detection. Take a look at the logs and look for evidence of things such as malware that was detected that is no longer being detected (this can indicate the signature was removed from the scanner's database), out-of-cycle signature updates that don't look like they were initiated by the software company, and large gaps in the scanning process. If you note that the virus scanner logs a daily scan of the system and it mysteriously stopped for a two-week period, that can be an indication that malware has done something to stop it.

Hostname Lookup Files Malware can attempt to disable the update capabilities of the virus scanners and other anti-malware tools by routing away the traffic of the computer from the scanner updates site to some other malicious update server. This is commonly accomplished by modifying the HOSTS or LMHOSTS file in the Windows system directory. Take a look at these two files: By default, there should be an active entry for the loopback and not much else. If you notice several errant entries, make a note of the last created and modified times of the file, as that can help to determine when the malware was placed on the computer.

Hash Analysis   If none of the above has worked, your next task is to look to see if any operating system files have been modified. The best way to do this is to use the National Software Reference Library (NSRL) hash set for the operating system in question. If you compare the reference hashes provided by the NSRL to the system files on the computer, you will be able to tell if any of the vital files have been modified or changed, an indication that they have been taken over by malware. Tools such as EnCase and SMART allow you to apply this NSRL set to the image to find out which files are out of sorts.

NOTE   The NSRL can be found online at www.nsrl.nist.gov. All the NSRL hash sets can be found on this site and downloaded for your use.

What to Do After You've Found It   Once you find the entries and files that you believe are malware, it's time to start figuring out when it was placed on the system and how it got there.

When Was It Placed on the System?

Popularity:	8
Simplicity:	5
Impact:	10
Risk Rating:	8

Generally, your next question after "Is there malware on the system" is "How long has it been there?" You can make use of some traditional computer forensic techniques to determine this. Just as with any other kind of malicious activity, you want to create a timeline to show when the events happened and what exactly occurred. Several tools in your forensics examiner's toolbox can help with this process.

Determining When the Malware Was Placed on the System

Once you know how the malware is being started, you can quickly gather a few datapoints. For one, you know the name of the file that contains the malware and you can find it on the file system. Second, if the startup is occurring through a registry key, you can go to that key and look at the created and last-written times. Look at the created time on the file and the registry keys. This should indicate when the malware was actually placed on the machine. Once you know this time, look for other events that occurred around the same time. Check the virus scanner logs for that day and see if anything anomalous happened. Look for other files that have the same created or modified times as the malware, as that can indicate whether additional files have been infected or what the malware may have been targeting.

Where Did It Come From?

Popularity:	8
Simplicity:	5
Impact:	10
Risk Rating:	8

Next, you can begin to identify where the malware may have come from. Malware generally initiates from Internet downloads, infected software, or some type of third-party device plugged into the machine. Using the same type of forensic techniques used to look at the Internet history, software installations, and external device history can be very beneficial in these investigations.

Determining the Entry Vector of the Spyware

With the multitude of ways that malware can get on the machine, it is prudent to take a look at multiple data points to narrow down the potential entry vectors for the malware. Let's take a look at several different areas that you can look at.

Internet History   By far the most common entry vector we see is by some kind of Internet download. In addition, reviewing the Internet Explorer history has the added benefit that normally e-mail attachments and other file system activities can be captured by these logs as well. Your first task when presented with malware after finding the date and time it was placed on the system is to look at the Internet history for that timeframe. If you see that a suspicious Web site was being accessed at the same time the malware was placed on the machine, you should investigate the site and see if the malware did in fact come from that site. It is also common for the history to show the location of the malware as it existed in the Internet cache, even if the virus scanner has already removed it. As another added bonus, oftentimes malware will beacon back home using the Internet Explorer API. This means that any calls home or files it downloads may be logged in the Internet history as well.

The main caveat with performing this Internet history analysis is to make sure that you carve the history and cache out of unallocated space before beginning. You may miss something if you deal with only active files, as the history may have aged out or, as a hiding mechanism, the malware may have cleared the Internet history and cache.

Installed Software   In Chapter 18, we discussed how to identify what software was installed and when it was installed. This can be helpful in malware analysis, as the malware may have come from what the user thought was legitimate software. One example of this would be an application that assists a user in placing many different types of emoticons and smileys in e-mail. The user downloads it for free, thinking the people who wrote it are the greatest for giving it away for free, but the software actually installed a backdoor on the user's system.

External Devices   I can fondly remember back in 1992, when a friend brought the latest video game to my house on floppy disk. We put the disk into my computer, and 10 minutes later, the entire computer's hard drive had been erased, having fallen victim to a virus. Before the prevalence of e-mail and the Internet, such disks were the main transmission method for malware. Although it isn't nearly as prevalent as it once was, malware that uses USB and flash drives as the infection mechanism still exists. Take a look at the USBSTOR areas and see if any devices were attached around the time that the malware found its way onto the machine.

E-mail Messages   In the late 1990s–early 2000s, e-mail was the transmission method of choice. E-mails would come into your Outlook inbox, promising nude photos of Britney Spears. You would click to open the e-mail and it would then send itself to everyone in your address book. The various e-mail clients have been armored quite a bit to help prevent such widespread transmission, but you still see it used from time to time, especially when the malware is targeted toward a particular group or company. Look for suspicious e-mails in the inbox that may have been opened around the same time as the malware hit the system.

What Does the Malware Do?

Popularity:	8
Simplicity:	5
Impact:	10
Risk Rating:	8

Now that you know what the malware is, how long it has been on the computer, and where it came from, you can start to look at what it was actually doing. Is it remote-control software that allows a hacker to take over a computer? Does it act as merely a processing center to crack passwords or send e-mails? Is it capturing information and sending that data to other servers on the Internet? Determining what the malware touched and the interactions of the software can be vital in the investigative process.

Determining Malware Capabilities

Determining what malware was doing and which areas of the computer it touched can be a very complex process. Entire books have been written on how to sandbox the malware and watch how it interacts with the system. While this is definitely an effective methodology, in some situations, this may not be possible. For instance, if you can't find the malware itself, only evidence that it was on the computer, you will have nothing to sandbox. Also, some of the more advanced malware can detect when it is being monitored and "self destructs" to protect its intentions. Let's look at some of the things you can look for without having to run the malware that may help in identifying the malware's purpose.

Prefetch Files   If you know the filename of the malware and it is a standalone .exe file, look for the .pf file in the PREFETCH folder (discussed earlier in the book). Note the created and last written times, as those can indicate when the malware was first and last run. Also of note is the content inside the prefetch files. As you know, the prefetch exists to assist with the caching of support files for the executable. This means that the .pf file will contain the actual names of files that the executable uses. In some cases, this can point you toward networking, user, and disk subsystems. Also, look for the filenames of temporary-looking files. These can be the data stores that the malware uses to store keystrokes and other user information before transmitting them to a central server.

Temporary Files   Look for files that were created or modified either the first time or the last time the malware was run. This may require recovering what you can in the way of deleted files. It is not uncommon for malware to "bundle up" a day's worth of keystrokes or logs and then encrypt them and upload them to a predetermined server. However, it is also common for this data to live unencrypted in the page file and temporary files. If you believe you know a particular key phrase or a document that was taken, run the phrase or sets of terms from the document as a keyword search across the hard drive. This can help in locating these files and can tell you what else may have been taken.

Operating System Changes   Look for operating system files or registry keys that were created or modified during the created time or last modified time of the malware. This can help identify whether the malware has taken over any kernel-level subsystems or has otherwise left itself a backdoor in case something happened to the malware proper. In addition to looking for things that were created or modified in concert with the execution, you should also look to the NSRL hash set to see if anything on the computer has been modified from the known good installation.

Internet History and Network Logs   In addition to determining when the malware was downloaded to the computer, checking the network logs and Internet history can also be valuable in determining what the software was doing. Look for evidence of the malware calling home or downloading updates. In addition, if you have a web proxy, you can actually use the proxy logs to determine the volume of data that may have been uploaded out of the company. These logs can also be key in determining the external IPs where the data was sent, which will be important if and when the investigation is taken to the next stage and authorities are involved.

Traditional Hacks

With all the talk of malware and bot attacks these days, it is easy to forget that sometimes you are dealing with a good-old-fashioned "hacker sitting behind a keyboard" attack. For these types of hacks, your understanding of how to re-create user activity can be a huge boost in the investigation of what the hacker was able to do on the system. Let's take a look at some of the various audit trails we use in traditional forensics and see how they apply to determining the actions of a hacker.

Tracking Hacker Activity

Popularity:	8
Simplicity:	5
Impact:	10
Risk Rating:	8

Much as with malware, the first question you will hear when you notify someone that a hacker broke into their system is "What did they do to my computer/network?" Just as with IP theft or any other type of fraud, you can use the forensic artifacts on the system to determine what exactly the hacker did.

 ## Reconstructing the Hack

You want to look in several places to determine what happened in a hack. Some of the places that we start with are the same ones we have discussed in the book, but with a slightly different twist.

Event Logs   Depending on the level of auditing turned on in the policy, event logs can either be a real boon or completely worthless. If full auditing of the user accounts is turned on, you can tell whether a brute-force attack on the password was employed, what username the hacker was using to gain access to the computer, and what other accounts may have been compromised. Also, as applications may have been changed or modified by the hacker, these changes may be logged in the application and system logs.

Prefetch Files   The PREFETCH folder can be invaluable in determining what tools the hacker employed. Generally, a hacker will download a toolkit in short order after gaining access to a system, which can include tools to download company files and crack passwords. If you find prefetch files for these tools, be sure to review the contents of the .pf file as well. The file will contain the directory from which the tool was run, and this can be extremely helpful in determining where the hacker stored his toolkit. In addition, if the hacker used a utility such as RAR to package up data before sending it off the computer, the prefetch file for RAR can actually contain the names of the files that were placed in the archive.

User Assist Logs   Just as if a user is logged into the computer, when a hacker runs software on the computer it is logged in the user assist logs. These can also be extremely helpful in determining not only what the hacker did on the computer, but also what username and privilege level he used to do his deeds. In matters for which the hacker actually took control of a user account, I have found these logs to be invaluable in the investigation process.

File System Analysis   As discussed in Chapter 9, you can look for evidence of wiping and information hiding in many ways. These methodologies can be extremely helpful in the investigation of a hack. Look for mass deletions or evidence of shredding utilities being used. Frequently, when a hacker is alerted that he may be detected or has finished what he came to do, he will then undertake efforts to destroy the evidence and cover his tracks. And just as with any user who is trying to cover his tracks, evidence will be left over and you may actually be able to determine what was affected.

Internet History   As stated previously, one of the first things a hacker does when he takes control of a computer is to download his toolkit onto the system. Sometimes, if he took control using a remote desktop type of application, he may literally open Internet Explorer and download the toolkit via the Web. This activity will show up in the Internet history, just like any other kind of network activity. In addition, any files that he opened on the system may be contained in this history as well. If you know the user account that he took control of, take a look at the Internet history for that user and see if anything was accessed.

MONEY LAUNDERING

Once the hacking has generated profits for the criminals, they generally cannot use the money as it comes in. Because of the traceability of assets, some form of money laundering usually occurs before the money is dispersed. This laundering can take several forms: shell companies set up to make the money transfers look legitimate, individuals used as fronts who don't know about the underlying criminal activity, and even moving the money to banks with dubious jurisdictional status. All of these are efforts either to shield the true origins of the money or block authorities from freezing the assets.

Anti-Money Laundering Software

Some software packages out there can assist banks and other financial institutions with anti-money laundering (AML) compliance and money laundering detection. For instance, in the United States, the Bank Secrecy Act requires all financial institutions to report any cash transactions greater than $10,000.01. This software will automatically detect these transactions and report them to the appropriate authorities. In addition, the software can perform historical analyses and other types of statistical reviews of accounts to determine whether the patterns match that of potential money laundering. If you are lucky enough to be working with a financial institution that is mandated to use this type of software, the data it provides can go a long way toward helping with the investigation. Unfortunately, most of the cases where laundering becomes an issue will involve international institutions, who purposefully do not use these tools.

The Mechanics of Laundering

Let's take a step back and discuss the different ways that money laundering can be set up and run. It can be as simple as moving money from one bank to the other, or it can be a multinational network of individuals and shell companies designed to make asset tracing as difficult as possible. A few of the different ways that money can be laundered are discussed here.

Resale of Non-traceable Assets

This sounds a lot more complex than it is. Say you have stolen 1000 iPods. You then turn to eBay or Craigslist and sell them off, 5 to 10 at a time, at a discounted rate; the only requirement is that you accept only cash. You have now effectively laundered the theft of the iPods into usable cash that would be extremely difficult to trace. This is most commonly employed on smaller scale situations in which a petty thief has stolen a few high-value items such as electronics or computers.

Use of Fake Identities

In the anti-money laundering circles, there exists a term "KYC," or Know Your Customer. What this means is the banks are required to validate the identity of the individual who owns the account. The reason for this is as follows: If an organization can find an institution that doesn't adhere to these standards, the organization can use false identities to create accounts in which to place the misbegotten money. Using these fake identities, the money can then be withdrawn in the form of cash, clean of the transactions prior. When investigators try to find the person who withdrew the money, the trail ends when they realize that the credentials used by the person opening the account were falsified and there is no way to find them.

Shell Companies

According to the Financial Crimes Enforcement Network (FinCEN), the term "shell company" refers to non-publicly traded corporations, limited liability companies (LLCs), and trusts that typically have no physical presence (other than a mailing address) and generate little to no independent economic value. These organizations are generally used to make the financial transactions look legitimate.

Suppose you have a shell company that purports to provide software services. The criminals will pay this company for services rendered, usually in transactions structured to avoid detection (this is known as "smurfing"). The shell company will then pay the ultimate recipient of the money, creating a buffer between the recipient and the crime conducted to gain the money. While most of these shell organizations are internationally based, there are domestic examples as well. For instance, shell companies and shell nonprofits are commonly used by terrorist organizations to get money to terrorist cells in western countries without the transactions that would alert counter-terrorism forces.

Foreign Banks

Foreign banks generally go hand in hand with shell companies. Some banks in various jurisdictions focus on account privacy above all else. These banks will fight tooth and nail against any kind of subpoena or request for account information. If a shell company deposits money into one of these banks and then disperses the money from the bank to individuals, it can be almost impossible using traditional financial asset tracing methods to determine where the money flowed.

The Role of Computer Forensics

Traditional money laundering investigations have focused on asset tracing by way of financial transaction records. Computer forensics offers a new dimension for these reviews. Now, investigators can look not only at the financial transactions, but also the activities of the criminals on a larger scale. Let's look at several ways that computer forensics can assist with money laundering investigations.

Finding Evidence of Non-traceable Assets

Popularity:	*8*
Simplicity:	*5*
Impact:	*10*
Risk Rating:	*8*

We have all heard the stories about criminals using eBay and Craigslist to launder stolen goods. What used to occur in back alleys and in flea markets now occurs online. The good news is that if you get access to the computers the criminals used, you can use computer forensic techniques to look for the ways in which this money was laundered.

Web Site Analysis

Using the web history forensics we have discussed throughout this book, you can reconstruct the transactions that were undertaken by the criminals. Once they are reconstructed, you can look for evidence of large numbers of transactions online. If they have placed hundreds of items on an online auction site, that may be a clue. In addition, look for other, non-obvious things. One case we worked involved the purchase of rare jewels and precious metals with the intent of laundering the money. If something catches your eye and seems out of place, run it by the financial investigators or counsel with which you are working.

Evidence of Shell Companies

Popularity:	8
Simplicity:	5
Impact:	10
Risk Rating:	8

The traditional picture of a shell company is an empty office sitting on an island in the Caribbean, with money hidden in an offshore bank. While such organizations still exist, increased globalization has changed the structure and location of these companies. Finding their names and locations is now harder than ever. However, by performing a forensic review of the individuals believed to be involved, you can look at a few things to help determine the names and structures of these companies.

Finding Shell Companies

In addition to traditional asset tracing, general user activities can serve as tip-offs to finding shell companies. Take a look at the e-mail of the individuals believed to be involved. We have experienced situations in which shell companies have been discovered because the person embezzling money sent the company information in an e-mail to an accomplice.

Laundering Accounting Ledgers

Popularity:	8
Simplicity:	5
Impact:	10
Risk Rating:	8

Organizations or individuals who engage in money laundering on a widespread basis will generally need some method for tracking the money as it flows through the laundering process. Just as with embezzlement and fraud, it is common for the criminals to maintain an alternate ledger that monitors this flow of money through the process.

Finding the Ledgers

Chapter 17 covered how to find these alternate ledgers. The thing to remember here is that the criminal may not anticipate the need to hide the ledger, as he may not believe he will get caught. Before going through the process of deep diving on any file that appears to be a ledger, you should do a basic search for any non-hidden financials. Also, remember to look at the web history as well. This can provide a tip-off that may denote that the criminal is actually using an online service to manage the money laundering, even something as simple as online banking.

Finding Fake Identities

Popularity:	8
Simplicity:	5
Impact:	10
Risk Rating:	8

I remember distinctly one of the first cases I ever worked had a laundering component. The individual gave fake Social Security numbers to his friends to use when withdrawing funds. They would then go on to forge identification documents to satisfy the banks, and they were off to the races. This matter was blown wide open when we found the forged ID documents and detailed e-mails describing the SSNs that the friends were supposed to use when they would transfer the money.

Things to Look For

The standard computer forensic techniques we have discussed throughout the book all come into play here. Look for communications that can denote mechanisms to carry out the fake IDs. For instance, as discussed above, we found false SSNs in e-mails addressed to friends, along with instructions on how to move money. While these days you'd be hard pressed to find that in an e-mail, such information may exist in cell phone records or chat logs. Also, look for evidence of document forgery. This will generally come in the form of modified scans of pictures or modifications of the types of documents required for obtaining a government ID.

CHAPTER 21

CONSUMER FRAUD

Fraud perpetrated against everyday individuals or consumers continues to rise in the United States and throughout the rest of the world. The digital age and the prolific use of e-mails and the Internet have both depersonalized fraudulent scams against consumers and significantly enhanced the ability of individuals to commit frauds on a mass scale, especially frauds perpetrated primarily through the Internet or e-mail. In the not too distant past, many frauds were committed by skilled con artists who would draw people into their confidence to get in on a "once-in-a-lifetime" opportunity. Today, however, con artists rely on the Internet and mass e-mails to reach a broad audience of individuals all over the world in an effort to get people to part with sensitive information about their lives, bank accounts, and other private information, as well as to part with their hard-earned dollars.

Most people have experienced, or at least heard of someone receiving, the now infamous e-mail from a Nigerian doctor, lawyer, or some other individual needing help to transfer money into the United States. For a limited amount of assistance, and a small amount of the consumer's money, the e-mail promises significant risk-free returns. Unfortunately, this was a scam. Countless Americans fall prey to such "too good to be true" type frauds each year.

If it sounds too good to be true, it probably is. That old saying rings true too often as consumers fall victim to various frauds every day. In reality, frauds are not limited to those gullible victims who fall for the Nigerian e-mail scam, but they can also affect many successful and sophisticated investors who fall for sophisticated and elaborate investment frauds that offer the opportunity to get into a unique venture with the potential for significant or "too good to be true" returns. Unfortunately, it can be easy to turn a blind eye to the details and the obvious risks of these proposed ventures.

As this book is written, Wall Street is embroiled in controversy surrounding the ongoing investigation of Bernard Madoff in what may turn out to be one of the largest investment frauds ever perpetrated. As facts unfold daily regarding the handling of billions of dollars of investments managed by Madoff and his investment company, it is becoming clearer that he may have perpetrated one of the largest Ponzi schemes ever, right under the nose of the SEC, other investment funds that provided capital to him for investment, and many successful, wealthy, and sophisticated individuals who had invested with him for years.

This story, on a smaller scale, is being repeated elsewhere around the country as investors come to grips with not only the realization that their investment portfolios have significantly decreased in value from the downturn in the global economy, but that in reality the funds have been squandered, lost, and/or used for other purposes without their knowledge as part of some ongoing investment fraud. If there is one lesson to be learned, it's that anyone can fall victim to consumer fraud.

While much of the focus of this book has been on evaluating the need for computer forensics skills and professionals from the corporate perspective, it is important to point out that frauds are also perpetrated against individuals. While consumer fraud in many cases affects individuals, sometimes the frauds encompass a broad range of consumers. While much computer forensics work focuses on corporate events and occurrences, it is not uncommon for computer forensics specialists to be retained to assist in matters involving both large and small frauds against consumers, especially where the frauds may involve a group of consumers and the potential loss of large sums of money.

WHAT IS CONSUMER FRAUD?

Consumers fall victim to countless types of frauds every year. Although the various fraudulent schemes have changed over time, they all involve the use of deception to separate consumers from their money. The most common, and widespread, of frauds these days involves identity theft, a rampant problem in the United States. Billions are spent each year to protect and secure personal information and data, including Social Security numbers, bank accounts, credit card information, and other personal information that can be used by skilled individuals to take out credit (such as loans, credit cards, and so on) using someone else's identity.

Consumer fraud is perpetrated by various means. Fraudulent operations typically make prolific use of the telephone and now e-mail and the Internet to perpetrate their schemes. Prior to the rapid expansion of the Internet, the telephone was the primary means of contact in consumer frauds. However, today contact through the Internet and e-mail has far surpassed the use of the telephone. In addition, where fraud perpetrated through the telephone required contacting consumers one-by-one, the use of mass e-mails and Internet sites has vastly increased the number of people exposed to the various types of consumer fraud. Each year, billions of dollars are estimated to be lost due to identity theft, fraudulent telemarketing, various scams through e-mail and the Internet, fraudulent business opportunities, and various forms of mortgage and investment fraud.

Consumer fraud is the primary domain of the Federal Trade Commission (FTC). The FTC's Bureau of Consumer Protection states, as one of its primary goals, "to protect consumers against unfair, deceptive, or fraudulent practices in the marketplace." The Bureau of Consumer Protection has the authority to conduct investigations, sue companies and individuals that violate the law, and develop rules aimed at protecting consumers. It also serves as a repository for information collected from complaints about identity theft and other forms of consumer fraud that may be prevalent across the country.

RAMIFICATIONS

The ramifications of consumer fraud are not unlike those of other frauds—they can cost consumers billions of dollars in losses, undermine the public trust in the safety and protections in the marketplace, and cost the government and corporations billions to ensure that adequate protections are in place to guard against the many unlawful practices targeted at consumers.

Impact to Consumers and the Public

In 2007, the FTC received close to a million complaints and disclosed that consumers had reported losses in excess of $1.2 billion. It is important to point out, however, that these were the "reported" losses to the FTC. Many, if not most, consumer frauds happen to individuals who have little to no recourse against the perpetrators. Once the fraud is discovered, little evidence typically exists to track down the suspected perpetrator other than a defunct telephone number or e-mail address.

Education and prevention remain key for numerous organizations to protect consumers from the many forms of consumer fraud. In addition to the FTC, organizations such as the Better Business Bureau, Internet Crime Center, National Consumers League, Social Security Administration, and the US Postal Inspection Service all work to educate consumers about the risks of consumer fraud and preventive steps that consumers can take to guard against falling victim to scams.

Regulatory Environment

As with any area of significant abuse or fraud, once it reaches a certain level or impacts a sufficient number of people, rules and laws are typically enacted in an effort to provide additional protections to consumers. The FTC is responsible for enforcing numerous laws aimed at protecting consumers from false advertising and telemarketing scams to an individual's right to receive a free credit report. However, various law enforcement and regulatory agencies have similar focus in their respective areas. In addition, as concerns unfold regarding the Madoff investment fraud and others like it, the SEC may implement additional rules to provide enhanced protections to individuals and their investments through various types of private investment management companies.

Investigations and Litigation

As described, many consumer frauds go unreported. People quickly realize after they've parted with their money and fail to receive anything in return that they may have been had. All too often, they have little recourse against the suspected perpetrators as the true identity of the perpetrators is likely not known. Professional con and scam artists are experts at putting people at ease and convincing them of the veracity of their product offering, investment opportunity, or other ruse underlying the fraudulent scheme. In addition, it is not difficult these days with the help of specialized software to produce professional-looking documents, mailers, forms, and Internet sites that further compel potential victims to inquire about the "too good to be true" opportunity. Unfortunately, once payment has been made, most victims have little chance of getting it back.

While most consumer frauds typically involve amounts of under $100, certain types of fraud (mainly investment and mortgage fraud) can cost consumers, as well as other parties impacted by the frauds, significantly more. Many victims may have lost millions of dollars. When frauds of this nature are exposed, they quickly garner the attention of investigative and regulatory agencies that will engage to expose the fraud, recover funds for those damaged, and punish the parties responsible. As with various types of corporate fraud discussed, the agencies may include the FBI, Department of Justice, SEC, US Attorneys, and others, and may lead to various civil lawsuits by the injured parties. When investigations and lawsuits of this nature occur, the computer forensics specialist plays a significant role in uncovering the specifics of the fraudulent scheme, identifying the use and potential whereabouts of the money received during the scheme, and developing evidence to support the actions of various individuals and entities in perpetrating the scheme.

TYPES OF CONSUMER FRAUD

There are many types of consumer fraud, and the types of fraud are constantly changing. Consumer fraud varies in size and the scope of the people affected. The more significant consumer frauds involve the theft of an individual's identity, access to some form of credit or monetary accounts, and frauds involving the investment process and the mortgage loan origination and underwriting process. In this chapter, we focus on three areas of consumer fraud that have been, and continue to be, more prevalent in today's business environment: identity theft, investment fraud, and mortgage fraud.

Identity Theft

Popularity:	10
Simplicity:	9
Impact:	10
Risk Rating:	10

Identity theft has become the most widespread and prevalent form of consumer fraud in recent years. The schemes used to victimize consumers are ever-changing. Most forms of identity theft involve the theft of credit card data, while others involve the unauthorized receipt of utilities or other services in someone else's name. Others still may involve someone receiving loans or other forms of monetary gain using someone else's identity. However, while identity theft is widespread, the frauds are typically concentrated on one individual at a time and fairly limited to certain transactions. While identity theft typically doesn't rise to the level at which an individual's savings are completely wiped out, they can be costly to consumers in terms of monetary losses and damage to the individual's credit rating, which often can be difficult and time-consuming to correct.

What to Understand

When identity theft is suspected, you must first determine the potential sources of the stolen information. Identity theft often results not from the unauthorized access to private financial and other information resident on personal computers or computer networks and databases, but from the interception of credit card offers or other information in snail mail. Many schemes rely on using personal information gleaned from stolen or improperly discarded personal information that is later used to gain access to credit cards, bank accounts, or other services that provide value to the perpetrator at the potential cost of the consumer. In these instances, computer forensics may have only a limited role, if any. However, it is not uncommon for the source of the illicitly obtained information to be computer based, which may require an evaluation of how access to the information in question was achieved.

Identity theft can also begin with the theft of customer data, as described in Chapter 16. As with customer data, when identity theft is confirmed or even suspected, standard protocols are recommended for identifying, reviewing, and evaluating personal consumer information to determine whether any of the information has been put at risk, and if so, to determine how the information was accessed and by whom. As with the potential theft of information in electronic format, what to look for will depend on the type and format of information suspected to have been stolen and how that information was maintained and secured.

Important information in relation to a person's "identity" (such as name, address, date of birth, Social Security number, driver's license number, bank account numbers, and so on) are maintained by numerous organizations with which an individual may have dealings over the years. In addition to an individual's employer, banks, hospitals, insurance agencies, universities, and even the local video rental establishment may keep records unique to a person's identity. In reality, the source of the theft of an individual's identity may not be easily determinable and may have resulted from something as simple as someone gaining access to an individual's Social Security number and receiving a credit card in that person's name. So much information about an individual's identity is dispersed throughout multiple organizations and entities that trying to source the potential theft may be a fruitless task. However, the information stolen may be more acute, such as specific access to bank and/or investment accounts.

When specific information is suspected to have been stolen, and the potential sources of that information are reasonably narrow in scope, you need to understand what security procedures exist to protect the information and how that protection may have been circumvented to evaluate the relative risk of a perpetrator gaining access to the information and to narrow the potential source of the theft. As a general preventive measure, users should be cautious when providing personal information to unsecure Internet and bill pay sites, in maintaining important passwords and account access information in unsecure formats and locations, and in responding to requests for personal information relative to various applications to join Internet sites, clubs, or other types of services (such as video rental stores).

Unfortunately, the list of potential suspects and access points for identity theft may be significantly greater than you might realize. In reality, finding the source of the identity theft and tracing it to a potential suspect may be relatively impossible. Still, where information is significantly specific to one account or unique type of information, the exercise may be warranted, if only to understand what precautions and preventive measures should be put in place to avoid subsequent occurrences. Ultimately, preventing identity theft through the practice of safe and secure management of both hard-copy and electronic personal information is the best bet, as well as periodic monitoring of one's credit report to identify suspicious credit transactions and stop identity theft before the damage becomes too great.

What to Look For

What to look for depends on the circumstances surrounding the personal information in question. However, several areas of information are typical sources of identity theft that warrant more careful inspection.

Detecting Spam Attacks

Popularity:	8
Simplicity:	7
Impact:	8
Risk Rating:	8

Take a look at a victim's inbox. Then look at the number of spam e-mails that are in the junk mail folders. Think about how you could best determine which of those hundreds of e-mails was accessed by the victim when their identity was stolen. Finding out whether a spam message was the vector of attack could be an extremely difficult task due to the shear volume you must deal with.

How to Find the Spam Message

Your best bet is to start elsewhere and see if you can link it back to an e-mail, but if your only lead is an e-mail, following are some tips on what to look for.

How Many People Were Involved?   If more than one person was the victim of identity theft and it is believed that the method used was a spam message, look for commonalities between the users. We are starting to see a lot more custom-crafted and targeted messages in these types of crimes. It is not uncommon for an entire organization to receive the same malicious e-mail in hopes that a few people will believe that it is pertinent to their business operations and follow through. If multiple people have been compromised in the same fashion and have uploaded to the same server around the same time, chances are they were all victims. Identifying the general timeframe can help as well. Use near–de-duplication technologies and tools such as Equivio or Trident to assist with this process. While it will take some time to get to a single e-mail using this methodology, it can at least give you a place to start.

What Did the User Look At?   Another thing that can help in identifying a specific spam message is to look at what e-mails the user opened and read. This can significantly reduce the number of e-mails that you have to review. Depending on what e-mail client the individual used, this can be dealt with in several different ways. If the e-mail was received using a tool such as Outlook, look in the message store metadata for the is_read flag. This flag is used by the tool to identify which e-mails should be marked as unread to assist the user. From a forensics standpoint, you can use this flag to help determine what e-mails the user opened and read. If the e-mail was believed to come in via webmail, perform the standard webmail retrieval and review the cache for the likely culprit.

Interview the Victim   This isn't exactly a technical solution, but in these types of situations it can be extremely helpful. If you know the general timeframe when the theft occurred, talk to the victim about what she read and accessed during that time period. Ask general questions like "Did anything jump out at you as being off?" or "Do you remember any of your services contacting you about a bill around those days?" You'd be amazed how much the right question can replace hours and hours of forensic analysis.

Phishing Web Sites

Popularity:	10
Simplicity:	8
Impact:	9
Risk Rating:	9

Phishing is the act of getting an individual to give up personal information under the premise that it is needed for some official reason (such as a request supposedly from a bank asking for a person's SSN). Generally, the net result of a spam e-mail is directing the user to a phishing Web site. These sites are designed to appear as though they were affiliated with a large financial institution or utility company, and they require some form of payment. The user thinks she is paying a PayPal or cable bill and dutifully enters private information into an online form. Unfortunately, the information isn't going where it is represented to be going. In fact, it's going to a hacker Web site located in Eastern Europe or China, for bundling and selling on the black market. These phishing Web sites can be extremely difficult to detect after the fact due to their perceived similarity to the sites they purport to be affiliated with. The user may not even realize she went to a malicious site.

Detecting and Finding Phishing Access

The good news for the forensic examiner is that phishing generally takes place over the Web and as such, you can use the standard Web site review process to find the phishing sites. Perform the standard history and cache extraction, just as with any other web activity review.

Looking at the Internet History and Cache   From here, you can start looking for URLs that are designed to look as though they came from a popular site but in fact reside on a third-party site. For instance, it is not uncommon to see URLs that look similar to this:

http://80.84.121.35/.www.eBay.com/. This URL is clearly designed to look like a legitimate eBay site, when in fact it leads to a Web site located at 80.84.121.35. As shown in Figure 21-1, the page is designed to look like the eBay login page. The unsuspecting user then enters her username and password for her eBay account and the criminals enter the information into a database that they will later use to conduct auction fraud.

Understanding this process and what to look for is vital when you're performing a web activity review looking for phishing sites. Be aware that the URL is going to be intentionally designed to look like something it isn't. In addition, an incredible amount of resources are out there to help you identify phishing sites. One such resource, www .phishtank.com, actually keeps a list of all known or suspected phishing sites on the Net. If you run across a suspicious site in your review that is no longer in operation, PhishTank offers search capabilities that let you determine whether the site had been identified as a phishing Web site.

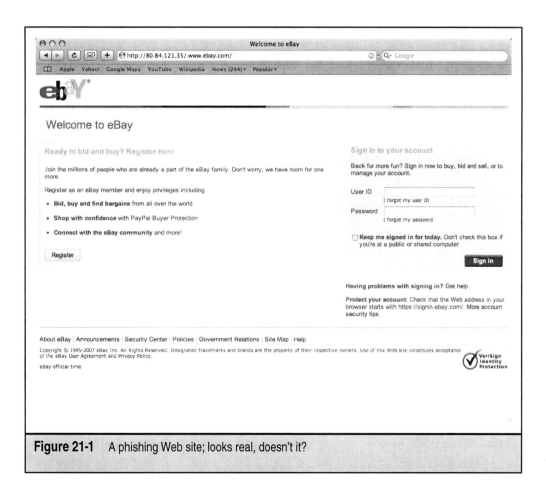

Figure 21-1   A phishing Web site; looks real, doesn't it?

Looking at the Network Logs   If you are dealing with an organization that has centralized logging of web traffic, these logs can be a real asset in these types of investigations. If you find a site through the analysis of the web history on a single computer, you can use the central logs to determine whether anyone else visited the same Web site and may have fallen victim to the same type of crime. Alternatively, if you can't find anything in the web history but you believe phishing occurred, use the logs to find the malicious site. Compile a list of all sites visited during the suspected time period and compare them to a phishing black list to see what bubbles up. These logs can also tell you how much interaction the victim had with the site, as it is common for these proxies to log the data size and duration of the interactions.

Match Up the Timeline with E-mails   One thing that can be very helpful in these types of reviews is to correlate data between the e-mails and the web history. If you see that a spam e-mail purporting to come from eBay was read on a certain day, look for web traffic around that time to see if any Web sites could have been accessed from that e-mail. Look at the URLs contained in the e-mail to get at least a starting point for the web history review.

Going the other direction can also be helpful. Study the suspicious URL metadata and try to determine what caused the user to access the site. Do you notice similarities among e-mails that were opened around that time? If so, did anyone else in the organization receive the same e-mail and visit the same site? Put together a timeline of activity not only on the user's computer, but across the entire organization.

Identity Theft Malware

Popularity:	8
Simplicity:	6
Impact:	6
Risk Rating:	7

We discussed malware at length in Chapter 20, but it bears a bit more discussion in the specific context of identity theft. Malware is placed on a machine with the explicit purpose of stealing personal information and uploading it to a central server. While we discussed a couple of entry vectors in Chapter 20, some others are worthy of your attention in the context of identity theft. We have encountered manually installed malware on public machines (in coffee shops, copy stores, libraries, and so on) to steal people's passwords and other personal information. This is a much different infection vector than the traditional "visiting a shady Web site" or "clicking on the wrong link" and requires some additional techniques.

Finding the Source of Manually Installed Malware

If you are tasked with finding how a public terminal was infected, you should start by asking several preliminary questions:

- *Did the machine have Internet access?* If it didn't, then you narrow down what you have to look at initially. If it did, your first step is to perform a traditional malware analysis, like that discussed in Chapter 20.

- *Who had access to the physical box?* Depending on how the terminal was set up, the public may or may not have been able to plug USB drives or other external storage devices into it. If the public had access, you need to start by looking at the records of external device usage. If not, look to the network and Internet to see if a device could have been attached from another computer or over the Internet.

- *Where was the data going?* Depending on the malware, the data may have been uploaded onto the Internet, or it could have been stored on the computer, for the hacker to pick up at a later point in time.

Locally Installed Malware   If you suspect the malware did come from a USB drive, you can take a few additional steps to close the loop on the malware analysis. Perform the steps discussed in Chapter 20 to find out when the malware was installed. Then use the USB drive techniques discussed throughout the book to see what drives were plugged into the computer when the malware was installed. This can be extremely important in these matters, as the USB drive can be used to get information off the system as well. (In one case, a hacker periodically returned to the computers and downloaded stolen information from the computer to a thumb drive and then reset the data repository on the compromised computer.)

If you have performed the standard network analysis and it doesn't appear that the malware is transmitting information out to an external server, or the computer isn't connected to the Internet in that way, look for the repeated accesses by way of thumb drive or CD-ROM. The information has to be getting off the computer in some form or fashion; otherwise the malware is all for naught.

 ## Theft of Personal Records by an Insider

Popularity:	5
Simplicity:	9
Impact:	10
Risk Rating:	8

We covered how to identity theft of customer data in Chapter 16, and those principles apply here as well. The data is usually stored in some type of a centralized location, such as a database, mainframe, or customer relationship management (CRM) system where it can be managed uniformly. The one twist between IP theft and identity theft is that, in our experience, there is more of a remote access component in insider identity theft. This can change the way you conduct your investigation, as you will want to check a few extra nooks and crannies in addition to the standard places we discuss in Chapter 16.

Detecting Remote Transfer of Personal Data

In addition to looking for the standard methods of getting data off a computer used in IP theft, you should look for remote connections into the databases or data repositories. For instance, if the data is stored in an SQL server, look at the access and firewall logs to see if any long-duration connections to the database were made. Also, since the database stores personal information, regulations may mandate that logging and auditing are kept at a higher level than for general databases. Consult with counsel about this and work with them to determine what additional audit logs may exist that can help you find the stolen information.

Investment Fraud

Popularity:	7
Simplicity:	5
Impact:	10
Risk Rating:	7

While identity theft is the most prevalent form of consumer fraud, investment fraud accounts for the most significant amount of dollar losses to consumers. Individuals invest in all types of offerings including traditional investments in stocks, bonds, CDs, and other investment products, as well as nontraditional investments in such things as rare stamps, coins, precious metals, and art. Investments in publicly traded stocks and bonds, as well as private offerings of certain other types of investments, fall under regulation by various entities including the SEC, the Commodities Futures Trading Commission, state securities regulators, and various aspects of the stock exchanges in which the respective security or commodity may be traded. However, investments in other more nontraditional types of investments may not be regulated to any significant degree. Regardless of the many safeguards and regulations in place, investment fraud appears to cover the entire spectrum of investment types and vehicles.

Along with the victims of telemarketing fraud and other Internet and e-mail scams, investors often fall victim to investment opportunities that seem too good to pass up. A recurring theme in many of the investment scams exposed today, especially those that have been ongoing for some time, is that each promised and reported above-market returns over a long period of time.

Most investment frauds involve some legitimate business front or purpose and the purchase of an existing security or putting funds into an existing investment fund. The fraud comes in how the money is actually used versus what is believed by the investor.

Common investment frauds involve either pyramid or Ponzi schemes, or so-called "pump-and-dump" schemes. In pyramid schemes, the investment in a security or through an investment firm promises a high-rate of return, where such returns do not exist or are more highly improbable than promised. The scheme is sustained either through the reporting of fictitious returns to investors or through the use of money from new investors to pay off existing investors. The scheme was made famous by Charles Ponzi in the 1920s; he became a millionaire overnight by offering a high rate of return for an investment that was essentially a sham. Pump-and-dump schemes involve the manipulation of the stock price of a security through false information that entices investors to buy the stock, driving up the price, only to have it falter after the truth is revealed. By that time, the perpetrators of the fraud have long cashed out their stock at the higher price and typically a hefty profit.

What to Understand

As investment fraud can take many forms, it is important that you understand the nature of the alleged scheme, or at least the nature of the hypothesized scheme. Investigating investment fraud in many respects is about following the actual trail of money and comparing it to the represented trail reported to investors. Often the fraud involved deception between what investors are being told about the use of their funds and how that money is actually being used. The main forms of investment fraud involve the misuse of invested funds.

You should understand the details around the proposed security or investment vehicle. What was promised? What type of investment or investment vehicle is involved (stocks, bonds, commodities, or other nontraditional investments)? What was the described structure of the investment (direct purchase and ownership, purchase through another investment entity, purchase through a fund)? What were terms and conditions of the initial investment and its return or redemption of proceeds from the investment? What documentation was provided to support the initial investment, as well as periodic reporting (monthly, quarterly, annually) on the investment's performance? What documentation should exist with the responsible regulatory authority to support the investment made, as well as legality of the investment security or vehicle? Answers to these types of questions typically provide initial guidance on what to look for, which is discussed next.

What to Look For

Where you start looking depends on the answers to the preceding questions. However, we've found that investment frauds typically require that we look for information in several general areas. As with any fraud, identifying the deception in investment fraud is the key to exposing the fraud and gathering evidence against those suspected of the wrongdoing. As described, the typical deception in investment fraud is the misrepresentation of how an investor's investment is being used, as well as the promised return on that investment. To that effect, investment frauds typically involve the use of fraudulent monthly, quarterly, and annual performance reports sent to investors.

In addition, investment frauds may also involve the fraudulent reporting of fictitious stock or other security trades to investors, as well as false or fictitious regulatory filings.

In addition, because of the complexity of investment frauds, the number of potential investors involved, as well as the amount of money that may be involved, successfully sustaining an investment fraud may likely entail a significant amount of effort and ability to track effectively what is being fraudulently reported from one period to the next. In other words, those perpetrating investment frauds have to keep track of the fraud, especially where the investment fraud may be embedded into an otherwise legitimate and ongoing business. For a fraud to be successful, there often needs to be a clear distinction to the perpetrators between what's real and what's not.

The third general area involves following the money. When investor funds are suspected of not being used or determined not to be used as represented, the question quickly turns to Where is the money? Sometimes that answer may not be concealed as the success of an investment fraud typically revolves around the ability to keep the deception going, not how the money is actually being used. However, in other circumstances the money may be off-book or taken off-book from an otherwise legitimate business, in which case identifying the location of financial records, bank accounts, wire transfers, and the like may require significant investigative skills and undertakings.

With respect to the general areas described so far, we have used computer forensics in the investigation of investment frauds in the following ways.

Finding the Second Set of Books

Popularity:	6
Simplicity:	9
Impact:	8
Risk Rating:	8

As discussed earlier, it's not uncommon for the individuals perpetrating the fraud to run a second set of books that keep track of everything they are doing. One of the vital roles that computer forensics plays in this type of investigation is assisting with the identification and location of the alternate ledgers, be they Excel spreadsheets, QuickBooks files, Act! Databases, or other forms. The fundamentals of computer forensics still apply.

Where to Look for These Records

We discussed in Chapter 18 where to look for alternate ledgers and second sets of books. This type of fraud is a bit different because it is institutional, and the perpetrators may not feel the need to hide the books in the same way as a single employee who is embezzling money. Let's review that list with some pointers specific to this type of fraud.

Changing a Filename This is the most simple example. Instead of calling the ledger mysecondsetofbooks.xls, the individual renames the file pinkbunnies.jpg, with the hopes that whoever may be looking for the financials will pass right by this file, thinking it's a picture of bunnies. You can use a file signature analysis to combat this tactic. One quick and easy way to do this is with the file command on your UNIX flavor of choice (or cygwin). However, the granularity of what types of files it can detect and differentiate leaves a bit to be desired. If you have access to a commercial forensics tool such as EnCase, you can use the file signature facilities in the software to perform this analysis quickly and easily.

Encrypting a File   Many ledgers are hidden using encryption. The individual knows the file is bad, and if the information inside the file gets out she will be in a lot of trouble, so she take steps to encrypt it. What method she actually uses varies based on the file type and the complexity of the user. Most people will just use the password protection features of the software used to create the file (for instance, applying a password to an Excel spreadsheet) and let that be it. Others may use more advanced forensic techniques. Utilizing a tool such as Access Data's PRTK can be crucial in not only cracking the password but also the identification of what type of scheme was used to encrypt it.

External Media   The use of some type of secured thumb drive, while less common in this case than in employee embezzlement, can still provide relevant results. We have described in detail in other chapters how to identify that thumb drives were used and how to locate what files may have been stored on them. Performing this same analysis—but this time with a focus on looking for accounting-related files in the link files, temp files, and registry keys—can be an extremely fruitful path of investigation. It can also help you determine who was involved, as it is common for these thumb drives to be passed around between the conspirators.

File Type Searches   Because the fraud in these matters is generally institutional, the answer may be right in front of your face. They may not hide the second set of books because they think there's no reason to do so. It is their computers and their networks, and they know what goes in and comes out. As such, you shouldn't neglect to perform simple searches across the user shares and computers to see what comes back with respect to financial databases.

Falsification of Official Documents

Popularity:	6
Simplicity:	9
Impact:	8
Risk Rating:	**8**

Same story, second verse. Just as with other types of corporate fraud, corporate officers often forge documents such as quarterly or annual statements to make them look as though everything is on the up and up. Computer forensics can assist you in answering two questions: What are they using to create these falsified documents? How are they deriving the numbers to put into them?

Finding Falsified Documents

Because these documents are generally publicly distributed, you have the advantage of knowing exactly what they contain. You can put together a keyword list that, when run across the universe of documents, should bubble up the majority of the falsified documents. Once you have a list, you can look for a few things from a forensics standpoint that can advance the investigation.

Authorship History   As discussed in Chapter 12, office documents can be a treasure trove of metadata information. Use this information to determine who developed these records and talk to them. Find out what process they used to create the documents and how they arrived at the numbers. Ask about approval processes and who saw the document before it went out. Also look at the revision history, and if the document had been e-mailed to anyone, and talk to those individuals as well.

Data Sources   If the document links to other files (such as an Excel spreadsheet that has database input, for example), run that link to ground. See exactly where it is connecting to and what information is contained within the data source. Look for other similarly structured data sources that may contain the true set of books.

Other Disk Activity Around the Modified Times   Look at the MAC times for the files in question, and use those times to see and correlate other activities on the computer. Look for programs that were run in the User Assist, determine whether thumb drives were connected or if LNK files show other documents or databases being accessed at the same time. These documents were not created in a vacuum. Just like legitimate financial records, these documents generally have some source and inputs. By accurately mapping out how these documents are created, you can help complete the picture of how the fraud occurred and what other important data sources may be out there.

Mortgage Fraud

Popularity:	8
Simplicity:	6
Impact:	10
Risk Rating:	8

The housing and mortgage banking business is a trillion dollar industry in the United States, but it is also big business for perpetrators of mortgage fraud. In 2008, the FBI estimated that annual losses due to mortgage fraud in the United States exceeded $4 billion. With more than a decade-long housing boom in the United States fostered by continued economic expansion, rising home values, low mortgage rates, and weakening underwriting standards, among other factors, mortgage fraud has become much more prevalent and pervasive in recent years. Just how much more did not become evident until the beginning of the melt-down in the subprime mortgage markets in 2007 and the ensuing financial crisis and economic recession in the United States and around the world. With heightened scrutiny on so-called subprime mortgages (mortgages taken by borrowers with lower credit ratings than "prime" borrowers) in recent years, regulators, politicians, the media, and the general public became more keenly aware of the various types and pervasiveness of mortgage fraud in the mortgage lending arena.

The FBI defines mortgage fraud as the "material misstatement, misrepresentation, or omission relied upon by an underwriter or lender to fund, purchase, or insure a loan." As with all frauds, mortgage fraud is founded upon deception. Mortgage fraud encompasses a broad range of frauds by individuals and entities to profit from the overall mortgage industry. Some frauds are perpetrated by consumers against lending institutions, while others are targeted at consumers in addition to the lending institutions. In the latter, both parties typically suffer.

Given the size of the US mortgage market and the destabilizing effects resulting from unsound lending practices and efforts to undermine the mortgage financing system, mortgage fraud is a chief concern for the federal government and an acute focus of the FBI. The FBI describes mortgage fraud in two main categories: fraud for housing and fraud for profit. Fraud for housing is typically perpetrated by consumers on lenders and financial institutions where the fraud is in the misrepresentation of material information typically in relation to loan eligibility requirements (such as income, employment, and so on) so that the consumer can qualify for a loan to purchase or refinance a home. While pervasive, especially given the deteriorating underwriting standards over the years, fraud for housing accounts for a small minority of the overall losses experienced each year.

Fraud for profit schemes typically involve industry insiders who take advantage of the consumer and the lenders, as well as weaknesses in underwriting and the overall loan process. The FBI estimates that more than 80 percent of all reported losses resulting from mortgage fraud involve collaboration or collusion among industry insiders (such as real estate agents, mortgage brokers, loan officers, appraisers, loan underwriters, and so on). Fraud for profit schemes include so-called equity skimming schemes and property flipping, among numerous others, and also may involve identity theft (such as the use of someone else's identity to secure a mortgage loans). Often these schemes involve the fraudulent receipt of proceeds from the sale of a home (funded through a lender and secured by a mortgage) where the perpetrators of the fraud either skim a large amount of proceeds from an overinflated loan value or flat out have no intention of repaying the loan.

What to Understand

Mortgage frauds can range from simple misrepresentations of information on a loan application to complex schemes involving multiple parties collaborating to steal from lenders, as well as from consumers. Mortgage fraud can occur at almost every point in the process of a mortgage loan, from the initial sales listing to a loan origination and closing. The first point to understand is at what point in the process the mortgage fraud is suspected to have occurred and what relevant parties were involved at that stage of the process.

In fraud for profit schemes, the seller is often the primary perpetrator of mortgage fraud. A seller, with assistance from others, may be able to orchestrate a higher appraised value for a property than warranted, may be able to steer a prospective buyer to a loan officer willing to overlook deficiencies in a borrower's overall loan application and qualifications as a buyer, or may make other arrangements with borrowers to bypass more standard and stringent underwriting criteria. Sellers may also be able to manipulate the entire lending process by fronting straw buyers and falsifying information in each step of the process. Sellers in this situation often have help from someone "inside" the process, including real estate brokers, appraisers, loan officers, or underwriters friendly to the seller. In other situations, sellers sometimes recruit unsuspecting buyers to participate in their schemes with the promise of quick-and-easy returns through acquiring and flipping real estate. However, these unsuspecting investors are often left holding an overvalued property with an extensive mortgage that the investor neither intends to live in nor can afford.

Your next step is to understand what documentation or information in the loan process may be misrepresented (such as overstated property values, overstated borrower income, and so on). Fraud for housing schemes typically involve a misrepresentation or omission with regard to some part of the loan application—namely, a borrower's qualifications. Common borrower misrepresentations include false claims of their personal income, liabilities, or assets to make them appear more creditworthy.

Regardless of the mortgage fraud scheme, the misrepresentations, omissions, or other deception likely occur in one of several areas, including the borrower's qualifications to receive the loan, the value of the property in question, or the underlying credit score and credit-worthiness of the borrower. Most mortgage fraud schemes involve the manipulation of one or more of these processes, often with the assistance of sellers, appraisers, loan officers, and others.

What to Look For

Understanding in what part of the loan process the mortgage fraud may have occurred, who the suspected perpetrator is, and whether the perpetrator may have had, or would necessarily had to have had assistance from insiders, will determine what you look for in investigating the fraud. You'll often focus on identifying altered documents, as well as identifying collusion with insiders through communications, payments (such as kickbacks), or other conflicts of interest.

As with other types of fraud, attempts may have been made to conceal the existence of altered documents or inappropriate relationships, and this is where computer forensics often plays a substantive role. Other examples of specific areas that may yield results in an investigation of mortgage fraud include the following.

Check/Bank Statement Forgery

Popularity:	*6*
Simplicity:	*9*
Impact:	*8*
Risk Rating:	*8*

With the advent of "low doc loans," demonstrating proof of income was significantly reduced. Where you once had to fill out books' worth of forms relating to your assets, you now just needed a check stub and a printed bank statement. We have found in multiple investigations that the loan officer, due to job quotas and other pressures, decided to scan in these documents and change the numbers around to ensure that the person applying for the loan would, in fact, get approved.

Detecting Proof of Income Forgery

Follow the paper. Find out how the paper got into the computer and figure out how it got out. If the forgery involved a check stub, generally the stub would be scanned in and modified using a photo-manipulation tool such as Photoshop to bump up the claimed salary. This modified scan would then be printed out with the modified numbers and sent in as proof of income. Similarly, look for the same type of activity for any bank statements. Some have even gone so far as to type up completely forged letters from the employer stating the title and salary of the individual to justify the modified salary on the pay stub. The key is to look for the repository of these types of documents, or at the very least the process by which they were modified. Look at the User Assist logs and see what types of applications are clustered together (scan, modify, print, and so on) and when and how often they were run. If you have reason to believe that entire letters were forged, set up a keyword search using the individual's name, employer, and any other types of unique identifiers and run them in the unallocated space to see what comes up.

Also, since check forges will generally involve images, think about performing a data carving on the unallocated space and pagefile to see if any images remain on the system.

Communications Chatter

Popularity:	*10*
Simplicity:	*8*
Impact:	*7*
Risk Rating:	*8*

Rarely does this type of fraud occur in a vacuum, as much as those being investigated would like you to believe it does. As such, examining the communications among loan officers can provide vital insights into how these frauds may have been perpetrated and just how much formality went into them. While e-mail and chat searches have been discussed in the earlier parts of the book, several aspects of these types of investigations can help you speed up the process and better identify what you need to find.

 ## What Communications to Look For

In our experience, those committing fraud within an institution that permits it will usually ask for advice as to how to set up the fraud or with case specific issues. (For instance, Mr. Clark makes X number of dollars, but it takes Y to get the house. What's the best way to manipulate the documents so that Mr. Clark appears to make I?) In addition, the first thing you will hear when you walk in the door to perform one of these types of reviews is that a rogue agent was doing stuff on his own to keep his job. This is something that you will need to run down quickly, as it can affect the overall scope of the investigation.

Understand the timeframes in which these activities were supposedly occurring—not only timeframes in terms of years, but timeframes in terms of when the negotiations occurred and where it was most likely that these communications took place. Understanding the timeframe will help you focus on the pertinent e-mails. The suspect may think that doing it over the phone or using voicemail ensures that it's not permanent. Also, some of the more "churn-and-burn" mortgage houses may have used call centers. If so, they probably had the phone calls of the officers recorded just as with any other type of call center. You saw this phenomenon come to light with the investigation of Enron. The company recorded activity on the trading floor phones, and several of the conversations were used in the criminal trials to show the depths of the fraud.

Focus intently on the communications with an eye toward who else was involved. A single e-mail or chat log can change the complexion of the investigation.

 ## Data Destruction

Popularity:	8
Simplicity:	6
Impact:	6
Risk Rating:	7

Throwing a single loan officer under the bus seems to go hand in hand with data destruction in these investigations. While it's rare to find an institutional mandate to destroy data, we have found that sometimes when players get word that a subpoena is coming their way, they will take steps to "destroy" what they believe to be evidence that may incriminate them. Of course, whether it is actually destroyed is left up to the forensic investigator to decide. We have talked extensively throughout the book about how to detect data wiping and data destruction, but a few points unique to mortgage fraud are worth mentioning.

Data Destruction in Mortgage Cases

The key here is not to look for destruction only by those who are accused of the fraud, but also those who associate with the suspects—such as supervisors. Check out these people to see if any surreptitious activities occurred around the same time as reports were being investigated. Also, if data destruction is found, pay close heed to what data was destroyed. In one of our investigations, the e-mails themselves were destroyed, but we were able to figure out by looking at residual metadata who the e-mails were to and what were the subject lines and times. That gave us two opportunities: we were allowed to retrieve those e-mails from the other inboxes; and, secondly and most important, we were able to ask the question of why the suspect was deleting those particular e-mails from those particular individuals, especially when it was supposedly a one-man "rogue" operation.

TYING IT TOGETHER

Consumer fraud is a pervasive and growing problem in the United States. With billions of dollars in fraud losses every year, various federal and law enforcement agencies have made combating consumer fraud a major initiative. However, with the ever-increasing use of e-mail and the Internet to commit fraud, as well as the complexity of the frauds being perpetrated and the ease by which documents can be altered or falsified, law enforcement and regulatory agencies have their work cut out for them. Increased investigative efforts have been underway for quite some time, as have efforts to broaden and strengthen the scope of applicable laws and regulations and the penalties for violating those laws.

As consumer fraud has become more sophisticated, so have the efforts to track, investigate, and uncover those frauds. The existing arsenal of computer forensics tools combined with skilled investigative techniques mean that many of these frauds can be uncovered and evidence identified to bring them to a halt and hold the guilty parties accountable for their actions. While frauds may become more complex and sophisticated, one fundamental truth remains: evidence always exists, and whether it's in falsified information and documents or in separate sets of books and records, evidence is typically concealed in some way. It is the objective of skilled computer forensics specialists to assist in lifting the veil of that concealment.

APPENDIX

SEARCHING TECHNIQUES

L earning effective search techniques is one of the single most important things you can do as a forensic investigator. As anyone who has conducted an investigation on a large dataset can tell you, if you choose the wrong search criterion, you will either completely miss the data you are looking for or you will spend hours, if not days, searching through masses of false positives. To search effectively, you must consider not only the key phrases that you are looking for, but also the context in which they may be stored in the document. To search for the context as well as the keywords, you will have to understand something more than how to perform simple keyword searches.

REGULAR EXPRESSIONS

The easiest and quickest way to search effectively is by using regular expressions (regex). Most of the forensics tools available today support some subset of the regular expressions language. The most famous regex may be the old DOS holdover, *.*.. To translate loosely, this means any amount and kind of characters, a period, and then any amount and kind of characters after the period.

Theory and History

If theory isn't your thing, skip this section. Regular expressions were developed by an American mathematician named Stephen Kleene. They were created as a notation for an algebra that described what he called "the algebra of regular sets." This was later placed into what became known as the Chomsky hierarchy of languages, which is a formal linguistics model that places every grammar from the regular expression language to the English language into a hierarchy. This hierarchy can then be used to tell how easy or how difficult it is to parse that grammar. Regular expressions are some of the easiest to parse, with the English language being one of the most difficult.

The Building Blocks

Before we start constructing regular expressions to see how powerful they are, let's look at some of the common operators that will be the fundamental building blocks.

Symbol	Meaning
?	Matches any character zero or one time.
*	Matches a preceding regular expression zero or more times; also known as the Kleene star.
+	Matches the preceding regular expression one or more times.
{number}	Matches the preceding regular expression *number* of times.
. (period)	Matches any character one time.
^	Matches the start of a string; also used in some languages for negation.

Symbol	Meaning
$	Matches the end of a string.
[ ]	Used to indicate a set; for instance, [0,1] matches all 0's or 1's.
[^]	Used to indicate an exclusive set; for instance, [^0-1] will match everything except for 0's or 1's.
"\"	Used to escape special characters.
|	The regex equivalent of a logical or; A|B matches either A or B.
(...)	Matches whatever is inside the parentheses.

Constructing Regular Expressions

The following regex matches numbers in the format of currency ($2.50, for example). This shows that regular expressions can get messy and can become completely unreadable.

```
\\$[1-9][0-9]*(\\.[0-9]{2})?|\\$0?\\.[0-9][0-9]
```

Let's work with the symbols listed in the preceding table to see how to create effective searching tools. The utility that will be used throughout this appendix is called *grep*, the open source regex processor. It is extremely powerful and uses the same syntax used in Perl and other scripting languages.

Simple Text Matching

Let's start by doing a simple keyword search. If, for instance, we want to search for all HTML files, we would use the following:

```
\.html
```

Note the use of the \ operator to escape out the period (.), since the period itself is an operator. This works well enough for files ending in .html; however, some HTML files have the extension .htm as well as .html, so we want to be able to search for both. In this case, we want to use the | operator, so this becomes

```
\.html | \.htm
```

This will give us all the files ending in either .html or .htm. Now, to extend this regex a bit, let's match only the files that are either index.htm or index.html. Two different regular expressions will match this:

```
index\.html | index\.htm
```

or

```
index\.(html|htm)
```

While the first example may be a bit easier to read, the second regex is less prone to error. We have also introduced the () operator. Think of this as the grouping operator. If we left it out, the regex would match either index.html or htm, but not index.htm:

```
Index\.html|htm
```

A lot of your problems when debugging these regular expressions will come because you are not grouping correctly. Practice makes perfect.

A More Complex Example

Let's construct an alternative regex to the one listed earlier that searched for financial numbers. First, we construct the regex to match $:

```
\$
```

Easy enough. Now to introduce the [] operator, which allows us to define a set of characters we want to match. To match a single digit, we use this regex:

```
[0-9]
```

This will match a number 0 through 9. Let's combine the two regular expressions:

```
\$[0-9]
```

What we now have is a pattern that will match $1 or any other number besides 1. However, there is a "gotcha" here. This will check only for one digit, not multiple digits. If we want to do that, we must add either a + or a * to the end, as shown:

```
\$[0-9]*
```

Now we have something that will match an arbitrary number of digits, but will also match $, since the Kleene star allows for zero as a positive match. Be very careful when doing repetition operators like this. In this case, to reduce the number of false positives, we actually want to use the + operator, not the * operator, to force at least one number after the $.

```
\$[0-9]+
```

Say we want to enforce formatting where we know there is a decimal point and two trailing numbers ($250.00). To match this, we want to extend this regular expression a bit:

```
\$[0-9]+\.
```

This will match the ($250.) part of the number. To add in the two places after the decimal, we can do it in one of two ways:

```
\$[0-9]+\.[0-9][0-9]
```

or

```
\$[0-9]+\.[0-9]{2}
```

The introduction of the {} operator shows another way the regex can be shortened and made even more unreadable. The number inside the brackets defines how many times the previous element can be repeated. In addition, if you want to do a range of repetitions, say two to four repetitions, you would write it like this:

```
\$[0-9]+\.[0-9]{2,4}
```

Here, the format is {x,y} with x being the minimum and y being the maximum number of occurrences.

INDEX

▼ F

▼ G

J

▼ N

▼ **T**

U

 V

Stop Hackers in Their Tracks

**Hacking Exposed,
6th Edition**

**Hacking Exposed
Malware & Rootkits**

**Hacking Exposed Computer
Forensics, 2nd Edition**

**24 Deadly Sins of
Software Security**

**Hacking Exposed
Linux, 3rd Edition**

**Hacking Exposed
Windows, 3rd Edition**

**Hacking Exposed
Web 2.0**

**Hacking Exposed:
Web Applications, 2nd Edition**

**Gray Hat Hacking,
2nd Edition**

**Hacking Exposed
Wireless**

**Hacking Exposed
VoIP**

**IT Auditing: Using Controls to
Protect Information Assets**